FLORIDA

SRA Imagine It!

Level 5

Themes

Heritage

Energy at Work

Making a New Nation

Our Corner of the Universe

Going West

Call of Duty

FLORIDA

Level 5

Program Authors

Carl Bereiter	Jan Hirshberg
Andy Biemiller	Anne McKeough
Joe Campione	Peter Pannell
Iva Carruthers	Michael Pressley
Doug Fuchs	Marsha Roit
Lynn Fuchs	Marlene Scardamalia
Steve Graham	Marcy Stein
Karen Harris	Gerald H. Treadway Jr.

McGraw Hill SRA

Columbus, OH

Acknowledgments

Grateful acknowledgment is given to the following publishers and copyright owners for permissions granted to reprint selections from their publications. All possible care has been taken to trace ownership and secure permission for each selection included. In case of any errors or omissions, the Publisher will be pleased to make suitable acknowledgments in future editions.

Unit 1—Heritage

From THE LAND I LOST, TEXT COPYRIGHT © 1982 BY HUYNH QUANG NHUONG. ILLUSTRATIONS COPYRIGHT © 1982 BY VO-DINH MAI. Used by permission of HarperCollins Publishers.

"Our Song" from MEMORIES OF THE SUN by Angela Johnson. COPYRIGHT © 2004 ANGELA JOHNSON. Used by permission of HarperCollins Children's Publishing.

"The Dancing Bird of Paradise" by Renee S. Sanford. Reprinted by permission of CRICKET magazine, November 2001, Vol. 29, no. 3, copyright, © 2001 by Renee S. Sanford.

Reprinted with the permission of Simon & Schuster books for Young Readers, an imprint of Simon & Schuster Children's Publishing Division from FROM MISS IDA'S PORCH by Sandra Belton. Text copyright © 1993 Sandra Belton.

Abridged from IN TWO WORLDS: A Yup'ik Eskimo Family, by Aylette Jenness and Alice Rivers. Text copyright © 1989 by Aylette Jenness and Alice Rivers. Photographs copyright © 1989 by Aylette Jenness. Reprinted by permission of Houghton Mifflin Company. All rights reserved.

"I Look at You" Copyright 1999 Kelly Hill. Originally appeared in WHEN RAIN SINGS: POEMS BY YOUNG NATIVE AMERICANS (1999, Simon & Schuster/National Museum of the American Indian, Smithsonian Institution).

"Mama's Glory" from CROWNING GLORY. Copyright © 2002 by Joyce Carol Thomas. Used by permission of the author.

Unit 2—Energy at Work

"The Sparks Fly" © 2004 by Ruth Ashby from THE AMAZING MR. FRANKLIN OR THE BOY WHO READ EVERYTHING. Permission to reprint granted by Peachtree Publishers.

"Tailing Tornadoes" from STORM CHASERS by Trudi Strain Trueit. Copyright © 2002. All rights reserved. Reprinted by permission of Franklin Watts an imprint of Scholastic Library Publishing, Inc.

Reprinted with the permission of Simon & Schuster Books for Young Readers, an imprint of Simon & Schuster Children's Publishing Division from JAKE DRAKE KNOW-IT-ALL by Andrew Clements, illustrated by Dolores Avendano. Illustrations copyright © 2001 Dolores Avendano.

From THE WIND AT WORK, © 1997 by Gretchen Woelfle. Used with permission of Chicago Review Press.

WHAT ARE FOOD CHAINS AND WEBS? By Bobbie Kalman. Copyright © 1998. Reproduced with permission of Crabtree Publishing Company.

"Landscape" by Carl Sandburg from GOOD MORNING, AMERICA published by Harcourt, Inc. © 1928, renewed 1956.

Unit 3—Making A New Nation

From . . . IF YOU LIVED AT THE TIME OF THE AMERICAN REVOLUTION by Kay Moore, illustrated by Daniel O'Leary. Text copyright © 1997 by Kay Moore, illustrations copyright © 1997 by Scholastic Inc. Reprinted by permission.

Reprinted with permission of the National Geographic Society from THE MIDNIGHT RIDE OF PAUL REVERE by Henry Wadsworth Longfellow. Illustrations by Jeffrey Thompson. Illustrations copyright © 1999 National Geographic Society.

"The Master Spy of Yorktown" from BLACK HEROES OF THE AMERICAN REVOLUTION, text copyright © 1976 and renewed 2004 by Burke Davis, reprinted by permission of Harcourt, Inc.

From SHH! WE'RE WRITING THE CONSTITUTION by Jean Fritz, copyright © 1987, Illustrations copyright © 1987 by Tomie dePaola. Used by permission of Paperstar, an imprint of Penguin Putnam Books for Young Readers, a division of Penguin Putnam Inc.

Text copyright © 2000 by Russell Freedman. All rights reserved. Reprinted from GIVE ME LIBERTY! By permission of Holiday House, Inc.

Unit 4—Our Corner of the Universe

"The Universe" from THE UNIVERSE by Seymour Simon. COPYRIGHT © 1998 by Seymour Simon. Used by permission of HarperCollins Publishers.

"Circles, Squares, and Daggers" by Elsa Marston. Reprinted by permission of the author.

From THE MYSTERY OF MARS by Sally Ride and Tam O'Shaughnessy. Copyright © 1999 by Sally K. Ride and Tam E. O'Shaughnessy. Published by arrangement with Random House Children's Books, a division of Random House, Inc., New York, New York. All rights reserved.

From APOLLO 11: FIRST MOON LANDING by Michael D. Cole. Copyright © 1995 by Michael D. Cole. Published by Enslow Publishers, Inc., Berkeley Heights, NJ. All rights reserved.

EXPLORE MORE: ELLEN OCHOA REACHING FOR THE STARS by Claire Daniel. Copyright © 2005 The McGraw-Hill Companies, Inc. Used by permission.

"Sun", from SPACE SONGS by Myra Cohn Livingston (Holiday House). Copyright © 1988 Myra Cohn Livingston. Used by permission of Marian Reiner. Illustration copyright © 1988 by Leonard Everett Fisher. All rights reserved. Reprinted from SPACE SONGS by permission of Holiday House, Inc.

"A Lunar Lament" by Ann Pedtke. Reprinted by permission of CRICKET magazine, January 2004, copyright © 2004 by Carus Publishing Company.

Unit 5—Going West

From BUFFALO HUNT. Copyright © 1988 by Russell Freedman. All rights reserved. Reprinted by permission of Holiday House, Inc.

From MY NAME IS AMERICA: THE JOURNAL OF WONG MING-CHUNG, A CHINESE MINER, CALIFORNIA, 1852 by Laurence Yep. Copyright © 2000 by Laurence Yep. Reprinted by permission of Scholastic Inc.

BILL PICKETT: RODEO RIDIN' COWBOY, text copyright © 1996 by Andrea Davis Pinkney, illustrations copyright © 1996 by Brian Pinkney, reproduced by permission of Harcourt, Inc. This material may not be reproduced in any form or by any means without the prior written permission of the publisher.

From GHOST TOWNS OF THE AMERICAN WEST by Raymond Bial. Copyright © 2001 by Raymond Bial. Reprinted by permission of Houghton Mifflin Company. All rights reserved.

SRAonline.com

Printed in the United States of America.

Send all inquiries to:
SRA/McGraw-Hill
4400 Easton Commons
Columbus, OH 43219

ISBN: 978-0-07-609657-2
MHID: 0-07-609657-2

1 2 3 4 5 6 7 8 9 RRW 13 12 11 10 09 08 07

Program Authors

Carl Bereiter, Ph.D.
University of Toronto

Andy Biemiller, Ph.D.
University of Toronto

Joe Campione, Ph.D.
University of California, Berkeley

Iva Carruthers, Ph.D.
Northeastern Illinois University

Doug Fuchs, Ph.D.
Vanderbilt University

Lynn Fuchs, Ph.D.
Vanderbilt University

Steve Graham, Ed.D.
Vanderbilt University

Karen Harris, Ed.D.
Vanderbilt University

Jan Hirshberg, Ed.D.
Reading Specialist

Anne McKeough, Ph.D.
University of Toronto

Peter Pannell
Principal, Longfellow Elementary School,
Pasadena, California

Michael Pressley, Ph.D.
Michigan State University

Marsha Roit, Ed.D.
National Reading Consultant

Marlene Scardamalia, Ph.D.
University of Toronto

Marcy Stein, Ph.D.
University of Washington, Tacoma

Gerald H. Treadway, Jr., Ed.D.
San Diego State University

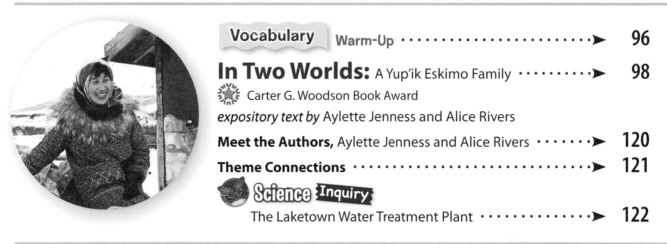

Unit 2 Table of Contents

Energy at Work

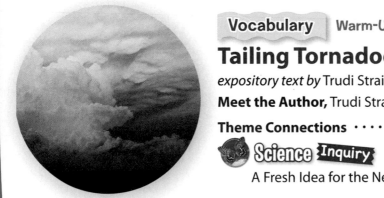

Unit 3 Table of Contents

Making A New Nation

Unit 4 Table of Contents

Our Corner of the Universe

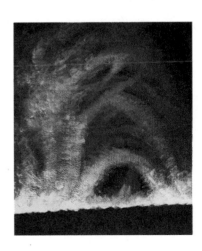

Unit 5 Table of Contents

Going West

Unit 6 Table of Contents

Call of Duty

Heritage

How do you define heritage? How do you think others define heritage? How does heritage affect who you are? What types of things are passed down from generation to generation?

Theme Connection

Look at the illustration.

- What parts of the illustration show heritage?

- How do you think the illustration relates to the theme Heritage?

- In what ways does the illustration depict preserving and celebrating one's heritage?

BIG Idea

How has your heritage influenced your life?

19

Read the article to find the meanings of these words, which are also in "The Land I Lost: Adventures of a Boy in Vietnam":

✦ assumed
✦ apparently
✦ persecuted
✦ unjustly
✦ reality
✦ propped
✦ edible
✦ lingered
✦ logic
✦ inspired

Vocabulary Strategy

An **appositive** is a noun that follows another noun to modify or name it. Authors sometimes use apposition to clarify the meanings of words. Look at the word *persecuted*. Find how the author uses apposition to define the word.

Vocabulary
Warm-Up

Standing offstage, Molly felt her knees shake a little as she waited anxiously for her cue. Each year, the fifth graders at her school performed a Thanksgiving play. Molly had signed up for an audition, had acted well enough to earn a part, and then had attended every practice. She had assumed that when opening night arrived, she would be ready to burst onstage. Apparently, Molly realized, stage fright could affect even the most prepared actor.

The play's first act was set in England. It showed how the Pilgrims were persecuted, or treated unjustly, because of their religious beliefs. For the second act, students had built a version of the Mayflower out of plywood. Onstage, the wooden boat appeared to float gently on the waves. In reality, students standing out of sight pulled it back and forth with ropes.

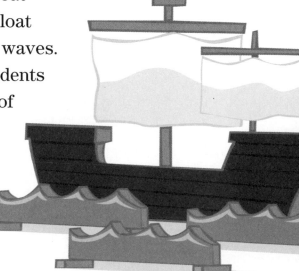

For Molly's scene, the set builders had used a piece of plywood on top of four logs to create a table. The table, propped against the backdrop, was piled high with food.

Molly thought the food would be fake, but a lot of it had come from the grocery store. For instance, the popcorn was edible, but when Molly had tried some earlier, it tasted pretty stale.

Molly's friend Charley played the lead role. As she waited, Charley gave his speech thanking the Native Americans for their help. He lingered near the table, slowly circling it and gesturing to the food. Then Charley stopped and held up a bowl. This was Molly's cue.

She had practiced hard and memorized all of her lines. Logic told Molly everything should go smoothly. Still, her heart beat as swiftly as a bird's.

Molly strode onstage and quickly glanced at the audience. She could not believe how easily she spotted her parents. Seeing the smiles plastered across their faces calmed Molly's nerves, and she was inspired, and put on her best performance yet. Molly had a sense that things would turn out okay.

GAME

Substituting Synonyms
Using a thesaurus, find a synonym for each selection vocabulary word. On a separate sheet of paper, rewrite the sentences from the selection that contain vocabulary words, but substitute a synonym for each vocabulary word.

Concept Vocabulary

The concept word for this lesson is *culture*. *Culture* is the collection of beliefs, customs, stories, and art shared by a group of people. Large nations, such as the United States of America, contain many different cultures. People can also be part of more than one culture.

Genre

An **autobiography** is written by a person about her or his own life.

Comprehension Skill

 Author's Point of View

As you read, identify who is telling the story by deciding whether it is the main character speaking from a first-person point of view or a narrator speaking from a third-person point of view.

The LAND I LOST:

Adventures of a Boy in Vietnam

by Huynh Quang Nhuong
illustrated by Johanna van der Sterre

Focus Questions

What memories does the author carry
with him of his boyhood in Vietnam?
Why are these memories important to him?

I was born on the central highlands of Vietnam in a small hamlet on a riverbank that had a deep jungle on one side and a chain of high mountains on the other. Across the river, rice fields stretched to the slopes of another chain of mountains.

There were fifty houses in our hamlet, scattered along the river or propped against the mountainsides. The houses were made of bamboo and covered with coconut leaves, and each was surrounded by a deep trench to protect it from wild animals or thieves. The only way to enter a house was to walk across a "monkey bridge"—a single bamboo stick that spanned the trench. At night we pulled the bridges into our houses and were safe.

There were no shops or marketplaces in our hamlet. If we needed supplies—medicine, cloth, soaps, or candles—we had to cross over the mountains and travel to a town nearby. We used the river mainly for traveling to distant hamlets, but it also provided us with plenty of fish.

During the six-month rainy season, nearly all of us helped plant and cultivate fields of rice, sweet potatoes, Indian mustard, eggplant, tomatoes, hot peppers, and corn. But during the dry season, we became hunters and turned to the jungle.

Wild animals played a very large part in our lives. There were four animals we feared the most: the tiger, the lone wild hog, the crocodile, and the horse snake. Tigers were always trying to steal cattle. Sometimes, however, when a tiger became old and slow it became a maneater. But a lone wild hog was even more dangerous than a tiger. It attacked every creature in sight, even when it had no need for food. Or it did crazy things, such as charging into the hamlet in broad daylight, ready to kill or to be killed.

The river had different dangers: crocodiles. But of all the animals, the most hated and feared was the huge horse snake. It was sneaky and attacked people and cattle just for the joy of killing. It would either crush its victim to death or poison it with a bite.

Like all farmers' children in the hamlet, I started working at the age of six. My seven sisters helped by working in the kitchen, weeding the garden, gathering eggs, or taking water to the cattle. I looked after the family herd of water buffaloes. Someone always had to be with the herd because no matter how carefully a water buffalo was trained, it always was ready to nibble young rice plants when no one was looking. Sometimes, too, I fished for the family while I guarded the herd, for there were plenty of fish in the flooded rice fields during the rainy season.

I was twelve years old when I made my first trip to the jungle with my father. I learned how to track game, how to recognize useful roots, how to distinguish edible mushrooms from poisonous ones. I learned that if birds, raccoons, squirrels, or monkeys had eaten the fruits of certain trees, then those fruits were not poisonous. Often they were not delicious, but they could calm a man's hunger and thirst.

My father, like most of the villagers, was a farmer and a hunter, depending upon the season. But he also had a college education, so in the evenings he helped to teach other children in our hamlet, for it was too small to afford a professional schoolteacher.

My mother managed the house, but during the harvest season she could be found in the fields, helping my father get the crops home; and as the wife of a hunter she knew how to dress and nurse a wound and took good care of her husband and his hunting dogs.

I went to the lowlands to study for a while because I wanted to follow my father as a teacher when I grew up. I always planned to return to my hamlet to live the rest of my life there. But war disrupted my dreams. The land I love was lost to me forever.

These stories are my memories. . . .

When she was eighty years old grandmother was still quite strong. She could use her own teeth to eat corn on the cob or to chew on sugar plants to extract juice from them. Every two days she walked for more than an hour to reach the marketplace, carrying a heavy load of food with her, and then spent another hour walking back home. And even though she was quite old, traces of her beauty still lingered on: Her hands, her feet, her face revealed that she had been an attractive young woman. Nor did time do much damage to the youthful spirit of my grandmother.

One of her great passions was theater, and this passion never diminished with age. No matter how busy she was, she never missed a show when there was a group of actors in town. If no actors visited our hamlet for several months, she would organize her own show in which she was the manager, the producer, and the young leading lady, all at the same time.

My grandmother's own plays were always melodramas inspired by books she had read and by what she had seen on the stage. She always chose her favorite grandson to play the role of the hero, who would, without fail, marry the heroine at the end and live happily ever after. And when my sisters would tell her that she was getting too old to play the role of the young heroine anymore, my grandmother merely replied: "Anybody can play this role if she's young at heart."

When I was a little boy my grandmother often took me to see the opera. She knew Chinese mythology by heart, and the opera was often a dramatization of this mythology. On one special occasion, during the Lunar New Year celebrations—my favorite holiday, because children could do anything they wanted and by tradition no one could scold them—I accompanied my grandmother to the opera.

When we reached the theater I wanted to go in immediately. But my grandmother wanted to linger at the entrance and talk to her friends. She chatted for more than an hour. Finally we entered the theater, and at that moment the "Faithful One" was onstage, singing sadly. The "Faithful One" is a common character in Chinese opera. He could be a good minister, or a valiant general, or someone who loved and served his king faithfully. But in the end he is unjustly persecuted by the king, whose opinion of him has been changed by the lies of the "Flatterer," another standard character.

When my grandmother saw the "Faithful One" onstage she looked upset and gave a great sigh. I was too interested in what was happening to ask her the reason, and we spent the next five hours watching the rest of the opera. Sometimes I cried because my grandmother cried at the pitiful situation of the "Faithful One." Sometimes I became as angry as my grandmother did at the wickedness of the "Flatterer."

When we went home that night my grandmother was quite sad. She told my mother that she would have bad luck in the following year because when we entered the theater, the "Faithful One" was onstage. I was puzzled. I told my grandmother that she was confused. It would be a good year for us because we saw the good guy first. But my mother said, "No, son. The 'Faithful One' always is in trouble and it takes him many years to vindicate himself. Our next year is going to be like one of his bad years."

So, according to my mother's and grandmother's logic, we would have been much better off in the new year if we had been lucky enough to see the villain first!

My grandmother had married a man whom she loved with all her heart, but who was totally different from her. My grandfather was very shy, never laughed loudly, and always spoke very softly. And physically he was not as strong as my grandmother. But he excused his lack of physical strength by saying that he was a "scholar."

About three months after their marriage, my grandparents were in a restaurant and a rascal began to insult my grandfather because he looked weak and had a pretty wife. At first he just made insulting remarks, such as, "Hey! Wet chicken! This is no place for a weakling!"

My grandfather wanted to leave the restaurant even though he and my grandmother had not yet finished their meal. But my grandmother pulled his shirt sleeve and signaled him to remain seated. She continued to eat and looked as if nothing had happened.

Tired of yelling insults without any result, the rascal got up from his table, moved over to my grandparents' table, and grabbed my grandfather's chopsticks. My grandmother immediately wrested the chopsticks from him and struck the rascal on his cheekbone with her elbow. The blow was so quick and powerful that he lost his balance and fell on the floor.

Instead of finishing him off, as any street fighter would do, my grandmother let the rascal recover from the blow. But as soon as he got up again, he kicked over the table between him and my grandmother, making food and drink fly all over the place. Before he could do anything else, my grandmother kicked him on the chin. The kick was so swift that my grandfather didn't even see it. He only heard a heavy thud, and then saw the rascal tumble backward and collapse on the ground.

All the onlookers were surprised and delighted, especially the owner of the restaurant. Apparently the rascal, one of the best karate fighters of our area, came to this restaurant every day and left without paying for his food or drink, but the owner was too afraid to confront him.

While the rascal's friends tried to revive him, everyone else surrounded my grandmother and asked her who had taught her karate. She said, "Who else? My husband!"

33

After the fight at the restaurant people assumed that my grandfather knew karate very well but refused to use it for fear of killing someone. In reality, my grandmother had received special training in karate from my great-great uncle from the time she was eight years old.

Anyway, after that incident, my grandfather never had to worry again. Anytime he had some business downtown, people treated him very well. And whenever anyone happened to bump into him on the street, they bowed to my grandfather in a very respectful way.

One morning my grandmother wanted me to go outside with her. We climbed a little hill that looked over the whole area, and when we got to the top she looked at the rice field below, the mountain on the horizon, and especially at the river. As a young girl she had often brought her herd of water buffaloes to the river to drink while she swam with the other children of the village. Then we visited the graveyard where her husband and some of her children were buried. She touched her husband's tombstone and said, "Dear, I will join you soon." And then we walked back to the garden and she gazed at the fruit trees her husband had planted, a new one for each time she had given birth to a child. Finally, before we left the garden my sister joined us, and the two of them fed a few ducks swimming in the pond.

That evening my grandmother did not eat much of her dinner. After dinner she combed her hair and put on her best dress. We thought that she was going to go out again, but instead she went to her bedroom and told us that she didn't want to be disturbed.

The family dog seemed to sense something was amiss, for he kept looking anxiously at everybody and whined from time to time. At midnight my mother went to my grandmother's room and found that she had died, with her eyes shut, as if she were sleeping normally.

It took me a long time to get used to the reality that my grandmother had passed away. Wherever I was, in the house, in the garden, out on the fields, her face always appeared so clearly to me. And even now, many years later, I still have the feeling that my last conversation with her has happened only a few days before.

Meet the Author

Huynh Quang Nhuong

Huynh Quang Nhuong was born in My Tho, Vietnam. He was a first lieutenant in the South Vietnamese Army and was wounded during the Vietnam War. He came to the United States for medical treatment. Once in the U.S., he became a naturalized citizen. He now makes his home in Columbia, Missouri.

Nhuong is the first Vietnamese writer to write both fiction and nonfiction in English. He says, "I hope my books will make people from different countries happy." *The Land I Lost: Adventures of a Boy in Vietnam* was Nhuong's first book for children. It was published in five different languages and has received awards worldwide.

Meet the Illustrator

Johanna van der Sterre

Johanna van der Sterre has always loved to create characters. Since she was young, she has always thought that creating art was more interesting than watching television. When she learned that some people create art as their careers, she was very excited and began practicing all the time. It did not matter whether she was better than anyone else or not—she just kept on drawing. When van der Sterre is not drawing or painting, she goes on camping trips with her husband and two dogs.

Theme Connections

Within the Selection

1. What is something the author's father taught him?

2. What were some special memories the author had of his childhood? Why were these memories so important to him?

Beyond the Selection

3. How do the people in your family help one another?

4. What is something you learned from a member of your family?

Write about It!

Tell a story about the oldest member of your family.

Remember to draw your family tree to add to the **Concept/Question Board**.

Children of the Pear Garden

Chinese opera dates back more than a thousand years to the Tang Dynasty. The ruler of that time, Emperor Xuanzong (pronounced *swan song*), loved music and theater. He was inspired to help support a school for music called the Pear Garden. Today Chinese opera actors are still known as "children of the Pear Garden."

In those days, opera was more than just entertainment. There were no schools, so opera was used for teaching people about Chinese history and culture. Most operas also had a moral lesson.

As Chinese opera evolved through the years, hundreds of different styles were formed. Each area of China had its own version of opera.

In the late 1700s, the Chinese people threw a huge party for the eightieth birthday of Emperor Qianlong (pronounced *chin long*).

At this rare event, many opera styles were seen in one place. One troupe decided to combine the best parts of each style. Beijing opera was born. It contains music, dancing, acting, miming, and acrobatics.

Chinese opera uses few props. Most of the time the stage has only a carpet, a table, and one or two chairs. The costumes and makeup are elaborate, though. Their colors are used to give a sense of each character's personality. For example, red stands for goodness. A face painted white means a character is dishonest and sly.

Actors tell much of the story through movement. Emotions are shown by the way they hold their arms and legs. Every gesture has some meaning. Apparently, you have to stay alert at a Chinese opera!

Think Link

1. Write your own caption for the photograph. Make sure the caption relates to the text.

2. Who are the children of the Pear Garden?

3. As China changed throughout history, so did its opera. How do you think Chinese opera is changing today?

Try It!

As you work on your investigation, think about how you can use captions to explain photos and illustrations.

Read the article to find the meanings of these words, which are also in "Our Song":

- ✦ ignores
- ✦ delicate
- ✦ lavender
- ✦ quivers
- ✦ surrounded
- ✦ Senegal
- ✦ traders
- ✦ ship
- ✦ mist

Vocabulary Strategy

Context Clues are hints in the text that help you find the meanings of words. Look at the words *quivers*, *traders*, and *ship*. Use context clues to find each word's meaning.

Vocabulary
Warm-Up

It is hot, and I am bored. Listening to my radio would at least help pass the time, but Mom said no. I am supposed to interact with the customers and watch for shoplifters. But everyone who walks in here mostly ignores me. They scan the shelves filled with my mom's delicate little pillows, occasionally picking up one to sniff it. She sprinkles crushed lavender inside each pillow.

Mom took off to get food. I am hoping for an enormous stuffed burrito.

At least it is shady underneath our booth. A guy wearing sunglasses enters and walks right into one of the booth's poles—I guess his eyes are not adjusted yet. The entire tent quivers for a second. Then he mumbles an apology, puts his shades on top of his head, and turns toward the shelves.

I watch the family in the booth next to ours for a few minutes. Dad stands proudly in the middle of the tent surrounded by colorful shirts and dresses. The dyed fabrics are covered with bold block patterns and busy stripes. The family is originally from Senegal. Mom told me that in Africa they were traders, exchanging clothes for food and other necessities. Now they make only some of the clothes they sell. The rest are manufactured by friends back in Senegal, who then ship the clothes overseas. I notice that the son, who is about my age, watches his father closely. When he is old enough, he will inherit the business.

My mom rushes back into the booth carrying pitas filled with who-knows-what. I notice her hair and clothes are soaked—it is hot, but not that hot. She describes a booth filled with a cool mist of spraying water. I am definitely going there after lunch.

Word Charades Divide into two teams and choose one student from each team to sit facing the class. Reveal a vocabulary word to everyone but the two seated students. Then have the class describe the word without saying the word itself. The first of the two students to predict the word scores a point for his or her team. Continue with different vocabulary words and different students until all of the words have been used.

Concept Vocabulary

A *pilgrimage* is a journey to a sacred or very special place. Many Americans make pilgrimages to important historical landmarks that were part of our nation's fight for independence. People of the Islamic faith try to make a pilgrimage to the holy city of Mecca at least once in their lives. Why do you think pilgrimages are important to certain people?

Genre

Realistic Fiction contains characters, settings, and conflicts that can exist in real life.

Comprehension Strategy

☆ Clarifying

As you read the selection, remember that it is important to monitor your reading for words and ideas that you do not understand and to clarify them right away.

Our Song

by Angela Johnson

illustrated by Linda Pierce

Focus Questions

How does the song connect Josie with her great-great-grandmother? Why is Josie excited about visiting Senegal?

I've always heard the song. I can't ever remember a time when the song didn't come real soft and sweet out of my great-great-grandma, or Ole Ma, as we all call her.

She always sings it for me and me only. She says it's an old song from Senegal about a girl who lived a long time ago. She only sings it in her village language though.

So I sit and listen and dream the song is about me, and I sure do like that I'm named after her.

She has black-and-white pictures of people from her village in Senegal, Africa, all over her room. There are rugs on her floor she says her sister from Africa sent her, baskets and rugs from back home.

Ole Ma says on days when the wind blows she thinks that she can imagine all the food smells and wood smoke from her village.

She says it gets carried on the breeze.

Anyway, Ole Ma's room is the only one in the house where I can play basketball. She let me put a net on the back of her closet door. She even has shoot-outs with me sometimes. Ole Ma is my biggest fan. Nobody else at home understands me and my moods except her.

Ole Ma says, "Child, will you be playing that round-ball game on the television one day like those other girls?"

And that is when I sit down by her feet. Ole Ma has big feet like me. I always tickle them and make her laugh.

She says that her big feet are what helped her get a husband. Even though she wasn't looking for one, just running around her village in Senegal with her friends when all of a sudden a boy who would turn out to be great-great-grandaddy fell at her feet. He tripped over her feet.

She was the same age as I am now. Ten.

They would be friends for ten years, then marry.

But Ole Ma hardly ever talks about that kind of stuff to me; all she wants me to do is get good grades and one day play basketball on television.

She says that boys are different now, and I don't understand that. They all seem the same to me when I beat them at basketball or outrun them.

Ole Ma says that everything was different in her village when she was young. I always wonder what it was like, but even though she tells some stories, she ends each one by saying, "But all that's not important, my girl, how is school and everything that moves around you?"

The first time she said that I turned around 'cause I thought she saw something.

I said, "You see something, Ole Ma?"

Ole Ma just laughed and reached down from her old chair and squeezed my face. Then she sang the song that she says her Ole Ma taught her.

In all the times Ole Ma has sung the song to me, which was probably from the time I was a real little baby and she'd just moved in with us, I'd never thought about learning the song.

All the words are in another language that I don't understand. But I like the words, whatever they are.

Ole Ma sang the song for me the time my arm got broken after I tried to make a jump shot on a junior high boy who said girls couldn't play real basketball.

I made the shot, though.

She sang the song for me when I fell off the roof after my best friends, Buddy and Charlotte, bet each other they could land in my mom's lavender bushes.

Charlotte said, "We're not even asking you, Josie, 'cause we already know you'll do it."

The next thing any of us knew, I was in the lavender, then in the backseat of my brother Jamal's car, then in the hospital with Charlotte and Buddy yelling at each other that it wasn't like they included me in the bet or anything.

The nurses all knew me, and when they called me by name, Jamal just put his head in his hands and stayed that way for a while.

Momma says Old Ma was delicate when she was my age and probably doesn't understand the trouble I get in. She says I should be more like Ole Ma was.

But all that's not important 'cause now Ole Ma is laughing as I tickle her feet and lean against her as she starts to sing her song. The wind blows through her curtains and I can smell my momma's flowers in the yard.

I fall asleep to the sound of Ole Ma's song.

Just like that.

Ole Ma says that it has been a long time coming, but now is the time. We are going back to where she grew up in Senegal.

She said it at the dinner table last night, and I was the only one there who was surprised.

My sister, Nita, kept moving her head to whatever was on her headphones. Jamal smiled. Momma and Daddy looked across the table at me and then smiled down at the other end at Ole Ma.

Even though I had a mouth full of food I still spoke. "When?"

Mama laughed. "We'll be leaving around your winter break in a couple of months."

I was happy. "Africa is so far away I'll probably need to miss a whole lot of school—right? I mean, we don't just want to go for a couple of days, then come right home, do we?"

Daddy says, "I don't think two weeks is such a short time by plane. And anyway, we'll make sure you don't miss any school, Josie. We all know how much that would upset you."

Daddy is always trying to be funny, but it doesn't matter.

I will finally see where my Ole Ma is from. I get to see the place her husband fell over her big feet and the places she ran around with her friends. I am going to Africa.

I run around the village my Ole Ma grew up in.

I run around the village with my cousins. Cousins that I sort of knew I had, cousins that Ole Ma talked about around the table and in her chair before she went to sleep at night. But they were always dream cousins to me.

These are the real cousins.

They are the cousins that show me the secret places in the village. They show me where they go when they want to hide from the adults. They show me the field that they all play soccer in. They also show me (when we stand on top of my cousin Leo's house) where they bag groundnuts (peanuts) to ship off to everywhere in the world.

There are mountains and mountains of them as we stand on the roof and look off into the blue sky.

It's the end of December and it's warm enough in my Ole Ma's village to be wearing a tank top and shorts. I am. It's warm enough to be standing outside with no shoes, even though Momma yells at me about that and makes me put a hat on my head.

None of the other kids are wearing hats.

And I want to run barefoot like them.

Even though my cousins can't speak much English, they smile and pat me on the back when I try to speak some French; 'cause they can speak it and I took it when I was in second grade. But mostly we just point or laugh.

My cousin Leo's village is outside a city called Dakar. Tomorrow we are all going there for market day. I can't wait. Leo talks about the food and all the traders and the excitement of the market. It won't be like the grocery stores back home.

I wake up beside Leo and his little sisters Doni and Victoria on the covered mats in the backyard. Sleeping outside in December! The sky is just starting to turn pink when I hear our song. Ole Ma's song is being hummed by somebody I can't see, and it isn't Ole Ma.

So I go looking.

First I should tell how Ole Ma has done nothing but smile and be surrounded by people who visit our cousins' little house and sit and talk and talk way into the night.

She smiles at me when I run past her with a soccer ball or kneel beside her when we eat our dinner, at least I call it dinner.

Sometimes some of the older village women stop me when I'm running past with my cousins and call me Little Goat. I just smile 'cause they all seem to know me as Ole Ma's great-great-grandchild.

I'm used to it now like I'm used to carrying a soccer ball everywhere I go. And I'm getting used to the dry desert village and people who speak a different language and kind of look like me.

At home when I watched shows on television and they would show Senegal I'd always search for a tall girl who looked just like me. Now I see a lot of people who look like me and are related.

Anyway, Ole Ma is so happy to be back in her village. To be back home.

On this early morning, though, even before the chickens start to move again, I hear Ole Ma's song.

When I start walking down the center of the road I don't think much about it. Nobody is out yet and I pretty much know every place. But I don't think I remember the little hut at the end of the village road.

Someone is up besides me. She comes out of the mist that circles the little hut. She dances around, then runs around. She starts talking to people I can't see in the hut, then runs ahead of me.

"Hey, wait for me," I call.

But she doesn't, so I follow her. I follow her over the dusty village road and around a few huts that I never noticed before.

Even when I catch up to her she doesn't seem to notice I'm there. She looks about my age and I think I've seen her someplace before. . . .

She just starts climbing a tree and swinging from it. The mist is all around her, and then she is gone.

A few minutes later I'm watching the girl come out of the mist as she ties scarves around her head and saddles up a goat and starts galloping around the village.

It looks like fun, but she still ignores me when I call her. With all the noise she's making, you'd think she would have woken somebody up by now, but it's still.

The girl in the mist is standing on top of one of the huts I'd never seen before, the mist surrounds her, and she's gone.

My stomach quivers.

Then Ole Ma's song whistles through a breeze, so I follow it, down the winding dirt road and into the mist. They are there.

The girl from the mist is sitting on the ground tickling an old woman's feet and smiling as she is being sung to, but this time I can hear the song in English.

The old woman sings:

"Good girl child flying over us all.

Good girl child flying to be free.

Jumping girl child, hop over the mountains.

Jumping girl child, hop over the trees.

Don't have to sit down, girl child.

Don't have to be like the rest.

Don't have to keep your feet on the ground

Girl child,

Just keep on flying and doing your best.

The old woman grabs the mist girl's face and squeezes it in her old hands and calls her Josiabi. They look up through the mist at me, smile, then disappear.

I love the color of Senegal. I love that my Ole Ma's hand in mine, as we walk through the village she ran through as a girl, is warm and holds mine tight.

I like my whole family more, and I don't even know why. Daddy says it's because I've made room for more family and I've got heart space now.

I don't know about that.

I do know that when I look at Ole Ma from now on I will see Africa. I will know where we all come from.

But most important, I will know who Ole Ma really was when I hear our song, and learn in the old way to sing it one day to my great-great-granddaughter. So one day she'll say she's always heard the song and can't remember a time when it didn't come soft and sweet from her great-great-grandma.

Meet the Author

Angela Johnson

Angela Johnson has always loved a good story. Her grandfather would thrill her with his tales, but it was her fifth-grade teacher who inspired her to write. After hearing her teacher share the adventures of *Harriet the Spy,* Johnson bought a diary and began writing every day. However, Johnson has not limited her writing to just novels. She has also written picture books and poetry. When not writing, Johnson enjoys gardening, taking long walks, and watching old movies.

Meet the Illustrator

Linda Pierce

Pierce grew up watching her mother, a professional artist, draw and paint. Wanting to be like her mother, Pierce began drawing as soon as she could hold a pencil. She has never looked back. Pierce loves to draw faces. It is always a challenge to show feelings in a person's face. If she was not an illustrator, she says she "would be a full-time portrait artist . . . There is beauty in every face!" Pierce creates art in a light-filled studio above her garage. Her dog, Mandy, always keeps her company.

Theme Connections

Within the Selection

1. What is one way that Ole Ma keeps her childhood memories from Senegal alive?

2. Who was the mysterious girl in the mist?

Across Selections

3. What does Josie have in common with the narrator of "The Land I Lost"?

4. Name one way that village life in Senegal is similar to village life in Vietnam.

Beyond the Selection

5. Why do you think the children in the village have to work?

6. Why do some people pass names down from one generation to the next?

Write about It!

Describe a memory that you would want to share with a grandchild someday.

Remember to choose a poem or song about heritage to add to the **Concept/Question Board**.

THE LAND OF SENEGAL

The terrain in Senegal—the westernmost country in Africa—consists mainly of gently rolling hills. Depending on which part of the country you are in, though, the hills may be covered with trees, grasses, or dry, sandy soil. The different landscapes determine where and how people live.

Most of Senegal is part of a much larger terrain called the Sahel. The Sahel stretches across the middle part of Africa. It lies between the Sahara to the north and more fertile land in the south. Savanna—grassland with a few trees scattered across it—covers much of the Sahel.

The savanna of eastern Senegal is very dry. Farming is quite difficult. Most people who live there are nomads who raise cattle or sheep. During the driest months, they travel far to the south to find more fertile land for their herds.

About the size of South Dakota, Senegal is the westernmost country of the semi-arid lands known as the Sahel.

Many more people live in northern Senegal. This region contains much of the nation's farmland. Nearly three-quarters of the Senegalese people work in agriculture. As in much of Africa, though, droughts make farming unpredictable. Many people look for more reliable wages in Senegal's capital, Dakar.

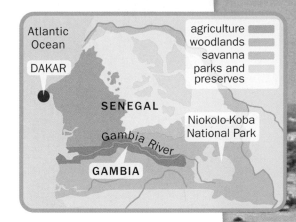

Senegal has a variety of ecosystems that determine how humans use the land.

Nearly a quarter of the Senegalese people live in or near the coastal city of Dakar. Many of them take jobs in the fishing industry. Like any big city, Dakar also has factories and businesses that provide work.

The giant Gambia River flows across southern Senegal. It creates a huge swampy area of mangrove forests. This unique ecosystem supports lots of wildlife, especially birds. The nation has always been at the forefront of conservation efforts.

Think Link

1. What is the name of the terrain by which Senegal is completely surrounded?

2. Why does one-quarter of Senegal's population live in or near Dakar?

3. What industries provide jobs for the people of Senegal?

Try It!

As you work on your investigation, think about how you can use a map to show the shape and location of an area.

Read the article to find the meanings of these words, which are also in "The Dancing Bird of Paradise":

✦ ascend
✦ sweltered
✦ kimono
✦ internment
✦ barrack
✦ donned
✦ startled
✦ phonograph
✦ soloed
✦ enrich

Vocabulary Strategy

An **appositive** is a noun that follows another noun to modify or name it. Authors sometimes use apposition to clarify the meanings of words. Look at the word *barrack*. Find how the author uses apposition to define the word.

Vocabulary
Warm-Up

Once more, Shiro called for his great-grandfather and again received no reply. "He must be out in the garden," he suggested to his friend Simon.

The boys began to ascend the stairs to the second floor. Shiro was showing Grandpa Juro's "remembering room" to Simon.

The walk to Grandpa Juro's house was not far, but the boys had sweltered in the summer heat the whole way. Now the house's air conditioning dried the sweat that ran down their backs.

Upstairs, Shiro led Simon to a closed door. He turned the knob and the door swung open. The room's walls were covered with posters, and books and records lined the shelves. Toys and knickknacks were everywhere. Directly opposite the open door, a colorfully patterned robe with huge sleeves and a wide cloth belt hung on the wall.

"That's Grandma Moriko's kimono," Shiro said.

Shiro explained that his great-grandparents had been confined to a camp during World War II. The kimono was one of the few family treasures they had taken with them to the internment camp.

Barrack life at the camp was boring. Each barrack—a plain, temporary house—was exactly like the next. Grandma Moriko often donned the kimono to perform tea ceremonies. The ceremonies helped make life more interesting.

Suddenly a hand gripped Shiro's shoulder. The boys turned quickly, their startled faces showing alarm. Grandpa Juro stood behind them smiling.

He walked to the phonograph and placed a record on it. Soon jazz filled the room. One by one, each musician took a turn and soloed.

"Now that's what I call music," Grandpa Juro said. "This remembering room certainly does enrich my life. It always adds some happiness to my day."

GAME

Define It! Form two teams with your classmates. Have a volunteer define a vocabulary word. The first team to guess which word is being defined gets a point. Spell the word correctly to receive a bonus point. If the team is unsuccessful, the other team gets a chance to spell the word for a point. The game is over when all of the words have been defined and spelled.

Concept Vocabulary

The concept word for this lesson is *inheritance.* An *inheritance* is something that is passed from one generation to the next. It might be money or a piece of furniture, but it can also be knowledge or physical characteristics. What kind of inheritance have you received?

Genre

Expository Text tells people something. It contains facts about real people, things, or events.

Comprehension Skill

☆ Making Inferences

As you read the selection, use the information from the text, as well as your own knowledge, to "read between the lines." This knowledge will help you form a better understanding of the people and events being described.

The Dancing Bird of Paradise

by Renée S. Sanford

illustrated by Cheryl Kirk Noll

Focus Questions

Why does Haruno travel to Japan? How does Haruno help to preserve the heritage of her people while they are living in the internment camps?

Seven-year-old Haruno's black eyes sparkled with delight as cousin Yuki's kimono swished and flared to the lilting Japanese music coming from the old phonograph in the corner. The year was 1931, and fifteen-year-old Yuki was visiting her grandfather's farm in a beautiful valley near San Francisco, California.

That evening Haruno and Yuki's aunts and uncles and friends looked forward to performing a kabuki play—a style of Japanese theater that tells stories with song and dance. The old hall would be filled with farmers and their families who now lived in America but who still enjoyed the bright costumes and exciting drama of kabuki.

Yuki had learned several native Japanese dances she now practiced and planned to perform at intermission.

"Come, Haruno," Yuki beckoned to her small cousin. "You may be young, but you are big enough to learn this dance." Haruno jumped up quickly and followed Yuki's every move with her head and hands, just as she had followed her with her eyes.

"Very good!" Cousin Yuki exclaimed when the music ended. "I will ask your mother—maybe she will let you perform with me this evening."

Haruno did dance with her cousin Yuki during intermission, and the whole audience clapped and cheered. A gentleman from the big city was watching and was especially impressed. "This child has tremendous talent," he told Haruno's mother. "She should go to the Tachibana Dance School in Tokyo, Japan. She will learn the beautiful Japanese dances and become a great dancer."

Haruno knew only that she loved to dance, but her parents did not forget the gentleman's words. Five years later, when she was only eleven years old, she boarded a ship with her grandparents and returned with them to Japan. Each day she went to school and then to her dance lesson. Twenty minutes was all she had alone with her teacher, but she stayed much longer each afternoon, watching and copying the other students, learning their dances as well as her own.

Sometimes Haruno was lonely for her family—her parents, her two brothers, and her three sisters. She wrote them letters about her life in Japan: about living with Grandfather and Grandmother, about learning to read and write in Japanese, and about learning to dance. Then her cousins would come to visit, and the days would be filled with fun and laughter—just like back home.

As Haruno grew older and prepared to finish high school, she didn't notice that anything was different, but Grandfather did. One day he called for Haruno to come and speak with him.

"Haruno," he said, "it is time for you to go home. Things are changing. Very soon I feel that Japan and the United States may be at war."

Haruno was startled. She loved both of her countries; how could they ever fight each other? But she knew Grandfather was wise and that she must listen to him.

Grandfather continued, "Before you go, you must receive your dancing name. You have worked long and hard, and I want you to take back to America something valuable from your time in Japan."

The very next week, Haruno stood poised before the headmaster of the dance school. As soon as he nodded, she began to dance with all her heart and skill. The music died away, and she waited to hear the report. "Yes, Haruno," he said with a smile. "You have danced magnificently. You will receive your dance name to show that the Tachibana Dance School honors you as one of its own."

Haruno's dance teacher came to her side. "My name is Saho—bird of paradise—and I have taught you well. So I give you a name that shows you are my student. You will be Sahomi Tachibana—a beautiful bird of paradise who learned to dance at Tachibana."

In November 1941, Haruno—Sahomi—sailed back across the ocean to her home in California. Just as Grandfather had feared, within a few weeks the United States and Japan were fighting in World War II.

Overnight the Japanese people living in America were accused of being spies. Because Japanese-Americans looked different from most other Americans and because so many people in the United States had never met a Japanese person, non-Asian Americans were afraid of them and thought they might help Japan in the war. So, even though Japanese-Americans loved their new country and were very loyal, the United States government ordered them to move from their homes on the West Coast and sent them to live in internment camps.

It was not fair, but Sahomi knew they had no other choice. Her family had lived as good, orderly citizens. In a good and orderly way, they boarded the bus that took them to the distant Tanforan Assembly Center.

When they arrived, Sahomi choked back a feeling of sickness as she set down her suitcase and looked around. The center had been a racetrack, and the smell of horses still hung heavily in the stalls that had been converted into places for people to live. She blushed with embarrassment every time she needed to use the bathroom and had no place to go but the doorless latrines everyone had to share.

After a few months, Sahomi and the other Japanese-Americans were told to board a train headed for Delta, Utah. Three days later they arrived at the Topaz Relocation Center. Like the Tanforan Assembly Center, this internment camp, too, was far different from Sahomi's comfortable homes in California and Japan. Here, the bathroom stalls had doors, but everyone still lived very close together. Families crowded into long rows of barrack apartments. Each room was lit by a single bulb hanging in the middle of the ceiling and heated by potbellied stoves that burned coal and wood. Only the latrines and laundry rooms had running water. Families shared meals at long tables in a large dining hall and reported for roll call each morning.

Because they were living in the middle of the Sevier Desert, the internees sweltered through the blistering summer heat. They also shivered through frigid winter nights. During dust storms, fine sand blew through the cracks in the walls and coated the few belongings that Sahomi and her family had brought with them.

The people still enjoyed being entertained, so they asked whoever had a talent to share it. "Please teach our children to dance," some parents asked Sahomi. Once again, Sahomi had a stage on which to perform. This was not what I expected, she thought, but I can still share the dances of Japan with people around me. If I ever want to be a professional, I can never stop dancing, even when life is hard and unfair.

The children at Topaz went to school in the internment camp. After class, an eager group would gather around Sahomi as she patiently taught them the delicate steps of the dances that were as familiar as her own thoughts. When she taught her students, Sahomi explained the story and meaning behind each dance. They learned the Dance of the Old Ruined Castle on a Moonlit Night and acted out the parties in the beautiful gardens of a castle in Japan. For the Cherry Blossom Dance, Sahomi showed the children how to flutter their fans like the fragrant pink mist that surrounds Japan's mountains in springtime.

After much practice, her students were ready for their first recital. Because of the oppressive summer heat, the children did not dress in the traditional heavy kimonos. "You may be dressed simply," Sahomi told them as they stood ready to ascend the stage, "but you must dance your very best. Make the beauty of the land and stories of Japan come alive to everyone who sees you." Parents and friends smiled their appreciation as they were transported to a different, more beautiful time through the children's dances.

After three long years, the American government realized what a terrible mistake it had made by imprisoning loyal citizens. The war was ending, and the Japanese-American people were allowed to move anywhere they wished. Sahomi's father wanted to see what the East Coast was like, so Sahomi moved with her family to Pennsylvania. At first, she could only get a job as a cook, even though she didn't really know how to cook. But she kept taking dance lessons—she wanted to learn ballet—and kept performing and teaching.

Then Sahomi took a big step—she moved to New York City and began classes at Studio 61 in Carnegie Hall. There she studied ballet and modern dance under the famous dance teacher Martha Graham. But the greatest lesson she learned was that her first love and talent was for Japanese dance. Like the brilliant bird of paradise, she donned beautiful costumes and shone brighter than any other dancer of her kind.

Sahomi began teaching privately at a Buddhist temple, but her talent was no secret. One day, Eleanor Roosevelt, the president's wife, came to see her perform. Then, in 1966, Sahomi started her own Tachibana Dance School in New York City.

Every time Sahomi performed or taught, new opportunities came her way. With her husband, Frank, as her biggest fan and enthusiastic agent, she began touring, performing for women's clubs and universities in forty of the fifty states. She performed and helped direct dances for Broadway plays and soloed as a dancer for big city orchestras.

Several times Sahomi traveled to Japan to learn more dances. She shared these dances in many performances when she returned. Everywhere Sahomi went, people loved to watch her graceful performances. They did not look down on her anymore because she was Japanese. They knew that she had a beautiful gift to share with them.

Sahomi Tachibana is a grandmother now, but she is still performing and teaching the graceful dances of Japan. She has won many awards, but she is most proud of the honor of watching her students become better and better. "It's a lifelong study," Sahomi says. "I am trying to teach my pupils whatever I have so that it will enrich their lives more. At least I have done that much. I have given something."

Even when the bird of paradise can no longer perform, her students will continue to pass on Sahomi's gift of Japanese culture to those around them.

What a beautiful gift it is!

Meet the Author

Renée S. Sanford

Sanford is a freelance writer living in Oregon. As a girl, she learned the importance of heritage when her family took in a Vietnamese family after the fall of Saigon. Today, she still enjoys reaching out to people of other cultures and backgrounds and learning about their lives. In turn, Sanford also likes to share her culture just like the young Sahomi shared her love of kabuki dancing in the selection. Sanford is an avid reader and enjoys traveling with her husband and children.

Meet the Illustrator

Cheryl Kirk Noll

Cheryl Kirk Noll's favorite things to draw are people. Since high school, she has been filling sketchbooks with quick drawings of people, both real and imaginary. She most enjoys creating illustrations for stories from long ago or far away. Noll's inspiration for her illustrations often comes from the art of the country or time period where the story takes place. She enjoys working on the sun porch of her home where she can observe nature and her surroundings as she works.

Theme Connections

Within the Selection

1. Why is Haruno given the name "Sahomi"?

2. Why is it important to Sahomi to teach Japanese dance?

Across Selections

3. Compare and contrast the importance of grandparents in the lives of the people and characters in the first three selections of the unit.

4. In what other selection are the characters' lives affected by war?

Beyond the Selection

5. Why is it important to preserve one's cultural heritage after moving to a new place?

6. What other cultures use clothing and dance to display and preserve their heritage?

Write about It!

Imagine you are going to interview a relative you have never met. What would you ask him or her?

Remember to look for a photograph or make a drawing of a family reunion to add to the **Concept/Question Board.**

Genre

Genre

Expository Text tells people something. It contains facts about real people, things or events.

Feature

Italics are typed words that slant to the right. A word is put into italics when that word itself is being written about. Italics are also used for foreign words, titles of books and movies, and the names of vehicles.

Chanoyu:
The Japanese Tea Ceremony

How long does it take to drink a cup of tea? If you are in a hurry and the tea is not too hot, it will take you only a few minutes. During a Japanese tea ceremony, though, it might take hours.

The tea ceremony is a Japanese ritual that has been performed for hundreds of years. Making, serving, and drinking tea is treated as an art form. Every detail is meant to create a pleasing and relaxing event.

Called *sadō*, or "the way of tea," this ritual is a way to take a break from the stress of an ordinary day. It is like an intermission from regular life. During the ceremony, the focus is on experiencing the moment. The rest of the world stays outside the tearoom.

People do drink tea at tea ceremonies, but that is only part of the ritual. Greeting guests, serving food, and even sitting have to be done properly. Guests should also know how to act. For example, they must bow in thanks at specific times.

A *chawan*, or tea bowl, will often look imperfect and may even be cracked.

The person serving the tea wears a kimono and uses special tea-making equipment. For example, a bamboo ladle, called a *hishaku*, carries water. A bamboo spoon, called a *chasaku*, scoops the powdered green tea. Probably the most important item is the *chawan*, or tea bowl.

The dishes and utensils are often passed down through many generations. Each piece is treated carefully and with great respect. Part of the ritual is showing your guests just how important these items are by the way you handle them.

Tea ceremonies can be held almost anywhere, but a proper tearoom has *tatami* mats on the floor. A special area of the room, called the *tokonoma*, contains a scroll hanging on the wall and a vase filled with flowers.

It may seem like a lot of effort for a cup of tea, but the soothing nature of the tea ceremony will enrich your life.

Think Link

1. Why did the author use italics for certain words in this selection?
2. What is one reason people perform tea ceremonies?
3. What kinds of ceremonies or rituals do you perform with your family?

Try It!

As you work on your investigation, think about how you might use italics.

Read the article to find the meanings of these words, which are also in "From Miss Ida's Porch":

+ concert
+ finest
+ claim
+ trolley
+ civilizations
+ forbidden
+ magnificent
+ spellbound
+ section
+ attitude

Vocabulary Strategy

Context Clues are hints in the text that help you find the meanings of words. Look at the words *concert, trolley,* and *section.* Use context clues to find each word's meaning.

Vocabulary

Warm-Up

Kendra and her parents waited for the doors of the theater to open. Mr. and Mrs. Fernandes spoke quietly to each other, but Kendra was too distracted to listen. She could not take her eyes off the crowd milling around them. There were so many different ways people could dress up for an evening out!

A few feet from where the family stood, a narrow stone pyramid—nearly as tall as the theater—towered over them. A plaque at its base told how the monument had been built to honor the man who paid for the theater.

Finally, the crowd began moving toward the doors. The concert was about to begin. One of Brazil's finest samba bands had come to town to perform, and Mr. Fernandes could not wait. Born in Rio, he had danced to samba music at many celebrations during his youth. He wanted Kendra to claim samba as part of her heritage too.

As a special treat, the Fernandeses had taken a trolley to the theater. Streetcars had once been common all over the city. Over the years, though, buses had replaced them. The trolley was now a unique attraction for the city's residents.

Soon after Kendra and her parents found their seats, the lights dimmed and the curtain rose. Kendra learned from the program that samba's roots were African. It grew out of music and dances that slaves had carried from their African civilizations. Samba had even been forbidden in Brazil at one time.

As soon as the band began playing, dancers dressed in magnificent costumes ran onstage. Their colorful headdresses and costumes—covered in sequins and feathers—shook and glittered with each move leaving the audience spellbound. One by one, each section of the audience stood and danced. Kendra and her parents joined the crowd by dancing and clapping along with the lively rhythms. The joyous attitude of the performers was infectious. No one ever sat back down.

GAME

Substituting Synonyms

Using a thesaurus, find a synonym for each selection vocabulary word. On a separate sheet of paper, rewrite the sentences from the selection that contain vocabulary words, but substitute a synonym for each vocabulary word.

Concept Vocabulary

An **anecdote** is a short, true story about a real event in someone's life. Although an *anecdote* is about a specific event or experience, it is told to teach a bigger lesson or truth about life. Think of an anecdote to share with the class. What lesson about life does your anecdote teach?

Genre

Realistic Fiction contains characters, settings, and conflicts that can exist in real life.

Comprehension Strategy

 Adjusting Reading Speed As you read the selection, remember to slow down or reread any sections of the text that you find difficult to understand.

FROM MISS

Focus Questions

Who saw Marian Anderson perform in Washington D.C.? Why was it significant that Marian Anderson sang at Constitution Hall?

IDA'S PORCH

by Sandra Belton

illustrated by Meryl Treatner

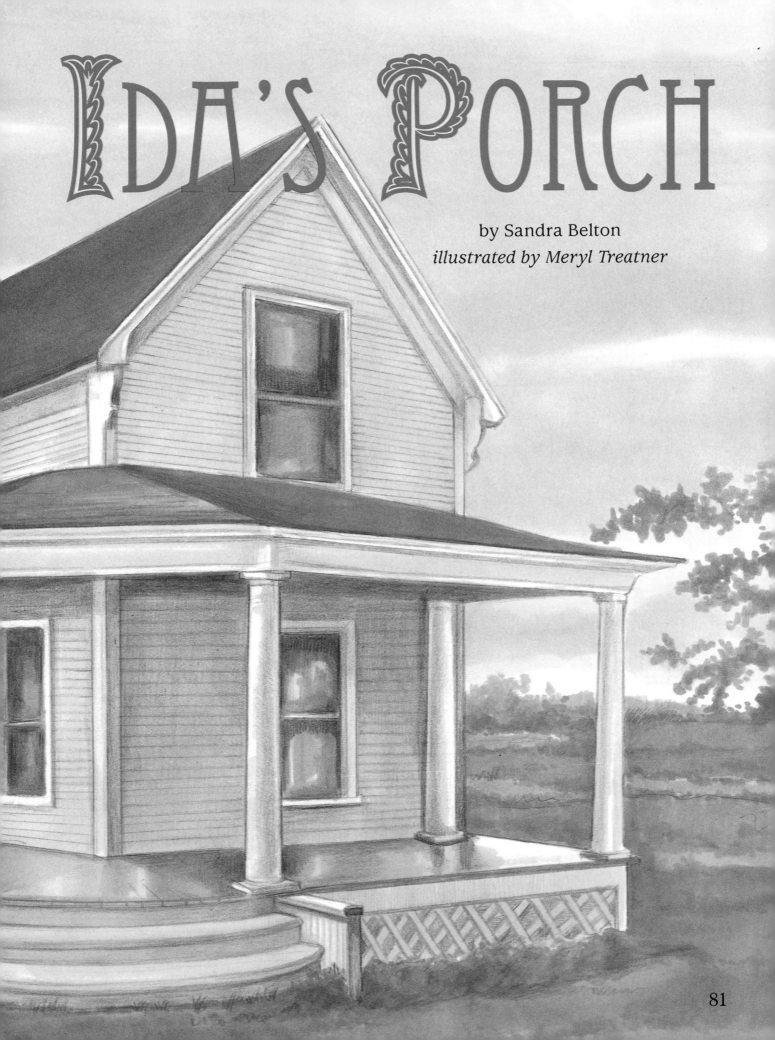

Shoo Kate has just finished telling the story of her visit as a child to the Lincoln Memorial to hear Marian Anderson perform one glorious Sunday morning. Ms. Anderson was scheduled to sing at Constitution Hall, but the hall's owners cancelled her performance because she was black. So, Ms. Anderson decided that the concert would take place at the Lincoln Memorial instead so that everyone who wanted to see and hear her sing could attend.

Shoo Kate's remembering had kind of put a spell on us. On everybody listening. Even Punkin was real still, and she was usually moving around like a doll on strings. When my father and my sister Sylvia walked up on the porch, we all jumped. Nobody had heard them coming.

"Goodness, you all gave me a fright." Miss Ida got up. "Hi, Sylvia. Here, take my seat, J.S.," she said to Daddy. "I'll get more chairs from the house."

"No need, Ida," Daddy said. "A few folks are going to be leaving very soon and there'll be plenty of room."

Daddy looked over at me and Freda. I knew that the very best time was about to be over for us.

"Hey, J.S., what you been up to?" Daddy and Mr. Fisher were shaking hands.

"I just been walking down to the corner to make sure Sylvia and her friends know it's time to come home."

"Sylvia don't know nothing when Peewee's around." I just had to say that. My sister thinks she's something special just 'cause bony ole Peewee said she was cute.

"Shut up!" Sylvia wanted to hit me. I just knew it.

"Don't speak that way to your sister," Daddy said to Sylvia. "And you, missy," he said pointing to me, "if you want to get your extra few minutes here, I think you'd better have kinder thoughts for Sylvia."

"There's been some wonderful thoughts on this porch tonight, folks. Let's keep the good words going." Miss Ida always makes things okay.

"J.S.," she said, "you missed a wonderful story. Shoo Kate was telling us about the time she saw Marian Anderson."

"Oh, yeah," Daddy said, like he was remembering something. "You told me a little about that, Shoo Kate. I wish I had been here to hear the whole story."

"Tell him the story, Shoo Kate. We'd love to hear it again. Right, Freda?" I wanted so much to make the best time last.

"Good try, baby, but it won't work tonight." Daddy hardly ever let my tricks work on him.

"I have another chapter for that story, however. Want to hear it?" While he was talking, Daddy winked at Shoo Kate. I thought he was fooling.

Miss Ida sat up in her seat. Like she felt the same as me. Wanting the evening to go on.

"Come on, J.S., sit down and take your turn this evening." Miss Ida motioned for us to make room for Daddy.

Then my daddy started his remembering.

"I had an uncle—Uncle Henry—who lived in Washington," Daddy began. "He taught at Howard University there, for many years.

"Uncle Henry was a big man, well over six feet tall. He had wide, full eyebrows that came together like a hairy *V* whenever he frowned. And Uncle Henry frowned easily. Especially when one of us was messin' up. His voice was like a drum—booming, deep. His voice, his frown, and his attitude could put the fear of God in you. Uncle Henry didn't play!"

Daddy chuckled.

"I dearly loved Uncle Henry, though. We all did. In fact, he was probably the favorite of everybody in the family. Whenever there was going to be a family gathering, we all wanted it to be at Uncle Henry's. At Uncle Henry's you knew that there would be lots to do, lots to eat, and best of all, lots and lots of Uncle Henry."

Daddy has a deep voice, too. A good telling voice.

"Uncle Henry had worked hard to get where he wanted to be in life. And he was one of the lucky ones: He got there. Yep, Uncle Henry was a grand old guy. One of those people you hope will go on forever."

Daddy looked out into the darkness. I think he was seeing Uncle Henry in his mind. I think I was, too.

"Whenever us nephews and nieces were gathered around the breakfast or dinner table, Uncle Henry would claim the floor, but we didn't mind at all. Uncle Henry was a magnificent storyteller! And though we didn't know it then, his stories were like fuel for our young minds.

"Uncle Henry firmly believed that the knowledge of our history—the history of black folks—was the most important story that we could ever be told. I can just hear him now: 'You can know where you are going in this world only if you know where you've been!'"

Mr. Fisher slapped his hand on his leg. "Now that's a man after my own heart!" he said.

"*Shhhhh*, Fisher. Let J.S. go on," Shoo Kate said.

Daddy did. "Uncle Henry held us spellbound with his stories. He told us about the great civilizations of Africa that existed thousands of years ago, and—"

"Tell us about that!" T-Bone moved real close to Daddy.

"That's a story for another time, T," Daddy said. "I'll be sure to tell you, but I'd better get on with this one now.

"One of Uncle Henry's stories described how he had been there that Sunday at the Lincoln Memorial. But that same story had another part, a part that told something that had happened *before* that famous Sunday.

"You see, another important event had taken place in that same spot seventeen years earlier—the dedication of the Lincoln Memorial. Uncle Henry had been there then, too."

"Wow!" said T-Bone and Punkin. I knew how they felt.

"It wasn't as much of a 'wow' as you might think, kids. At the dedication of this monument to the man known as the Great Emancipator, the black folks who came had to stand in a special section. A section off to the left of the monument. Away from the white folks, who could stand dead center, right in front."

Daddy had started breathing hard. It sounded loud. Everything else was quiet. Except Daddy's breathing.

"Anyhow, during one of our visits to Uncle Henry, Marian Anderson was going to be giving another concert. It was very important to Uncle Henry that all the nieces and nephews have a chance to go."

"So, you heard a concert at the Lincoln Memorial, too, right?" T-Bone sure was making it hard for Daddy to get on with his story. I wanted to put some tape over his mouth.

Daddy smiled. "No, as a matter of fact, I didn't. The concert I went to was held at Constitution Hall."

"What?" All of us were surprised at this twist.

"That's right," Daddy said. His breathing wasn't so loud now. "It was 1965, over twenty-five years since that concert at the Lincoln Memorial. Marian Anderson was now at the end of her career as a singer. This concert was taking place so she could say farewell to Washington audiences.

"Constitution Hall was still one of the finest concert stages in Washington, a stage now open to all performers, no matter what their color. It had been that way for years. But that concert and that magnificent singer were special. Very special."

Everybody was looking at Daddy as he went on.

"Many of the people in the hall that night were African Americans. Some of these black people had also been standing on the grass under the sky that Sunday morning. And some, like Uncle Henry, had been out there on the grass for the dedication in 1922. Now these same people were sitting in the forbidden hall, some of them in the best seats in the house!

"When Marian Anderson came onto the stage, the applause of the crowd was like the roar of a thousand pounding seas. It went on and on and on. But above the noise, there was one thing I heard very clearly."

"You heard your Uncle Henry, right?" Miss Ida was smiling at Dad. And her eyes were sparkly. Like raindrops are sparkly when I can look through them on my window and see the sun.

My dad's voice was real soft. "I did, Ida. I could hear Uncle Henry. But I think I would have known what he was saying even if I hadn't heard him. Just like I can hear him right now: 'You can know where you are going in this world only if you know where you've been!'"

In the quiet after Daddy stopped talking, I looked out into the velvet black sky. I tried to imagine the sound of a thousand pounding seas. I tried to imagine some other things, too. Like how it might have been to ride on a trolley. Or to spend the night in the same house with a famous person. Or to go to a famous monument and not be able to stand where I wanted to.

My dad's story brought the end to the very best time that evening.

Like we always did, Freda, T, Punkin, and I said good-night to all the grown-ups and walked each other home. I walked Freda home and then she walked me home, and then I walked her home again. Sylvia told on us like she usually does, so I finally went home for good to go to bed.

Just before I go to sleep is the very, very last part of the very best time. After I'm in bed and my light is turned off. I can look out my bedroom window and see Miss Ida's porch.

Most of the time the grown-ups are still there. I can hear them talking and laughing, but it's soft and far away.

These sounds feel good. They keep the very best times close. So close that they're with me when my eyelids stop cooperating and just drop. I think the very best times go with me into my dreams . . .

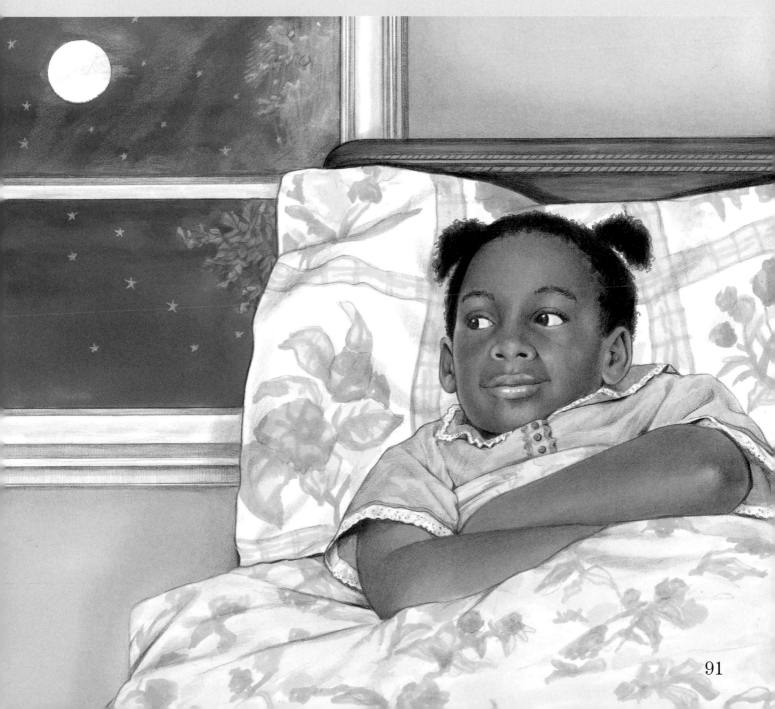

Meet the Author

Sandra Belton

Sandra Belton grew up in a segregated town in the hills of West Virginia. Belton and her friends spent Saturdays at the local library, one of the few places where black and white children were treated the same. While she loved the library, Belton soon realized that she wanted more books about black families. Her experiences inspired her to write stories about her childhood. She currently lives with her husband and son in Chicago.

Meet the Illustrator

Meryl Treatner

Treatner has made art since she was old enough to hold a crayon. She studied art at college, and her first job was drawing pictures in a courtroom. Later she drew pictures for newspapers, and finally she started working on children's books. Treatner's rat terrier, Emmy, has modeled for many of her books. Emmy lives with Treatner and her three children.

Theme Connections

Within the Selection

1. Why did the children love seeing Uncle Henry even though he was so serious?
2. Why do you think the audience at Constitution Hall applauded for such a long time?

Across Selections

3. How are "The Land I Lost," "Our Song," and "From Miss Ida's Porch" similar?
4. How is this story different from "The Land I Lost"?

Beyond the Selection

5. Uncle Henry says, "You can know where you are going in this world only if you know where you've been." What do you think he means?
6. How does storytelling help preserve history?

Write about It!

Retell a story you have heard from an older relative.

Remember to look for pictures of famous monuments or opera singers to add to the **Concept/Question Board.**

93

A Time Line of the American Civil Rights Movement

Genre

Expository Text tells people something. It contains facts about real people, things, or events.

Feature

Time Lines show a series of events placed in the order of time that they occurred.

1900

1905 The Niagara Movement is founded by W.E.B. DuBois and other prominent African Americans.

1909 The Niagara Movement changes its name to the National Association for the Advancement of Colored People.

1910

1939 Marian Anderson performs at the Lincoln Memorial.

1941 President Franklin Roosevelt signs the first federal law prohibiting racial discrimination.

1940

1942 Congress of Racial Equality (CORE) is formed.

1944 United Negro College Fund is started.

1947 Sixteen members of CORE (eight black men and eight white men) are arrested and jailed for traveling together in the segregated South.

1945

1948 President Truman ends segregation in the United States armed forces.

1950

1954 In Brown vs. the Board of Education, the Supreme Court rules that segregation is illegal.

1955 Rosa Parks refuses to give up her bus seat and sparks the Montgomery Bus Boycott led by Martin Luther King Jr.

1955

1957 President Eisenhower orders federal troops into Little Rock, Arkansas, to enforce integration of the public schools.

1960 Four students in Greensboro, North Carolina, stage the first sit-in at a segregated lunch counter.

1960

1961 Interracial groups of students, many of them members of CORE, take part in the Freedom Rides through southern states.

1963 Hundreds of thousands of people participate in the March on Washington. They hear Martin Luther King Jr. tell the world "I have a dream."

1964 President Johnson signs the Civil Rights Act.

1965 Thousands of protestors march in Alabama for voting rights.

President Johnson signs the Voting Rights Act.

1965

1968 Martin Luther King Jr. is assassinated.

1970

During the 1920s and '30s, classical singer Marian Anderson wowed fans around the world with her magnificent voice. Her talent was not enough, though, to overcome some people's prejudices.

In 1939, Anderson was forbidden to perform at Constitution Hall in Washington, D.C. The Daughters of the American Revolution—the group that owned the concert hall—banned her because of her race. Thousands of DAR members, including First Lady Eleanor Roosevelt, resigned in protest when they heard about this decision.

Eleanor Roosevelt and Secretary of the Interior Harold Ickes made plans for Anderson to sing at the Lincoln Memorial instead. Nearly eighty thousand people attended this famous concert.

Think Link

1. In which year did the first sit-ins occur?

2. What organization banned Marian Anderson from singing at Constitution Hall?

3. Choose an event from the time line, and search online to discover why it was an important event in the Civil Rights Movement.

Try It!

As you work on your investigation, think about how you might use a time line to display events in the order they occurred.

Read the article to find the meanings of these words, which are also in "In Two Worlds: A Yup'ik Eskimo Family":

- ✦ lagoon
- ✦ freighter
- ✦ vast
- ✦ withered
- ✦ inhabit
- ✦ luxury
- ✦ tilted
- ✦ fluent
- ✦ role
- ✦ sewage

Vocabulary Strategy

Context Clues are hints in the text that help you find the meanings of words. Look at the words *freighter* and *inhabit*. Use context clues to find each word's meaning.

Vocabulary
Warm-Up

Imagine sitting on the beach of a deserted island. You stare across the clear blue water of a lagoon, looking out toward the open sea. The tiny shape of a freighter carrying its cargo slides quietly across the horizon. Then you think, *Boy, I am thirsty!*

The island does not have any streams or lakes, but a vast ocean surrounds it, filled with saltwater you cannot drink. You tried watering some of the island's plants with it, but they just withered and died. How will you be able to inhabit the island? At that moment, thunder rumbles in the sky and you get an idea. *I will collect rainwater!*

Believe it or not, living in a city is not that different from the island. Freshwater is just as precious. Thousands of people gathered in one place would have trouble surviving without a complex system to bring them clean water.

Many of the lakes, rivers, and streams that provide cities with water are filled by rain and snow. The rest of our water comes from underground. It either bubbles up naturally from springs, or we dig wells to reach it.

Some parts of Earth do not have easy access to freshwater. It is a luxury item. Engineers have to find ways to get water from one place to another. One early example of this engineering is the Roman aqueduct. It looked like a giant bridge stretching across the land. It was tilted slightly so that water flowed many miles to where it was needed.

Some engineers travel all over the world supplying clean water to the people who need it. Many of the engineers are fluent in more than one language. They also play an important role in cleaning sewage from water that people have already used.

Although the planet is swimming in saltwater, the amount of freshwater is limited. We need to be careful that Earth does not become a desert island.

GAME

Fill in the Blanks
On a separate sheet of paper, complete the following sentences with selection vocabulary words.

1. Because they had not been watered, Russ's crops _____ in the hot sun.
2. Deirdre got the _____ she wanted in the school play.
3. Someday, humans may _____ another planet.

Concept Vocabulary

The concept word for this lesson is **generations.** *Generations* are a way to distinguish people of one time period from another. For example, you and others who are about the same age are considered one generation, and the people your parents' age are a different generation. What historical events were happening during your great-grandparents' generation?

Genre

Expository Text tells people something. It contains facts about real people, things, or events.

Comprehension Skill

 Compare and Contrast

As you read the selection, compare and contrast characters, events, settings, and ideas to help you better understand the text.

98

In Two Worlds:

A Yup'ik Eskimo Family

by Aylette Jenness and Alice Rivers

Focus Questions

What is life like for the Yup'iks in the present day? Why do they continue to teach their children the old ways?

The Past Long Ago

Alice and Billy Rivers live with their children in the small town of Scammon Bay, Alaska, on the coast of the Bering Sea. They are Yup'ik Eskimos. Their story really begins long, long ago.

Alice and Billy's parents, grandparents, great-grandparents, great-great-grandparents—all their ancestors for several thousand years—have always lived here. They were part of a small group of Yup'ik Eskimos whose home was this vast area of tidal flats bordering the sea, with inland marshes, ponds, creeks, and rivers lacing the flat treeless tundra, broken only by occasional masses of low hills.

Each year, as the northern part of the earth tilted toward the sun, the long hours of sunlight here melted the snow, melted the sea ice, melted the rivers, melted, even, the frozen land down to the depth of a foot or so. Briefly, for a few months, birds came from the south to lay their eggs and raise their young. The fish spawned, plants grew, berries ripened. And then the earth tilted away from the sun. Days grew shorter, the sun weaker, temperatures fell. The rain turned to snow, plants withered, birds flew south. Ponds, creeks, rivers, and finally even the Bering Sea froze, and layers of snow covered the whole landscape. Fish, sea mammals, and land animals all moved beneath thick blankets of ice and snow.

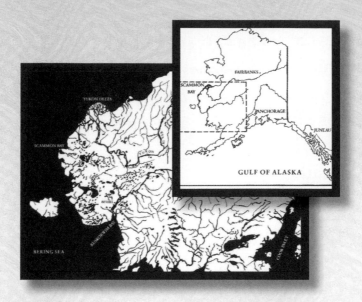

The small, scattered groups of Yup'ik Eskimos knew exactly how to survive here. Living as single families, or in small groups of relatives, they moved with the seasons to catch each kind of fish, bird, or mammal when and where each was most easily available. They harpooned the whales that migrated north along the coast in spring and south in the fall. They shot and snared birds nesting on the tundra, and they gathered the birds' eggs. They netted saltwater fish coming to lay their eggs in the rivers and creeks, and they caught freshwater fish moving beneath the ice of inland creeks. They trapped small mammals on the land for meat and for fur clothing. They knew where to find and how to catch dozens of different fish and animals for food, for clothing, even for light and heat for their small homes.

They had fire, but they didn't know how to use it to make metal. Everything they had they made themselves, with their hands, with stone, bone, or ivory tools—their many intricate snares and nets and traps, their boats and sleds, their homes and their clothing. Life was hard and precarious. Nothing was wasted.

Their mark on the land was light. Today their old sites are nearly part of the earth, not easy to see. These Yup'ik Eskimos didn't build monuments to gods or leaders. They believed that animals had spirits, and that the spirits survived the animals' death to inhabit other animals. After killing a seal, they put water in its mouth to show their caring and respect for it and to ensure that its spirit would return in the form of another seal another time. They made up stories and dances of awe, fear, and pleasure in the animals they knew so well.

They shared with each other, and no one was much better or worse off than anyone else. Families, or groups of families, had rights to certain places for hunting or fishing, but no one owned the land or its resources.

They knew no outsiders, no one different from themselves. During those hundreds and hundreds of years, their way of life changed very little. People followed in the footsteps of their ancestors, children learning from their parents the vast body of knowledge necessary for survival in this environment.

But during the last fifty years, their lives have changed enormously. And these changes are within the memory of the older people living here now.

Listen to Alice Rivers's mother, Mary Ann, describe her childhood. She speaks in Yup'ik, and one of her daughters, Leota, translates into English.

Mary Ann Remembers

"I was born, as I was told, in the late fall. My mother delivered me outside in the tundra, out in the open. My mother told me that after I was born I clutched some tundra moss and grass in my hand. I do not know why I was born outside, but it must have been because my mother was out in the tundra.

"When I was first aware of my surroundings, we lived on the other side of the mountains of Scammon Bay. The name of the place where I was born is called Ingeluk, and I think it's called this name because we are surrounded by small hills. We were the only people living in that area. We were secluded away from other people. There was my father, my mother, my two older sisters, and one older brother, and I am the youngest in the family.

"We lived in a sod house. The insides of our house had braided grass hanging on the walls as paneling. We had only one window, which was made out of dried seal guts, and it made a lot of noise when it was windy. Our floor was plain, hard, dried mud. Our beds were dried grass, piled high to keep us warm. We had no blankets. We mostly did with what we had at hand, and we used our parkas to keep us warm. I remember we had one kettle, a small half kerosene tank for our cooking pot, and the plates we had were carved from wood by my father.

"For light, we used seal oil when we had the oil, and it smoked a lot. Other times we had no light because we had no oil. I remember my mother cooked whitefish, and she carefully skimmed off the oil from the pot we had, and what she took out of the cooking pot we used in our oil lamp. The oil from the fish made pretty good light; it never smoked like the seal oil did. There were lots of stories being told, that's what we did during the evenings.

"Our main diet was fish, caught in my father's traps. There were times that we were really hungry. We were very poor. Sometimes when we woke up in the morning, we had nothing at all to eat.

"We didn't have any kind of bread. We did not know what coffee and tea were.

"I saw my first white man when we were traveling by our skin boat. I did not know who he was, but later on I was told that the white man was trading goods for fur or skins. Maybe I was fifteen years old when I saw an airplane.

"I liked the life we used to live a long time ago, but we were always in need of something. I would say we live in comfort now. I don't go in hunger now. I say both lives I led were good, and I like both."

Mary Ann grew up and married a man who lived nearby, Teddy Sundown. They began to raise their family in Keggatmiut, as Scammon Bay is known in Yup'ik. It was a good site, and a number of families settled there. They built their small log houses on the lower slope of a range of hills that rose out of the flat tundra. A clear stream, racing down the hillside, flowed into the river that wound along the base of the hills, and finally emptied into a wide, shallow bay of the Bering Sea. Mary Ann and Teddy still moved to seasonal camps to fish, trap, and hunt, but as the village grew, they began to spend more and more of the year there.

The United States government set up a school in Scammon Bay and hired a Yup'ik teacher. All of the children were expected to attend school.

Missionaries had come to convert the people from their traditional religion, and the village was divided between Catholics and Protestants. Two churches were built.

Alice was the fourth child born to Mary Ann and Teddy. She is shown at the age of ten, standing on the far right of her family. She speaks of growing up in Scammon Bay.

Alice Remembers

"Our home was a one-room building. Our beds were together—Mom and Dad's bed and our bed. All of us kids slept together in one bed. No table—the tables came later on. We used to eat sitting on the floor, Eskimo way. Mom used to cook bread on top of the stove, 'cause there was no oven. To me it used to be the best bread I've eaten. Then as I grew older, we got a stove and oven, and she started baking bread.

"We ate bread, birds, dried herrings, clams, mussels, fish—boiled and frozen—seals, mink, muskrats. There were two stores. We bought shortening, flour, tea, coffee—just what we needed.

"We were always together. We'd go to church every morning. Mom would wake us up early, we'd go to Mass. We never used to be lazy, we used to just go, get up and go, get up to a real cold morning, and by the time we were home, the house would be nice and warm.

"Right after church we used to go straight to school, all of us. I remember that learning to write my name was the hardest thing. I was maybe about six. We had Eskimo teachers. It was one room, and everything was there.

"After school, we'd have lots of things to do—bringing some wood in, dishes to wash, house to clean, babies to watch, water to pack. We had aluminum pails with handles. We used to run over to the stream and pack water until we had what we needed. In the winter we had to keep one hole in the ice open the whole winter. This was one of the things I used to do with my sisters, not only me.

"Planes came in maybe once a week with mail. We didn't know about telephones. We had a radio, just for listening. I think we listened to one station all the time. No TV.

"The teachers had a short-wave radio. If someone got sick, they would report us to the hospital. They would give us medication or send us to the hospital in Bethel."

Alice Grown Up

By the time Alice was an adult, Scammon Bay was a village of a hundred and fifty people, with twenty-five log and frame homes. For transportation, each family had a dog sled and team, and a boat for use in summer.

The government began to take a larger role in the Yup'ik villages. A new school was built, with living quarters for non-Eskimo teachers from outside of Alaska. Children were taught a standard public elementary school curriculum, which had little reference either to their own lives or to what they knew and didn't know about life outside Scammon Bay. They were forbidden to speak Yup'ik in school, in the belief that this would help them to learn English, and that learning English was very important.

A postmaster was hired from among the village men, and a custodian for the school. A health aide was trained, and a small clinic built and stocked. More planes came to Scammon Bay, and it became easier to fly someone needing hospital care out—as long as the weather was good.

Government money became available for low-income families and for the elderly and disabled. There were few opportunities to earn cash, but almost all of the men in Scammon Bay were able to earn some money by hunting or trapping seals, mink, muskrats, and beaver and selling the skins to be made into luxury fur coats outside of Alaska.

In summer they netted salmon in the river mouths north of Scammon Bay and sold this valuable fish to processors, who marketed it throughout the United States as smoked fish, or lox.

Each summer a freighter came up the coast from Seattle, Washington, with supplies for the villages. Everyone began to buy more factory-made goods. Some families bought stoves that burned fuel oil instead of relying on brush wood they cut nearby. Some bought windmills, which produced enough electricity for one or two light bulbs in their homes. Some bought snowmobiles, which enabled them to travel farther than they could by dog team to hunt and trap, but which, unlike dogs, required money for fuel and new parts.

And for the first time in the long history of the Yup'ik Eskimos, some people began to travel away from their homeland. Some teenagers went to boarding school in the state of Washington. Some men went to National Guard training, and some families moved away permanently, settling in Alaskan towns and cities, or even as far away as Oregon and California.

But most remained in Scammon Bay, and some new Yup'ik people came to live there from other towns.

Now

Alice's life today is both very similar to that of her mother at the same age—and very different. Scammon Bay has grown and changed in many ways.

There are three hundred and fifty people in Scammon Bay now, living in fifty-six houses. Most of the old log homes are now used for storage, and many people, like the Riverses, have new houses provided by the government at low cost. A dish antenna relays television to all the homes. Satellite transmission enables families to make telephone calls anywhere in the world. Huge storage tanks hold fuel to run an electric generator that provides enough power for each home to have all the lights that people want. A water and sewage disposal system required building a water treatment plant and a lagoon on the tundra for waste water. The dump, full of cans, plastic, fuel drums, and broken machinery, is a reminder of the difficulty of disposing of modern trash.

For some years the state government made a great deal of money from taxes on oil found in Alaska, and this money paid for many of the modern conveniences in Scammon Bay and other rural towns. An airstrip was built so that planes could land more easily at all times of the year; it is regularly plowed in winter.

Three small planes a day fly into Scammon Bay, bringing everything from cases of soft drinks to boxes of disposable diapers and, of course, the mail. A huge new gym has been built, and a new clinic, a preschool center, town offices, and a post office. The school is now run by the state, not the federal government, and goes all the way through the twelfth grade.

In spite of the changes, the traditional pattern of living from the land is still powerful. This can be seen most clearly as people move to seasonal camps during the summer months.

School

During the school year the family's life falls into very different patterns from those of summer. Billy begins his winter rounds of hunting and fishing, going out by snowmobile nearly every day to get food or firewood for the family. Alice goes to work as the school cook, and the Rivers children go to their classrooms each morning.

Billy Junior, in the second grade, is learning to type. He says proudly, "I've already finished typing one book, and now I'm on another. We can read any kind of books. Now I'm on a hard one."

In Sarah and Isaac's combined third and fourth grade class, Clifford Kaganak teaches Yup'ik. Here he writes words in Yup'ik on the chalkboard, and the class practices reading and translating. They want to be fluent in both of their languages—English and Yup'ik.

Down the hall, Jennifer Allison Keim works with the older Rivers boys—Oscar, Jacob and Abraham. Jacob enjoys using the computers, but generally the boys would rather be out hunting and fishing—or using the school skis. Jennifer says, "My goals are for the kids to be educated to the point where they can protect themselves from outsiders, so if something comes their way that they have to deal with, they'll know how to weigh and measure and make decisions."

The teachers all know that the school has a great responsibility to prepare the kids for the outside world, and they also want to encourage a sense of pride in Yup'ik Eskimo culture. Some students want to go on to college after graduating from high school in Scammon Bay, and the teachers work hard to make this happen.

On the Weekends

During the school year, traditional ways of life are practiced mostly on the weekends. The end of each school week marks the beginning of two days of hunting and fishing for the whole Rivers family.

Alice says, "On the weekends, we get to go traveling with Billy. Usually we decide what we're going to do ahead of time, what's going to happen. Like if we want to go fishing, we go fishing, or hunting ptarmigans. We're out most of the day Saturday doing this and that."

This is where Billy becomes the teacher, training the kids in both the oldest methods of hunting and fishing, and the newest. Since the children spend so much time in school, this is an important time for them to learn how to survive as Eskimos.

"I teach my boys the way I've been taught, the way my dad taught me. What I think that's wrong, I try to do it better than my dad. And when I make a mistake, I try to correct it to my boys, so they'll do it better than I did.

"I start taking them out as soon as they're old enough—like in the boat, when they're old enough to sit down and take care of themselves. I tell them little things like taking the anchor out, putting the anchor back up. As soon as they understand our words, we teach them from there. If they show you something that they know, you'll know they learned it—and then they can start doing it by themselves.

"Each one of them that goes with me, I talk to them, I tell them about little things—what's dangerous, what's not dangerous. I tell them about melting ice—even though it looks good on the surface, some places you can't see when it's covered with snow, it's thin. That's where they fall through. I teach them what thin ice looks like, and how it looks when it's safe.

"Oscar's been going with me first, 'cause he's the oldest one, then Jacob. One of them will know more, the one that pays attention more, just like in school. The one that doesn't listen, or doesn't pay attention, he'll make more mistakes or get more scolding.

"Oscar was about seven or eight when I first let him shoot a gun. He got his first seal when he was maybe eight or nine. In the boat I did the driving, and I had him do the shooting. He got a young mukluk that was a baby in springtime. He shot it, and after he shot it, he looked at me, looked back, and he smiled. 'I catch it.'"

Oscar remembers this very clearly. He says, "My grandpa divided the seal up in circles and gave it to the old people." This is the traditional Yup'ik way of sharing a boy's first catch with the elders, still carried on, though motorboats have replaced kayaks, and rifles are used in place of thrown harpoons.

The Future

Alice and Billy know very well that life is changing fast here in Scammon Bay, and they want their children to be prepared for this.

Alice says, "When I was a kid, I used to do things with my mom. I used to watch her sew. Now I try to have Mattie knit, crochet, make things, but she thinks it's too boring. She knows how to do it, but she can't sit and look at one thing for a long time. I can't even teach her how to sew a skin. She doesn't have any patience.

"Now there's so many other things going on. In our time there was no basketball, no Igloo [community center], hardly any dances."

Billy says, "When I was Billy Junior's age, I used to run maybe twenty or thirty times around a pond with my little wooden boat. Just run around, play with it, put mud inside of it, and run around. I'd never think of TV, it wasn't in my mind.

"Everything is not the same here in Alaska, not like before. Things are changing. Things are getting more expensive. Most of the people are depending on more jobs. I mean working, you have to have a job.

"I talk to the kids, I just say what we'd like them to do. I tell them, 'If you go to school, and be smart over there, and try to learn what you're taught, you guys will have good jobs, and good-paying jobs. I want you to have good-paying jobs, so we'll have the things that we need, anything we need'; like this I talk to them.

"I'd be happy to have them travel to see other countries, to have them learning something that's Outside—*if* they have a job. 'Cause Outside there's many people without jobs, no home. Here it's okay, as we help each other here in the villages.

"We get after the kids for not doing their homework. We want them to be more educated, more than us. I mean, learn more. I only went up to the fifth grade."

Alice agrees. She adds "I want them to learn other ways—Outside ways. And I want them to learn our ways, too—hunting for our kind of foods. We can't have store-bought food all the time. I want them to learn both ways."

Looking down on Scammon Bay from the hill, it seems like a very small settlement, nearly lost in the huge expanse of tundra around it. From this distance it doesn't look so different from the Scammon Bay of Alice's childhood. Yet it is invisibly connected to the whole world now. And so is the Rivers family.

Meet the Authors

Aylette Jenness and Alice Rivers

Aylette Jenness, a writer and photographer, met Alice Rivers when they were both young women. At the time, Aylette had moved to Alaska to write *Gussuk Boy* and *Dwellers of the Tundra,* books about the people of Scammon Bay. After finishing the books, Aylette left Alaska. When she returned for a visit more than twenty years later, she met up with her old friend, Alice Rivers. Alice told her about how different things were in Scammon Bay since she had lived there twenty years ago. The two decided to work together on the story of how Alice's family had grown and changed, and how the little community on the Bering Sea had changed as well. Rivers's mother, Mary Ann Sundown, also contributed to the book by telling about the way people lived during the years she was growing up near Scammon Bay.

Theme Connections

Within the Selection

1. How is modern life for the Rivers family different from their life in the past? How is it the same?

2. Why do you think the traditions practiced by Alice, Billy, and their children are important to them?

Across Selections

3. What do the fathers in this story and "The Land I Lost" have in common?

4. How are the Riverses different from the other families described in this unit?

Beyond the Selection

5. What stories have your older family members told of how life has changed since they were young?

6. Do you think the changes that came to Scammon Bay were good or bad? Why?

Write about It!

Ask an older family member to explain how life was different when he or she was young. Write about how you would feel living at that time.

Remember to look for historic photographs of your city or town to add to the **Concept/ Question Board.**

Science Inquiry

The Laketown Water Treatment Plant

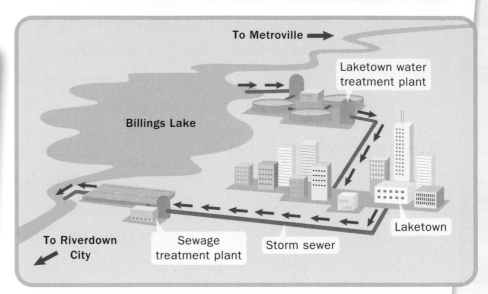
Genre

Expository Text tells people something. It contains facts about real people, things, or events.

Feature

Diagrams are drawings that are used to show how something works or the relationship among things.

What We Do

Each day we treat about forty million gallons of water. Fifteen hundred miles of pipes bring this water to the 300,000 residents that inhabit Laketown.

Treating the Water

Water pumped from Billings Lake flows into giant tanks here at the plant. Then a chemical called alum is added. Alum causes pieces of dirt in the water to stick together. Paddles in the tanks stir the water to help the alum do its job. As the dirt clumps, it becomes heavy and sinks to the bottom of the tank. The water moves slowly through a series of tanks and leaves the dirt behind.

Next the water flows through filters made of sand and gravel. They remove even the smallest particles of dirt. The last step is to add chlorine.

122

It kills any germs that are living in the water. Now it should be ready to drink, but we test it first.

Sewage Treatment

Just south of us on Billings Creek, another one of our plants treats Laketown's sewage. First the wastewater travels through a series of screens with increasingly smaller holes. This process removes the biggest pieces of solid waste. Next the sewage moves into large tanks. The remaining solids sink to the bottom, but grease and oil float to the top where they can be skimmed off. In the next tank, bacteria are added to the sewage. They eat any organic materials left in the wastewater. Finally chemicals are added to finish cleaning the water before it is pumped back into the river.

Think Link

1. Why is alum added when treating water?

2. If Laketown's wastewater is not treated properly, where will the dirty water go? Use the diagram to help answer this question.

3. Where does the water you use in your home or school come from? Use the Internet to discover which water treatment plant supplies your neighborhood and where it gets its water.

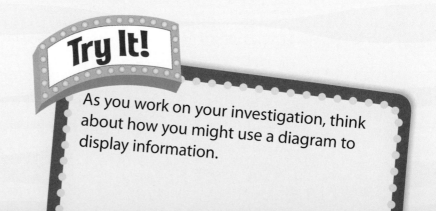

Try It!

As you work on your investigation, think about how you might use a diagram to display information.

I Look at You

by Kelly Hill

I look at you and my mind drifts back to
    A time of peace and honesty
    A time of honor
    A time when all our people
        spoke our Native language
        and were proud to wear
        eagle feathers and beads.
    A time of dancing and giving thanks
        for all that Mother Earth
        gave our people:

        buffalo that roamed the grasslands
        fish that swam in clear blue rivers and lakes
        trees that our canoes were made from
        horses our people rode
        natural spring water pure and cool
        berries, roots, and bulbs, grown in rich soil
        rocks people used to tan hides
        stones our people used for arrow tips
Then I wish our people had that time again
    A time of peace and honesty
    A time of honor.

125

Mama's Glory

by Joyce Carol Thomas
illustrated by Nicole Tadgell

Mama says, "I wear my hair natural
In memory of a faraway place."
Her hair is thick and soft
A frame around her face

Her hair is a continent
Her glory on earth
"My Africa," she says
"Our ancestors' place of birth."

She picks it with a comb
'Til it stands sculpted and round
I like the way it looks and feels
A halo of a crown.

Test-Taking Strategy: Writing an answer to a question

Sometimes you will be asked to write an answer on a test. The answer may be as short as one sentence or as long as a whole page. Be sure to read the directions and question carefully so you know what you are supposed to do.

Writing an answer to a question

Read these directions and questions. They would follow a story that you would have read. Think about what you should do.

> **What are the ways that the family got ready for the storm? Use details and information from the story to support your answer.**

The story was probably about a big storm and what a family did. That means **you should answer the question based on what you read.** When you write your answer, you should use details from the story to show what the family did to get ready.

Here's a different kind of writing task. Read the directions carefully.

Your school does not have a track team for girls and boys. You and your friends want the school to start one. Write a letter to the school board explaining why your school should have a track team.

This writing task asks for your ideas. You have to think about the question and write a letter using your own thoughts.

In both kinds of writing, you should plan your writing before you begin. Think about what you want to say, and then write in a way that makes it easy for the reader to understand you.

Tortillas on Saturday

"Why do you make tortillas every Saturday, Mama?" Berto asked. "Why not just buy them at the store like you do every other day?"

Berto's mother rolled the ball of tortilla dough in her hand. She shaped it a little and then put it on the tortilla press. She had already covered the bottom with a piece of clear plastic wrap. She put another piece of plastic wrap carefully on top of the ball of dough. She pulled down on the handle slowly, counted to two, and then opened the press.

The dough was now flat and covered on both sides with plastic wrap. She removed the wrapped tortilla and put it aside. She slid a cooked tortilla from the flat pan called a *comal* onto a towel. Mama then peeled the plastic from the flat tortilla, turned it over in her hand, peeled off the plastic from the other side, and placed it on the *comal*.

Mama repeated the process dozens of times. Berto and the other children loved watching her do it. When Mexican music was playing on the radio while she worked, he said it was like seeing a music video.

129

"When I was a little girl, my grandmother made tortillas every Saturday." Mama paused for a moment as she spoke. She looked out the window as if she could see her *abuelita*. "That was a long time ago. You could not buy tortillas in many places in the United States. Now you can. I loved watching *Abuelita* and loved eating her tortillas even more. For years, Grandmother did not even have a press—she made them flat with her hands. I can remember the year we bought her a tortilla press for Christmas. I could not tell if she was happy or sad. She liked the press because it made her work so much easier. I think she felt a little sad because she was giving up a tradition. She had flattened tortillas by hand her whole life."

Berto's sisters came into the room and pulled chairs up to the table. They kneeled on the chairs and grabbed handfuls of dough. They made them into round shapes. Berto did the same thing.

"Not too many," said Mama. "The dough will dry out. Be patient. You will all have a turn."

Mama helped each of the children flatten and cook a tortilla. They could almost do it themselves. They had watched or helped every Saturday since they had been born. Mama hoped that when they grew up, their children would remember their *abuelita* when they made tortillas on Saturday.

GO ON

1. Read this sentence from the story.

   Mama repeated the process dozens of times.

   What does the word *repeated* mean in this sentence?

   Ⓐ told about

   Ⓑ cooked

   Ⓒ did again

   Ⓓ dropped

Test Tips

- Read the directions carefully.

- Skim the story, but do not try to memorize it.

- Skim the questions and do the easiest ones first.

2. Why was the tortilla dough covered with plastic wrap?

   Ⓕ So it could be flattened by hand.

   Ⓖ So it could be rolled into a ball.

   Ⓗ So it would not stick to the comal.

   Ⓘ So it would not stick to the press.

3. The last paragraph of the story is mostly about

   Ⓐ Mama's hope for the future.

   Ⓑ the children's ability to make tortillas.

   Ⓒ the importance of being careful.

   Ⓓ why *Abuelita* liked her tortilla press.

4. How would you answer Berto's question "Why do you make tortillas every Saturday, Mama?" Use details and information from the passage to support your answer.

STOP

Energy at Work

How does energy affect our lives? What are some different forms of energy? Where does energy come from? What are some alternate or unique sources of energy?

Theme Connection

Look at the photo of Nikola Tesla, a nineteenth-century scientist and inventor, working in his laboratory.

- What do you see in the photo?
- How does the photo relate to the theme Energy at Work?
- What questions do you have after looking at the photo?

BIG Idea

How does energy affect your life?

Read the article to find the meanings of these words, which are also in "The Sparks Fly":

+ demonstration
+ retirement
+ attracted
+ donors
+ inefficient
+ dissolve
+ insulators
+ electrocuted
+ vents
+ charged

Vocabulary Strategy

An **appositive** is a noun that follows another noun to modify or name it. Authors sometimes use apposition to clarify the meanings of words. Look at the word *donors*. Find how the author uses apposition to define the word.

Vocabulary
Warm-Up

Dr. Gupta entered the room to loud applause. Scientists from around the world had gathered to watch a demonstration of his newest invention. It was the doctor's final project before heading into retirement. He was ready for some time off.

Dr. Gupta had hinted for years that his machine would use very little energy to produce a lot of power. It would forever change how humans used Earth's resources. This news had attracted reporters to the laboratory as well.

The donors, people who had supplied Dr. Gupta with money for his project, could not wait to see the doctor's work.

"Ladies and gentlemen," Dr. Gupta began. "Many machines are very inefficient. They waste a great deal of energy to create only a small amount of power. My machine is the solution to this problem."

Dr. Gupta poured sugar into a large beaker of water. He stirred the mixture well so that the sugar would dissolve into the liquid. Then he poured it into a small metal box.

Wires coated in plastic ran from the box to a large battery. The plastic coatings were insulators. They did not carry an electrical charge. The wires were covered in plastic so that people would not get electrocuted or killed by electricity.

Dr. Gupta flipped a switch on the box, and it whirred to life. A meter showed that the battery's power was draining away.

"As the machine burns sugar water for fuel," Dr. Gupta explained, "exhaust flows out of these vents." He pointed to small openings on the box's side. "That is wasted energy."

Dr. Gupta covered each vent with a hose and sent the exhaust back into the top of the machine. Suddenly, the meter showed that the battery was being charged. The machine was making extra electricity and refilling the battery!

The crowd jumped to their feet, showering the doctor with applause. They had just witnessed the world's most efficient motor.

Substituting Synonyms
Using a thesaurus, find a synonym for each selection vocabulary word. On a separate sheet of paper, rewrite the sentences from the selection that contain vocabulary words, but substitute a synonym for each vocabulary word.

Concept Vocabulary

The concept word for this lesson is **curiosity.** *Curiosity* is wanting to know things. People who have curiosity are not satisfied until they have the answer. They love to learn. How did Benjamin Franklin's curiosity lead to the events in the selection? What role does curiosity play in other selections in the unit?

Genre

Expository Text tells people something. It contains facts about real people, things, or events.

Comprehension Strategy

☆ **Asking Questions**

As you read the selection, ask yourself what you want to learn. It is important to revisit the questions to see if they have been answered in the text.

Focus Questions

How did Benjamin Franklin contribute to our knowledge of energy? In what ways can energy benefit humankind?

THE SPARKS FLY

by Ruth Ashby

illustrated by Dick Smolinski

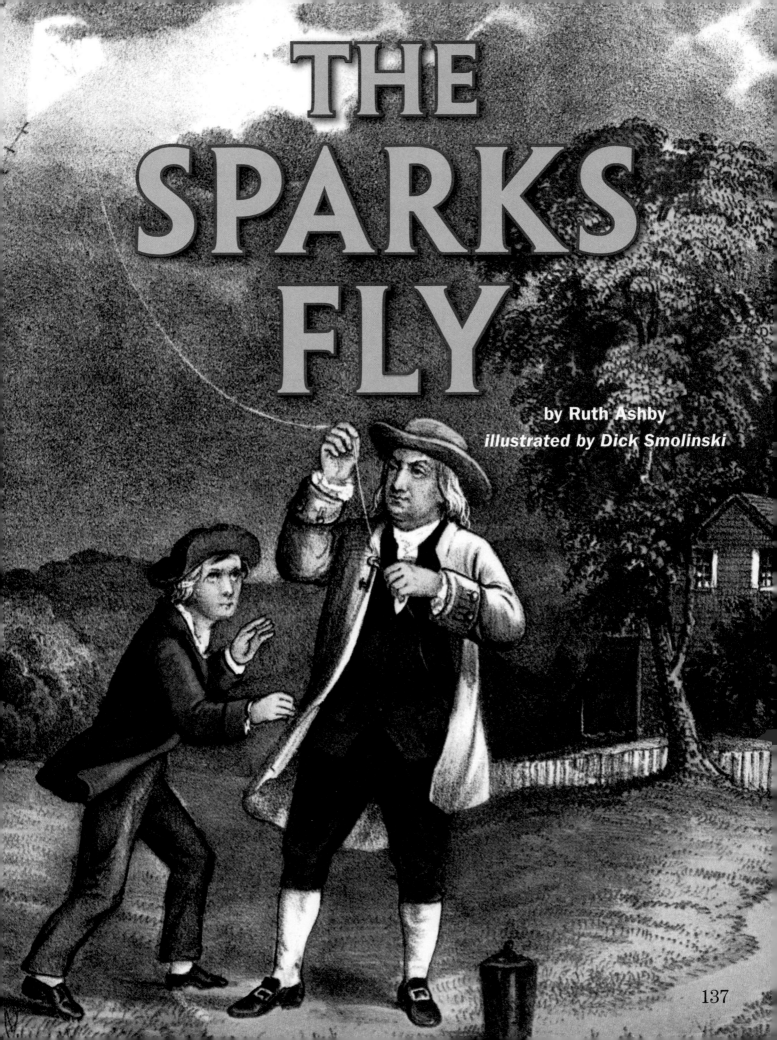

Throughout his life, Ben Franklin continued to ask questions. Why? How? What? Why does salt dissolve in water? Why are voyages from America to England so much faster than voyages from England to America? How do crabs reproduce? How do ants tell each other where to find food? What causes earthquakes?

Two years before his retirement, Ben had tried to find an answer to the old Junto question, "How can smoky chimneys be cured?" Heating a home in the 1700s was dirty and inefficient. Most colonial fireplaces spewed black smoke into the room. Meanwhile, most of the heat escaped up the chimney.

Franklin designed a stove he hoped would solve these problems. A wood fire in the metal stove would heat the air in an inner metal box. This warm air would then flow out through vents in the side of the stove. But the smoke would be carried out a pipe and up the chimney.

Franklin was very proud of his "Pennsylvania Fireplace." In his advertisements, he claimed that it made the room "twice as warm with a quarter of the wood." He could have made a lot of money from his invention. But he refused to patent it. He wished to serve others "freely and generously," through his inventions.

In order to satisfy his curiosity about the natural world, Franklin dove into every science book the Library Company ordered. He had always been interested in the sciences—in chemistry, mathematics, astronomy, biology. But nothing captured his curiosity the way electricity did.

Not much was known about electricity in the early 1700s. Somehow, people realized, "electrical fire" could be caused by rubbing glass or certain other materials. Sparks would fly out—*hiss, crackle, pop!* And if someone touched the electrified object, he or she could get a small shock—or a big one. Sometimes the jolt would be so great the person would be weak or sore for days.

Traveling showmen used electrical fire to entertain. First they filled a glass container with water, coated it with metal foil, and stopped it up with a cork. A metal rod stuck through the cork was set in the water. This was called a Leyden jar. After the jar was charged with a spark, anyone who touched it would get an electric shock.

In one famous demonstration, a French scientist in Louis XV's court sent a jolt of electricity through 180 soldiers holding hands. As the force passed though them, they all jumped at once. The audience loved it. The king laughed uproariously when the scientist gave the same demonstration with 800 monks.

Franklin had his first opportunity to see the mysterious force in action when he visited Boston in 1743. There a Scottish physician named Dr. Archibald Spencer was thrilling audiences with his electrical demonstrations.

Spencer would rub a long brass tube with his hand, then hold it near pieces of gold leaf. The gold pieces would whirl wildly in the air. Some of them leaped toward the tube—others darted away.

Then, in the climax of the show, Spencer suspended a young boy from the ceiling with silken ropes.

The audience held its breath.

Dr. Spencer rubbed a glass tube near the boy's feet. The boy's hair stood on end.

Franklin held his knuckles out towards one of the boy's fingers. *Flash!* A spark crackled between them.

Franklin was intrigued. I wish my friends could see this, he thought. He invited Dr. Spencer to come to Philadelphia, and advertised the lectures in the *Gazette.* On May 3, 1744, an announcement read: "A course of experimental philosophy [science] begins in the Library-Room, next Monday at five o'clock in the afternoon."

By 1744, the Library Company had moved to the second floor of Philadelphia's new State House, which later became known as Independence Hall. The rooms housed a collection of more than 400 books and a mini-museum. Thomas Penn's print of an orrery had been the first exhibition. Then came an air-pump from John Penn. Other donors sent fossils, dead animals preserved in glass jars, tanned skins, and all sorts of other strange and interesting objects. The Company owned both a microscope and a telescope, which were often borrowed by scientists.

The Library Company was the perfect place to hold scientific lectures. It was also the perfect place for Franklin to perform his own first experiments in electricity.

Franklin asked the Library's agent in London, Peter Collinson, to send any information he had on electricity. In 1747, Collinson shipped the Library a long glass tube and instructions for using it. Then Franklin and his friends started their experiments. During the winter of 1748–49, Franklin lived and dreamed electricity.

Franklin decided to have some fun. He made a little spider of burnt cork, with spindly linen legs. Inside the cork he placed a bit of lead. Then he hung the spider from a bit of silk thread and waited for visitors.

When anyone approached the table—the spider leapt up! The onlookers would jump back, startled. Back and forth the electric spider sprang between an electrified jar on one side of a table and a wire on the other. It looked alive!

Another time, Franklin electrified a painting of King George II. If someone touched his gilded crown, they got a "high-treason" shock!

Such "electrical amusements" could be really dangerous. Once Franklin himself was nearly electrocuted. He linked two jars together, and touched one of them by mistake. *Flash!* He felt a "universal blow from head to foot throughout the body."

His chest was sore for a week afterward. Luckily, Franklin had taken the shock through his hand. If it had come through his head, he realized, he might not still be alive to tell the story.

Playing with electricity was not all fun and games. Franklin made some very important discoveries and invented new ways to describe what he had observed:

- Sometimes objects with an electric charge attracted other objects. Sometimes they pushed them away. Electricity, Franklin decided, must contain equal amounts of *plus* and *minus* charges. Electricity was either *positive* or *negative.*

- Some materials, such as metal or water, carried the electrical charge easily. These were *conductors.* Other materials, such as wax or silk, did not carry the electric charge. They were *insulators.*

- If charged glass and lead plates were wired together, electricity could be stored for later use. These Franklin called electrical *batteries.*

- Electricity was attracted to pointed objects, such as metal rods. This observation would lead to one of Franklin's most famous inventions.

Franklin sent news of his experiments to Peter Collinson in England. Collinson, in turn, read his letters to the most important scientific organization in England, the Royal Society. Everyone began to speak of this clever American.

Ben thought that what he had learned might help other scientists make still more discoveries. So in 1751 he put the letters together into an eighty-six page pamphlet and published it. *Experiments and Other Observations on Electricity Made at Philadelphia in America* by Mr. Benjamin Franklin was an immediate hit on both sides of the Atlantic.

Franklin was having the time of his life.

Meet the Author

Ruth Ashby

Do you like learning about cats, tigers, or sea otters? Maybe you prefer reading about how people lived 200 years ago? If you enjoy reading nonfiction or a biography, then Ruth Ashby probably has a book for you. In addition to being a writer, Ashby has also worked as a teacher and a book editor. She lives in New York with her husband, daughter, and pets.

Meet the Illustrator

Dick Smolinski

Dick Smolinski began drawing at the age of five and he has not stopped since. By copying comic strips as a boy, he learned the basics of illustrating. As a young man in the U.S. Air Force, he enjoyed a job drawing for the base newspaper. He decided after he was discharged that he would become an illustrator. He enjoys drawing people, especially sports figures and scenes from history with period clothing and lifestyles.

"It's really fun when the picture begins to take on a life of its own and goes beyond what I had imagined." As he works in his home studio, he has two Sheltie dogs close by and often uses them as models when a drawing calls for a dog.

Energy at Work

Theme Connections

Within the Selection

1. Why do you think people used electricity for entertainment in Franklin's time?

2. Why do you think Benjamin Franklin invented and discovered so many things?

Beyond the Selection

3. How has the world changed since electricity became an energy source?

4. Can you think of a reason why electricity is not a good energy source?

Write about It!

Describe what a day in your life would be like without electricity.

Remember to look for pictures of electronic devices to add to the **Concept/Question Board.**

Science Inquiry

The Science of Energy

Energy Everywhere

When you think of energy, you might think of electricity, coal, oil, and other resources that run the machines we use. In science, though, energy is less specific. Energy is the ability anything has to do work. A battery has energy, but an ordinary piece of paper does too. The difference is that we can use the battery's energy more easily than the paper's.

Forms of Energy

Energy falls into two categories: kinetic energy and potential energy. Kinetic energy is caused by motion. For example, a ball flying through the air has energy because it is moving. You will get a smashing demonstration of the work it can do if it hits a window!

Potential energy is when an object works against a force. Hold a ball in your hand, and it has potential energy. It is working against the force of gravity. When you release it, the potential energy turns into kinetic energy because the ball begins to move toward the ground.

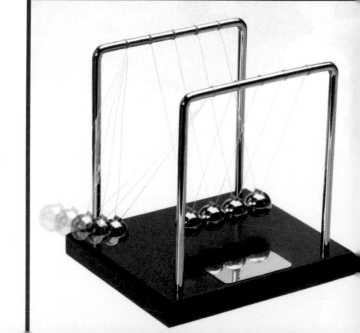

148

Thermal energy is a special form of kinetic energy. The movement—or kinetic energy—of atoms and molecules causes it. The more quickly the atoms and molecules move, the more thermal energy the object has. Every object in the universe has thermal energy, even ice.

Heat: Energy on the Move

Thermal energy wants to spread evenly. It will always flow from areas with more of it to those that have less. That moving energy is called heat.

When you hold warm bread, you feel its heat. The bread's atoms are more active—they have more thermal energy— than the atoms in your hand. Heat is the thermal energy flowing into your hand from the bread.

When you touch ice, the reverse happens. Thermal energy from your hand flows into the ice. The molecules in the frozen water are moving more slowly than the atoms in your hand. Cold is the feeling of energy leaving your body.

Think Link

1. Explain potential energy.

2. How did the selection's headings help you answer the previous question?

3. Explain thermal energy, and provide some examples of thermal energy on the move.

Try It!

As you work on your investigation, think about where you might use headings.

Read the article to find the meanings of these words, which are also in "Tailing Tornadoes":

- ✦ layer
- ✦ survey
- ✦ prediction
- ✦ severe
- ✦ alert
- ✦ raging
- ✦ inspiration
- ✦ stovepipe
- ✦ spiraling
- ✦ opposing

Vocabulary Strategy

Context Clues are hints in the text that help you find the meanings of words. Look at the words *prediction, severe,* and *spiraling.* Use context clues to find each word's meaning.

Vocabulary

Warm-Up

Bundled in a thick, hooded sweatshirt, Megan stepped outside. The extra layer helped. It blocked the cold, steady breeze that lingered from the storm. With the hood pulled up, Megan's hair could not whip against her face and into her eyes. She wanted to survey the storm's damage and did not need her hair getting in the way.

Before the storm hit, weather forecasters had all made the same prediction. The storm was rolling across the country and growing into something severe—something serious and even dangerous. The newscasters warned people to stay alert. They needed to be prepared to take shelter at any minute.

By the time the storm blew into town, the wind and rain were raging. Streets flooded, electric lines went down, and buildings were damaged. The sound of sirens was enough inspiration to get Megan's family into the basement. They huddled around a battery-powered radio and listened to news updates.

Now it was morning, and Megan stood on the back porch. She saw that her dad's workshop was gone. The heavy wood-burning stove that heated it during winter had not budged, but the shop's roof was gone, and the walls lay in ruins. Megan saw the stovepipe across the yard. The black metal tube was wrapped around a tree.

Wind pushed garbage into a fenced corner of the yard and sent bits of paper spiraling into the air. It reminded Megan of a tiny tornado. She wondered if a real one had visited the night before.

Megan made her way to the front of the house, stepping over broken limbs that littered the yard. She saw a huge pine leaning heavily against another tree. The pine had nearly fallen onto a house, but the opposing tree had stopped it.

Seeing the damage along her street, Megan knew the neighbors would be leaning on each other as well.

GAME

Building Sentences Write each selection vocabulary word on a separate slip of paper, and place the words in a box or another container. Without looking, remove a word from the box, and use it in a sentence. Write the sentence on the board or a sheet of paper. Then have a different student choose another word and use it in a sentence. Once all of the words have been used, discuss whether they were used correctly in the sentences.

Concept Vocabulary

The concept word for this lesson is *atmosphere.* Earth's atmosphere is a layer of gases surrounding the planet. Although the atmosphere has oxygen, it is made mostly of nitrogen. Weather is a result of temperature differences within the atmosphere. In the selection, how does the atmosphere aid the storm chaser? How does atmosphere connect with the theme Energy at Work?

151

Genre

Expository Text tells people something. It contains facts about real people, things, or events.

Comprehension Strategy

☆ **Adjusting Reading Speed**
As you read the selection, remember to slow down or reread any sections of the text that you find difficult to understand.

Tornadoes

by Trudi Strain Trueit

Focus Questions

How do storm chasers help us understand weather? Why is chasing storms dangerous?

It is just after dawn in Norman, Oklahoma, when Greg Stumpf steps outside to read the sky. A low layer of broken gray clouds races northward. On the ground, the air is muggy with barely a breeze. All signs point to a day of wild weather ahead. Greg is a storm chaser, and it is time for the hunt.

Greg is a meteorologist, a scientist who studies weather, and he works for the National Severe Storms Laboratory (NSSL). He has tracked tornadoes, also called twisters, for more than fifteen years. For most people, tailing storms is not a full-time job. Many chasers, like Greg, are meteorologists who follow storms in their spare time or chase together as part of a research team. Although storm chasing can be exciting, Greg's main goal is to help people learn more about these raging columns of wind.

It is late May, the height of chase season in Tornado Alley, a region in central North America that sees more tornado activity than anywhere else in the world. Tornado Alley stretches north from Texas to Nebraska, northeast to Ohio, and into Canada. Greg is in the best place at the best time to spot a tornado, but there are no guarantees he will see one today. There never are.

After his quick survey of the early morning sky, Greg logs on to his computer to check weather conditions from the radiosondes. A radiosonde, also called a weather balloon, is a package of weather sensors attached to a helium-filled balloon. As the radiosonde rises, it sends information about humidity (the amount of moisture in the air), temperature, and winds to meteorologists at the National Weather Service (NWS). Eventually, the balloon bursts, and the radiosonde parachutes to the ground.

Downloading new weather information onto the laptop, Greg and Bill discover that their target area has moved south toward Olney, Texas. They must change course. Three miles (5 km) outside of Olney, they spot towers, cumulonimbus clouds that signal severe thunderstorms. On the radio, the Storm Prediction Center issues a tornado watch for the area. They are getting closer!

Another 10 miles (16 km) down the road, Greg and Bill "go visual," following the storm by sight. The tops of the clouds are flattening out, becoming anvil clouds. Wind shear is pushing the clouds in a counterclockwise direction. A supercell is developing.

Soon, a long, gray wall cloud drops from below the storm. A wall cloud, which ranges from 1 to 4 miles (2 to 6 km) wide, is sometimes seen just before a funnel cloud forms. Wall clouds only produce tornadoes less than half the time, but Greg and Bill are hoping now is one of those times.

Experience tells the two chasers that the safest place to set up their camera gear is on a hill about 3 miles (5 km) east of the storm. Tornadoes usually move southwest to northeast at an average speed of 30 miles (50 km) per hour. Moving straight east should keep the chasers out of the storm's path—but nothing is certain.

Greg and Bill snap photographs and roll video to use later for scientific study. Soon the wall cloud begins to swirl. Spinning air, also called a vortex, is invisible by itself. If it contains cloud droplets or debris, a funnel cloud can be seen. When the funnel cloud comes in contact with the ground, it becomes a tornado.

The chase team cannot see a tornado yet, but that does not mean one is not there. A tornado can be causing damage on the ground even when no funnel cloud is visible. Sometimes a twister is wrapped in rain, making it very hard to spot.

Brown dust and debris are flying up from the ground. The chasers see the tornado! Greg's heart takes an extra beat as he watches the dizzying whirlwind suck up dirt in its path. The dark gray column spins faster, getting tighter and tighter until it looks like a stovepipe. Greg calls in over the ham radio to report the tornado's position to the local weather service office.

The twister grows until it is about 0.25 mile (0.5 km) wide. This is wider than the average tornado, which measures about 50 yards (45 m) across. Amazingly, there is hardly any noise. Because air in motion is silent, a tornado's sound depends on what it hits and what the air is passing through. A twister spiraling across a field sounds like a rushing waterfall, while one barreling through metal or wood roars louder than a train engine. Although he has seen more than a hundred tornadoes, Greg never tires of this awesome sight. "It's an adrenaline rush," he says. "Pure wonder, inspiration, and excitement."

As the tornado passes to the west, in front of the Sun, its color changes from dark to light gray. Soon the tornado starts to rope out, becoming very skinny before finally disappearing. It is all over. From beginning to end, the tornado lasted 15 minutes, a few minutes longer than most.

For the next several hours, Bill and Greg follow the remaining thunderstorm, taking pictures of the sunset and lightning bolts. By the time they are finished, it is nearly 10:00 P.M. The team has been chasing for 12 hours and is still 3 hours from home base. They are exhausted but thrilled.

Being hit by a tornado is not the main threat storm chasers face. Odds of this happening are low, as experienced chasers know how to keep a safe distance from twisters. Wind, lightning, hail, heavy rain, and chaser fatigue—getting very tired—are more dangerous than the twisters themselves. Some chasers have fallen asleep at the wheel after a long day on the road. Bill and Greg play the radio loudly and take turns driving to keep alert.

Today, skill, timing, and patience paid off. Luck was also on their side. As a light rain begins to fall, the chase team turns for home.

Trudi Strain Trueit

As a news reporter and weather forecaster, Trudi Strain Trueit has contributed to stories on many of the national news channels. Trueit shares these adventures in her many nonfiction works about nature, weather, and wildlife. (Thankfully she has seen only one tornado!) When not working or writing, Trueit enjoys rock collecting and learning about history. She is married and lives in Washington.

Theme Connections

Within the Selection

1. Why do you think it is important to study tornadoes?
2. Name one thing that indicates a tornado could form.

Across Selections

3. How is this selection similar to "The Sparks Fly"?
4. How are the storm chasers similar to Benjamin Franklin?

Beyond the Selection

5. Do you think it is possible to use tornadoes as a source of energy? Why or why not?
6. What are some other examples of powerful natural events?

Write about It!

Describe the most powerful storm you can remember and how it made you feel.

Remember to look for magazine or newspaper articles about tornadoes to add to the **Concept/Question Board.**

A Fresh Idea for the New Century

Humans are mostly liquid. Nearly three-quarters of the human body is water. Earth is a similarly wet place. Nearly three-quarters of its surface is covered in water. The problem is that almost all Earth's water—97 percent of it—is salt water. Humans need freshwater.

Unfortunately, the small amount of freshwater on Earth has limited availability. Only a third of it is in lakes, rivers, or reservoirs. The rest is frozen into glaciers and ice caps. In the end, only one percent of Earth's water is ready for human use. That makes it a very precious resource. Do you think it would be nice if we could make more?

Actually, freshwater is being made all the time. When the sun shines on the ocean's surface, solar energy causes evaporation. The very thin top layer of water changes from a liquid into a gas called water vapor. It rises into the air and leaves the salt behind.

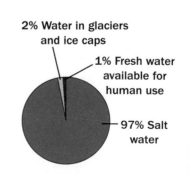

2% Water in glaciers and ice caps

1% Fresh water available for human use

97% Salt water

6.5 billion humans have to share the same small sliver of Earth's water.

As water vapor floats high into the atmosphere, it cools. The water molecules start gathering together and form droplets. The gas is changing back into a liquid. This is called condensation. As more and more droplets form, they create a cloud.

Carried by wind and Earth's rotation, clouds move water around the world. Inside a cloud, water droplets keep gathering molecules. When a droplet becomes too heavy to float, it falls to the ground as rain. This is called precipitation. In cold temperatures, droplets can freeze and fall as hail or snow.

On the ground, water runs into rivers, lakes, and reservoirs. Eventually it returns to the ocean. Water is fresh for a limited time.

During the twenty-first century, humans must solve the freshwater problem. As the human population increases, more water will be needed. Although humans have found ways to change salt water to freshwater, these ways are expensive and use a lot of energy. A cheaper, more efficient method must be found.

Think Link

1. How does the chart help demonstrate the scarcity of fresh water?

2. What is precipitation?

Try It!

As you work on your investigation, think about how you might use charts to display information.

Read the article to find the meanings of these words, which are also in "Jake Drake, Know-It-All":

+ observe
+ negative
+ positive
+ hypothesis
+ squinted
+ munchkin
+ crane
+ electromagnets
+ practically
+ conclusions

Vocabulary Strategy

Sometimes you can use **word structure** to help you find the meanings of words. Look at the word *electromagnets*. Use word structure to find the word's meaning.

Vocabulary

Warm-Up

Jeremy perched on his toes so he could observe what his father was doing under the hood. Mr. Howard disconnected the black cable that carried the negative electrical charge from the car's battery. Then he removed the red cable that carried the positive charge and carefully removed the battery.

"What is wrong?" Jeremy asked.

"I have a hypothesis," his dad replied. He explained his idea and how he would check to see whether it was correct. "The first step is to remove a couple of parts."

An hour later, three pieces of the motor lay next to the battery. Mr. Howard squinted into the bright sky, deciding what to do next.

Finally he said, "We should go to the junkyard."

Soon they were strolling between stacks of cars searching for parts. Jeremy felt like a munchkin walking through a giant maze.

A giant crane towered above them. A long cable hung from its arm and carried a large metal disk. The crane hoisted the cable, and Jeremy saw that a car was stuck to the bottom of the disk.

"Cranes like that use electromagnets," Mr. Howard explained. "Electricity turns the disk into a gigantic magnet."

Suddenly, the car fell crashing to the ground.

"That is what happens when the electricity is shut off."

Jeremy and his dad spent practically the entire afternoon at the junkyard. When they returned, Jeremy helped his mother prepare supper, and Mr. Howard worked on the car.

Finally Jeremy's dad came into the kitchen.

"I tried all the parts and reached similar conclusions," he said. "None solved the problem. So I tested the battery, and guess what I discovered? It is dead."

As Mr. Howard washed his hands, everyone began laughing.

Word Charades
Divide into two teams and choose one student from each team to sit facing the class. Reveal a vocabulary word to everyone but the two seated students. Then have the class describe the word without saying the word itself. The first of the two students to predict the word scores a point for his or her team. Continue with different vocabulary words and different students until all words have been used.

Concept Vocabulary

The concept word for this lesson is **experiment**. An *experiment* is a special test used to find out if an idea is correct. Experiments need to be carefully planned, and all of the results should be recorded. What is the experiment performed in the selection? What problem does the experiment try to address?

Genre

Realistic Fiction contains characters, settings, and conflicts that can exist in real life.

Comprehension Strategy

 **Summarizing**
As you read the selection, summarize the sections of the text to gain a clear understanding of how the pieces of the text fit together. This strategy will help you focus on the important items within each section and in the selection as a whole.

Jake Drake
Know-It-All

by Andrew Clements
illustrated by Fian Arroyo

Focus Questions

What kind of project do Jake and Willie work on for the science fair? How are Jake and Willie similar to other scientists or inventors?

On Friday morning, I had my dad drive me to school. That way, I got there about ten minutes before the buses. I didn't talk much in the car.

When we were almost there, Dad said, "So, how's the science fair coming? It's next week, right?"

I shook my head. "Nope. It's the week after. And I guess it's okay."

"Anything I can help with? I've never made electromagnets, but I think I understand how they work."

I smiled and said, "Thanks, but I'm supposed to do the work myself. It says that in the rules."

We pulled up at the front door of the school. Dad said, "I'm sure you're doing a terrific job. But maybe I could at least look things over."

I said, "Sure. That'd be good."

Dad leaned over and gave me a kiss on the cheek. "Have a great day, Jake."

I went into the office and asked Mrs. Drinkwater for permission to go to my room before the first bell. Mrs. Drinkwater is the school secretary. She's a good person to know. Even though Mrs. Karp is the principal, I think Mrs. Drinkwater runs my school most of the time. Because if you want to find out anything, you talk to Mrs. Drinkwater. Unless you're in trouble. Then you talk to Mrs. Karp.

When I got to my room, Mrs. Snavin was sitting at her desk using a calculator.

I guess my shoes were too quiet, because when I said, "Mrs. Snavin?" she jumped about a foot and let out this little squeal. "Oooh!—It's you, Jake. That gave me a fright."

I said, "Sorry, Mrs. Snavin. But I have to talk with you. You know Willie, my friend in Mrs. Frule's class? I want to be partners with him for the science fair."

Mrs. Snavin frowned. "The fair is the week after next. I think it's a little late to be choosing up partners."

I reached into my backpack and pulled out the science fair booklet. I said, "It doesn't say anywhere in here that you have to pick partners by a special time. It just says that you have to sign up on time, and it says you can work by yourself or with one partner. And Willie and I both signed up before Christmas."

Mrs. Snavin was still frowning. "Why has it taken this long to decide you want to work together?"

I said, "That's my fault. Willie wanted to be partners right at the start, but I said no. But now I want to. So will it be okay?"

Mrs. Snavin took a deep breath and let it out slowly. She was looking through my booklet. "Well . . . it doesn't seem to be against the rules. So, it'll be all right. I'll get the master list from the office and change it later today."

I said, "Thanks, Mrs. Snavin." Then I went back to the side doors to wait for the buses.

Willie was on bus four, but it was a while before he got off.

"Hey, Willie! Over here!"

He saw me and waved. He moved through the crowd of kids to where I was waiting. "Hi, Jake!"

We walked into the gym, and I said, "Guess what?"

"What?" he said.

"I've got a new partner for the science fair."

Willie looked at me and squinted. "What do you mean? Who?"

I grinned. "You! You're back in the science fair. You're my partner!"

Willie said, "No way!"

And I said, "Way! I talked with Mrs. Snavin already, and it's not against the rules or anything."

Willie smiled this smile that almost covered his whole face.

Then the smile stopped, and he squinted again. "But you said you wanted to work by yourself."

I said, "Yeah, but now I don't. I wasn't having much fun, either."

The first bell rang, and everyone began to move for the doors.

I said, "Tell you what. Get a pass to go to the library for lunch recess, and we can talk about it, okay?"

Willie said, "Yeah . . . okay. See you in the library." And then he smiled his big smile again. It's a great smile.

When you have a partner to work with, and it's a good partner, everything is more fun. It just is.

After Willie and I talked at the library we decided to work on the magnets. He had been making a project about how different balls bounce. It's because Willie loves basketball and almost every sport. He's not very good at sports, but he still loves them. So he wanted to observe Ping-Pong balls, golf balls, tennis balls, and basketballs bouncing. Then he wanted to guess why they bounced in different ways, and then try to prove it.

It was kind of an interesting idea, but Willie hadn't done much with it.

When I told him about the electromagnets, he got all excited. "You mean a regular nail turns into a magnet?"

I said, "Yeah, only I've got two giant nails this long! And you know at a junkyard? They have electromagnets on the end of a crane that can pick up whole cars, and when they shut off the power, BAM, the whole car falls to the ground!"

Then I told him about everything we had to do. And Willie got more and more excited. He said he would ask his mom if he could come over on Saturday. Then we could work all day on it.

"That'll be great. And there's one more thing," I said. "I've been keeping the project a secret. Especially from Kevin and Marsha."

Willie nodded slowly and began to grin. "Yeah, I like it. That means we know something that they don't know, right?"

See what I mean? How Willie got the idea right away?

Me and Willie are like that. We're good partners. We laugh at the same kinds of stuff, and when he needs help or I need help, we stick together.

Like magnets.

You know how people say "two heads are better than one"? Well, it's true, especially if the other head is Willie's head.

When he came over to my house on Saturday morning, we got right to work. First, I showed Willie what I had written down. And I told him how it was my idea to see what made a magnet more powerful: more wire or more batteries. I had the idea, but I hadn't a guess about it yet. In the scientific method, that's called the hypothesis.

Willie looked at the stuff, and he looked at my notes. Then he said, "More electricity makes an electromagnet stronger than more wire."

I said, "How do you know that?"

Willie shook his head. "I don't. That's our hypothesis. 'More electricity makes an electromagnet stronger than more wire.' We have to prove whether that's true or false."

See what I mean about two heads? In a minute, Willie had a big part of the problem all worked out. I wrote the hypothesis in our notebook. Then came the fun part. I know that might sound weird, but making those electromagnets was really fun.

We talked and we argued about stuff, and we tried six different ways of winding wire on the nails. And Willie figured out a great way to keep track of how much wire we were using.

We decided to put 150 feet of red wire onto one of the nails. We would put 300 feet of blue wire onto the other nail. That was Willie's idea, too, to put twice as much wire onto the second nail. That way, if more wire makes a stronger magnet, maybe the blue magnet would be twice as strong.

We started winding wire onto one of the nails. We kept the wire pulled really tight. It was harder than I thought it would be. And if I'd had to do it all by myself, it would have been really boring.

By lunchtime we had only finished the nail with the red wire, the short wire.

For lunch we had chicken noodle soup and grilled cheese sandwiches. Dad made lunch because Mom and Abby were at the mall taking some clothes back. Gram had given Abby a sweater that went all the way down to her knees. It made her look like a Munchkin.

Dad said, "It's been pretty quiet up there. How's it going?"

Willie said, "We've been winding wire around a nail."

Dad said, "If it's taking too long, you could bring your things down to the workshop. I bet I could figure out how to make the nail spin around. That way, you could just hold the spool of wire and it would almost wind itself. Sound good?"

Willie started to nod his head, but I said, "That sounds great, Dad, but we'd better do the second nail like we did the first one. They should look the same way."

I felt a little sorry for my dad. He really wanted to help. It was hard for him to keep out of the way.

Then I said, "But when we're done winding the second nail, would you look at them for us?"

Dad said, "You bet. Just give a holler when you need me."

And I could tell it made my dad feel good to be invited.

When Willie and I finished winding the wire, we looked in one of the books to see how to hook the batteries together. And that's when I called my dad. Because if you hook big batteries together wrong, it can start a fire. And it said in the rules that if anything might be dangerous, ". . . an adult should be present."

Dad was great. He didn't try to change anything we were doing. He didn't say we should wind the wire some other way. And instead of being a K-I-A/D-I-A and telling us how to hook up the batteries, he made us think about it. Then we had to tell him how we wanted to do it.

We told him, and Dad said, "That's exactly right. You guys have got it all figured out." And then he left. Mom would have been proud of him.

Willie and I decided our first trial should be with just one battery. So we hooked the wire from each end of the red magnet onto the battery—one wire to the positive terminal and the other to the negative terminal.

But we didn't have anything to lift with the magnet. So we unhooked the wires and went downstairs and into the kitchen.

I said, "We need something that's made of iron or steel."

And Willie said, "And we have to know how much it weighs. Because it said in the science fair booklet to measure everything. So we have to measure the weight of what we pick up."

I opened the door to the basement, but Willie said, "Wait a minute."

Willie's been to my house so many times, he knows where everything is. He opened the pantry, and right away I knew what he was doing. He was going to get some cookies. But instead he grabbed a can off a shelf and said, "Tuna!"

"Tuna?" I said.

"Yeah," said Willie. "Tuna. This can of tuna weighs one hundred and seventy grams. And this can of soup weighs three hundred and five grams. And the cans are made of steel! Here, take some."

So I grabbed eight cans of soup, and he grabbed four cans of tuna.

If I told you every step of our experiment, it would make you crazy. About how we tried two batteries on the red magnet. And then tried to see if we could pick up a can of soup with the flat end of the nail. And how we used duct tape to stack two cans on top of each other so we could try to pick up two cans. And how we hooked the two batteries up to the blue magnet and then tried to lift soup again. And how we wrote down everything we tried. And then how we hooked up all four batteries and . . . but like I said, if I just told it all, you'd go nuts. Because me telling it wouldn't be as fun as really doing all this stuff with Willie, and he was cracking jokes and making faces, and coming up with all these good ideas.

It was a great afternoon. And when Willie's dad showed up to take him home, our science fair experiment was practically finished. I mean, we still had a ton of work to do. And posters to make. And conclusions to write.

But Willie and I knew what we knew, and we knew why we knew it.

It had been an afternoon of pure fun.

Which is what science is supposed to be in the first place, right?

Right.

Meet the Author

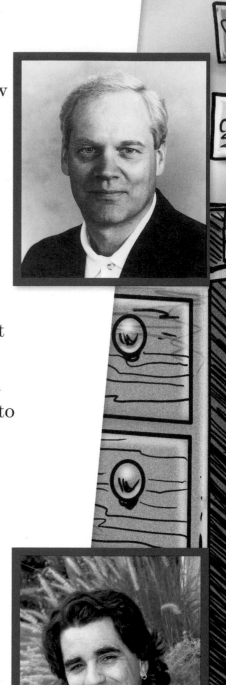

Andrew Clements

Reading has always been a family activity for Andrew Clements. As a child, his favorite place during the school year was the school library. In the summer, he and his family would vacation in the Maine woods where he had no television or telephone but plenty of books. Perhaps it is no surprise that now Clements writes his books in a small shed in his Massachusetts backyard, furnished with only a desk, laptop computer, wood stove and small air conditioner.

Clements has worked as a teacher and an editor, but writing has been a rewarding career for him: "Good books make good things happen in real life. They can make a big difference. So when I was given a chance to start writing for children, I jumped at it."

Meet the Illustrator

Fian Arroyo

Fian Arroyo loves to draw in his shorts and tee shirt with his music playing as loud as he wants it. Being paid to do what he loves is a bonus. His job can require long hours to meet project deadlines, but he always makes time for his family and hobbies—skateboarding and saltwater fishing.

He suggests to young illustrators to "draw, draw, draw and then draw some more!" He advises young illustrators to see all the different types of illustrations there are in books and magazines, and even on television. However, it is also important to develop one's own style of drawing.

Theme Connections

Within the Selection

1. Why did Jake and Willie need a hypothesis?

2. Why did Jake measure and record everything he did?

Across Selections

3. How is Jake like Benjamin Franklin?

4. Compare Jake's experiment to some of Benjamin Franklin's experiments.

Beyond the Selection

5. What do you think electromagnetism can be used for?

6. Why is it best that good scientists are not know-it-alls?

Write about It!

Describe a science experiment you have done or one you would like to do.

Remember to look for pictures of scientists to add to the **Concept/Question Board.**

Science Inquiry

The Scientific Method

Biologists, physicists, and chemists are just a few of the many different kinds of scientists. The best scientists have a couple of things in common. First, they love to learn. More importantly, however, scientists know that sloppy research cannot be trusted. For this reason, the scientific method was developed.

The first step in the scientific method is to observe the world and ask questions about what you see. When you discover a question you cannot answer, turn it into a statement. In other words, answer the question with your best prediction. This statement is called a hypothesis.

A hypothesis needs to be a simple sentence that can be proven true or false. For example, you might wonder: *Why do green leaves turn yellow?* One hypothesis would be: *Green leaves turn yellow when plants do not get enough light.*

The next step is to create experiments that will test your hypothesis. Record everything you do, even the smallest details.

What did the experiments show? Did they prove the hypothesis? If not, you can plan different experiments and try again. Just changing one small part of the experiment might make a big difference in the outcome. As always, record everything that happens. When the experiments are done, it is time to draw conclusions. The results often lead to a new hypothesis.

184

The final step in the scientific method is to share the results. Careful records allow other scientists to test the experiments and confirm the results. Once a hypothesis has been proven true many times by different scientists, it becomes a theory. After a theory has been proven true for many years—and it has never been proven false—it becomes a law. By working together, scientists help each other—and the rest of us— understand the universe.

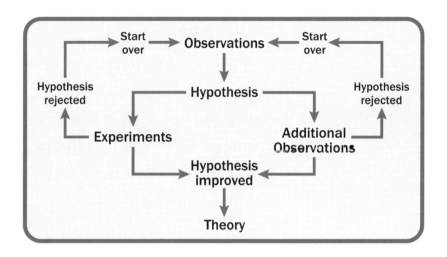

Think Link

1. What is the difference between a hypothesis and a theory?

2. Why is it so important to keep records about each step and about the results of an experiment?

3. *Vanilla ice cream tastes better than chocolate ice cream.* Is this statement a hypothesis? Why or why not?

Try It!

As you work on your investigation, think about where you might use diagrams.

Read the article to find the meanings of these words, which are also in "The Wind at Work":

+ gusty
+ propel
+ revolving doors
+ fossil fuels
+ flickering
+ converts
+ economical
+ reliable
+ currents
+ expands

Vocabulary Strategy

Context Clues are hints in the text that help you find the meanings of words. Look at the words *gusty, fossil fuels,* and *flickering.* Use context clues to find each word's meaning.

Vocabulary
Warm-Up

As Jamila opened the car door, a sudden burst of wind nearly ripped her presentation from her hand.

Once outside, Jamila braced herself against the gusty breeze. The wind would die down, but then it would suddenly blow stronger. Each gust would propel Jamila a few steps forward before she regained her balance.

The school was strangely quiet. Jamila was not used to being there on a Saturday. She tried using the revolving doors to get inside, but they would not turn. When she tried one of the regular doors, though, it pulled right open.

Jamila was on her way to a meeting about saving energy at school. The school's energy comes mostly from fossil fuels, like coal and oil. These fuels come from plants and animals that died millions of years ago, so their supplies are limited.

Jamila entered the classroom and found it buzzing with laughter and conversation. As soon as she sat down, the lights began flickering. Mrs. Hanson was switching them on and off to signal the start of the meeting.

Each student presented an idea for saving energy. Jamila's presentation was about CFLs, or compact fluorescent lightbulbs.

"If the school converts a quarter of its lightbulbs to CFLs," Jamila explained, "it will save a huge amount of energy.

"CFLs cost more at first, but over time they are more economical. They use less energy, and they are more reliable than regular bulbs. They last ten times longer."

Jamila held up a bulb and added, "CFLs run on the same electrical currents as any other bulbs. They don't need special lamps."

Her idea was a big hit.

"If this idea expands and spreads to other schools," Mrs. Hanson observed, "the savings will be tremendous. Good job, Jamila!"

Team Effort With your classmates, form two teams. One student from each team stands, and then the teacher defines one of the vocabulary words. The two students try to determine which word is being defined. The student who correctly answers first earns one point for his or her team. Have students take turns so that everyone has a chance to play.

Concept Vocabulary

The concept word for this lesson is **conservation**. *Conservation* is the careful protection of our world's natural resources. *Waste* and *abuse* are the opposites of conservation. As nonrenewable energy sources become scarce, we have to plan carefully how resources are being used. What form of conservation is discussed in the selection? How does *conservation* connect with the theme Energy At Work?

Genre

Expository Text tells people something. It contains facts about real people, things, or events.

Comprehension Skill

 ### Cause and Effect

As you read, remember that a cause is *why* something happened and an effect is *what* happened.

The Wind at Work

by Gretchen Woelfle

Focus Questions

How did people harness the power of the wind several hundred years ago? How do people harness the power of the wind today?

Night fell on the flatlands of Holland. The wind howled, rain slashed to earth, and waves broke higher and higher on the beach. Flashes of lightning revealed a high wall of earth built to hold back the sea. Waves crashed against this dike, throwing water to the fields beyond and washing away parts of the dike.

The Dutch called the sea the Waterwolf, and tonight the Waterwolf was on the prowl, trying to steal their lands. All night long flickering lanterns moved along the top of the dike as villagers kept watch. If the dikes broke, the Waterwolf would swallow their farms and homes.

By morning, the rain subsided and the wind dropped. The storm was over. The dikes had held. Tired Dutchmen stumbled home to bed.

But there was no rest for the windmillers. All night they had worked the windmills to pump water from the overflowing canals back out to sea. Now they had to drain the flooded fields to save the crops. For days and nights, giant windmill sails would turn—pumping and pumping until the fields were dry. The wind that nearly destroyed the land would now help to save it.

The History of Wind Power

Wind is created by the sun as it warms the earth unevenly. Warm air expands and rises. Cool air rushes in to take its place. This air movement is what we call the wind.

For more than a thousand years people have harnessed the wind with windmills. People used the wind to propel sailboats on the water long before they built windmills on land. Billowing sails filling with wind replaced the hard work of men rowing and paddling. Eventually, wind-powered machines moved on land and saved a lot of heavy labor. The wind-filled windmill sails then turned a shaft, wheels, gears, and finally, millstones, water pumps, or other machines.

warm air

cool air

Before the invention of windmills and water mills, men or animals turned heavy *millstones* by trudging around and around in a circle, hour after hour, day after day, crushing grain to make flour. It was mind-numbing, body-breaking work.

The wind is not a perfect source of energy. It can be steady or gusty. It can change direction in a few seconds. It can grow to the force of a hurricane or die completely. Scientists can predict daily and seasonal wind patterns, but these patterns won't tell if or how much the wind will blow tomorrow afternoon. Even so, the wind has been reliable enough for many uses through the centuries.

Jacob van Ruisdael. *The Mill Near Wijk.* c. 1670. Oil on canvas. 83 × 101cm. Rijksmuseum, Amsterdam.

Like the wind itself, *windmills* have come and gone. From A.D. 1200 to 1900, windmills were the most powerful machines in Europe. They ground grain, pumped water, pressed oil, sawed wood, and performed many other tasks. In the 1800s windmills were replaced by steam engines. Only nine hundred Dutch windmills remain out of ten thousand that stood two hundred years ago. In America, six million windmills pumped water on the dry Western plains until the 1940s when electric and gasoline engines did away with most of them. Today a new kind of windmill turns in the wind.

Many people think of Dutch models when they think of windmills, but windmills come in many shapes and sizes. Ancient Persian-style mills looked like revolving doors. Modern *wind turbines* look like giant airplane propellers. All can harness a powerful energy source to work for us.

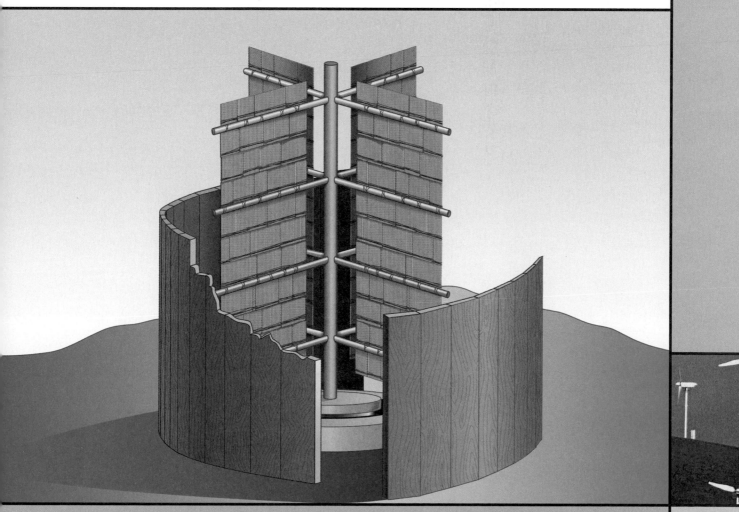

Wind Power Today

Thousands of wind turbines stand in the deserts and hills of California today. Thousands more are scattered across Canada, Europe, and the rest of the world. They are new versions of an old idea.

From far away, wind turbines look like toy pinwheels that catch the sunlight as they spin. Up close, these pinwheel giants stand on one-hundred-foot towers with whirling blades up to one hundred feet in diameter. A generator behind the blades converts wind energy to electricity. Underground cables carry electric currents to power lines that feed the electricity to nearby towns and cities.

Clean, Renewable Energy Source

Wind power is a renewable source of energy, so we will never run out of it. It's clean, safe, and free for all to use.

Currently, most of the energy we use comes from burning coal, oil, and natural gas. These are called *fossil fuels.*

Wind power is a clean, economical energy source that can help reduce environmental pollution. Wind turbines could produce 10 percent of America's electrical power in the near future. This would save about 900,000 tons of coal, oil, and gas from going up in smoke every year.

Wind power is found in more places around the globe than fossil fuels. It is a clean, *renewable energy* that we will never use up. Some people discovered this a thousand years ago. Others don't know about it yet. But whether you've heard it or not, there's good news in the wind.

Science Inquiry

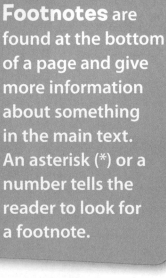

Fossil Fuels: Ancient Technology

Emily Ross: Today I am speaking with Dr. Liz Guzman about fossil fuels. Let me begin by asking you to explain what they are.

Dr. Liz Guzman: Fossil fuels come from the remains of dead plants and animals. As millions of years passed, these remains became buried beneath the earth's surface. Then heat and pressure turned them into coal, oil, and natural gas. Nearly 80 percent of the energy humans use to run the world is made by burning fossil fuels.

ER: So they are very important?

LG: Yes, but that is a problem. Fossil fuels are a limited resource. For example, oil takes millions of years to make. Even if we do not completely run out, oil will become too expensive.

ER: Can people use electricity instead?

LG: Well, we burn fossil fuels to make most of our electricity too. People need to start using less energy. For example, they can start by using appliances that have the Energy Star* label.

The U.S. government places the Energy Star label on products that have the highest energy efficiency.

ER: What else can be done?

LG: Drive less, carpool more, and avoid buying things with lots of packaging that you'll just throw away. Using CFLs** instead of regular lightbulbs can make a big difference. Recycle and reuse as often as possible. These things will help, but unfortunately they won't solve the big problem.

ER: What do you mean?

LG: We have to use more reliable energy sources—ones that will not run out. We need renewable energy sources because they do not run out.

ER: Do you have any suggestions?

LG: Solar, wind, and water power are the most realistic alternatives. They are all renewable sources of energy.

**CFLs, or compact fluorescent lightbulbs, use four times less energy than regular bulbs, but they last ten times longer.

Think Link

1. What is a CFL?

2. What are the three main fossil fuels?

3. In addition to being renewable energy sources, solar power and wind power cause little or no pollution. Can you think of any reasons they might not be good energy sources?

Try It!

As you work on your investigation, think about where you might use footnotes.

Read the article to find the meanings of these words, which are also in "What are Food Chains and Webs?":

+ ecosystem
+ food chain
+ food web
+ ridges
+ algae
+ absorbs
+ diet
+ omnivores
+ predators
+ scavenger

Vocabulary Strategy

An **appositive** is a noun that follows another noun to modify or name it. Authors sometimes use apposition to clarify the meanings of words. Look at the word *absorbs*. Find how the author uses apposition to define the word.

Vocabulary

Warm-Up

Sand crunched beneath the bus's wheels as it slowed to a stop. Then the door swung open, and twenty excited students ran out.

"Welcome to the beach!" announced their teacher, Miss Jasper. "First let's talk about why we are here."

The class had come to the beach to study the ocean's ecosystem. An ecosystem involves plants and animals and how they interact with one another. Miss Jasper asked someone to define a food chain.

"It is the order in which creatures eat, and then get eaten, by one another," one of the students answered.

"Exactly," Miss Jasper agreed, "but an ecosystem is actually a food web. A food web is made of many chains that cross and connect with each other."

Miss Jasper led her students down the windy beach. It was covered by dozens of low ridges that ran off into the distance.

"At the bottom of this food chain are algae," she began. "They are tiny plants, without roots or leaves, that float in the water. Each one absorbs, or takes in, sunlight and turns it into energy. Tiny animals called krill live on a diet of algae."

Miss Jasper explained that many fish are omnivores. They eat plants, but they are also predators that eat krill and other fish.

"The ocean is filled with predators," she continued. "Squid eat fish, seals eat squid, and then sharks eat seals."

"Is anything in the ocean a scavenger?" someone asked.

"Yes," Miss Jasper replied. "Sharks often eat dead fish they find floating around, and crabs eat dead animals that sink to the ocean floor."

Suddenly a seagull screamed and dove into the water. It came up with a fish in its beak.

"Even something that does not live in the ocean," Miss Jasper pointed out, "can be part of its ecosystem."

Fill In the Blanks
On a separate sheet of paper, complete the following sentences with selection vocabulary words.

1. My baby sister does not have teeth yet, so her _____ is made of only soft foods.

2. Foxes are _____ because they eat mice and berries.

3. The tractor crawled through the field and left _____ in the dirt behind it.

Concept Vocabulary

The concept word for this lesson is *balance*. *Balance* is an important part of every ecosystem, and each animal and plant plays a role. When a new animal is introduced into an ecosystem, or one is taken away, all the other animals are affected. In the selection, how is balance important to food chains and webs? How does balance connect to the unit theme Energy At Work?

What Are

Food Chains and Webs?

by Bobbie Kalman and
Jacqueline Langille

Focus Questions

How is energy transferred between
plants, herbivores, and carnivores?
What would happen to an ecosystem if
one part of the food chain disappeared?

The diagram below shows the levels of a food web. There are many plants on the first level because sunlight provides the energy plants need to survive. Fewer herbivores can survive than plants because energy is lost as it is passed along the food web. At the top of the pyramid, there is only enough energy to keep a few carnivores alive.

Plants make up the first level of all food chains and webs in the world. Green plants are primary producers, or the first food-makers in a food chain or web. They make all the food energy found in an ecosystem. People and other living things could not survive without the food energy made by plants.

Plants use sunlight to make food. They use the sun's energy to make different types of sugar. Using the energy from sunlight, they combine water with carbon dioxide, a gas found in air. This food-making process is called photosynthesis. When a plant needs energy to grow, it uses up some of the sugar to feed itself.

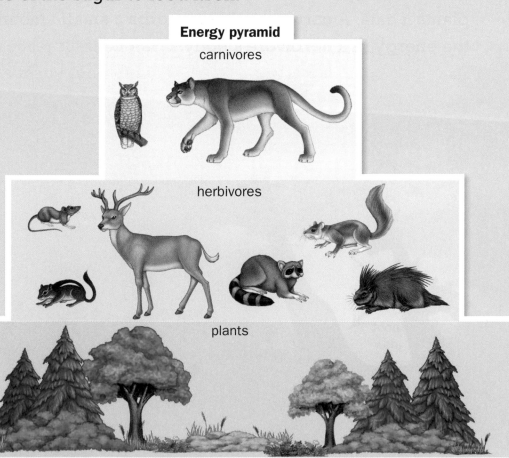

Energy pyramid

carnivores

herbivores

plants

For photosynthesis to occur, plants use more than just sunlight. They use a green substance found in their leaves, called chlorophyll. Chlorophyll catches the energy from sunlight. Plants take carbon dioxide from the air through their leaves and absorb water and nutrients from the soil through their roots.

Food is an important product of photosynthesis, but photosynthesis also makes large amounts of oxygen, a gas in air. Animals need oxygen to survive. Without plants, the earth's air would soon run out of oxygen and people and animals would die.

During photosynthesis, plants also take large amounts of carbon dioxide from the air. Even though this gas is a natural part of air, it can be harmful. Too much carbon dioxide could make the earth heat up more than normal and harm most living things.

Plants are an important part of water ecosystems. A water food chain starts with tiny floating plants called phytoplankton. They change the sun's energy into food, just as plants do on land. They also provide fish with the oxygen they need in order to survive underwater.

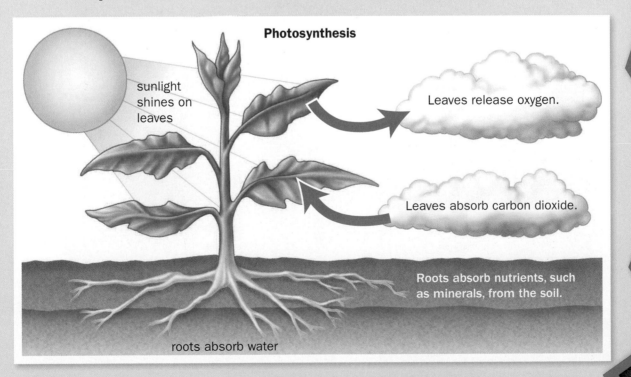

Photosynthesis

sunlight shines on leaves

Leaves release oxygen.

Leaves absorb carbon dioxide.

Roots absorb nutrients, such as minerals, from the soil.

roots absorb water

Seaweeds such as kelp are the largest ocean plants. Like phytoplankton, seaweeds are types of algae. Algae are water plants that do not have roots, stems, or leaves. They only grow in shallow water, where sunlight can reach them.

In some ecosystems, animals must eat plants to get water as well as food. Deserts are ecosystems that receive very little rain. Desert plants, especially cacti, are good at storing water. The stems have waxy coverings to keep water from leaving the plant. Spines on the stems protect the plants from being eaten. In order to get at stored water, some animals have special mouths that can bore into desert plants. Other animals eat the parts of the plants that hold water and try to avoid getting pricked by the spines.

Some plants do not get all the nutrients they need from the soil, so they consume, or eat, insects! More than 400 types of plants are meat-eaters. These plants make their own food using the sun's energy, but insects give them the extra nutrients they need to help them grow bigger and healthier.

Herbivores, or animals that eat mainly plants, are at the second level of all food chains. They are also called primary consumers. Consumers are animals that eat to get food energy. Primary consumers are the "first" consumers in a food chain. Herbivores include small squirrels that eat nuts and berries and huge elephants that eat grass and tree bark.

Herbivores have a hard time getting energy out of plants because grass, buds, leaves, and twigs are difficult for their bodies to digest, or break down. Most herbivores have to eat a lot of plants to get the energy they need. Elephants and cows must spend most of their time eating in order to get enough nutrients and energy to stay healthy. Many grass-eating animals have ridges on their teeth for grinding their food into small pieces so their body can digest it more easily.

Some herbivores have to re-chew their food in order to break it down enough for their bodies to absorb its energy. The food comes back up into their mouths after it has been in their stomachs for a while. They chew this food, called cud, again before swallowing it a second time. Sheep, cows, and deer are examples of animals that chew their food twice.

Carnivores are animals that eat mainly other animals. Most carnivores feed on herbivores, so they are called secondary consumers. A few carnivores eat other carnivores. They are called tertiary consumers. Some carnivores can be both secondary and tertiary consumers. For example, in the food web, a lynx is a secondary consumer when it eats a rabbit, which is a herbivore. When a lynx eats a weasel, another carnivore, the lynx is a tertiary consumer.

Most carnivores are predators. A predator is an animal that hunts and kills other animals for food. The animal that a predator eats is called prey. A huge variety of animals are predators, from spiders that eat flies to lions that hunt zebras. Predators are very important in an ecosystem. Without them, the number of herbivores would increase until there were no longer enough plants to eat. Predators often eat only sick and weak animals, leaving more food for healthy animals and their babies.

Each type of predator has a different way of catching food. Some, such as wolves, track their prey over long distances. A few, including lions and leopards, stalk, or sneak close to, their prey and then chase and catch it. Other predators wait quietly while watching for any movement nearby. When prey comes close, they grab it. Frogs and some birds hunt this way.

A type of carnivore that feeds mainly on dead animals that it finds is called a scavenger. Scavengers such as vultures help keep an ecosystem clean. They often eat the leftovers from a predator's meal. Scavengers are an important part of a food web because they keep the food energy in a dead animal's body from being wasted.

Omnivores are animals that eat both plants and animals. In most types of ecosystems, omnivores do not have difficulty finding food because they eat almost anything they find. An omnivore can belong to several levels of a food web at once, depending on what type of food it eats. Bears, pigs, raccoons, and humans are some examples of omnivores.

Most omnivores are opportunistic feeders, which means they eat whatever is available. Their diet, or the type of foods they eat, changes depending on the time of year. Bears, for example, often eat fish in the spring and berries in the fall. An omnivore's diet also changes depending on whatever it finds nearby. Ostriches usually eat grass, but they readily eat any lizards they find crawling in the grass.

All living things die. If herbivores or carnivores do not eat them, the bodies of dead plants and animals are usually eaten by decomposers. Decomposers are living things that get all their food energy from dead material. They form the detritus food web. Detritus is material that is decomposing, or breaking down. Bacteria, worms, slugs, snails, and fungi such as mushrooms, are examples of decomposers.

Decomposers recycle important nutrients and help keep them moving through food webs. Without fungi and other decomposers, nutrients would stay locked up in dead animals, branches, logs, and leaves. They could not be used by plants to grow. If plants could not grow, they would not survive. Without plants, all other living things would slowly starve.

Decomposers are very small, so many kinds are needed to help break down large pieces of dead material. On land, animals such as snails, mites, and earthworms eat parts of dead plants, herbivores, and carnivores in order to start the breakdown process. In water, small crustaceans such as crabs and insect larvae, or babies, are an important part of the detritus food web.

Decomposers get the energy they need from dead material, but they also help keep the ecosystem clean for other living things. Without decomposers to feed on dead material, an ecosystem such as a forest would soon be buried under piles of dead plants and animals.

Bobbie Kalman and Jacqueline Langille

Bobbie Kalman has lived around the world. She was born in Hungary, worked as a teacher in the Bahamas and Germany, and now lives in Canada. At her father's urging, Kalman wanted to be a pharmacist when she was younger, but her love of books caused her to be a teacher and writer instead. Kalman is a very detailed writer and says that writing takes "endless rounds of rethinking and rewriting. Anything before the twentieth draft is usually not even worth reading." To aid her in the writing process, Kalman has teamed up with writing partner Jacqueline Langille to create interesting and educational nonfiction books for children.

Theme Connections

Within the Selection

1. How do you think humans are part of a food chain?

2. How have humans affected the food web?

Across Selections

3. How is the energy in a food chain different from the energy in the wind?

4. Can you think of a way in which wind might contribute to a food chain?

Beyond the Selection

5. By following the food chain backward, what is the energy source for all living things?

6. What would happen if all the plankton in the oceans died?

Write about It!

Choose an animal. Describe the role it plays in its food chain and its ecosystem.

Remember to draw a simple food-chain diagram to add to the **Concept/Question Board.**

Science Inquiry

Urban Predators

Humans chopped down many trees and paved a lot of land to build cities. Look around your neighborhood. It is easy to see how different the landscape is now compared to when it was a forest, prairie, or desert.

Most people live in an urban ecosystem. It supports some animals better than others. For instance, squirrels, raccoons, and deer find food in cities' green areas, like parks and yards. Many urban animals also forage through human garbage. The food chain does not end with these animals, though. Who are their urban predators?

Birds of prey are commonly seen in cities. Hawks and owls help control the populations of mice and other small rodents. Peregrine falcons have even settled in some cities. They nest on the window ledges of skyscrapers. The steep, towering buildings resemble cliffs, which are the falcons' homes in the wild.

If you are outside at night, you may be lucky enough to see a fox. Foxes are becoming a common sight in many U.S. cities. These cat-sized canines follow tree-lined creeks and drainage ditches deep into urban areas. They hunt small rodents, but their diet also includes large insects.

216

Wolves were once the top canine predators in America. During the early part of the twentieth century, though, they were hunted almost to extinction. Today, coyotes have taken their place. As the suburbs spread farther into the countryside, humans and coyotes share more of the same land. Sometimes coyotes even live in big cities. Some scientists estimate that two thousand coyotes live in Chicago. They hunt mice, rabbits, and their canine cousins, foxes.

The largest predator living and hunting in some urban areas has to be the puma. Also called mountain lions, these giant cats—some as big as eight feet long—mostly hunt deer. They avoid humans as much as possible. Mountain lion attacks are extremely rare.

A number of city buildings have nesting boxes to encourage the falcons to breed.

Think Link

1. Describe a simple food chain in the urban ecosystem.

2. What is something you learned by reading the caption to the photograph?

3. In the outskirts of many cities, deer populations have soared and become a problem. Why do you think this has happened?

Try It!

As you work on your investigation, think about where you might use captions.

Landscape

by Carl Sandburg

illustrated by Sandra Speidel

See the trees lean to the wind's way of learning.
See the dirt of the hills shape to the water's
way of learning.
See the lift of it all go the way the biggest
wind and the strongest water want it.

Focus Question How is a hurricane like an "agile dancer"?

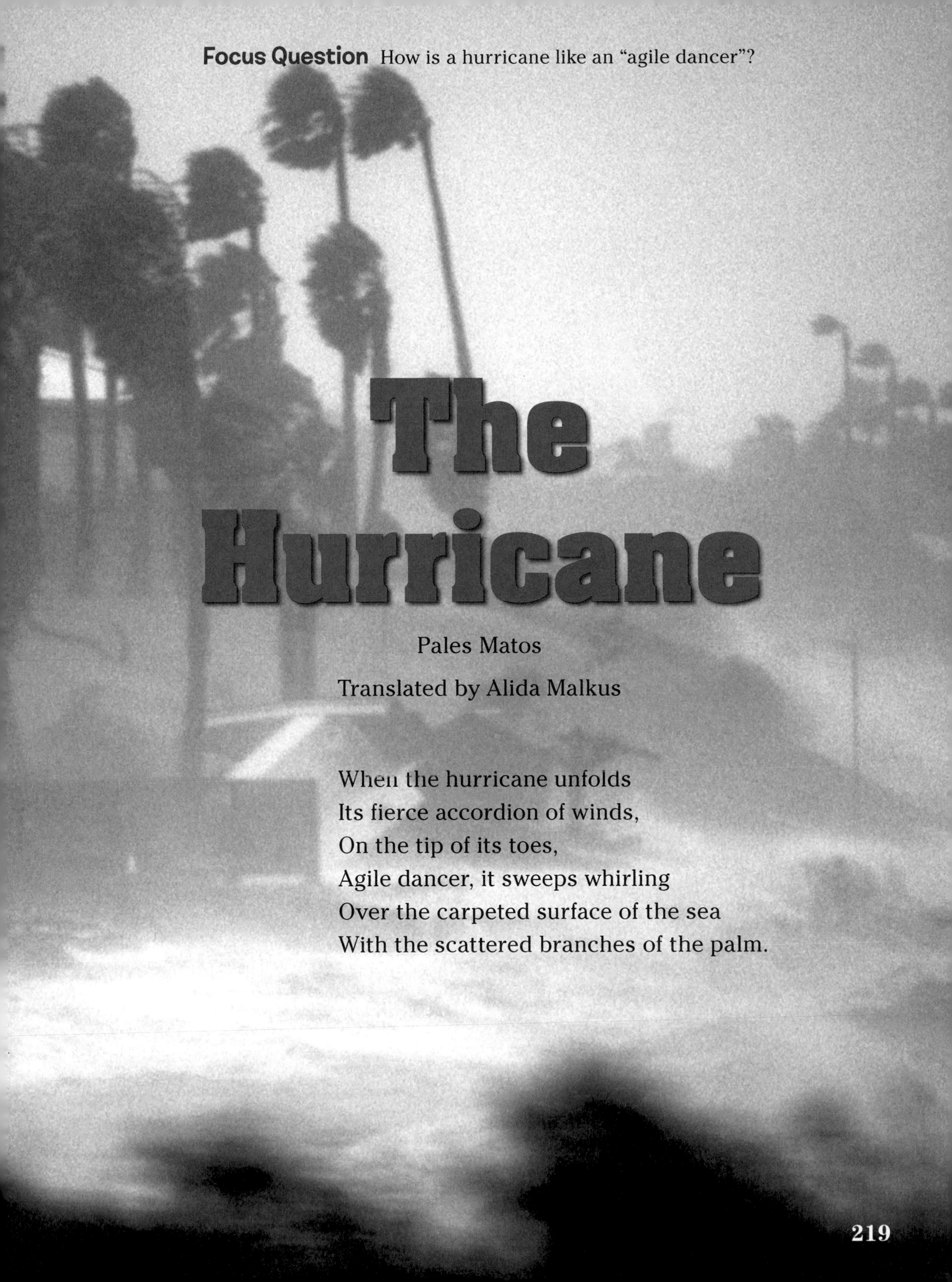

The Hurricane

Pales Matos

Translated by Alida Malkus

When the hurricane unfolds
Its fierce accordion of winds,
On the tip of its toes,
Agile dancer, it sweeps whirling
Over the carpeted surface of the sea
With the scattered branches of the palm.

Test-Taking Strategy: Analyzing questions

Think carefully about what the question is asking. Pay attention to important words in directions and questions. These important words will help you find the right answer.

Analyzing questions

Read each question on a test carefully. Each question or answer choice has important words. Try to understand the question before you choose an answer.

Read this item to yourself. Think about the important words in the question and answer choices. Decide which answer is best.

> **According to this article, how do plants help animals to breathe?**
>
> Some animals eat plants.
>
> Plants make oxygen that animals breathe.
>
> Some animals make homes in trees.
>
> Trees are good places for animals to hide.

The first part of the question reminds you to base your answer on the article. The other important words in the question are *help animals to breathe.* By reading the question carefully and thinking about what it is asking, you can figure out the right answer. Now look at the answer choices. Which choice is the best answer to the question? Only the second answer is about breathing. All the other answers are about other ways that trees help animals.

Analyzing a question will help you understand it better.

Electricity for Free

Some people get their electricity for free. It is perfectly legal. They do it by changing the light from the sun into electric energy.

Solar cells change light from the sun into electricity. The kind of electricity they make is called *direct current*. When you put a number of solar cells together, it is called an *array*. A solar array can charge batteries, run some motors, and power other electrical machines. Sometimes the direct current is changed to *alternating current*. This kind of electricity can run regular household devices. These include things like lights, televisions, or computers.

The first solar cells were made about fifty years ago. They were very expensive. Most people could not afford them. Solar power was mostly used in special projects like satellites or science stations in remote areas.

Over time, solar cells became cheaper to make. In the 1980s, they were used in things like calculators, watches, and small radios. These devices worked, but solar power was more of a gimmick than anything else.

All of that changed as people began to see that an energy crisis was on the way. Most electricity is made by burning fossil fuels. These are fuels like coal, oil, and natural gas. Fuels like these will not last forever. Another source of energy had to be developed. Solar power seemed like one of the good choices.

GO ON

Lots of money was given to research into solar power. This caused two things to happen. First, solar cells became more efficient. Second, the cost of the solar cells dropped. Solar power is still expensive compared to other ways of making electricity. However, it is getting cheaper.

A home solar power system is made up of a number of parts. The first is the solar panel. This is the group of solar cells that converts sunlight to electricity. The panels are usually put on the roof of the house.

The electricity made by the solar cells goes to one of three places. Part of it is changed to electricity that is used at once. Some of it is stored in batteries for use when the sun is not shining. The rest of it goes to an unusual place.

Sometimes the solar cells will generate more electricity than can be used at once or stored. This surplus energy is sent to the "grid." This is the system of wires that connects power stations and users. A family that owns a solar home will be paid for this extra electricity. That is not a bad deal, is it?

1. Read this sentence from the article.

   These devices worked, but solar power was more a gimmick than anything else.

   What does the word *gimmick* mean in this sentence?

   Ⓐ change

   Ⓑ task

   Ⓒ stunt

   Ⓓ deal

2. Which of these happened because more money was available to do research on solar power?

   Ⓕ The "grid" was invented to distribute electricity.

   Ⓖ Extra electricity was made by solar homes.

   Ⓗ Coal and oil were no longer needed to make electricity.

   Ⓘ Solar cells became more efficient.

3. What was the author's purpose in writing this article?

   Ⓐ to inform readers about the home use of electricity from solar cells

   Ⓑ to show how little research on solar power has been done in fifty years

   Ⓒ to tell a story about why some people save more money than others

   Ⓓ to explain the difference between alternating current and direct current

4. Why is solar power so important in today's world? Use information and details from the article to explain your answer.

Making a New Nation

What does it take to make a new nation?
Why would people want to do it? Who
would do it? How was our nation made?

Fine Art
Theme Connection

Look at the painting *The Declaration of Independence,* 1786–95, by John Trumbull.

- What historic meeting is depicted in the painting?

- What is the significance of that event?

- Who are some of the historic figures depicted in the painting?

- How does the painting relate to the theme Making a New Nation?

John Trumbull.
Declaration of Independence.
Oil on canvas. 12' × 18'.

BIG Idea

How do individuals make changes by working together?

Read the article to find the meanings of these words, which are also in ". . . If You Lived at the Time of the American Revolution":

+ colonies
+ loyal
+ protest
+ pamphlets
+ published
+ liberty
+ necessities
+ settlers
+ discharge
+ militia

Vocabulary Strategy

Context Clues are hints in the text that help you find the meanings of words. Look at the words *loyal, settlers,* and *honorable.* Use context clues to find each word's meaning.

Vocabulary
Warm-Up

Tom hunkered down deeper into the blankets. He was not cold—it was only October—but he felt safer buried beneath the folds. Outside, Tom heard whooping and cheering, and cannons were exploding in the distance. He expected the celebrating to go on all night. The colonies had just won their freedom.

What this event meant for Tom, however, was less clear. His father had stayed loyal to King George despite the protest of their neighbors. For example, Mr. Hanson had given them many pamphlets to read. The little books were published to tell the colonists why it would be better if they governed themselves. Tom had read a few of them. He agreed with the idea of liberty—of freeing the colonies from England's rule—but Tom's father did not. He believed England gave them too many necessities, like a strong army and a sure trading partner. Tom's father was convinced that without these things, the colonies would fail.

Earlier that day, word had reached Tom's town that the Patriots had won the war. By dinnertime, Tom's father announced that the family would return to England. Tom could not believe it. The Howes had lived in the colonies for nearly 150 years. They were among the earliest settlers to travel from England to America.

Tom's father explained that a treaty would be signed soon. It would declare that England no longer ruled the colonies. Even sooner, the army would begin the discharge of its soldiers, letting them return home. Many of the men from their town had fought in the militia against England. These were honorable men, deserving respect for how well they had fought, but Tom knew his father feared revenge. English soldiers had killed many of the Patriots, and the Howes were known Loyalists. They would be safer in England.

As another cannon blast echoed down the street, Tom pulled the blankets tight and tried to sleep.

GAME

Matching Game
Unscramble the letters to discover the selection vocabulary word that matches the definition. Write your answer on a separate sheet of paper.

1. small books that have paper covers — tlhmppaes
2. to object to — trostep
3. freedom from control by another country — triblye
4. printed a newspaper, magazine, or book — sledubphi
5. territories ruled by another country — sloonice

Concept Vocabulary

The concept word for this lesson is **rebellion.** *Rebellion* is something done to show disagreement with the people in power. Booing at a sporting event because you think the referee made a bad call is a minor form of rebellion. Fighting against a corrupt government is a more serious form of rebellion.

Genre

Expository Text tells people something. It contains facts about real people, things, or events.

Comprehension Skill

Classify and Categorize

As you read the selection, group similar things together to comprehend and recall the text. This skill will also help you see the relationships found in the text.

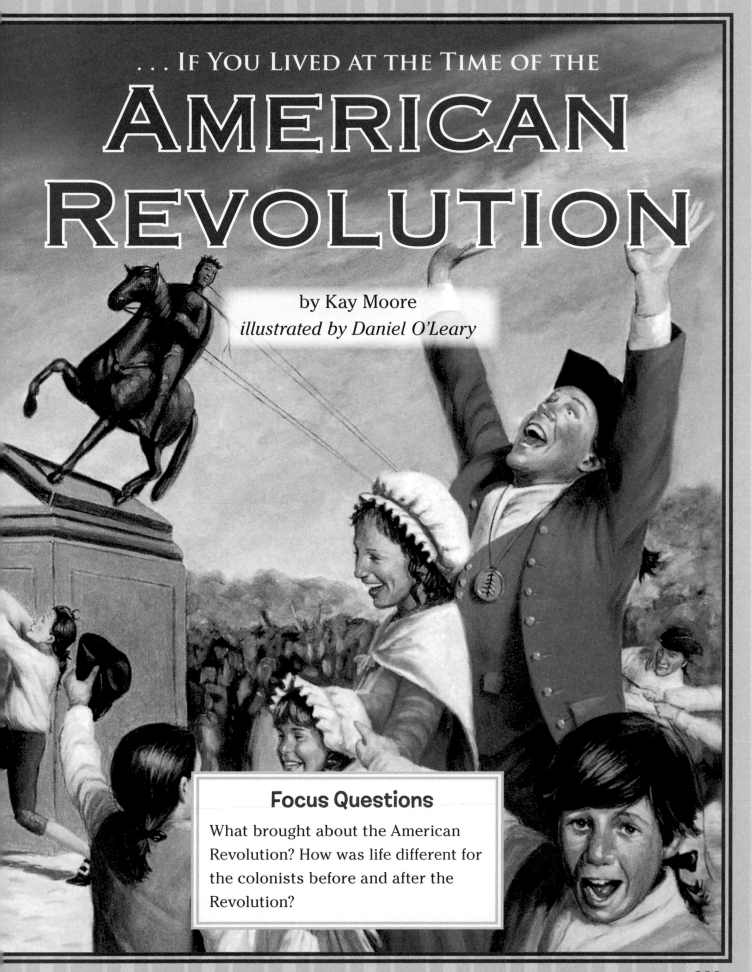

... IF YOU LIVED AT THE TIME OF THE

AMERICAN REVOLUTION

by Kay Moore

illustrated by Daniel O'Leary

Focus Questions

What brought about the American
Revolution? How was life different for
the colonists before and after the
Revolution?

Introduction

Have you ever wondered why the Fourth of July is a holiday? Before that date in 1776, the thirteen American colonies were part of an empire of more than thirty-two lands ruled by the King of England. The Declaration of Independence, which was signed by members of the Continental Congress on July 4, 1776, showed that the colonies wanted to be free. But it took a war for this to actually happen.

This war is called the "American Revolution." Some call it the "War of Independence" or the "Revolutionary War." It is usually viewed as a struggle between the American colonies and King George III of England, who ruled the British Empire. But it was also a "civil" war, a war that is fought between people of the same country.

There were people from many different backgrounds living in the British American colonies. Not all of them thought it was a good idea to break away from England. If you and your family remained loyal to the king, you were called Loyalists. If you and your family wanted to be free from British rule, you were called Patriots.

What was life like before the Revolution?

All thirteen American colonies ruled by England were along the Atlantic Ocean. About two and a half million people lived in the colonies.

You could travel on the Boston Post Road from Boston to New York, then on to Philadelphia. These were the three largest cities in the colonies. Other roads went south from Pennsylvania to South Carolina. All the roads were narrow and rough. It was better to travel by water if you could.

Mail went by stagecoach between New York and Philadelphia three times a week in spring and summer, and twice a week between Boston and Philadelphia. In fall and winter, service was less often.

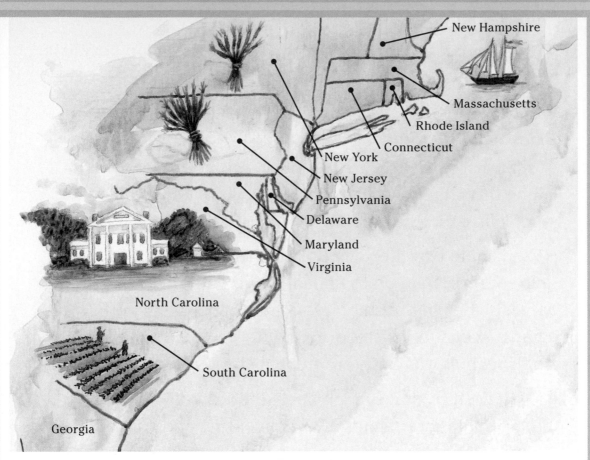

New Hampshire

Massachusetts

Rhode Island

Connecticut

New York

New Jersey

Pennsylvania

Delaware

Maryland

Virginia

North Carolina

South Carolina

Georgia

Each colony was interested only in its local problems. The colonies did not work well together.

The area called New England included the colonies of Massachusetts, New Hampshire, Rhode Island, and Connecticut. Shipbuilding, fishing, hunting for whales, and buying, selling, and shipping goods were important to these colonies.

The Middle Colonies of New York, Pennsylvania, New Jersey, and Delaware had soil that was good for growing many different kinds of fruits and vegetables. So much wheat was grown in Pennsylvania and New York that they were called "the bread basket of the empire."

In the South were the colonies of Maryland, Virginia, North Carolina, South Carolina, and Georgia. Here, tobacco was grown on large farms called plantations. In some areas, farmers grew rice, and indigo plants used to make blue dye.

What started the Revolution?

The first settlers in the colonies liked having British help and protection. British soldiers were there to help them fight Native American enemies and to keep other countries, such as France and Spain, from invading. It was like your mother watching over you. However, as you grow older, you will want more freedom to make your own decisions. That is how many of the colonists felt.

The colonists grew tired of following British rules. England controlled trade and told people where they could settle. They forced the colonists to provide housing and food for the British soldiers sent to protect them.

Since 1760, the colonists had also had to pay taxes for various products. Under a law called the Stamp Act (1765), the colonists had to pay extra money for newspapers, land deeds, card games, dice games, and even for graduation diplomas.

The colonists had no direct way to complain, since no one from the colonies was allowed to be a member of the British Parliament, which made the rules. James Otis, a Boston lawyer, stirred up the colonists when he said they should not pay taxes until they could send a person to speak for the colonies in Parliament. "Taxation without representation is tyranny!" he exclaimed.

After years of protest, the British took away all the taxes except the one on tea. This did not satisfy the Patriots. On December 16, 1773, angry Patriots, dressed as Mohawk Indians, dumped 342 crates of tea into Boston Harbor.

King George decided to punish Boston for the "Boston Tea Party" by closing the port. Nothing would go in or out of the city until the tea was paid for, and the city told the king it was sorry that this had happened.

Some people thought it was time for the colonies as a group to protest British taxes. In September 1774, men from the colonies met together in Carpenters' Hall in Philadelphia. Called the "Continental Congress," this group became the informal government of the colonies.

Bad feelings continued. Finally, British soldiers and Patriots fought at Lexington and Concord, Massachusetts, on April 19, 1775. This was the start of the American Revolution.

Who were the Loyalists?

About one-third of the people living in the colonies wanted to remain as citizens of England. They stayed loyal for different reasons:

1. They believed the king had the right to rule the colonies and that his laws were fair.

2. They were afraid of the British soldiers.

3. They had family in England and didn't want to put them in danger.

4. They felt that a government run by rich Patriots would be worse.

These people were known as "Loyalists," "Royalists," "friends of the government," "the King's friends," or "Tories."

Some Loyalists joined the British army and became regular British soldiers (called "Redcoats" or "Lobsterbacks" by the Patriots because of the color of their uniforms).

Others formed Loyalist units that fought with the British. Among these were the Loyal Greens, King's American Regiment, Queen's Loyal Rangers, and Royal American Regiment.

Many Native Americans, including the Iroquois and Seneca nations, joined the British side. So did thousands of African Americans. They had been slaves, brought over to the colonies from Africa against their will to work on plantations in the South, or born in the colonies as slaves. The British gave them their freedom in return for their help.

Soldiers from Germany, called "Hessians," were paid by the British to come and help their troops.

Many people who had recently come to the colonies from England, Scotland, Ireland, and Germany also remained loyal to the King of England.

There were so many Loyalists in New York City that it became known as the Tory capital of America. Delaware and the southern colonies also had a large number of Loyalists.

LOYALIST SOLDIERS

Redcoat

Freed Slave

Iroquois Brave

Member of the Royal American Regiment

Hessian

All types of people were Loyalists, including lawyers, merchants, ministers, government officials, farmers, and workers.

Who were the Patriots?

In the beginning, the Patriots were the people in the colonies who wanted England to remove taxes. But soon the word "liberty" was being heard. The Patriots no longer wanted to be "British Americans"—they just wanted to be "Americans." They supported the Continental Congress as a way to rule themselves. They started thinking of themselves as the "United Colonies."

Patriots were known by many names including "Rebels," "Liberty Boys," "Sons (or Daughters) of Liberty," "Colonials," and "Whigs." About one-third of the people living in the thirteen colonies were Patriots.

When war broke out, the "Continental Army" was formed with men from the colonies and a few men from Canada. Most Native Americans were on the British side, but some tribes helped the Patriots.

The Patriots enlisted slaves to fight for them after England had already taken on thousands of African-American soldiers. Although more blacks joined the British army, it is thought that about five thousand fought for the Patriots. Since slaves did not have last names, many gave themselves names such as "Liberty" or "Freedom." One unit from Connecticut included men named Sharp Liberty and Cuff Freedom.

In 1778, France joined the Patriots' side. They sent money, troops, and a navy.

Spain and Holland entered the war in 1779, supplying money to the Patriots.

Did everyone in the colonies take sides?

No. Many people tried to stay neutral (not choose a side) during the war. Some changed sides depending on what was happening.

Many families split because of different views about the war. Benjamin Franklin was a well-known Patriot. His son, William, was the Royal Governor of New Jersey and warned the people in that colony not to act against the king. William became the head of the Board of American Loyalists.

George Washington was the leader of the Continental Army. His older half brother, Lawrence, was a Loyalist.

Some people hoped to stay out of the war entirely. The religion of the Quakers and Mennonites did not allow them to fight, although some did take sides.

Others were not free to express openly their true feelings, but were expected to go along with the view of their households. These included slaves and indentured servants—men and women who had to work for someone else for a number of years to pay off a debt.

You could not always be sure how someone felt about the war. There were no lines dividing each side. Your family might be Patriots and your next-door neighbors Loyalists.

In some families, a couple of family members would travel to Britain and the rest would stay in the colonies. In this way, the family was sure to be on the winning side, no matter which side won.

***How would your life have changed after the
Declaration of Independence?***

The Declaration of Independence was written mainly by
Thomas Jefferson and adopted by the Continental Congress
in 1776. The Declaration listed twenty-seven ways the king
had hurt the colonies.

Patriots agreed with the Declaration. They now viewed the
colonies as thirteen states making one nation.

The Declaration divided many families, friends, and
neighbors. Some Patriots were against British taxes, but
didn't favor a total break with Britain. John Dickinson, a
member of Congress from Philadelphia, spoke out strongly,
saying, "Declaring our independence at a time like this is like
burning down our house before we have another."

Some of these Patriots began siding with the British and
even moved to England.

Men who wanted independence went to fight with
the Continental Army or with their local militia. In
Massachusetts, they were known as "minutemen" because
they could get ready to fight in a minute. More soldiers came
from Massachusetts and Connecticut than other areas.

With men away from home, family life changed.

Women had to run farms and manage businesses. Children helped harvest crops, and made sure animals were fed and watered. Sometimes, fathers and brothers would return home to help plant or harvest crops and then go back to their units and the fighting.

Money could be scarce for soldiers' families because soldiers often didn't get paid for over a year.

Did any women or children fight in the Continental Army?

Boys often went to war with their fathers or older brothers. At age sixteen, boys could join the army. Younger boys might have played the drum, bugle, or fife for the soldiers.

Nathan Futrell was a drummer boy in the North Carolina Continental Militia when he was seven years old.

At ten, Israel Task left his Massachusetts farm to be a cook and carry messages during battles.

Women and girls took care of the wounded, cooked food, and washed and mended uniforms.

Some women were part of the fighting, too. They carried pitchers of water to cool down the cannons and give the men drinks. These women were called "Molly Pitchers" by the soldiers. When her husband was hurt, Mary Hays stopped carrying water and took over his job loading and firing a cannon. After the war, she was awarded a pension of forty dollars a year for her service.

Families sometimes went with their men and the army. The armies didn't often fight in winter so General George Washington's wife, Martha, spent eight years in winter camp with her husband, returning to Mount Vernon, their Virginia home, each spring.

Was it hard to get money during the war?

Because of the war, gold and silver coins were hard to come by. And the war cost a lot of money! To pay for the war, the Continental Congress asked each state to print its own paper money. At first Patriots used the paper dollars in support of their cause.

However, this kind of money lost value because so much was printed and it was easy to copy. Many people called the paper money "shin plasters," because they felt it was only useful as a bandage for a sore leg. People began to say, "It's not worth a Continental" when they meant something was not worth very much.

This kind of situation is called inflation. It got so bad that in March of 1780, a paper dollar was worth just a fourth of a cent! And things kept getting worse. In May of 1781, it took 225 paper dollars to equal one gold dollar. A few weeks later, you needed 900 paper dollars to buy one gold dollar's worth of supplies.

It was said that it took a wagon-load of money to buy a wagon-load of food. Some soldiers even refused to be paid in the paper money at all; they wanted hard gold.

How did people get food and clothes?

You didn't need much money to buy food if you lived in the country. Most homes had a vegetable garden. Also, you could pick wild fruits, berries, and nuts. You could catch fish and hunt for deer and wild turkeys.

Nothing was wasted:

- Animal bones were saved and made into buttons.

- Goose feathers were used to stuff pillows.

- Reeds and twigs were woven into baskets.

- Old pieces of cloth and outgrown clothing were cut into squares and sewn into quilts. During the war years, quilt-makers invented patterns they called "Washington's Puzzle" or "Washington's Plumes."

Patriots who lived in cities often received food, clothing, and other necessities from relatives or friends who lived in the country. You could also trade with Patriot neighbors.

Sometimes you just did without.

How did you get news about the war and what was happening in the other colonies?

Getting news was important to the Patriots even before the war began. Each colony had set up a "committee of correspondence," who hired its own riders to carry messages by horseback. (This was long before the telephone, radio, television, or even the telegraph had been invented.)

Messages were delivered from one town to the next until all colonies received the news.

Sometimes, information was sent by ship instead of overland.

After the war began, the committees of correspondence formed "committees of safety." Their riders were constantly in danger of being captured by the British.

Children were sometimes used as messengers. One young messenger was nine-year-old John Quincy Adams, who later became the sixth president of the United States. He took messages from his mother, Abigail, in Braintree, Massachusetts, to his father, John, in Boston.

Another way to find out the news was from a newspaper. The *Boston Gazette* and the *South Carolina Gazette* were two papers that reported news with a Patriot view. The *Royal Gazette* (New York) was the best known of the Loyalist newspapers.

Most newspapers were printed only once a week and had four pages, with three columns on each page.

In small towns a "town crier," sometimes a schoolboy, might share news aloud. As more and more people learned to read, there was less need to have a town crier.

Pamphlets and books were also printed. Thomas Paine's *Common Sense* had sent the idea of freedom throughout the colonies when it was published in January of 1776. It was often re-read and shared during the war. On the last page in bold letters were the words, **"THE FREE AND INDEPENDENT STATES OF AMERICA."**

As thousands of people read the forty-seven pages, they saw themselves as the "United States."

More news could be found on posters, called broadsides, that were nailed to trees, poles, and buildings. Broadsides were used to get men to join the army and for various public announcements.

Who were the famous Patriots?

The most well known were the men who helped promote the idea of freedom.

George Washington

George Washington, a planter and soldier from Virginia, was chosen to be commander of the Continental Army. Called "the Father of Our Country," Washington was a strong leader who held the army together when the soldiers faced many problems.

Patrick Henry

Paul Revere

Patrick Henry from Virginia was known as "the Son of Thunder" because of his patriotic speeches. He started many people thinking about freedom when he said, "Give me liberty or give me death."

Paul Revere was a silversmith in Boston. He was a leader of the Sons of Liberty, a messenger, and a secret agent for the Patriots. On April 18, 1775, Revere made his famous midnight ride from Boston to Lexington, Massachusetts, to warn the citizens that the British army was on its way. Revere was captured, but he escaped safely. The next day, the battle of Lexington and Concord marked the beginning of the American Revolution.

John Adams, Benjamin Franklin, and **Thomas Jefferson** were the most well known of the committee who wrote the Declaration of Independence. Jefferson did most of the actual writing.

John Adams

Benjamin Franklin

Thomas Jefferson

Marquis de Lafayette

The **Marquis de Lafayette** was a rich Frenchman who decided to help the Patriots. His full name was Marie Joseph Paul Yves Rich Gilbert de Motier. At nineteen, Lafayette brought a ship and money to the colonies from France. He asked only to serve and would not take any pay. He was an excellent soldier and helped Washington throughout the war in many ways.

A schoolmaster who joined the army at the start of the war, **Nathan Hale** volunteered to spy for the Patriots, but was caught by the British. Before he was hung, he is reported to have said, "I only regret I have but one life to lose for my country."

Crispus Attucks was a black man killed during the "Boston Massacre" in 1770, when five people were shot by British soldiers. This event pushed many people to join the Patriots.

Nathan Hale

Crispus Attucks

Abigail Adams

Mercy Otis Warren

Women were also interested in rights and freedom.

Abigail Adams ran the family farm in Massachusetts while husband John was working in the Continental Congress in Philadelphia. She wrote letters to him, reminding him "not to forget the ladies" as Congress was writing laws for the new government.

Mercy Otis Warren was James Otis's sister. An excellent writer, she wrote plays that made fun of the British. Printed

Phillis Wheatley

in pamphlets, her plays were very popular. Later, she wrote three books that described the events of the American Revolution.

Phillis Wheatley was an African girl brought to the colonies as a slave. Bought by the Wheatley family, she learned to read and write, and wrote poetry. Phillis wrote a poem for General Washington and visited him at army headquarters. She is known as the first published black woman poet in America.

Deborah Sampson

Deborah Sampson dressed in men's clothes and joined the Continental Army in 1782 as Robert Shurtleff. She received an honorable discharge for her work as a soldier when her identity was discovered in 1783.

What ended the war?

After over six years of fighting, the British army gave up to the American forces at 2 P.M. on October 19, 1781, at Yorktown, Virginia. General Charles Cornwallis said he was too ill to surrender personally to General Washington. And so British General Charles O'Hara surrendered to American General Benjamin Lincoln at Yorktown. The British officer presented his sword and the American tapped it as an acceptance of surrender. The British fifes played the song, "The World Turned Upside Down." This was a good tune because life in America changed greatly after this day.

News of the surrender spread throughout the states by messengers, newspapers, and broadsides. It reached Philadelphia on October 22 and Boston on October 27. Towns celebrated with cannon salutes, bonfires, and fireworks. People kept the lamps in their houses lit all night. Loyalists had to keep their lights on, too.

It took until September 1783 for the final peace agreement to be written. The Treaty of Paris really ended the American Revolution. In the treaty, the new country was recognized and its boundaries decided. Fishing limits were set along the coast of Canada.

It was also agreed that Congress would recommend to the states that they restore property to any Loyalists who had not fought in the war. In most cases, the states did not do this.

Meet the Author

Kay Moore

Kay Moore is a freelance journalist who has worked as a feature writer and city editor at various newspapers. She also co-writes books with her husband, Louis Moore. She sees newspaper writing as being very different from book writing. Newspaper writing allows her to be in immediate contact with readers about issues that are important to them. Book writing involves a longer process, but she likes its "enduring nature." She says, "It stimulates me to know that a book preserves for posterity my values and interpretation of life."

Meet the Illustrator

Daniel O'Leary

O'Leary illustrates children's books, but he has done much, much more. He has been an artist for over twenty years. O'Leary creates art for television and movie ads. Sometimes he makes paintings for people who like art. Sometimes he illustrates product boxes. O'Leary is happy coming up with his own ideas, or using the ideas of others. Much of his art is very realistic, looking almost like photographs. O'Leary lives in New York City.

Making a New Nation
Theme Connections

Within the Selection

1. What was the main event that made a "new nation"?

2. List three people who contributed to the establishment of the United States and how they helped.

Beyond the Selection

3. What have you learned about your country's history from this selection?

4. How has this selection added to your understanding of the founding of our nation?

Write about It!

Write about a time when you thought something was unfair.

Remember to add your own questions about the founding of our nation to the **Concept/Question Board.**

Settling a Settled Land

The first European explorers to see America found a continent filled with natural resources. Soon, all of Europe had heard about this vast new land. Each country wanted to claim as much of the land as possible for itself. Each European nation treated the local populations they met in different ways.

By 1600—about one hundred years after Columbus arrived—Spain had a huge empire in America. Spanish settlements stretched from Texas, through Mexico, and across half of South America. After defeating the Incas and the Aztecs—the native peoples of Central and South America—the Spanish forced them to work in

United States

Mexico
Cuba
Haiti
Dominican Republic
Belize
Puerto Rico
Honduras
Guatamala
Nicaragua
El Salvador
Costa Rica
Venezuela
Guyana
Suriname
Panama
Colombia
French Guiana
Ecuador

Brazil

Peru

Bolivia
Paraguay
Chile
Argentina

Areas under effective Spanish control c.1600

mines and on farms. Most of what they took from the land, such as crops and gold, was shipped back to Spain. Europe watched the Spanish rulers grow rich from their new source of income. Soon, the other countries raced westward.

France settled where Quebec, Canada, is today. The settlers traded with Native Americans, especially with the Iroquois. French traders gave them European goods, such as tools. In return the French received goods such as furs and fish.

In 1607, King James I of England gave a large part of the American East Coast to one company—the Virginia Company. It controlled land from Maine to North Carolina.

Most of the English settlers wanted nothing to do with Native Americans. However, Jamestown, the Virginia Company's main settlement, sat on land belonging to the Powhatan tribes. They attacked and made war against the settlers. Similar conflicts between Europeans and Native Americans would continue for the next two centuries as the United States grew.

Think Link

1. Where did the Incas and Aztecs live?

2. Which Central American countries were once part of the Spanish Empire? Use the map to answer this question.

3. Why did the other European countries want to follow Spain to America?

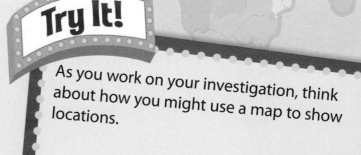

Try It!

As you work on your investigation, think about how you might use a map to show locations.

253

Genre

A **Narrative Poem** tells a story using traditional elements of poetry like rhyme, sound patterns, meter, and imagery.

Comprehension Strategy

⭐ **Visualizing** As you read the selection, visualize what you are reading as a way of making sure you understand and remember what is happening in the text.

The Midnight Ride of **Paul Revere**

by Henry Wadsworth Longfellow
Illustrated by Jeffrey Thompson

Read the article to find the meanings of these words, which are also in "The Midnight Ride of Paul Revere":

✦ assigned
✦ gleam
✦ sentinal
✦ mount
✦ weathercock
✦ muffled
✦ aloft
✦ magnified
✦ ledge
✦ spread

254

Vocabulary

Warm-Up

September 13, 2006

Dr. Horace Johnson
113 Solomon Road, Office G
Williams University
Tacoma, WA 98402

Dear Dr. Johnson,

Thank you again. I am so glad that out of all your ecology students you assigned this task to me. The landscape here in Montana is beautiful, and the Werners could not be nicer. This morning Mr. Werner took me out to see the eaglets for the first time. Let me describe how it went:

Before the sun had risen, the crowing of the rooster woke me from sleep. Then I ate a quick breakfast and headed outside. It was still pretty dark. Through the doorway of the barn I saw the gleam of a flashlight and knew where I could find Mr. Werner. He stood like a sentinel in the barn. He led two horses into the barnyard, explaining that they would be our transportation for the day. I needed a boost from Mr. Werner to help me mount my horse, but he swung up easily onto his.

As we left, he pointed to the barn's roof and pointed out the old weathercock, or weather vane, that was in the shape of a rooster. Its metal arrow swiveled slightly, showing that the wind blew toward the southeast. We rode down a gravel road for a while, and then turned and headed straight for the mountains. The long grass slowed the horses' muffled clopping. The sun had risen by then, but I had barely noticed until I caught sight of an eagle soaring aloft. With my binoculars, I magnified the eagle and watched it land on a ledge halfway up the mountainside. Next thing I knew, three eaglets poked their heads up out of the eagle's nest. What a beautiful sight!

It is encouraging to see that the number of bald eagles has increased so much after they nearly became extinct. They were saved because people spread the word about a threat to our nation's symbol. What if we could do that for all endangered animals?

See you soon!
Melinda Chou

GAME

Searching for Synonyms
Look at the list of words below. Using a dictionary or a thesaurus, find the selection vocabulary word that has the same or nearly the same meaning, and write your answers on a separate sheet of paper.

rooster	skyward
appointed	vane
muted	shelf
ascend	enlarged
shine	publicized

Concept Vocabulary

The concept word for this lesson is *movement.* A *movement* is a large group of people working together to change some part of society. For example, people in the Civil Rights movement fought hard so that African Americans would be treated equally and fairly in our country. The environmental movement wants humans to use Earth's resources wisely and not pollute the planet.

The Midnight Ride of Paul Revere

by Henry Wadsworth Longfellow
illustrated by Jeffrey Thompson

Focus Questions

Who was Paul Revere? Did Revere achieve what he set out to do?

Listen, my children, and you shall hear
Of the midnight ride of Paul Revere,
On the eighteenth of April, in Seventy-five;
Hardly a man is now alive
Who remembers that famous day and year.

He said to his friend, "If the British march
By land or sea from the town to-night,
Hang a lantern aloft in the belfry arch
Of the North Church tower as a signal light,—
One, if by land, and two, if by sea;
And I on the opposite shore will be,
Ready to ride and spread the alarm
Through every Middlesex village and farm,
For the country folk to be up and to arm."

Then he said, "Good Night!" and with muffled oar
Silently rowed to the Charlestown shore,
Just as the moon rose over the bay,
Where swinging wide at her moorings lay
The Somerset, British man-of-war;
A phantom ship, with each mast and spar
Across the moon like a prison bar,
And a huge black hulk, that was magnified
By its own reflection in the tide.

Meanwhile, his friend, through alley and street,
Wanders and watches with eager ears,
Till in the silence around him he hears
The muster of men at the barrack door,
The sound of arms, and the tramp of feet,
And the measured tread of the grenadiers,
Marching down to their boats on the shore.

Then he climbed the tower of the Old North Church,
By the wooden stairs, with stealthy tread,
To the belfry-chamber overhead,
And startled the pigeons from their perch
On the sombre rafters, that round him made
Masses and moving shapes of shade,—
By the trembling ladder, steep and tall,
To the highest window in the wall,
Where he paused to listen and look down
A moment on the roofs of the town,
And the moonlight flowing over all.

Beneath, in the churchyard, lay the dead,
In their night-encampment on the hill,
Wrapped in silence so deep and still
That he could hear, like a sentinel's tread,
The watchful night-wind, as it went
Creeping along from tent to tent,
And seeming to whisper, "All is well!"
A moment only he feels the spell
Of the place and the hour, and the secret dread
Of the lonely belfry and the dead;

For suddenly all his thoughts are bent
On a shadowy something far away,
Where the river widens to meet the bay,—
A line of black that bends and floats
On the rising tide, like a bridge of boats.

Meanwhile, impatient to mount and ride,
Booted and spurred, with a heavy stride
On the opposite shore walked Paul Revere.
Now he patted his horse's side,
Now gazed at the landscape far and near,
Then, impetuous, stamped the earth,
And turned and tightened his saddle girth;
But mostly he watched with eager search
The belfry-tower of the Old North Church,
As it rose above the graves on the hill,
Lonely and spectral and sombre and still.
And lo! As he looks, on the belfry's height
A glimmer, and then a gleam of light!
He springs to the saddle, the bridle he turns,
But lingers and gazes, till full on his sight
A second lamp in the belfry burns!

A hurry of hoofs in a village street,
A shape in the moonlight, a bulk in the dark,
And beneath, from the pebbles, in passing, a spark
Struck out by a steed flying fearless and fleet:
That was all! And yet, through the gloom and the light,
The fate of a nation was riding that night;
And the spark struck out by that steed, in his flight,
Kindled the land into flame with its heat.

He has left the village and mounted the steep,
And beneath him, tranquil and broad and deep,
Is the Mystic, meeting the ocean tides;
And under the alders, that skirt its edge,
Now soft on the sand, now loud on the ledge,
Is heard the tramp of his steed as he rides.

It was twelve by the village clock,
When he crossed the bridge into Medford town.
He heard the crowing of the cock,
And the barking of the farmer's dog,
And felt the damp of the river fog,
That rises after the sun goes down.

It was one by the village clock,
When he galloped into Lexington.
He saw the gilded weathercock
Swim in the moonlight as he passed,
And the meeting-house windows, blank and bare,
Gaze at him with a spectral glare,
As if they already stood aghast
At the bloody work they would look upon.

It was two by the village clock,
When he came to the bridge in Concord town.
He heard the bleating of the flock,
And the twitter of birds among the trees,
And felt the breath of the morning breeze
Blowing over the meadows brown.
And one was safe and asleep in his bed
Who at the bridge would be first to fall,
Who that day would be lying dead,
Pierced by a British musket-ball.

You know the rest. In the books you have read,
How the British Regulars fired and fled,—
How the farmers gave them ball for ball,
From behind each fence and farm-yard wall,
Chasing the red-coats down the lane,
Then crossing the fields to emerge again
Under the trees at the turn of the road,
And only pausing to fire and load.

So through the night rode Paul Revere;
And so through the night went his cry of alarm
To every Middlesex village and farm,—
A cry of defiance and not of fear,
A voice in the darkness, a knock at the door,
And a word that shall echo forevermore!
For, borne on the night-wind of the Past,
Through all our history, to the last,
In the hour of darkness and peril and need,
The people will waken and listen to hear
The hurrying hoof-beats of that steed,
And the midnight message of Paul Revere.

Historical Note

Henry Wadsworth Longfellow's stirring poem of the events leading up to the battle of Lexington and Concord made Paul Revere a folk hero for generations of Americans. But Longfellow's poem is not an actual historical account. In fact, Paul Revere never even made it to Concord. What was the true story of Paul Revere's ride? It goes like this:

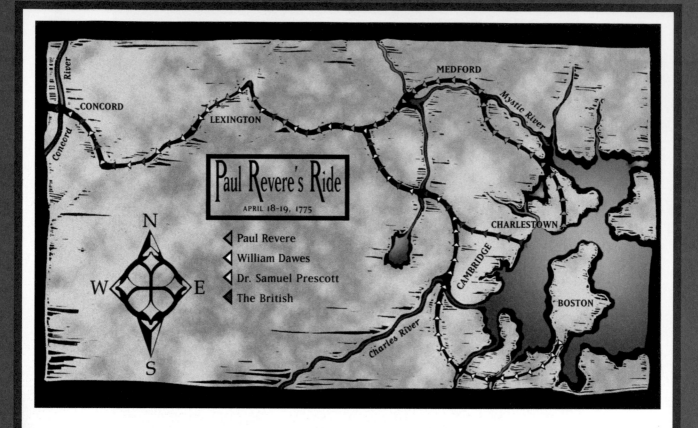

Paul Revere's Ride
APRIL 18-19, 1775

◁ Paul Revere
◁ William Dawes
◁ Dr. Samuel Prescott
◁ The British

The American Revolution had not yet started on the 18th of April in 1775. So far, the colonists had only been protesting and arguing to try to get England to treat them more fairly. But there were many who thought that the colonies should break away from England, and some had started to collect guns and ammunition so that they would be ready to fight if necessary. The British knew the rebels were preparing for war and were worried. Whenever they could, they seized guns and ammunition from the rebels to keep them from growing too strong.

On the night of April 18, a British force of about 700 men left Boston. They were planning to surprise the town of Concord and seize colonial ammunition stored there.

But patriots had been spying on the British troops for some time and had caught wind of the plan. That night silversmith Paul Revere and shoemaker William Dawes set off to sound the alarm. Besides alerting the countryside, they also hoped to warn two rebel leaders in Lexington: Samuel Adams and John Hancock.

Revere had been an active revolutionary for some time. He had helped plan the Boston Tea Party, and some think that he participated in it as well; he had spied on British troop movements around Boston; and he had ridden back and forth to Philadelphia several times, carrying news to and from the Continental Congress.

The weekend before, Doctor Joseph Warren, one of the last leaders of the independence movement still in Boston, had assigned Revere and Dawes to spread the news of the British troop movements. Worried that he might not get out of Boston safely, Revere asked a friend to hang signal lanterns in the tower of Christ Church in Boston. The signals would let patriots across the river know whether the British were marching out of Boston by land or rowing across the Charles River "by sea." That way, even if Revere was stopped from leaving Boston, others could carry the news to Lexington and Concord.

But in the end the signals weren't necessary. Revere avoided capture, and was rowed across the river by two friends. In Charlestown he borrowed a horse and set off for Lexington, stopping at each house to call the patriots to arms.

Arriving at Lexington at about midnight, Revere alerted Adams and Hancock and then was joined by Dawes, who had taken another route from Boston. They started for Concord. Just outside Lexington, another patriot, Dr. Samuel Prescott, joined them. The three men continued toward Concord, stopping at every house to spread the alarm.

On the way, a British patrol stopped the men and tried to arrest them. Prescott knew the area well and escaped immediately by jumping his horse over a stone wall. He galloped on to Concord. A little later, Dawes fled back to Lexington on foot. Revere was not so lucky. The British held him for a couple of hours and then let him go without his horse. He never got to Concord but did return to Lexington in time to witness the battle there.

The redcoats arrived in Lexington on the morning of April 19. About 70 patriots were ready, lined up on the village green, and the first battle of the Revolution began. No one knows who fired the first shot, but when the fighting stopped, eight patriots lay dead, and the redcoats had won.

The British marched on to Concord, sure that the militia there could be defeated as easily as the one at Lexington. But Prescott had arrived with his warning, and more than 300 patriots lay in wait at North Bridge. In the fighting, three redcoats and two rebels were killed. With more patriots arriving, the British turned around and retreated to Boston.

As the British marched back to Boston, they were met by patriots who had been roused by Revere, Dawes, and Prescott and were on their way to join the battle in Concord. When these patriots saw the British marching away from Concord, they attacked. By the time they reached Boston, the British had lost 200 men, and the Revolutionary War had begun.

Meet the Author

Henry Wadsworth Longfellow

Henry Wadsworth Longfellow was the most popular and widely read American poet of the world during his lifetime. He was also a college professor, a writer of textbooks, and a translator (he learned 11 languages). This poem is one of his most famous. Other poems of his include "Evangeline, A Tale of Arcadia," "The Courtship of Miles Standish," "The Song of Hiawatha," and "The Village Blacksmith." All of his poems are known for having truly American themes.

Meet the Illustrator

Jeffrey Thompson

Jeffrey Thompson likes to borrow from both old and new techniques when creating his illustrations. His artwork takes on the traditional look of being created with watercolors, woodcuts, and scratch boards, but he enhances their color using a computer program. Mr. Thompson's dream is to become a full-time author and illustrator of children's books.

Making a New Nation
Theme Connections

Within the Selection

1. Why did Paul Revere make his famous ride?

2. Who was actually there that night with Paul Revere?

Across Selections

3. Compare Paul Revere's role in this selection and in the Historical Note with the information you learned in ". . . If You Lived at the Time of the American Revolution."

4. Think about a short story you have read either in this book or outside of class. How does the form of a narrative poem compare to a short story?

Beyond the Selection

5. Have you read or heard any other poems based on people or events from the American Revolution? If so, what were their titles, and what stories did they tell?

6. What have you learned about Paul Revere's contribution to the making of our nation?

Write about It!

Describe the midnight ride of Paul Revere in your own words.

Remember to look for other articles about Paul Revere or Henry Wadsworth Longfellow to add to the **Concept/Question Board.**

Sing for Your Country

The word *patriotism* means "love for your country's laws and customs." This love is often shown by using symbols. The flag, Uncle Sam, and the Statue of Liberty are just a few of America's patriotic symbols. Songs and poems are also used to show patriotism. These songs include "America the Beautiful," "My Country 'Tis of Thee," and "The Star Spangled Banner."

Our national anthem was written during the War of 1812. In 1814, Francis Scott Key boarded the *H.M.S. Tonnant*, a British warship. He hoped to argue for the release of his captured friend, Dr. Beanes. While Key was on the ship, it set sail. The British were about to attack the United States at Fort McHenry.

Onboard the ship, Key watched the battle rage. When night fell, however, he could no longer see which flag flew above the fort—American or British. As the sun rose the next morning, Key got to witness a stunning sight: a giant American flag flying aloft over Fort McHenry.

Key was inspired to write a poem. He titled it "Defence of Fort McHenry." Within a few weeks, the poem was renamed and set to music. While its popularity quickly spread, it was not until 1931 that Congress and President Hoover named it the official song of our nation.

The "Pledge of Allegiance" is also often heard in public. Francis Bellamy wrote it in 1892. He wanted to honor the 400th anniversary of Columbus's trip to America. Here is what Bellamy wrote:

I pledge allegiance to my flag and the republic for which it stands: one nation indivisible, with liberty and justice for all.

In the 1950s, during the Cold War, the words *under God* were added to the pledge.

Think Link

1. Italics were used three times in the article. Explain why, in each instance, the author needed to use italics.

2. Use an encyclopedia or search online to find out what the letters *H.M.S.* stand for.

Try It!

As you work on your investigation, think about how you might use italics in your work.

Read the article to find the meanings of these words, which are also in "The Master Spy of Yorktown":

+ lessen
+ idle
+ invaders
+ civilians
+ commander
+ looting
+ revealing
+ precautions
+ portrait
+ prompt

Vocabulary Strategy

Context Clues are hints in the text that help you find the meanings of words. Look at the words *idle*, *precautions*, and *prompt*. Use context clues to find each word's meaning.

Vocabulary

Warm-Up

The rain fell like walls of water pushing across the dark street and beat a steady rhythm against the roof of Mac's car. The sound tried to lull Mac to sleep, but he was too alert. His only wish was that the storm would lessen so that he could see better.

Mac Schmidt had been waiting inside his car for nearly five hours. Sitting idle for that long would be hard for most people, but not Mac. He knew how essential it was to stay focused on those two windows across the street. They were his only view into Lido's third-floor apartment. Lido worked for a group of invaders spying inside the country. The army knew their goals, but civilians had no idea. An attack could come any day.

Mac's commander had asked him to monitor every move Lido made. Lido had been looting files from a government office where he worked undercover. Somewhere inside the apartment, Lido hid this stolen information. Mac's job was to catch Lido revealing the hiding place.

Sipping his coffee, Mac appeared to read a newspaper. Actually, his newspaper contained a screen connected to a camera pointing at the windows. Mac could not be obvious as he watched tenants coming and going from the building. He needed to take precautions so as not to be discovered.

Suddenly, Mac stiffened as lights came on in the windows and Lido wandered into view. He tossed his coat onto a chair and then quickly headed over to a large portrait hanging over the couch. Lido reached up and pressed the left eye of the woman in the painting. A small opening appeared in the wall next to the couch. Mac watched Lido place two folders inside and then press the other eye in the portrait. The opening closed.

Now Mac knew. He must be prompt about contacting his commander. Any delay and the government could fall.

Vocabulary Shuffle
Using a dictionary, find definitions for the selection vocabulary words and write each one on a separate index card. Shuffle the cards, and give half of them to another student. Take turns reading the definitions and trying to determine which word is being defined.

Concept Vocabulary

The concept word for this lesson is **espionage.** *Espionage* is the act of spying, or secretly trying to get information. What kind of groups or organizations spy on each other? What are they trying to find out? Do you think it is right to spy?

Genre

Comprehension Skill

The Master Spy of Yorktown

by Burke Davis

illustrated by Stephen Snider

Focus Questions

Who was James Armistead? What was his connection to the Marquis de Lafayette and Lord Charles Cornwallis?

In the spring of 1781, General Washington rushed a band of 1,200 men southward to meet British raiders who were looting and burning their way through Virginia. The commander chosen for this tiny force was the Marquis de Lafayette, one of the youngest major generals in history. The Frenchman was determined to halt the invaders, who were led by the newest of British generals, the American traitor Benedict Arnold.

Lafayette, who was only twenty-three years old, had come to America four years earlier as a volunteer, sailing in a ship he had bought for the voyage. As one of the richest men in France, Lafayette had done much to bring help from King Louis XVI to the American rebels—troops, ships, guns, money, and uniforms. And in Virginia, at last, his dream had come true, a chance to command an American army, however small.

George Washington

The Marquis de Lafayette

The young Frenchman soon found that his task was not easy. Virginia farmers hid their horses and wagons so that Lafayette's soldiers could not seize them for use against the enemy. The little army was often hungry, for people of the countryside refused to sell their meat and grain in exchange for the almost worthless American paper money. It was just as Governor Thomas Jefferson had warned Lafayette; Virginia was a state of "mild laws and a people not used to prompt obedience."

Lafayette also found that the enemy was too strong for him, since there were two British armies in Virginia, one under Benedict Arnold and another under Lord Charles Cornwallis. With better trained troops and thousands of horses stolen from Virginia plantations, the redcoats moved swiftly. The British burned the capital at Richmond, many warehouses full of valuable tobacco and supplies of rebel arms and food, and chased the Virginia legislature across the state. Governor Jefferson narrowly escaped capture and resigned his office. Lafayette complained to Washington, "I am not strong enough to get beaten. Government in this state has no energy and laws have no force. . . . The enemy can overrun the country."

Lord Charles Cornwallis

Still, the Frenchman refused to give up. His troops hung about the British, as closely as they dared without risking battle. And since he could not hope to defeat the enemy openly, Lafayette began sending spies into the enemy camps.

The most important of the American spies was a black man, JAMES ARMISTEAD, the slave of William Armistead, a farmer who lived near the town of Williamsburg. He was only twenty-one, even younger than Lafayette, but the Frenchman saw that his volunteer was brave as well as bright and felt that he would be loyal to the American rebels—even though he had not been promised his freedom for risking his life as a spy.

James Armistead went at once to the camp of Benedict Arnold, made his way to headquarters, and sent Lafayette word of everything he saw. The British were not suspicious of the smiling young black man who had come as a volunteer and was so willing to serve officers in camp and to guide them on the roads. But messengers went out to Lafayette almost daily, reporting what Armistead had seen. Making use of these secret reports, a band of Virginia soldiers sneaked into the British camp one night and almost captured Benedict Arnold himself. Still the redcoats did not suspect young James Armistead. Arnold and his officers felt sure that the black man would remain loyal to them because he wanted most of all freedom from his life as a slave.

When Benedict Arnold left Virginia and returned to the war in the north, James Armistead went into the camp of Lord Cornwallis, where he served as a waiter at headquarters. He continued to report to Lafayette almost daily, though the risk of death was now greater and his work was much harder. Cornwallis was a good general who was careful to see that his enemies had little chance to learn his plans.

As Lafayette reported, "His Lordship is so shy of his papers that my honest friend says he cannot get at them." The Frenchman further complained to Washington that he was forced "to guess at every possible whim of an enemy that flies with the wind and is not within the reach of spies."

But though Lafayette admitted that he was "devilishly afraid" of Cornwallis and was worried because his spies could not steal British maps and orders, he continued to camp very near the enemy, warned of every redcoat move by messengers from James Armistead. The armies trailed west through Virginia, and then back to the coast from the Blue Ridge Mountains, the British raiders leading, the Americans following stubbornly, a few miles in the rear. Cornwallis seldom realized that he was being followed, but Lafayette pretended that his tiny force was driving the British before it, in hopes of keeping up the morale of Virginia civilians.

James Armistead left no record of his life in the enemy camp during these weeks, but since he spent much time in the tent of Lord Cornwallis, he was certainly a trusted servant. He probably stood near the general during meals, serving food and drink and listening to the talk of officers, pretending that he did not understand their plans, and certainly did not dream of revealing them to Lafayette and the Americans. But often, by day and night, James Armistead whispered what he had overheard to other black men in the camp, and within a few hours Lafayette had word of British plans.

In July, when Cornwallis's army had moved to the east and was camped in the small city of Portsmouth, near Chesapeake Bay, James Armistead reported that a fleet of sailing ships had come to anchor in the harbor, ready to carry British troops to a new post. Lafayette expected news that Cornwallis had sailed, but for weeks there was no change. The ships lay idle at anchor day after day, and enemy troops remained in their camp at Portsmouth. At last, in early August, there was a warning from James Armistead: Cornwallis had sailed, no one knew where. The army of redcoats had disappeared from Portsmouth.

Within a few days, Lafayette's scouts learned the enemy's secret. Cornwallis was unloading his troops at Yorktown, a small tobacco port on the York River, within sight of the broad Chesapeake. Lafayette and his Americans moved nearer, to Williamsburg, where they could keep watch. They saw that Cornwallis was in no hurry to build defenses about the village. The weather was hot, and only a few men worked at digging trenches. Lafayette reported the news to Washington, who was still in the north.

Sometime during these days James Armistead returned to Lafayette's camp and no doubt told the French officer that he had been sent there by Cornwallis himself—as a spy for the British!

There was soon exciting word from headquarters. General Washington wrote Lafayette that "news of very great importance" was on its way. The commander urged the Frenchman to hold Lord Cornwallis in Yorktown and to prevent his army from escaping. Lafayette guessed the truth: Washington and the French commander in America, Count Rochambeau, were marching south with their troops, and at the same time French fleets were sailing for the Chesapeake. Cornwallis was to be cut off by land and sea.

Meantime, only Lafayette's small army could hold Cornwallis in place.

Lafayette reported to Washington, "I hope you will find we have taken the best precautions to lessen his Lordship's chances to escape."

By early September the trap was closing on Cornwallis. A French fleet defeated British warships at sea just outside the Chesapeake, drove them back to their port in New York, and anchored in the bay. By the middle of the month, Washington and Rochambeau and the first of their soldiers reached Williamsburg, where Lafayette welcomed them. Two weeks later the American and French armies, led by Lafayette's small force, marched the few miles to Yorktown and surrounded the village.

The allied soldiers dug trenches, ever closer to the enemy. Huge French cannon were hauled into place and began firing in early October. By October 19, after only ten days of shelling, Cornwallis surrendered. His army marched out from the battered lines of Yorktown and laid down its arms.

The battles of the Revolution were over. The broken-hearted Cornwallis himself did not ride out with his troops on the day of surrender, but remained in his headquarters in a cave beside the York River.

It was only two days later, when he had recovered, that Cornwallis left the village. In defeat he went to the headquarters of young Lafayette. The two generals were talking of the campaign, looking over the maps, when Cornwallis looked up to see the familiar face of James Armistead. The black spy wore an American uniform. The British general shook his head grimly, for it was only then that he realized that the volunteer who had served him so faithfully was in truth an American counterspy. The cunning and devotion of this young slave had played an important part in winning the final battle of the war.

One year after a treaty of peace had ended the war, Lafayette wrote a certificate praising the work of James Armistead as a spy:

This is to Certify that the Bearer By the Name of James Has done Essential Services to me While I Had the Honour to Command in this State. His Intelligences from the Enemy's Camp were Industriously Collected and More Faithfully deliver'd. He properly Acquitted Himself with Some important Commissions I Gave Him and Appears to me Entitled to Every Reward his Situation Can Admit of. Done Under my Hand, Richmond November 21st 1784   Lafayette

Soon afterward, James Armistead sent this certificate to the General Assembly of Virginia and asked that he be declared a free man. In his petition he said that he had volunteered to help against the British: ". . . during the time of his serving the Marquis Lafayette he often at the peril of his life found means to frequent the British camp, by which means he kept open a channel of the most useful communications to the army of the state . . . of the most secret & important kind; the possession of which if discovered on him would have most certainly endangered the life of your petitioner . . ."

Even now Armistead said he would not demand his freedom unless his master, William Armistead, could be paid a reasonable price "for the loss of so valuable a workman."

The Virginia General Assembly agreed. The state paid Armistead a fair price, and James Armistead became a free man. From that time onward, he called himself James Lafayette.

By the year 1819, when he was growing old, James Lafayette had become "poor and unable to help himself." Once more he turned for help to the assembly, which voted him $60, a large sum for those days. He was also granted $40 a year for the rest of his life, a pension such as those paid to privates who had served in the army during the Revolution.

One of the great days in James Lafayette's life came in 1824, when he was sixty-four years old, and the aging Lafayette visited Richmond on his final tour of America. Great crowds lined the streets to see the French hero who had made possible American independence, and thousands watched as the Marquis greeted James Lafayette as an old comrade.

It was during this visit to Richmond that James Lafayette sat for his portrait, painted by the well-known artist John B. Martin. The portrait still hangs in a Virginia museum, showing the lean, erect black spy, dressed in a handsome military coat as a reminder of the days when he had won his own freedom and helped to win that of his country as well.

It is thought that the friendship and faithful service of James Armistead Lafayette caused the Marquis to become a leader in the movement to end slavery and to extend help to the black people of many nations.

At the close of the Revolution, Lafayette suggested to Washington a plan "which might greatly benefit the black part of mankind." He suggested that they purchase "a small estate where we may try the experiment to free the Negroes and use them only as tenants."

This led Lafayette to other efforts to outlaw slavery. In Paris, five years later, he helped to found a society of The Friends of the Blacks, and for the rest of his life he supported efforts to give equal rights to men of all races.

James Armistead Lafayette was the best-known black spy in the American army, but he was by no means the only one.

A slave by the name of SAUL MATTHEWS served also as a
spy and guide in the British camp at Portsmouth. The white
colonel Josiah Parker said of him that he "deserved the
applause of his country" for his bravery. A Virginia historian
reported that this slave of Thomas Matthews "brought back
military secrets of such value to Colonel Parker that on the
same night, serving as a guide, he led a party of Americans
to the British garrison . . ." At another time, when Saul
Matthews's master and other white Virginia soldiers had fled
across the state border into North Carolina, Matthews was
once more sent to spy on the enemy and returned with plans
of British movements. Such distinguished officers as Baron
von Steuben, Peter Muhlenberg, and General Nathanael Greene
praised Matthews highly for his services.

Like James Armistead, he continued to work as a slave after
the war, but at last he too asked the legislature for help and
was granted his "full liberty" for his "very many essential
services . . . during the late war."

Others served in the same way, among them two slaves whose records included only their first names:

"*Antigua:* In March 1783 a slave by this name was lauded by the General Assembly of South Carolina for his skill in 'procuring information of the enemy's movements and designs.' He 'always executed the commissions with which he was entrusted with diligence and fidelity, and obtained very considerable and important information, from within the enemy's lines, frequently at the risk of his life.' To reward him, the assembly liberated his 'wife named Hagar, and her child.'" Antigua seems to have remained a slave all his life.

"*Quaco:* During the British occupation of Newport, Rhode Island, Quaco's Tory master sold him to a colonel in the king's army. Quaco fled to the Patriot lines with valuable information. In January 1782, the General Assembly of Rhode Island, saying 'the information he then gave rendered great and essential service to this state and the public in general,' declared Quaco free."

We will probably never learn more of the work of black spies during the Revolution, but it is certain that these secret services were so valuable that without them the struggle for the country's independence might have been lost.

Meet the Author

Burke Davis

Burke Davis's talent for writing led him to work as a newspaper editor, a reporter, and a columnist over a span of 25 years. He then wrote for Colonial Williamsburg for the next 18 years. During this time he also wrote numerous novels, biographies, history books, and children's books. Much of his writing focuses on the history of the United States. Some of his titles include *Getting to Know Thomas Jefferson's Virginia, Heroes of the American Revolution, Appomattox: Closing Struggle of the Civil War,* and *Gray Fox: Robert E. Lee and the Civil War.*

Meet the Illustrator

Stephen Snider

Stephen Snider has been a freelance illustrator for twenty years. He and his wife Jackie, who is also an illustrator, live and work out of their country home in southern Ontario. There they enjoy their six indoor cats, one barn cat, two dogs, two horses, and hundreds of birds.

Making a New Nation

Theme Connections

Within the Selection

1. What was James Armistead's job?

2. Who did James Armistead work for?

Across Selections

3. In "...If You Lived at the Time of the American Revolution," many important historical figures are introduced at the end of the selection. How does that information help you better understand this selection?

4. How does the structure of this selection compare to the previous selection, "The Midnight Ride of Paul Revere"?

Beyond the Selection

5. What have you learned about the contribution of enslaved men to the American Revolution?

6. How important was bravery to the American Revolution?

Write about It!

Describe some of the risks James Armistead took to help the Americans.

Remember to add your own thoughts about the contribution of spies to the American Revolution to the **Concept/Question Board.**

Women of the Revolution

The story of our nation's beginning often focuses on those men who founded our country and shaped the government. Many female patriots, however, were just as important to our country's freedom.

Prudence Wright

In 1775, the people in Peperell, Massachusetts, received word that British spies were using the road through town. Most of the men were off fighting the British near Boston, so Prudence Wright took matters into her own hands. She became the commander of thirty women from the area. They dressed in their husbands' clothes and guarded the bridge into town. Soon the women captured a British soldier and found papers in his boots. They seized the messages and imprisoned the soldier in a nearby building.

Deborah Sampson

Deborah Sampson wanted to help fight for America's freedom. The army did not enlist women, so she disguised herself as a man. "Robert Shurtleff" fought in the 4th Massachusetts Regiment from May 1782 until October 1783. Sampson was wounded more than once, but she treated herself.

When she became seriously ill, however, she finally had to see a doctor. Sampson's gender was found out, and she received an honorable discharge. Years later, with help from Paul Revere, Sampson received a lifetime pension just like other soldiers.

Sybil Ludington

The oldest daughter of Colonel Henry Ludington, Ludington is often called the "female Paul Revere." One night in 1777, a message reached the Ludington home. Nearby Danbury, Connecticut, was under attack by the British. American troops spread across the region needed to be told. Sixteen-year-old Ludington knew the area better than the army messenger, so she was sent to inform the men. That night, she rode her horse forty miles through the rain. Ludington was able to avoid the British and alert the troops. Today a statue in Carmel, New York, stands in her honor.

Think Link

1. After the war, who helped make sure Deborah Sampson was rewarded for fighting for America's freedom?

2. Reread one of the paragraphs from the article. Now write a new heading that would correctly describe the contents of that paragraph.

3. What are some other ways women might have contributed to the war for independence?

Try It!

As you work on your investigation, think about how you can use headings.

297

Read the article to find the meanings of these words, which are also in "Shh! We're Writing the Constitution":

+ eavesdroppers
+ concern
+ league
+ delegates
+ character
+ rumors
+ allegiance
+ contribute
+ central
+ accomplishment

Vocabulary Strategy

Sometimes you can use **word structure** to help you find the meanings of words. Look at the word *accomplishment*. Use word structure to find the word's meaning.

Vocabulary

Warm-Up

It all started one morning on the playground. Inez, Mark, and I stood in a tight circle a little bit away from the other students. Inez slowly looked around, making sure no eavesdroppers lurked nearby, trying to hear what she was about to say. Then Inez whispered her concern.

"You guys," Inez began, "we cannot let Brandon get elected to the Student League again this semester. You would be so much better, Mark. You are a way nicer guy and much more honest."

Each semester, our school holds elections for a student legislature. The chosen students work together as a group called Wilmont Elementary's Student League. With help from teachers and a few parents, they create the school's rules and plan a couple of events each semester. Mr. George, the principal, has final say over everything. We jokingly call him the *Supreme Leader*.

The students vote for three delegates to represent their grade level. Brandon was one of our delegates for both semesters of fifth grade. The problem is that he does not have good character. Brandon likes to spread rumors about his opponents. Last year, he told everyone that my friend Scott had stolen candy from the store. It was not true, but Scott lost anyway.

That day on the playground, Inez, Mark, and I formed an allegiance. We promised each other that we would contribute the time and effort needed to get Mark elected. We all shook hands.

The following weekend, Inez and I worked all day making posters. We had gathered quotes from other students about Mark's honesty. Getting the word out about Mark's good character was central to our plan.

When the elections were held two weeks later, Mark received the most votes. Brandon came in third, but that meant he would still be part of the league. We felt good about the result because we did what we could by supporting our candidate. Inez, Mark, and I were proud of our accomplishment.

Define It! Form two teams with your classmates. Have a volunteer define a vocabulary word. The first team to determine which word is being defined gets a point. Spell the word correctly to receive a bonus point. The game is over when all of the words have been defined and spelled.

Concept Vocabulary

The concept word for this lesson is **allegiance.** Having *allegiance* to a group or an idea means promising to be loyal and devoted to it. People recite the Pledge of Allegiance to show their loyalty and devotion to the ideas on which America was founded.

Shh! We're Writing the Constitution

by Jean Fritz

illustrated by Tomie dePaola

Focus Questions

Why did people living in the states not want a national constitution? How is democracy important to this system of government?

After the Revolutionary War most people in America were glad that they were no longer British. Still, they were not ready to call themselves Americans. The last thing they wanted was to become a nation. They were citizens of their own separate states, just as they had always been: each state different, each state proud of its own character, each state quick to poke fun at other states. To Southerners, New Englanders might be "no-account Yankees." To New Englanders, Pennsylvanians might be "lousy Buckskins." But to everyone the states themselves were all important. "Sovereign states," they called them. They loved the sound of "sovereign" because it meant that they were their own bosses.

George Washington, however, scoffed at the idea of "sovereign states." He knew that the states could not be truly independent for long and survive. Ever since the Declaration of Independence had been signed, people had referred to the country as the United States of America. It was about time, he thought, for them to act and feel united.

Once during the war Washington had decided it would be a good idea if his troops swore allegiance to the United States. As a start, he lined up some troops from New Jersey and asked them to take such an oath. They looked at Washington as if he'd taken leave of his senses. How could they do that? they cried. New Jersey was their country!

So Washington dropped the idea. In time, he hoped, the states would see that they needed to become one nation, united under a strong central government.

But that time would be long in coming. For now, as they started out on their independence, the thirteen states were satisfied to be what they called a federation, a kind of voluntary league of states. In other words, each state legislature sent delegates to a Continental Congress which was supposed to act on matters of common concern.

In September 1774, when the First Continental Congress met, the common concern was Great Britain. Two years later, after the Declaration of Independence had been signed, the concern was that the country needed some kind of government. Not a fully developed government because of course they had their states. All they wanted were some basic rules to hold them together to do whatever needed to be done. So the Congress wrote the Articles of Confederation which outlined rules for a "firm league of friendship." In practice, however, the states did not always feel a firm need to follow any rules.

The Congress, for instance, could ask the states to contribute money to pay the country's debts, but if the states didn't feel like contributing, no one could make them. Congress could declare war but it couldn't fight unless the states felt like supplying soldiers.

The trouble was that their president had no definite powers and the country had no overall legal system. So although the Congress could make all the rules it wanted, it couldn't enforce any of them. Much of the time the states didn't even bother to send delegates to the meetings.

By 1786, it was becoming obvious that changes were needed. People were in debt, a few states were printing paper money that was all but worthless, and in the midst of this disorder some people could see that America would fall apart if it didn't have a sound central government with power to act for all the states. George Washington, of course, was one who had felt strongly about this for a long time. Alexander Hamilton was another. Born and brought up in the Caribbean Islands, he had no patience with the idea of state loyalty. America was nothing but a monster with thirteen heads, he said. James Madison from Virginia wanted a strong America too. He was a little man, described as being "no bigger than half a piece of soap," but he had big ideas for his country.

In 1786 these men, among others, suggested to the Congress that all the states send delegates to a Grand Convention in Philadelphia to improve the existing form of government. It sounded innocent. Just a matter of revising the old Articles of Confederation to make the government work better. No one would quarrel with that.

But they did.

Rhode Island refused to have anything to do with the convention. Patrick Henry, when asked to be a delegate from Virginia, said he "smelt a rat" and wouldn't go. Willie Jones of North Carolina didn't say what he smelled, but he wouldn't go either.

But in the end the convention was scheduled to meet in the State House in Philadelphia on May 14, 1787.

James (or "Jemmy") Madison was so worked up about it that he arrived from Virginia eleven days early. George Washington left his home, Mount Vernon, on May 9 with a headache and an upset stomach, but he arrived in Philadelphia on the night of May 13th. The next morning a few delegates from Pennsylvania and a few from Virginia came to the meeting but there needed to be seven states present to conduct business. Since there were only two, the meeting was adjourned.

It was May 25th before delegates from enough states showed up. They blamed their delays on the weather, muddy roads, personal business, lack of money. Delegates from New Hampshire couldn't scrape up enough money to come until late July, but even so, they beat John Francis Mercer of Maryland. He sauntered into the State House on August 6th.

The most colorful arrival was that of Benjamin Franklin who at eighty-one was the oldest of the delegates. Because he experienced so much pain when he bounced about in a carriage, Franklin came to the convention in a Chinese sedan chair carried by four prisoners from the Philadelphia jail. (He lived in the city so they didn't have far to carry him.)

In all, there would be fifty-five delegates, although coming and going as they did, there were seldom more than thirty there at the same time.

The first thing the delegates did was to elect George Washington president of the convention. They escorted him to his official chair on a raised platform. Then the other members of the convention took their seats at tables draped with green woolen cloth. James Madison sat in the front of the room and as soon as the talking began, he began writing. Never absent for a single day, he kept a record of all that was said during the next four months, stopping only when he, himself, wanted to speak.

They knew that there would be many arguments in this room, but they agreed that they didn't want the whole country listening in and taking sides. They would keep the proceedings a secret. So before every meeting the door was locked. Sentries were stationed in the hall. And even though it turned out to be a hot summer, the windows were kept closed. Why should they risk eavesdroppers?

Members were not supposed to write gossipy letters home. Nor to answer nosy questions. Nor to discuss their business with outsiders. Benjamin Franklin was the one who had to be watched. He meant no harm but he did love to talk, especially at parties, so if he seemed about to spill the beans, another delegate was ready to leap into the conversation and change the subject.

For fifty-five men to keep a secret for four months was an accomplishment in itself. But they did. Of course this didn't prevent rumors from starting. Once it was rumored that the convention was planning to invite the second son of George the Third to become King of America. The delegates were furious. They might not be able to say what they were going to do, but they had no trouble saying what they were *not* going to do. And they were not inviting the second or third son of George the Third or of anyone else to be King of America.

If the people of the country were afraid of what might happen in the convention, so were the delegates themselves. They didn't call the document they were working on a "constitution"; they referred to it as "the plan." Because they knew that the country was sensitive to the word "national," they tried to stick to "federal," a word they were used to and one which didn't reduce the power of the states. But after Edmund Randolph, Governor of Virginia, had presented what came to be called the Virginia Plan, he spoke right out.

In the Virginia Plan, Randolph explained, there would be three branches of government. The executive branch would have a head who would be responsible for running the government. The legislative branch would be made up of two houses which would make laws. The House of Representatives would be elected directly by the people; the Senate, the smaller and supposedly more coolheaded body, would be elected by the House. Together they would be called the Congress. The third branch would be the judiciary headed by a Supreme Court, which would make sure that laws were constitutional and were properly obeyed.

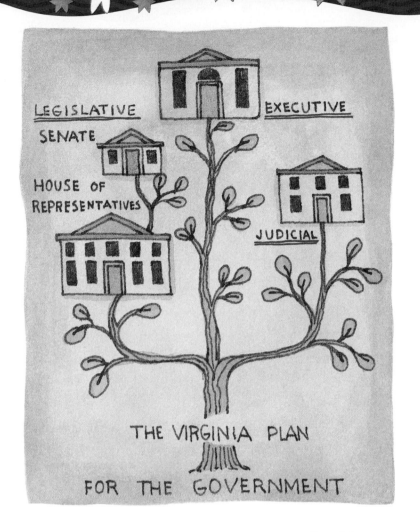

LEGISLATIVE

SENATE

HOUSE OF REPRESENTATIVES

EXECUTIVE

JUDICIAL

THE VIRGINIA PLAN
FOR THE GOVERNMENT

Edmund Randolph was a tall, handsome, likable man and nothing he said at first seemed alarming. Some of the states had constitutions that were similar to the one he described. Besides, the members knew that after Randolph's plan had been discussed, other members would have a chance to present their plans. But at the end of his speech Randolph did arouse his audience. It should be clear, he said, that his resolutions were not merely for a federal government but for a national government that would be supreme over the states.

There was a dead silence.

Pierce Butler of South Carolina was one of the first to recover. He jumped down hard on the word "national" but John Dickinson of Delaware said there was nothing wrong with the word. "We *are* a nation!" he declared.

No! For Elbridge Gerry of Massachusetts this kind of talk was scary. He was a thin, worrying sort of man who was sometimes called "Grumbletonian" behind his back. National? he sputtered. How could they think national? They had been sent here to revise the Articles of Confederation, not to destroy them.

As the meetings went on, all kinds of fear surfaced. The smaller states with fewer people were afraid of the larger states which had more people. In the past the votes of all states, no matter what their population, had counted the same. But a national government would be more concerned with individual people than with the states themselves. So what would happen to the small states now? And what kind of government were they forming? Some people were afraid of a "high-toned" or aristocratic government run by a small, privileged, wealthy group, the way a monarchy was usually run. Others were just as afraid of the common people having too much power. They weren't capable of governing, it was said.

Eventually the convention did agree on a national legislature to consist of two houses but before final acceptance, the word "national" was crossed out.

Still, there were so many questions to decide. What about the person who was to be the executive or head of the government? Should there be just one person? If so, would he seem like a king? Why not three people, each representing a different part of the country? But what if they fought among themselves? What if they couldn't reach an agreement? Should the executive be paid a salary? (Yes, said Madison. Don't count on patriotism.)

But who should pay the salary—the states or the government of the United States? How should the executive be chosen? By the people? By the states? By a branch of the United States legislature? By electors? By lot? (They had to vote sixty times before they could settle this question.) And how long should the executive serve? If he were thought to be guilty of misconduct, could they impeach him? Could they remove him from office?

Alexander Hamilton was one of the few who wanted the president to serve a long term, perhaps even for life. He thought it would be embarrassing to watch a lot of ex-presidents wandering around like ghosts. But suppose you had a long-term president, Franklin pointed out. And suppose he turned out to be a bad president. What then? Out of simple kindness they ought to provide some way to get rid of him. Otherwise, Franklin chuckled, the only thing they could do would be to shoot him.

In the end it was decided that there should be a single executive who would be paid out of the Treasury of the new government. He would be chosen by electors from each state, and he would serve four years. And yes, if it was necessary, he could be impeached.

But what if he should die while in office? Or be impeached? Who would take his place? So there had to be a vice president, the one who came in second in the presidential election. And since the vice president should do more than just wait around to see if the president would make it through his term, he was given the job of presiding over the Senate.

Mr. Randolph finished presenting his plan on May 29 and for the next two weeks—until June 13—the convention went over it. Some measures were voted on, some would be revised, and all would be discussed again and again. But there was also the chance that the whole plan would be scrapped for something else. After a day's recess, on June 15, William Paterson of New Jersey stood up. Only five feet two, he wasn't as impressive a figure as Mr. Randolph, but he was a cheerful, modest, likable man. Still, he didn't approve of a single idea of Mr. Randolph's. The government should be a federation of states as it was now, with each state having an equal vote, he said. It should consist of one legislative body with several executives at its head. According to Mr. Paterson, the Virginia Plan was impractical, illegal, and expensive. How could so many members of Congress, he asked, find the money to travel from all over the country to attend meetings?

J. MADISON   W. PATERSON

When James Madison answered Mr. Paterson, it was as if he were fencing. Madison danced all around Mr. Paterson's arguments, thrusting at first one point, then another until it seemed as if there were nothing left of William Paterson's plan. And there wasn't. When the delegates were asked to vote in favor of one of the two plans, Mr. Randolph's won. Seven states against three. (Maryland's delegation was divided.) Randolph's plan still had to be thrashed out, but the idea of a federation was dead. With this vote the delegates committed themselves to write a constitution for a new nation, whether all of them were willing to call it that or not.

Meet the Author

Jean Fritz

Fritz's fascination with historical figures began at a young age. Her father used to tell her tales about American heroes. She was so intrigued by these tales that she made it her hobby to find out everything she could about the famous people in them. She then turned her findings into stories. She now has many books filled with fascinating details about American historical figures.

Meet the Illustrator

Tomie dePaola

DePaola's true love is writing and illustrating books for children. He has illustrated over 80 children's books. More than 60 of these books also were written by him. Some of the titles for which he is most well known include *Tomie dePaola's Mother Goose*, *Tomie dePaola's Favorite Nursery Tales*, and *Watch Out for the Chicken Feet in Your Soup*. The last story was based on his Italian grandmother, who really did put chicken feet in her chicken soup!

Making a New Nation
Theme Connections

Within the Selection

1. Who was elected president of the convention?

2. Whose plan for government was adopted?

Across Selections

3. What historical figures in this selection are also mentioned at the end of ". . . If You Lived at the Time of the American Revolution"?

4. How does this selection fit in to the sequence of events in this unit? Write the events in sequential order.

Beyond the Selection

5. How do the actions of the Continental Congress affect you today?

6. Think about the last time you worked on a project with a group of people. What kinds of problems did you have with decision making and coordinating schedules?

Write about It!

Describe a time you solved a difficult problem.

Remember to look for articles about the Constitution to add to the **Concept/Question Board.**

Know Your Rights

When the Constitution went to the states to be approved, there was concern that the new government would be too powerful. Amendments were added that promised individual rights to each American. These first ten amendments are called the Bill of Rights:

First Amendment—Freedom of speech, press, religion, peaceable assembly, and to petition the government

Second Amendment—Right to keep and bear arms

Third Amendment—Protection from quartering of troops

Fourth Amendment—Protection from unreasonable search and seizure

Fifth Amendment—Due process, double jeopardy, self-incrimination, private property

Sixth Amendment—Criminal trial by jury and other rights of the accused

Seventh Amendment—Civil trial by jury

Eighth Amendment—Prohibition of excessive bail, as well as cruel or unusual punishment

Ninth Amendment—Protection of rights not specifically listed in the Bill of Rights

Tenth Amendment—Powers of states and people

Genre

A **survey** is a series of questions or statements. Surveys are given to people in order to gather a collection of responses. The responses can then be used to discover the group's opinions or ideas.

Feature

Boldface Print is text that is darker and thicker than the surrounding text. It is used to draw attention to certain words or phrases.

320

The Supreme Court uses the Bill of Rights to help decide cases. How do you feel about each issue listed below?

1. Students wearing armbands to school as a form of protest can be expelled by the principal. (*Tinker vs. Des Moines*, 1969)

The sitting justices of the Supreme Court of the United States

    Strongly Agree   Agree   Disagree   Strongly Disagree

2. To stop a crime wave, police can set up roadblocks and search all cars to find the robber. (*Indianapolis vs. James*, 2001)

    Strongly Agree   Agree   Disagree   Strongly Disagree

Think Link

1. Using a separate sheet of paper complete the above survey anonymously. Gather all students' responses, and discuss the survey results.

2. Why do you think the author chose to use boldface print?

3. How does the Bill of Rights protect individual rights?

Try It!

As you work on your investigation, think about how you might use boldface print.

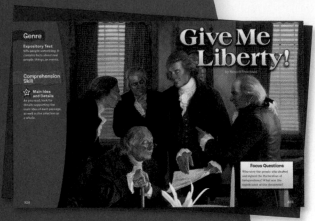

Read the article to find the meanings of these words, which are also in "Give Me Liberty!":

+ utter
+ bombarded
+ declaration
+ debate
+ treason
+ rights
+ retreat
+ exposing
+ composition
+ draft

Vocabulary Strategy

Context Clues are hints in the text that help you find the meanings of words. Look at the words *debate, composition,* and *treason.* Use context clues to find each word's meaning.

Vocabulary
Warm-Up

No one wanted to utter the words, but they were now said everywhere: *America is at war.* After Pearl Harbor was bombarded by Japanese warplanes, President Roosevelt signed a declaration of war. Soon, Akio Nakamura began worrying about his family.

A debate was heating up across the nation. One side argued that people of Japanese descent—including American citizens—might be spies and should be sent to special camps to be watched. The other side argued that no American citizens should be treated this way.

Akio wondered, *Why would anyone think we would commit treason?*

For three generations, the Nakamura family grew flowers near Sacramento, California. Akio's great-grandfather, Ichiro, came to America in the late 1800s to live a freer life. Japanese society was very strict.

At school Ichiro had read the writings of Thomas Jefferson.

THE COAST POST

Possible Japanese Camp

JAPANESE SPY?

Should we Imprison Japanese Americans to be Safe?

Jefferson's claim that everyone had the same rights made sense to him. Reaching America became his goal.

Ichiro arrived in California when he was twenty. He worked on a farm and saved every penny. He did not want to retreat to his old life in Japan.

Ichiro finally earned enough money to buy a small piece of land. The other farmers were angry that a Japanese man would compete with them. Ichiro knew he was exposing himself to their prejudices, but refused to cower or hide. Now the Nakamuras own dozens of acres and sell flowers in several cities.

Akio wrote a composition about Ichiro in his English class. Now he was writing a letter to the local paper. He had a rough draft finished so far. It described his great-grandfather's admiration of Jefferson's ideas. The letter also asked how locking up his family made the country safer.

GAME

Building Sentences Write each selection vocabulary word on a separate piece of paper, and place the words into a box or other container. Without looking, remove a word from the box, and use it in a sentence. Record the sentence on the board or a sheet of paper. Then have a different student choose another word and use it in a sentence. After all of the words have been used, discuss whether they were used correctly in the sentences.

Concept Vocabulary

The concept word for this lesson is **vigilance.** *Vigilance* is the act of being alert and watchful in order to avoid danger. In 1852, anti-slavery crusader Wendell Phillips proclaimed, "Eternal vigilance is the price of liberty." The citizens of a free country, such as the United States, must always be alert and watchful so that their freedoms are not taken away by those in power.

Genre

Comprehension Skill

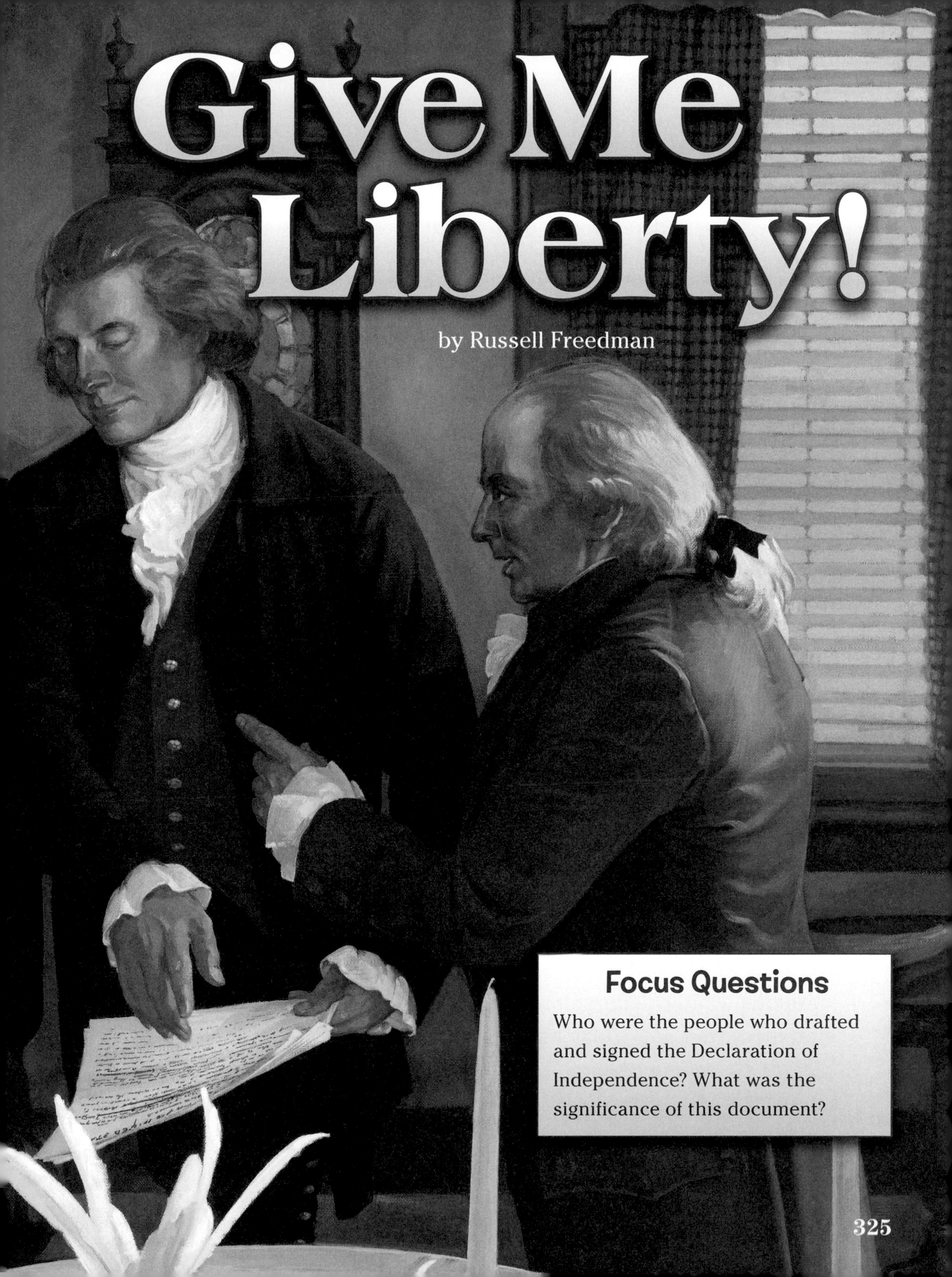

Give Me Liberty!

by Russell Freedman

Focus Questions

Who were the people who drafted and signed the Declaration of Independence? What was the significance of this document?

At age thirty-three, Thomas Jefferson was one of the youngest delegates to the Continental Congress. A tall, slim, quiet man with gray eyes and reddish hair, he could be lively and even vivacious among his friends. But in public he was so reserved, so soft-spoken and shy, he often seemed stiff or aloof. "During the whole time I sat with him in the Congress," said John Adams, "I never heard him utter three sentences together."

The Committee for Drafting the Declaration of Independence: Benjamin Franklin, Thomas Jefferson, John Adams, Robert R. Livingston, Roger Sherman

Though Jefferson did not say much, he was an avid scholar and an accomplished writer. Ever since his student days, he had practiced writing by condensing everything he read, striving to develop what he considered "the most valuable of all the talents, that of never using two words when one will do."

Adams wanted Jefferson to write the first draft of the statement we know today as the Declaration of Independence—a tough job, since the writer would have to come up with a document that all thirteen colonies could accept.

It seems that Jefferson tried to get out of the assignment. He wanted Adams to write the first draft. But Adams refused. Years later Adams recalled the following conversation:

"You should do it," said Jefferson.

"Oh, no!"

"Why will you not?"

"I will not."

"Why?" pressed Jefferson.

"Reasons enough," said Adams.

"What can be your reasons?"

"Reason, first, you are a Virginian and a Virginian ought to appear at the head of this business. Reason second, I am obnoxious, suspected and unpopular. You are very much otherwise. Reason third, you can write ten times better than I can."

So it was settled. Jefferson went to work in his rented rooms on the second floor of a brick house at the corner of Market and Seventh Streets in downtown Philadelphia. Every morning he would rise before dawn, soak his feet in a basin of cold water, have tea and biscuits, then sit down at a small portable desk he had designed himself and start writing.

"I did not consider it part of my charge to invent new ideas," he said later, "but to place before mankind the common sense of the subject."

There were plenty of ideas in the air for Jefferson to draw on. He was familiar with the writings of John Locke, an influential English philosopher who argued that people are born with certain natural rights and that governments should be run for the benefit of everyone, not just for their rulers. Like most Americans, Jefferson had read Thomas Paine's *Common Sense* and other revolutionary pamphlets. A number of state and local governments, including Virginia's, had already issued declarations of rights and resolutions on independence that could serve as his models.

Scratching away with his quill pen, he worked on the Declaration for about two weeks while attending daily meetings of the Congress—constantly writing and rewriting, ripping up his earlier drafts as he made changes. On one draft that still exists, he changed nearly one third of the words. Finally he showed his work to John Adams and Ben Franklin, who suggested additional changes before the draft was submitted to Congress on June 28.

An artist's impression of Thomas Jefferson working on the Declaration of Independence by candlelight

While Jefferson worked on his many drafts, news reached Philadelphia that British warships had bombarded Charleston, South Carolina, the South's most important seaport. A large British fleet had also been sighted off New York. And there was terrible news from Canada, where the invading Americans had been forced to retreat in total disorder, suffering from smallpox, malaria, and dysentery. Some five thousand American troops had been killed or wounded during the disastrous ten-month Canadian campaign.

With the alarming reports as a background, Congress began its final debate on independence. Before the delegates could consider Jefferson's declaration, they had to vote on Richard Henry Lee's resolution stating "That these United Colonies are, and of right ought to be, free and independent States."

On the steamy afternoon of July 1, John Dickinson of Pennsylvania rose to speak for the moderates. His voice trembled with emotion as he warned the delegates that independence was risky and premature. To abandon the protection of Great Britain would be "like destroying our house in winter and exposing a growing family before we have got another shelter." He argued that a way must be found to get along with England.

As John Adams began his reply, a summer storm crackled and exploded in the heavens above Philadelphia. Thunder shook the statehouse windows and lightning flashed against the darkening sky while Adams pleaded the cause of independence. No record of his words exists, but Jefferson remembered that Adams spoke "with a power of thought and expression that moved us from our seats."

When the vote was taken, only nine colonies voted for independence. Pennsylvania and South Carolina were opposed. Delaware's two delegates were divided. And New York's delegates abstained, saying they had no instructions from home.

The delegates who favored independence got busy behind the scenes. After a night of intense negotiations, Pennsylvania and South Carolina agreed to change their votes and go along with the other colonies. An absent Delaware delegate, Caesar Rodney, who also favored independence, rode eighty miles through heavy rain to reach Philadelphia and break the tie in his delegation's vote. New York, still lacking instructions, abstained again.

The final vote on July 2 was twelve colonies in favor of independence, none opposed. Two weeks later, New York's delegates were able to add their colony's approval, making the vote for independence unanimous.

Congress then turned to the wording of Jefferson's draft. During a three-day period, from late Tuesday, July 2, through Thursday, July 4, the delegates went over the document word by word. Jefferson, justly proud of his composition, squirmed in his seat, listening in unhappy silence as whole paragraphs were taken out, as new words and phrases were added. In all, nearly one hundred changes were made. Jefferson's text was cut by about a fourth. John Adams believed that Congress worked some real improvements into the text, but also "obliterated some of the best of it."

An early draft of the Declaration of Independence showing Jefferson's handwritten revisions

Jefferson and his fellow committee members presenting the Declaration of Independence to John Hancock, president of the Continental Congress

On July 4, 1776, swarms of horseflies from a nearby stable invaded the assembly room, encouraging the delegates to bring their deliberations to a close. The final version of the Declaration of Independence was voted on and approved unanimously. As soon as the vote was taken, a boy stationed at the statehouse door began to clap his hands and shout, "Ring! Ring!" At nearby Christ's Church, the old bellman was waiting for that signal.

That afternoon, the Declaration of Independence was signed by John Hancock, president of the Continental Congress. He said he would make his signature large enough so that King George would be able to read it without his glasses. Most historians believe that no other signatures were added until August 2, after the document had been copied onto a sheet of durable parchment, when every member present signed it. The remaining members added their signatures at later times.

One signer, Stephen Hopkins of Rhode Island, had a condition called palsy that caused his hands to shake. As he took up his pen to add his name to the Declaration, he said, "My hand trembles, but my heart does not."

Each man among them knew that by signing the Declaration of Independence, he had become a traitor to England. If captured by the British, he could pay with his life. The outcome of the Revolutionary War would decide whether the signers would be remembered as the founders of a nation or be hanged by the British for treason.

Pulling down the statue of King George III in New York City

Meanwhile, copies of the Declaration were printed and carried by express riders and coastal schooners to towns and villages in each of the thirteen states, where the text was read aloud amid "great demonstrations of joy." General George Washington and his troops heard it read in New York City on July 9. That evening a jubilant crowd pulled down a fifteen-foot-high gilded statue of George III on horseback. Later, the statue was melted down and the metal molded into 42,000 bullets for Patriot guns.

Although many changes were made to it by Congress, the Declaration of Independence remained essentially Thomas Jefferson's creation. Jefferson began by stating the purpose of the document: to explain why the colonies had voted to free themselves from British rule. "All men are created equal," Jefferson wrote. They have certain God-given rights, including the rights to "Life, Liberty, and the pursuit of Happiness." And governments are created to secure those rights.

A public reading of the Declaration of Independence

Jefferson then charged that King George III had repeatedly violated the colonists' rights, his purpose being "the establishment of an absolute Tyranny over these States." He gave a long list of examples, including "imposing Taxes on us without our Consent," "depriving us in many cases, of the benefits of Trial by Jury," "suspending our own Legislatures," and "waging War against us."

Today, Jefferson's indictment of King George as a tyrant may seem like ancient history. But the preamble to the Declaration, the opening statement, is recognized as a timeless affirmation of human rights and representative government.

Governments must have "the consent of the governed," Jefferson wrote. Whenever any government fails to protect the rights of its citizens, the citizens have the right to change it or to abolish it and to create a new government. That powerful idea has inspired popular resistance to tyranny in countries all over the world.

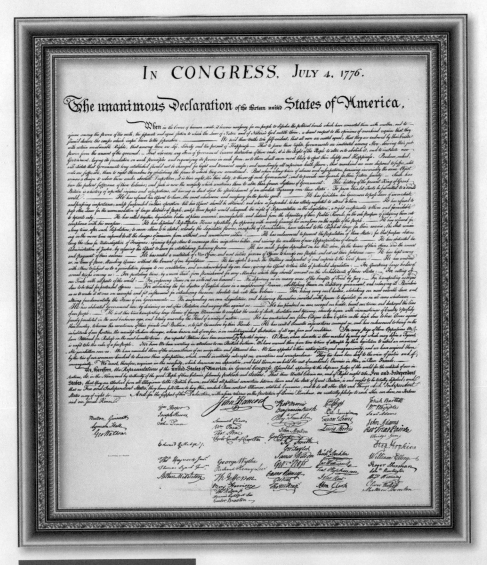

Declaration of Independence

Meet the Author

Russell Freedman

Russell Freedman seemed destined to be a writer. He grew up in a home frequently visited by authors. He later became a reporter and stumbled across a story about a sixteen-year-old boy who invented the braille typewriter. The story inspired his first book, *Teenagers Who Made History*.

Mr. Freedman travels widely to do the research for his books. When he is not writing, he enjoys attending films, concerts, and plays.

Making a New Nation
Theme Connections

Within the Selection

1. Who was the main author of the Declaration of Independence?

2. Why was it dangerous for the members of the Congress to sign the Declaration?

Across Selections

3. The people who signed the Declaration of Independence showed great bravery. Compare their actions to the actions of another historical figure in this unit.

4. How do the Declaration of Independence and the Constitution differ in purposes?

Beyond the Selection

5. What effects does the Declaration of Independence have today?

6. How were teamwork and compromise important to the founding of our nation?

Write about It!

Write about a time when you were given an important task.

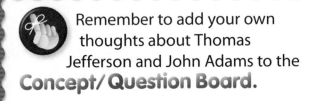

Remember to add your own thoughts about Thomas Jefferson and John Adams to the **Concept/Question Board.**

Genre

Expository Text tells people something. It contains facts about real people, things, or events.

Feature

Italics are typed words that slant to the right. Sometimes italics are used in place of quotation marks to indicate a quotation.

Plattsburg Volunteer Agency

How wonderful it is that nobody needs to wait a single moment before starting to improve the world.—Anne Frank

We in America do not have government by the majority. We have government by the majority who participate.—Thomas Jefferson

Declaration of PVA's Goals:

Our nation was founded on the belief that people can, and should, govern themselves. Our political rights, including the right to vote, are the most visible forms of this principle. However, civic duty should not be limited to politics and government. There are many ways Americans can contribute to the greater good of our society. We at PVA believe that every citizen has a duty to discover how he or she can help make our nation a greater place.

Volunteering Application

This application is designed to help us match your interests with groups seeking volunteers. Thank you in advance for your time and effort.

Last Name: *Vu*   First Name: *Sydney*

Age: *16*   Gender: M (F)

Address: *1444 Knottingham Dr.*
Pensacola, Florida 32509

How many hours per week would you be willing to help?
6

Which days are you available? *Monday, Tuesday, and Thursday*

What are your interests? Please check all that apply.

☑ Performing Arts   ☑ Writing   ☑ Politics

☑ Environment   ☑ Animals   ☑ Sports

☐ Food   ☐ Health   ☐ Other (Please specify)

The following groups are currently in need of volunteers. Please check the ones that you would be willing to help out.

☑ Plattsburg Pet Friends (animals)   ☑ Wild Animal Rescue (animals)

☑ Clean Parks Association (environment)   ☐ Elder Dance (activities for the elderly)

☐ Mobile Meal Patrol (helping the elderly)   ☑ Get Out and Vote! (civic duty)

You should receive a call within one week of submitting your application. Thank you for being a great American citizen!

Think Link

1. Why do you think most applications and other forms ask for your last name first?

2. Which part of this selection is in italics? Why?

3. Find the names of organizations in your community that use volunteers. Which ones would you be most willing to help?

Try It!

As you work on your investigation, think about how you might use italics.

Yankee Doodle

illustrated by Bandelin-Dacey

No one knows for sure who was the first to sing "Yankee Doodle." The story has it that members of the British army came up with the lyrics and set them to the tune of an old folk melody. They wrote the song to poke fun at the colonial militia, whose appearance and manners seemed rather unrefined to the British. Instead of being offended, the colonists thought it was funny and took the song as their own. "Yankee Doodle" grew to include over a hundred verses. The following lyrics are thought to be two of the song's original verses.

Chorus
Yankee doodle, keep it up
Yankee doodle dandy
Mind the music and the step
And with the girls be handy.

Father and I went down to camp,
Along with Captain Goodin',
And there we saw the men and boys
As thick as hasty puddin'.

There was Captain Washington
Upon a slapping stallion
A-giving orders to his men
I guess there was a million.

Chorus
Yankee doodle, keep it up
Yankee doodle dandy
Mind the music and the step
And with the girls be handy.

Our Corner of the Universe

What is the universe? What makes it up? Are we the only life forms in the universe? What do we know about our neighboring galaxies? Our neighboring planets? Our sun? Our moon? Why is it important to look beyond our own world?

Theme Connection

Look at the photo of the father and son viewing the night sky.

- What are the father and son looking at in the photo?

- What parts of the universe can you see in the sky at night?

- How did people in the past view the universe?

- How does the photo relate to the theme Our Corner of the Universe?

348

349

Read the article to find the meanings of these words, which are also in "The Universe":

◆ spokes
◆ disks
◆ galaxy
◆ spiral
◆ detect
◆ clusters
◆ infinity
◆ collapse
◆ bulges
◆ cosmic

Vocabulary Strategy

Context Clues are hints in the text that help you find the meanings of words. Look at the words *clusters* and *collapse*. Use context clues to find each word's meaning.

Vocabulary
Warm-Up

As Kyle hurried along in his wheelchair, the spokes inside the spinning wheels whirled into a blur. It looked like he floated on a pair of solid disks.

Kyle's mother had just dropped him off in front of Mason Hall. Somewhere inside was Ratnor Planetarium, but first he had to find it, and he was already late.

Kyle's science class had been studying the Milky Way Galaxy and its billions of stars. This field trip was the highlight of the unit. Now he was worried he would miss it.

Kyle rolled briskly down the ramp, which was shaped like a spiral, to reach the building's lower level. By the time he hit the bottom, the constant turning had made him a little dizzy.

There should be a sign somewhere, Kyle thought, but he did not detect anything. Clusters of college students stood around, each small group filled with busy chatter and laughter. Kyle wanted to ask someone for directions, but the older students made him nervous.

Kyle pressed a metal button to get inside the lower level and then rolled himself through the open doorway. Three long hallways greeted him, each one seeming to stretch off into infinity. Their shiny floors appeared endless.

Then a hand grabbed Kyle's shoulder, and he worried that he was somewhere he was not supposed to be. But when Kyle turned around, he discovered his friend, Aaron, leaning over him. Aaron looked like he was about to collapse. He held on to the wheelchair as if he might fall over any minute. Aaron's cheeks were red bulges as he huffed and puffed, trying to catch his breath.

"I have been running all over trying to find you," Aaron finally said. "I knew you did not want to miss this."

Aaron led Kyle down one of the hallways, and they quickly found the planetarium. Just as they entered, the artificial night sky above them began bursting with exploding stars. Kyle smiled as he leaned back to watch the cosmic scene.

GAME

Word Charades
Divide into two teams, and choose one student from each team to sit facing the class. Reveal a vocabulary word to everyone but the two seated students. Then have the class describe the word without saying the word itself. The first of the two students to predict the word scores a point for his or her team. Continue with different vocabulary words and different students until all the words have been used.

Concept Vocabulary

The concept word for this lesson is **physics.** *Physics* is the branch of science that studies the physical world and how objects interact in space and time. Physicists investigate an incredibly wide range of objects, from subatomic particles to stars and galaxies.

Genre

Expository Text tells people something. It contains facts about real people, things, or events.

Comprehension Skill

 Classify and Categorize

As you read the selection, identify subjects and their traits and then categorize them according to those traits.

Focus Questions

What is Earth's nearest neighbor in space? Do you think humankind will ever explore the entire universe?

THE UNIVERSE

by Seymour Simon

The universe is everything that exists, now and in the past. It includes the book you are reading and the ground beneath your feet, the animals and plants, oceans and continents, planets, stars, and galaxies, and the vast reaches of space. You are truly part of the universe. Every atom, every particle within you, is billions of years old.

If you wanted to write your complete address on a letter, to show where you live, it might look like this:

Your name

Street, city or town, zip code, country

Planet Earth

Solar System

Milky Way Galaxy

The Universe

There's no zip code for the universe, of course, but if there was one, it might be ∞, which is the symbol for infinity.

From Earth we can look into space and study the universe with telescopes and other instruments. The Moon is Earth's nearest neighbor in space, only about a quarter of a million miles away. That's very close in space, almost next door. Still, it's very far away compared to the distance between places on Earth's surface. You'd have to travel around the Earth ten times in order to match the distance from the Earth to the Moon. The Sun, the closest star to us, is over four hundred times farther away from us than the Moon is—about ninety-three million miles.

The nearest star after our Sun is much farther away than that. But measuring the distance between stars and planets in miles is like measuring the distance around the world in inches. We measure the distance to the stars in light-years: the distance that light travels in one year, which is close to six *trillion* miles. A spaceship speeding at ten miles per second would still take more than seventy thousand *years* to get to Alpha Centauri, the nearest star after the Sun—a distance of 4.3 light-years, or twenty-five trillion miles.

Mercury, Venus, Earth, and Mars are closest to the Sun and are called the inner planets. These rocky planets are much smaller than the giant outer planets: Jupiter, Saturn, Uranus, and Neptune, which are made mostly of gases. Pluto, the outermost and smallest of the planets, is 3.6 billion miles from the Sun.

Planetary nebulas come in a variety of shapes: from narrow jets of exploding gases to peanut-shaped clouds to bright globes surrounding stars. This Hubble Space Telescope image of a cosmic bubble is an hourglass-shaped planetary nebula around a distant star. The red rings are nitrogen gases. The potato-shaped inner rings of green and blue are hydrogen and oxygen. The hot star that gave birth to the nebula is a bit off center, to the left of the inner blue ring.

What look like spaceships from a science fiction movie are really the result of a dying star's final outbursts. These mysterious "space pods" are gigantic tadpole-shaped clumps of gas, each several billion miles across, twice the size of our Solar System. The cometlike tails fan out around the central star like the spokes on a wheel.

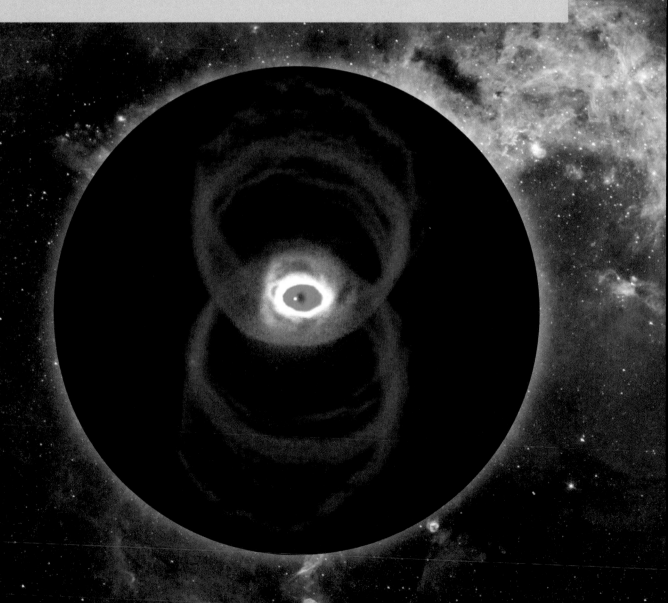

No one knows what will happen to the pods. Perhaps they will expand and disappear within a few hundred thousand years. Or perhaps the dust particles inside each gas ball will and stick together. Planets the size of Earth, but frigid and icy like the planet Pluto, might form over time. Thousands of these icy worlds might escape the dead star and roam the dark space between the stars forever.

Our Sun is just one of about two hundred billion stars in the Milky Way Galaxy, a vast spiral of stars about one hundred thousand light-years across. Viewed from the side, it looks like a lens, with a thick bright center of stars and flattened edges. All the stars we see in the night sky are in our galaxy. Other galaxies are much too distant for us to see their individual stars.

Our Solar System is about thirty thousand light-years away from the center of the Milky Way. The central galaxy is much more crowded than our lonely part of space. In one star cluster near the center of the Milky Way, there are one hundred thousand stars in one cubic light-year. But in our remote corner of the galaxy, there are no stars within four light-years of our Solar System.

This is a radio photo of a star called Sagittarius A*, near the center of the Milky Way. Hidden someplace within this photo there might be an enormous black hole marking the true center of our galaxy.

Among the strangest objects in the universe are black holes. A black hole is a region of space where matter is squeezed together so tightly and the pull of its gravity is so powerful that nothing can escape from it, not even light. It is impossible to see a black hole, but we can see vast amounts of matter being sucked into the hole, never to return. Black holes seem to come in two sizes: small and superlarge. The small ones are formed when stars collapse and are only a few miles in diameter. Most we cannot detect.

Scientists think that the superlarge black holes are probably at the center of most galaxies. This drawing shows a spiral of dust and gases eight hundred light-years wide being sucked into a giant black hole in the center of a nearby galaxy. The black hole contains more than one billion times the amount of matter in our Sun, all packed tightly together.

These discoveries have led to new mysteries: Does every galaxy have a black hole at its center? If there's a black hole in a galaxy, does that mean that all the stars in the galaxy will eventually disappear inside it? What starts a black hole, and does it ever end?

Does life exist on Earth-like planets in distant solar systems? Will the universe expand forever or finally stop and then collapse into a gigantic black hole? Searching for answers about the universe is like exploring a dark, mysterious ocean without being able to leave the shore. But with the Hubble Space Telescope and other new methods of gathering information, we are just at the beginning of a golden age of discovery. No one knows what fantastic places we will see.

Meet the Author

Seymour Simon

Seymour Simon taught science in the New York City schools for twenty-three years but now devotes all his time to writing. Simon is the author of nearly 150 science books written especially for students from preschool to junior high. Most of his books are about astronomy and animals. One reason his books are so wonderful is they contain many spectacular photos. He likes picture books because, unlike television, they can "freeze" images for as long as the reader wants to look at them. He hopes children will be as amazed as he is by the photos' subjects. He says, "Children need to develop a lifelong enjoyment and appreciation for science. Science is fascinating stuff, like dinosaurs, space, earthquakes, and the human body."

Theme Connections

Within the Selection

1. Why is it important that Earth's solar system is in a quiet part of the galaxy?

2. What do we know about the stars that are visible from Earth?

Beyond the Selection

3. Do you think life might exist in another part of the universe? Why or why not?

4. What makes studying the universe a difficult task?

Write about It!

Imagine you can watch stars forming inside a nebula. Describe what you see.

Remember to look for images of the planets in our solar system to add to the **Concept/ Question Board**.

Science Inquiry

A Lively Breakfast

If you were asked to describe the universe, what would you include? You might mention planets, stars, and the Milky Way galaxy. But the smallest things are part of the universe too.

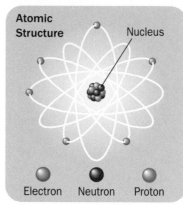

The neutrons in an atom have no charge.

Atoms are the building blocks of everything you see. All matter is made of atoms. Atoms are so small that a hundred million of them in a row would barely equal a centimeter.

Each atom is made of even smaller neutrons, protons, and electrons. A cluster of protons and neutrons forms the atom's center—the *nucleus*. Electrons whirl around the nucleus like planets orbiting a star.

Each electron has a negative charge. Each proton is positive. Usually the number of protons and electrons in an atom are equal, so the atom is neutral. When an atom has more electrons than neutrons its charge is negative. The atom wants to give away electrons so it can become neutral again. Negative atoms act like magnets. They pull neutral and positive atoms toward them.

Red objects have a negative charge.

This experiment shows what happens when atoms with too many electrons come into contact with neutral atoms.

Items needed:

- a dozen pieces of puffed or crispy rice cereal

- an old vinyl record album

- a piece of wool, like a sweater

1. Place the cereal on a flat surface.

2. Rub the wool against the record for about one minute.

3. Hold the record flat, a couple of inches above the cereal.

4. Don't move the record away yet. The cereal will hold on for a few seconds and then fall back to the table.

5. Be patient. The whole process will repeat several times.

Think Link

1. What is the center of an atom called?

2. How long should you rub the piece of wool against the record?

3. Using the diagram, explain why the pieces of cereal eventually fall off the record.

Try It!

As you work on your investigation, think about how you can use diagrams.

Read the article to find the meanings of these words, which are also in "Circles, Squares, and Daggers: How Native Americans Watched the Skies":

+ vertical
+ archaeology
+ observatories
+ abandoned
+ stargazers
+ calculations
+ devised
+ bull's-eye
+ solar
+ dramatic

Vocabulary Strategy

Sometimes you can use **word structure** to help you find the meanings of words. Look at the word *stargazers*. Use word structure to find the word's meaning.

Vocabulary

Warm-Up

The heat was oppressive. Montana Smith wiped his face, but seconds later, vertical lines of sweat streaked it again. He wondered aloud why archaeology had to be so hard.

"Studying these cultures always turns out complicated."

Montana was in the South American jungles searching for the lost observatories of the Mortecs. The places where they studied the stars had slowly disappeared.

Montana needed to find the sites that had been abandoned. He had discovered that these ancient stargazers knew when another meteor would hit Earth. The Mortecs' calculations had been carved into stones. By finding the stones, Montana could save the planet.

The plan he devised was simple enough. First, he would need to pay tribute to the local leader. He would then hire a guide and follow the route he had charted on a map.

But things never worked simply for Montana. Before long, an army began chasing him through the jungle. They wanted the stones for their own reasons.

Montana and his guide, Pedro, raced through the jungle, slashing at the thick leaves in their path. Montana called to his new friend, "Pedro! Do you see that marking up ahead? It looks like a bull's-eye."

Pedro held up a brown, crinkled sheet of paper. Solar rays streaming through the trees lit up a line of symbols written across the top. Pedro pointed to one that was shaped like a target.

They cautiously approached the stone circle and reached toward it. . . .

Suddenly everything went dark.

Then the lights came on, and an usher apologized. The film had broken but everyone would receive a refund.

"No way!" Chris exclaimed. "Right at the most dramatic part!"

Searching for Synonyms

Look at the list of words below. Using a dictionary or a thesaurus, find the selection vocabulary word that has the same or nearly the same meaning, and write your answers on a separate sheet of paper.

deserted
upright
invented
exciting

Concept Vocabulary

The concept word for this lesson is **solstice.** *Solstice* refers to the two times each year when the sun is farthest from the equator. In the Northern Hemisphere, the summer solstice occurs around June 21, when the sun is farthest north. The winter solstice occurs around December 21, when the sun is farthest south.

Genre

Expository Text tells people something. It contains facts about real people, things, or events.

Comprehension Skill

Compare and Contrast

As you read the selection, compare and contrast characters, events, settings, and ideas to help you better understand the text.

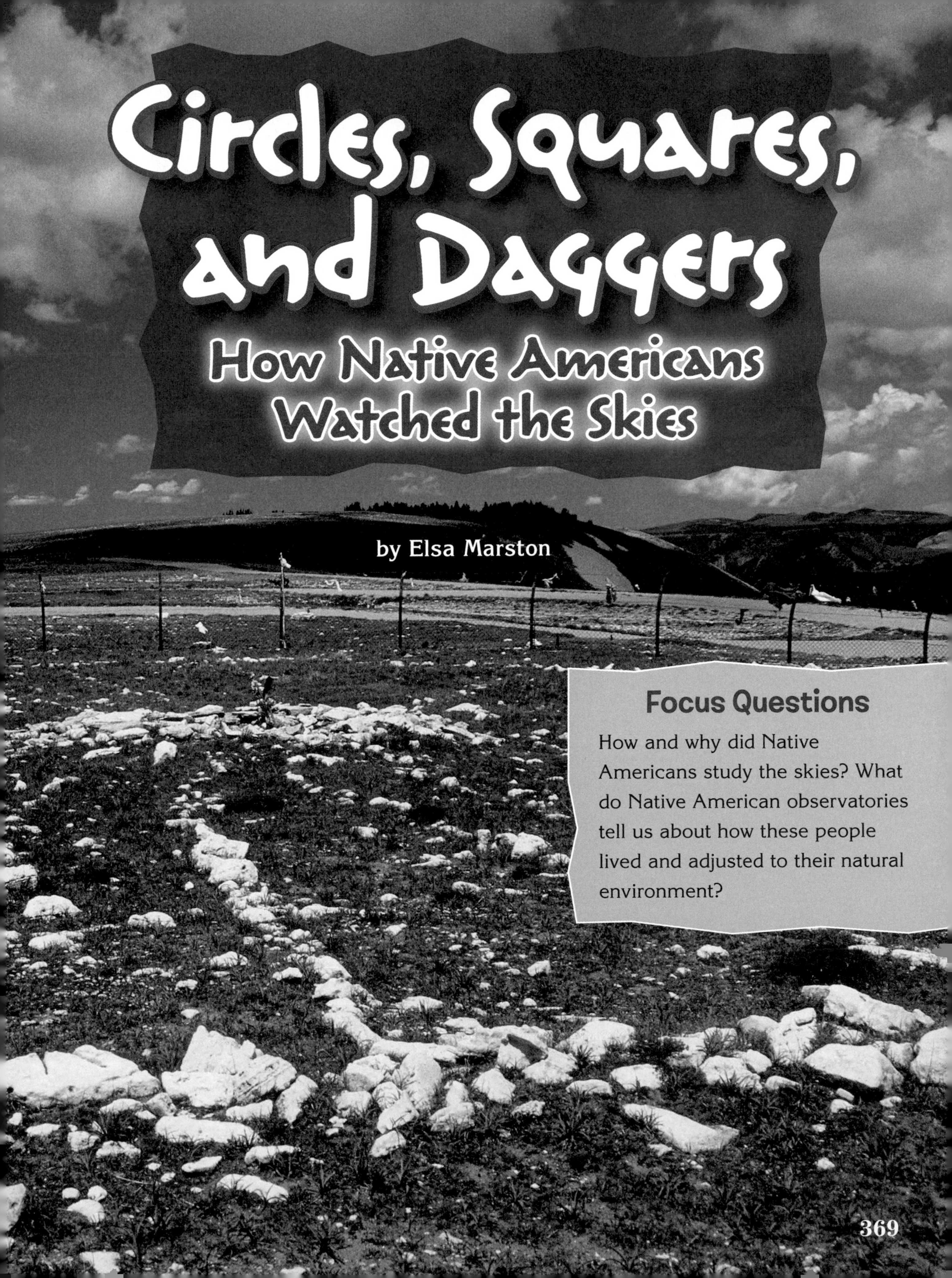

Circles, Squares, and Daggers

How Native Americans Watched the Skies

by Elsa Marston

Focus Questions

How and why did Native Americans study the skies? What do Native American observatories tell us about how these people lived and adjusted to their natural environment?

You have probably heard about stargazers of the past such as the ancient Egyptians, the builders of Stonehenge, and the Mayas. Did you know that Native Americans, too, made astronomical observatories—long before Europeans arrived?

The study of these ancient observatories is called *archaeoastronomy*. By combining astronomy with archaeology, we are beginning to understand how people of the past observed the skies.

Archaeoastronomy is a very new field. The Native American observatories have been discovered—or their purposes understood—only recently. Most of the sites had been abandoned centuries ago, and their original uses had been forgotten.

Let's look at some of the different ways Native Americans devised to follow the movements of the sun and, in certain cases, the stars.

Bighorn Medicine Wheel

Medicine Wheels

One of the most dramatic observatories lies on a windswept plateau high in the Bighorn Mountains of Wyoming. It is simply a circle of stones that looks something like a wheel, 80 feet across. In fact, it's called the Bighorn Medicine Wheel ("medicine" means holy or supernatural).

In the center of the wheel is a large pile of stones called a cairn. Twenty-eight lines of stones lead like spokes from the "hub" to the rim. Just outside the circle stand six smaller cairns.

Though the wheel had been known for about a hundred years, it was not until the early 1970s that its secrets began to come clear. An astronomer, John Eddy, discovered how the wheel "works."

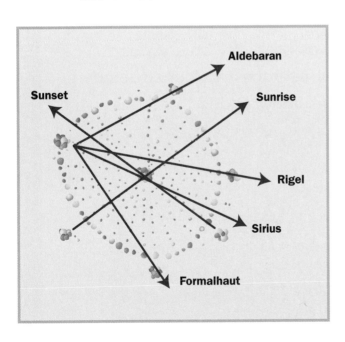

The Bighorn Medicine Wheel. The diagram shows cairns marking sunrise and sunset on the summer solstice and the rising of the bright stars Aldebaran, Rigel, Sirius, and Fomalhaut.

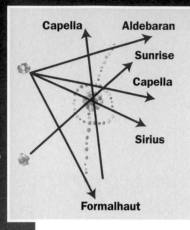

If you stand at a particular small cairn on the day of the summer solstice (usually June 21st), you will see the sun rise directly over the large cairn in the center of the wheel. At the end of the day, standing at a different pile, you'll see the setting sun line up with the center cairn. The medicine wheel tells almost exactly when the longest day of the year has arrived, the day we say summer begins.

The wheel shows other alignments as well. Pairs of small cairns were found to point to bright stars that shone briefly on the horizon on certain days before and after the summer solstice. These stars appeared roughly 28 days apart. Possibly the 28 "spokes" were supposed to help keep track of these intervals.

The Bighorn Medicine Wheel was probably built around 1700. The Ponca tribe claims that its ancestors constructed the original wheel. Other tribes probably added to it after moving into the area.

Moose Mountain Medicine Wheel

There is a similar medicine wheel in Saskatchewan, Canada. The Moose Mountain Medicine Wheel has cairns placed like those of the Bighorn Wheel. This gave a clue to its age. The point on the horizon where a star rises changes slightly over time. The wheel was dated by figuring out when bright stars rose closest to the points shown by the cairns. The calculations agreed with carbon dating for the site. The Moose Mountain Medicine Wheel was probably built around 2000 years ago!

Circles and Squares

At Cahokia, a major Native American site in western Illinois near St. Louis, archaeologists discovered traces of four large circles of wooden posts. They reconstructed part of one of these circles.

Seen from the center at dawn, the sun lines up with certain posts at the summer solstice and winter solstice (the shortest day of the year, usually December 21st). A third post is aligned with the rising sun at the spring and fall equinoxes (usually March 21st and September 21st, when day and night are of equal length).

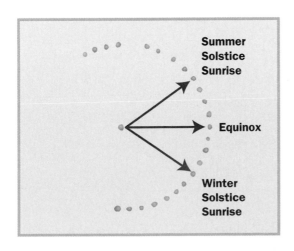

Summer
Solstice
Sunrise

Equinox

Winter
Solstice
Sunrise

At Cahokia, the sun rises over a post marker at the equinox. The diagram shows posts marking sunrises at the summer and winter solstices.

Another observatory was discovered near Kansas City, Missouri, in the early 1980s. Again, traces of posts were found, but this time in the shape of a square. About 35 feet long on each side, the square suggested a building such as a fort—except that the corners were open. A triangle of posts had stood in the center, and on the south side of the square was a double row of post marks.

A local astronomy society made a simple reconstruction of the square. They found that on the summer solstice, a person standing a certain distance from the center posts could see the sun rise and set through two of the open corners. The other two corners framed the sunrise and sunset at the winter solstice. On the equinoxes, the sun shone directly between the double lines of posts. Both observatories were made by Native Americans of the Mississippian culture, probably about a thousand years ago.

Cahokia

Sun Daggers

The Anasazi—a name that means simply "ancient ones"—lived in the beautiful but dry country of northern New Mexico, Colorado, Utah, and Arizona around 900 years ago. In Chaco Canyon, New Mexico, they designed an especially clever kind of observatory. It was discovered in 1977 by an artist, Anna Sofaer, who was examining rock carvings.

Near the top of Fajada Butte, a high rock that rises from the canyon floor, three large slabs of stone lean against a vertical rock face. About 9 feet long, they stand on end only a few inches apart, their narrow sides against the rock. On the shadowed rock behind them, two spirals have been cut.

At noon on the summer solstice, a tiny shaft of sunlight falls between two of the slabs. It makes a spot that looks like a dagger—cutting right through the middle of the larger spiral.

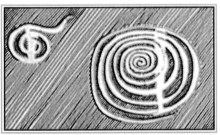
Fall equinox

Winter solstice

Spring equinox

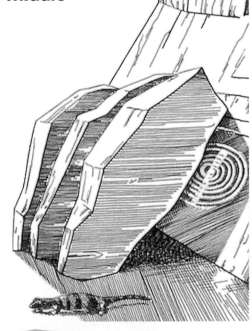
The solar marker in Chaco Canyon at noon on the summer solstice.

As the weeks pass, the "dagger" of sunlight moves to the right. Meanwhile, a second vertical streak of light appears. At the fall equinox, it cuts through the smaller spiral. By the winter solstice, the two "daggers" rest on the edges of the larger spiral. It's as though the spiral, now empty of sunlight, is a symbol of winter when the world is cold. Gradually, then, the sun daggers move to the left until, on the longest day of the year, the first one again strikes the center of the larger spiral.

All over the Southwest there are many such figures, called petroglyphs, cut in the rock. Spirals, crosses, rough outlines of humans, lizards, birds—all had meanings.

At many sites, the petroglyphs are touched by spots of sunlight, usually falling between two large rocks. Astronomer Robert Preston and his wife Ann, an artist, discovered many of these sites in Arizona. Light strikes the rock carving at the solstices, the equinoxes, or, in some cases, a point halfway between the fall equinox and the winter solstice.

"Sun Rooms"

The Anasazi thought of other ways to observe the travels of the sun. Between Tucson and Phoenix, Arizona, rises a three-story adobe building known as Casa Grande ("Great House"). At dawn, a person standing inside this ancient structure will see the sun shining through a small hole high in the east wall. The spot of light strikes the opposite wall, moves toward a small hole in that wall, and disappears into it. The spot of sunlight hits this bull's-eye only on the days close to the spring and fall equinoxes.

There is a different type of Anasazi "sun room" at Hovenweep National Monument in Utah. Attached to a large stone structure called Hovenweep Castle is a tower-like room. At sunset on the solstices and equinoxes, the sun's rays enter small holes and a door, shine through the room, and strike doorways in the inside walls. The archaeoastronomer who studied Hovenweep Castle, Ray Williamson, determined that the beams of sunlight could not enter the room in this way merely by chance.

Casa Grande a little after dawn, at the time of the spring equinox. Sunlight passes through holes in two different walls, one behind the other.

Why?

All over this country, Native Americans came up with ingenious ways to observe the skies. But *why* did they study astronomy?

The skies were the Native Americans' calendar. They had no fixed, written calendar as we do today. They relied on what nature would tell them about the changing times of the year. Important solar events such as the solstices and the equinoxes helped them know when to plant their crops, when to start preparing for the winter, when to move from one place to another.

The sun and stars told Native Americans when important ceremonies were supposed to take place. These ceremonies were usually concerned with the "return" of the sun and start of a new year, and with planting, harvesting, and hunting.

Hovenweep Castle

Other special occasions might have been for social purposes such as tribal rituals, gatherings of tribes, trade, or payment of tribute. For example, the most likely function of the Bighorn Medicine Wheel was to keep a calendar so large groups could assemble in summer for trading fairs.

It's probable that only special persons knew how to use the observatories and make the announcements awaited by the people. The observatories must have strengthened the power of the chiefs and religious leaders.

There is a deep religious meaning in Native American astronomy. The sun is a vital symbol in the beliefs of many Native American cultures. And something equally important: Native Americans' understanding of the heavens helped them feel in harmony with the universe—for in many Native American religions, human beings are only one small part of the world, living in peace with the rest of nature.

Today we are coming to recognize Native Americans' achievements in astronomical knowledge—and to appreciate the ways in which they used that understanding.

Meet the Author

Elsa Marston

Elsa Marston was born in Newton, Massachusetts. Although she is a writer and an artist, she has had a wide variety of jobs and interests. She has lived in Europe and the Middle East. She has taught English, been the head of an art gallery, and organized a jail improvement committee. She is also a nature lover and an active community worker. Her children's books are often based on experiences she has had. She says, "My basic philosophy in writing for young people is that I want to share what is important to me." Her favorite things to write about are the cultures of other people, both in the past and present. With her books, she hopes to "encourage an awareness of the world beyond here and now."

Theme Connections

Within the Selection

1. What is one reason why Native Americans needed to track the sun's movement?

2. How do we know that the observatories were important to Native Americans?

Across Selections

3. What do we know now about the universe that was probably unknown to the Native Americans who built the observatories?

4. How has technology changed from the time of early Native Americans to scientists today?

Beyond the Selection

5. How do you think Native Americans were able to build their observatories correctly without modern scientific instruments?

6. Why do you think the sun does not play as big a role in our culture today?

Write about It!

Describe the most beautiful sunrise or sunset you have seen, or tell about a time when you looked at the stars.

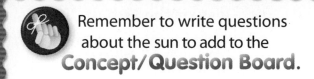

Remember to write questions about the sun to add to the **Concept/Question Board.**

Science Inquiry

Chasing the Moonlight

"The moon's an arrant thief, And her pale fire she snatches from the sun."
—William Shakespeare, from *Timon of Athens*

An Inuit legend from Greenland tries to explain the phases of the moon. Anningan, the moon god, and his sister, Malina the sun goddess, had a terrible fight. Malina spread dirt across Anningan's face so he would no longer shine as brightly as she did. Filled with anger, Anningan began chasing his sister across the skies. He was so involved in the chase that he forgot to eat and grew thinner and thinner. Finally, Anningan disappeared for a few days to eat. He gradually grew bigger until he was full once again, and the chase continued.

Of course, that is not really what happened. Shakespeare was a little closer to the truth with his dramatic description. The moon shines in the night sky because of sunlight reflecting off its surface. The moon is a sphere, so one half—the half facing the sun—is always lit.

The moon does not stay in one place, though. The moon appears in a different part of the sky because it has moved farther along in its orbit. As the moon travels around Earth, we see the area illuminated by the sun from different angles. As the moon moves counterclockwise around our planet, we see less and less of the lit half. Finally, the moon seems to disappear. We cannot see it because the unlit side of the moon now faces Earth.

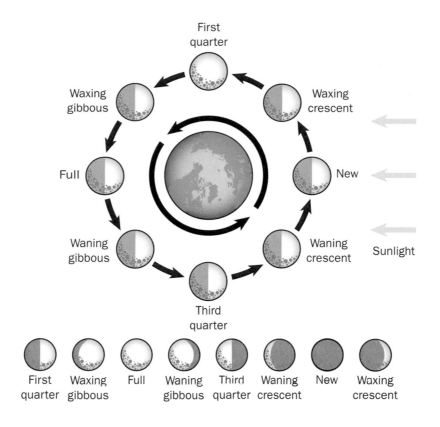

First
quarter

Waxing
gibbous

Waxing
crescent

Full

New

Waning
gibbous

Waning
crescent

Sunlight

Third
quarter

First
quarter

Waxing
gibbous

Full

Waning
gibbous

Third
quarter

Waning
crescent

New

Waxing
crescent

Think Link

1. When the moon is full, how much of it is being illuminated by the sun?

2. Which direction does the moon travel in its orbit around Earth, clockwise or counterclockwise?

3. Who wrote the quotation that begins this article?

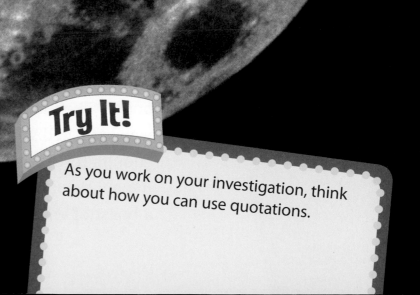

Try It!

As you work on your investigation, think about how you can use quotations.

Read the article to find the meanings of these words, which are also in "The Mystery of Mars":

- ✦ haze
- ✦ texture
- ✦ deflated
- ✦ analyze
- ✦ microscopic
- ✦ accumulate
- ✦ impact
- ✦ pressure
- ✦ harsh
- ✦ hospitable

Vocabulary Strategy

Context Clues are hints in the text that help you find the meanings of words. Look at the words *impact, microscopic,* and *harsh.* Use context clues to find each word's meaning.

Vocabulary

Warm-Up

The sun, hovering near the horizon, was a pale white ball glowing through the thick haze of a morning mist. Monika watched it through a large window and nervously wiped her warm, damp hands against her legs. The smooth texture of the spacesuit felt cool and refreshing. She took a deep breath, exhaled, and felt a little better after her lungs deflated.

Soon Monika Harold would become the first kid in space. Once the mist burned off, and the tower gave the okay, she and her parents would board the spacecraft. They were headed for Mars.

Mr. and Mrs. Harold were going to analyze a new mineral called *martianite.* Microscopic pieces of it swirled in the dust of the red planet. They needed to accumulate enough of the mineral to test it. The Harolds believed it might provide a new energy source. They hoped when martianite was smashed with enough force, the impact would release a burst of energy.

FiRST KiD iN SPACE!

384

Mr. and Mrs. Harold had fought hard to have Monika come with them. In the end, the government decided the time had arrived for a young person to travel in space. Monika's training had prepared her for the intense pressure of liftoff, and she knew the spacesuit would help. She was also ready for the ferocious sound of the rockets. But Monika was not so sure how she would handle the harsh emptiness of space.

The Harolds' first stop was a lunar station. It made the moon's surface habitable for humans. They also knew the other scientists would be hospitable, making them feel at home. After just a couple of days, though, Monika and her parents would leave for the long, lonely journey to Mars.

Turning from the window, Monika caught her mother watching her. They smiled at each other, and Monika had a new thought: *Maybe this trip will not be so lonely.*

GAME

Vocabulary Shuffle
Using a dictionary, find definitions for the selection vocabulary words, and write each one on a separate index card. Shuffle the cards, and give half of them to another student. Take turns reading the definitions and trying to determine which word is being defined.

Concept Vocabulary

The concept word for this lesson is *spacecraft. Spacecraft* are vehicles that travel in space. Sometimes they carry people, but more often they are unmanned. Spacecraft are used to put satellites into orbit around Earth and to explore our solar system.

Genre

Expository Text tells people something. It contains facts about real people, things, or events.

Comprehension Strategy

☆ **Summarizing**
As you read the selection, summarize the sections of the text to gain a clear understanding of how the pieces of the text fit together. This strategy will help you focus on the important items in each section and in the selection as a whole.

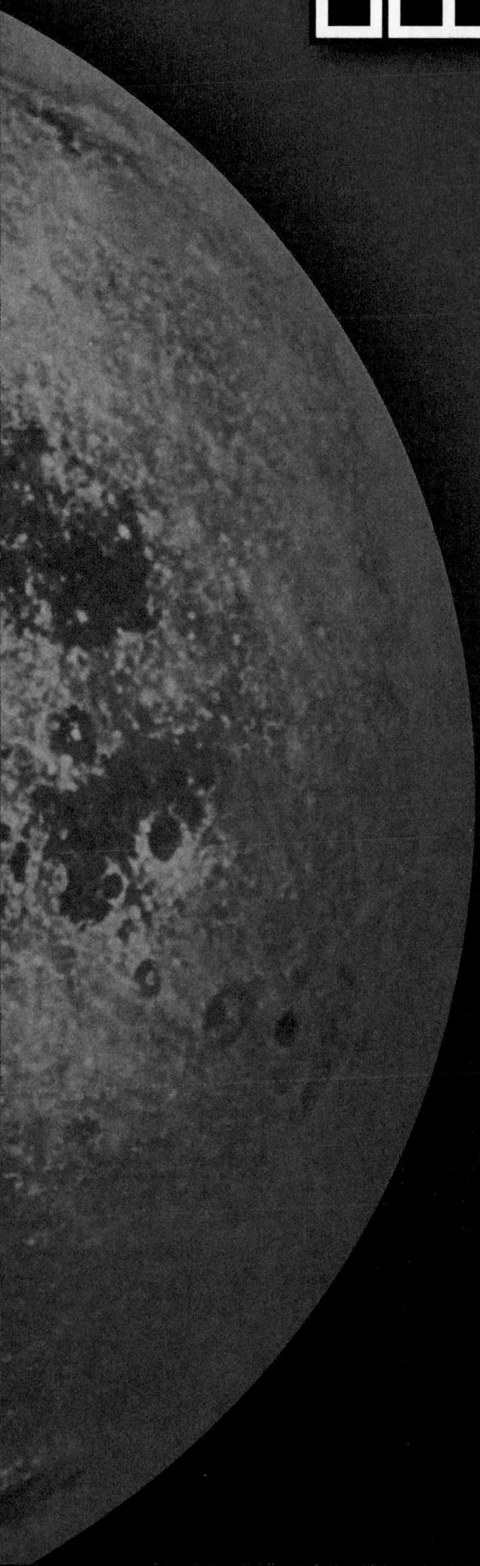

The Mystery of Mars

by Sally Ride and Tam O'Shaughnessy

Focus Questions

What information about Mars has been retrieved by the *Viking 1*, *Viking 2*, and *Pathfinder* landers? How is Mars like and unlike Earth?

In 1976 *Viking 1* and *Viking 2* settled softly onto the surface of Mars. They were the first spacecraft from Earth ever to visit the Red Planet. Twenty-one years later, *Pathfinder* dropped out of the Martian sky to join them. A parachute opened to slow it down, then giant air bags inflated to cushion it during impact. *Pathfinder* bounced hard more than 15 times before it rolled to a stop on the red Martian soil.

The *Viking 1* lander

Pathfinder landed in Ares Vallis, an ancient floodplain. Many of the rocks here were deposited by floods billions of years ago. This panorama also shows *Pathfinder's* deflated air bags and the ramp that its small rover, *Sojourner*, drove down to reach the surface. The rover is analyzing a rock a few feet from the lander. When *Sojourner* rolled down *Pathfinder's* ramp, it became the first rover ever to explore the Martian surface.

The *Pathfinder* lander. When the air bags that had protected it deflated, *Pathfinder* opened like a flower to reveal a camera, a weather station, and its rover, *Sojourner*. This photograph was taken by *Sojourner* after it had left the lander. The camera, at the top of the mast, is looking at *Sojourner*.

Although the *Viking* and *Pathfinder* landers arrived at different locations, they landed in similar terrain. Engineers did not want to risk landing these precious spacecraft on the edge of a cliff or the side of a volcano. They guided them to different sites on the gently rolling Martian plains north of the equator. The pictures the spacecraft sent back showed flat, windswept landscapes strewn with gray rocks and covered with fine red dust.

The two *Viking* landers could not move from their landing sites. They could reach out only a few feet with their robot arms to scoop up small samples of soil. *Pathfinder* carried the first rover to Mars. The rover, *Sojourner,* was about the size of a small dog. *Sojourner* traveled on six rugged wheels at the end of flexible legs. It moved at a snail's pace, but was able to travel several yards from the lander.

Sojourner had TV cameras for eyes and was steered by drivers back on Earth. *(Pathfinder)*

The little robot geologist dug its wheels into the red Martian dirt, churning up the soil to analyze its texture and clumpiness. It roamed through a garden of nearby rocks, ranging in size from pebbles to boulders, and nuzzled up to several of them.

The Martian rocks and soil seem to be made of about the same minerals, though in different proportions, as the rocks and soil on Earth.

This dry, dusty world does not look very hospitable. But many scientists have wondered whether there might be microscopic life on its surface. The *Viking* landers performed three important experiments that scientists hoped would answer that question. Their long robot arms scooped up samples of Martian soil and carried them inside the landers, where instruments analyzed the red dirt for evidence of life.

Sojourner's cameras took these close-up pictures of interesting rocks in the Rock Garden.

Above: A rock named Chimp, with small pebbles and wind streaks in the foreground.

Below: A pitted rock named Half-Dome. It looks as if it has been sandblasted by the Martian winds.

In planning these experiments, scientists assumed that Martian microbes would be similar to those on Earth: they would take in food molecules, grow, and release waste molecules. In one experiment, nutrients were added to soil samples. Then an instrument looked for the waste gas carbon dioxide, which might signal that living organisms had eaten the food.

This experiment did not find evidence of Martian life. Results from the other two experiments were also negative.

But are the building blocks of life present in the Martian soil? Another experiment looked for organic molecules, the molecules that make up living things. Samples of soil were heated, and instruments watched for gases that would be released if organic molecules were present. It was a great surprise when none were found. Scientists know that meteorites and interplanetary dust deliver a steady supply of organic molecules to the Martian surface. So even if there are no living organisms, there should still be some organic molecules. Scientists now suspect that they are being destroyed by harsh chemicals present in the Martian soil.

Spacecraft that have followed *Viking* have not carried experiments to look for evidence of life. The few *Viking* experiments are all scientists have to go by. Most scientists do not believe that there is life on the surface of Mars today.

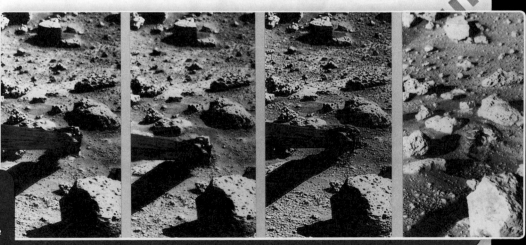

The *Viking 2* lander's robot arm scoops up a sample of soil and leaves its mark in the ground.

But many believe it is possible that primitive life exists beneath the surface, or that life existed on the planet long ago.

Earth is surrounded by an atmosphere that protects all the plants and animals on the planet from the extreme conditions in space. It shields us from the sun's radiation, helps keep our planet warm, and contains the oxygen that many of Earth's creatures need to survive.

Mars, too, has an atmosphere, but it is very different from Earth's. The Martian atmosphere is very, very thin and is made up almost entirely of carbon dioxide. Fine red Martian dust fills the thin air and creates a pink sky all year round.

Each of the landers set up a small weather station on the surface of Mars. While the stations operated, they radioed weather reports to Earth. Like the weather on Earth, the weather on Mars changes from day to day and from season to season. On some days the pink sky is mostly sunny, with light winds and wispy rose-colored clouds. On other days the sky is overcast, with strong winds and swirling cinnamon-colored dust.

Space shuttle astronauts took this picture of Earth's atmosphere at sunset. Storm clouds rise about eight miles above the planet's surface.

An unusually clear view of the Martian atmosphere. Thin layers of haze extend 25 miles above the horizon. (Viking)

The weather reports never included rain. There is very little water vapor in the Martian atmosphere. Martian clouds contain crystals of water ice, but the air is too thin and too cold for raindrops to form. In the early mornings, a thin veil of fog might fill the distant canyons, but there is no dew on the canyon walls. The rain that nourishes all life on Earth never falls on Mars.

Pathfinder's weather station. The windsocks on the far right are slightly tilted because they are being blown by the Martian wind.

During the late afternoon, clouds accumulate around and above Olympus Mons. *(Mars Global Surveyor)*

The Thin Air on Mars

The air on Mars is very thin. Because it is so thin, water cannot exist as a liquid on Mars' surface. If an astronaut on Mars poured a glass of water, it would soon boil away.

The boiling point of water (the temperature at which it turns into a gas) depends on the pressure of the surrounding air. You can see this yourself if you go camping in the mountains. Near sea level, water has to be heated to 212 degrees Fahrenheit before it will boil. As you climb up a mountain, the air gets thinner and thinner, so water boils at a lower and lower temperature. On a 5,000-foot-high mountain (and in the mile-high city of Denver), water boils at about 203 degrees Fahrenheit (a few degrees lower than at sea level). At the top of Mount Everest, the highest mountain on Earth, water boils at only about 160 degrees Fahrenheit.

When spacecraft measured the air pressure on the surface of Mars, they found that it is the same as it would be on a mountain more than three times as high as Mount Everest. When the air is that thin, water boils at very low temperatures— temperatures near its freezing point. That means that water on Mars exists either as ice or as water vapor (a gas), but not as a liquid.

Wispy clouds about 10 miles high, made of water ice condensed on particles of red dust. (*Pathfinder*)

Mars is very, very cold. Even on bright summer days, temperatures may only reach 10 degrees Fahrenheit—22 degrees below the freezing point of water. When the sun goes down, the temperature falls to a frigid 110 degrees below zero. Earth's atmosphere helps keep our planet warm overnight. But on Mars the atmosphere is so thin that after the sun sets, the planet's heat quickly escapes to space.

If you were standing on Mars on a summer morning, your feet would be warm, but your ears would be freezing! As the sun warms the soil, the air a few inches above the ground is heated to nearly 50 degrees Fahrenheit. But just a few feet off the ground, the temperature plummets.

Winters on Mars are so cold that nearly 20 percent of the planet's air actually freezes out of the sky. Carbon dioxide gas in the air turns to ice and is trapped in Mars' polar icecaps until spring. Then when the temperature warms, the carbon dioxide goes back into the air as a gas.

Frost covers the Martian landscape near the *Viking 2* landing site in Utopia Planitia in the Elysium region.

A section of the north polar cap. Layers of white ice and reddish orange dust form terraces around both the north and south polar caps. *(Viking)*

Mars is a windy planet. Dust devils whirl across the surface, lifting red dust high into the sky. During some parts of the year, ferocious winds stir up huge dust storms in the Southern Hemisphere that can grow to cover the entire planet. These dust storms are far worse than any on Earth and can completely block our view of the planet's surface for weeks at a time.

Over the ages, Martian winds have created complex sand dunes over much of the planet. Some dunes appear to be ancient remnants of an earlier time when the air was thicker and the wind could more easily blow sand around. Other dunes appear to be still active today.

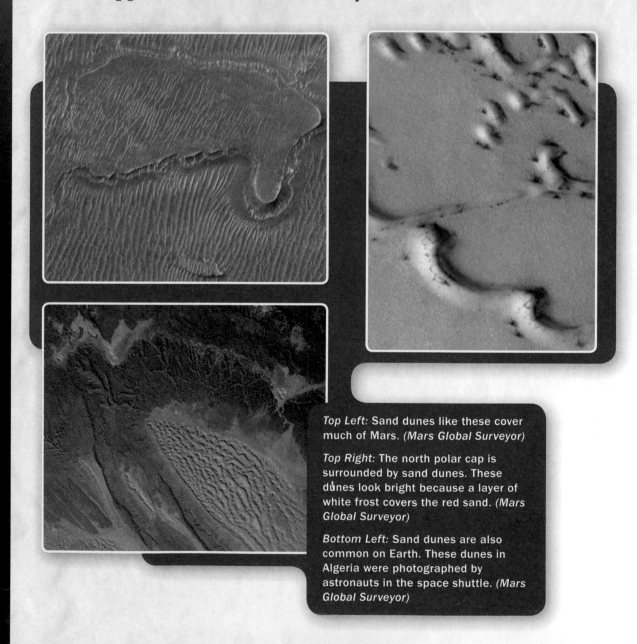

Top Left: Sand dunes like these cover much of Mars. *(Mars Global Surveyor)*

Top Right: The north polar cap is surrounded by sand dunes. These dunes look bright because a layer of white frost covers the red sand. *(Mars Global Surveyor)*

Bottom Left: Sand dunes are also common on Earth. These dunes in Algeria were photographed by astronauts in the space shuttle. *(Mars Global Surveyor)*

When the first astronauts visit Mars, what will they find? Though an astronaut could not survive without a spacesuit, she would feel more at home on Mars than anywhere else in the solar system. She could stand on a rocky surface, scoop up a gloveful of dirt, and explore extinct volcanoes and ancient canyons.

She would need the spacesuit to protect her from the thin Martian air and the extreme cold. The spacesuit would be bulky, but not heavy. Because Mars is smaller than Earth, the pull of gravity on its surface is lower. She and her spacesuit would weigh about one-third what they weighed on Earth.

As the astronaut hiked across the rugged, rocky terrain, her boots would leave deep footprints in the dusty red soil. Fine red dust would cling to her spacesuit. Even on days when the wind was calm, she would look up at a pink sky loaded with red dust. As she headed back to the warmth of her spacecraft at the end of the day, she would look past the silhouettes of crater rims at a dimmer setting sun.

The planet she was exploring would seem strangely familiar. But it would be missing the air and water that make Earth habitable, and the plants and animals that share her home world.

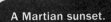

A Martian sunset.

Meet the Authors

Sally Ride

Sally Ride never set out to become the first American woman in space. She really wanted to play professional tennis. Dr. Ride gave up her tennis dream to study physics because, her mother says, she could not make the tennis ball go exactly where she wanted it.

Ms. Ride became an astronaut by answering an ad she saw from NASA. Of the eight-thousand people who responded to the ad, she and five other women were selected for a group of thirty-five new astronauts.

In 1983, Dr. Ride became the first American woman to travel to space. On the *Challenger* she performed experiments and tested the shuttle's robotic arm, which she helped design. Now retired from NASA, Sally Ride is a physics professor at the University of California where one of her goals is to encourage young women to study science and math.

Tam O'Shaughnessy

Tam O'Shaughnessy and Sally Ride have been friends since they were teenagers competing in junior tennis tournaments. Dr. O'Shaughnessy has played professional tennis, taught high school biology, and written several scientific books for young readers. She is a Professor at Georgia State University, where she researches ways to help children learn to read. Dr. O'Shaughnessy has collaborated with Dr. Ride on two other children's science books.

Our Corner of the Universe

Theme Connections

Within the Selection

1. How does Mars's thin atmosphere affect the planet?
2. What characteristics do Earth and Mars have in common?

Across Selections

3. In what way is the wind on Mars similar to the wind on Earth?
4. According to "The Universe," to which category of planets does Mars belong?

Beyond the Selection

5. Why is a robot like *Pathfinder* useful in space exploration?
6. Why do scientists want to know whether life did or did not exist on Mars?

Write about It!

Describe a possible use for a robot.

Remember to look for newspaper or magazine articles about Mars or outer space to add to the **Concept/Question Board.**

Science Inquiry

Welcome to Sol!

| Visitors | New Residents | Businesses |
| News | Government | |

Today's Weather
Surface temperature: 10,000°F
Core temperature: 27,000,000°F
Solar winds: 1,000,000 m.p.h.

An important note to new visitors:

You may be tempted to visit one of Sol's sunspots. These dark patches on the sun's surface are much cooler than the surrounding areas. However, at any moment a solar flare may erupt. These ferocious explosions are unpredictable.

FAQ

Why is it so hot?

Sol is a nuclear furnace. It has burned for 4.6 billion years and should burn for at least seven billion more. Earth's nuclear reactors make energy by breaking up the nuclei in atoms. This is called *fission*. The sun's energy is created through *fusion*. Fusion occurs when two nuclei are forced together and create a new, heavier nucleus. The intense pressure inside the sun helps this happen.

Fusion in the sun starts with hydrogen atoms. Once they fuse, the heavier element helium is formed. The impact of each fusion creates a tiny amount of energy. Every second, though, seven hundred million metric tons of hydrogen fuse together. About five million metric tons of energy in the form of heat and light are created *each second*. Now that is hot!

Did you know?

One million Earths could fit inside Sol.
Sol is 333,000 times heavier than Earth.

Meet the Neighbors!

Alpha Centauri 3	4.22 light-years
Barnard's Star	6 light-years
Wolf 359	7.8 light-years

Alpha Centauri 3 is actually a cluster of three stars. They are known as Alpha Centauri A, B, and C. Like Sol, Alpha Centauri A is an average yellow star, but B is an orange star. Both A and B are about the same size as our sun. However, C is a red dwarf star and is only about the size of Jupiter.

Think Link

1. Which pieces of text on this Web site are most likely to be links?

2. What is the difference between *fission* and *fusion*?

3. Use the Internet to learn why stars vary in color.

Try It!

As you work on your investigation, think about how you can use Web sites to help in your research.

Genre

Narrative Nonfiction
is a story that includes
real people, places,
and events.

Comprehension
Skill

Drawing
Conclusions
As you read the selection,
use information in the
text to draw conclusions
about characters and
events.

APOLLO 11:
First Moon Landing
by Michael D. Cole

Focus Questions
How are astronauts similar to the
early land and sea explorers? How do
astronauts help us learn more about
the universe?

Read the article to find the meanings of these words, which are also in "Apollo 11: First Moon Landing":

✦ bulky
✦ focused
✦ depressed
✦ module
✦ thrust
✦ tranquility
✦ hatch
✦ mankind
✦ sensations
✦ awe

Vocabulary Strategy

Context Clues are hints in the text that help you find the meanings of words. Look at the words *bulky* and *module*. Use context clues to find each word's meaning.

Vocabulary

Warm-Up

"Kaysar!" Mrs. Mansoor yelled. "Sit down so we can all see."

Kaysar headed back to the soft, bulky couch where his family sank cozily into the cushions. Everyone was focused intensely on the television.

Kaysar depressed the remote control button to turn on the sound. There was no question in his mind now—walking on the moon was the most important event of his lifetime.

For several days, Kaysar and his classmates had been discussing the coming moon landing. Their teacher explained how the astronauts, sitting in the command module were perched on top of a giant rocket. The rocket's thrust would propel them into space. Then the module would break away from the rocket and hurtle the astronauts into the moon's orbit. A smaller module would take two of the astronauts down to the moon's surface.

Most days the Mansoor household shook with the loud activities of four kids. Today, though, the room's tranquility underscored the importance of the event.

As they all watched, Neil Armstrong exited the lunar module's hatch and stepped down the ladder. Armstrong planted his foot on the surface and declared it a giant leap for mankind.

The family began chattering about NASA's accomplishment, but Kaysar knew the journey was hardly over. Even after the astronauts returned to Earth, they would need to be debriefed. Scientists would ask about the sensations they felt in space. But Kaysar thought the worst part would be the quarantine. Scientists needed to be sure they had not caught some sort of space disease. Even after surviving a trip all the way to the moon and back, the astronauts still might not live. Kaysar was in awe of their bravery.

Fill in the Blanks
On a separate sheet of paper, complete the following sentences with selection vocabulary words.

1. The _____ in my mouth and face disappeared after the dentist gave me novocaine.
2. The loud blaring of the car's horn disturbed the _____ of the neighborhood.
3. It was freezing, but Javier's _____ coat kept him warm.
4. The cook popped his head out of the _____ and told the ship's crew to come to lunch.

Concept Vocabulary

The concept word for this lesson is **odyssey.** An *odyssey* is a voyage that results in some kind of discovery or change, usually for the good. Often odysseys are physical journeys to another place, but they can also be educational and intellectual.

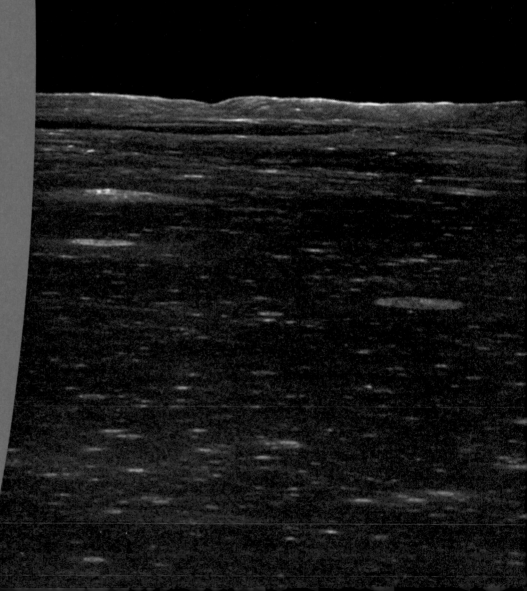

Genre

Narrative Nonfiction is a story that includes real people, places, and events.

Comprehension Skill

 Drawing Conclusions

As you read the selection, use information in the text to draw conclusions about characters and events.

APOLLO 11:
First Moon Landing

by Michael D. Cole

Focus Questions

How are astronauts similar to the early land and sea explorers? How do astronauts help us learn more about the universe?

It was warm on the morning of July 16, 1969, at Cape Kennedy in Florida. On launchpad 39A sat the mighty Saturn V rocket—the most powerful machine ever built. At the top of the towering rocket—363 feet above the ground—three men waited to begin mankind's most historic journey.

In the right couch was Michael Collins. He was the command module pilot. He would not land on the Moon, but he would orbit the Moon in the command module. The other two astronauts would make the landing on the Moon in the lunar module.

Awaiting liftoff, the Saturn V rocket sits on the launchpad.

Collins was born in Rome, Italy, in 1930 while his father was stationed there with the U.S. Army. Collins had been an air force test pilot and had already been in space before. He flew in the *Gemini 10* mission, and he had walked in space. He was married and had two daughters and a son. Collins liked to joke that because there was no TV set on the command module, he would be one of the few Americans who would not see the Moon landing.[1]

[1] John Barbour, *Footprints on the Moon* (New York: The Associated Press, 1969), p. 184.

In the middle couch was Edwin E. Aldrin. He would co-pilot the lunar module, which was named *Eagle.* Everyone called him "Buzz." It had been his nickname since his childhood in Montclair, New Jersey. He was thirty-nine years old, and he also had been an air force pilot.

Aviation was in Aldrin's blood. His father had been a colonel in the U.S. Army Air Corps and was a friend of Orville Wright and Charles Lindbergh. His mother's maiden name was Marian Moon. Aldrin had been in space on *Gemini 12.* He held the record for the longest spacewalk. He was an intelligent and serious man who spoke in the precise manner of an engineer. He was married, with two sons and a daughter.

In the left couch was mission commander Neil A. Armstrong. He was from Wapakoneta, Ohio, where he had earned a pilot's license before he was old enough to drive a car. After flying as a Navy pilot he became an astronaut. He commanded the *Gemini 8* mission. Armstrong was probably the best pilot among all the astronauts. He was married and the father of two sons. His boyish smile made him look much younger than his thirty-eight years. Because he was mission commander, he would be the first person to walk upon the Moon.

Armstrong, Collins, and Aldrin pose for a picture in front of the mighty Apollo/Saturn V rocket which would carry them to the Moon.

Neil Armstrong, Michael Collins, and Buzz Aldrin will always be remembered for their heroic and historic flight aboard *Apollo 11*.

These three men were about to experience an extraordinary adventure. All three had been in space before. All had been proud to serve their country in the space program. But they knew this mission was different.

People all over the world were waiting for the launch. They hoped *Apollo 11*'s historic mission to land on the Moon would be a success. People everywhere felt that a part of themselves was going with those three astronauts. Armstrong, Aldrin, and Collins could not escape the fact that this time they did not just represent their country. This time they represented the human race.

The three astronauts suited up in their bulky spacesuits. Then they made the five-mile trip to the launching pad in a large van. It went over a special remote route to avoid the incredible traffic jam that had been building around the Cape for days. Beaches and parks were full of camper trailers. Lakes and waterways were full of boats anchored where they could watch the launch. All of them, and the nearly one billion people around the world who were watching the exciting countdown on television, waited to witness the historic moment when *Apollo 11* began its journey to the Moon.

"Two minutes and ten seconds and counting, and the Moon at this precise second is 218,986 miles away," the announcer said over the Cape loudspeaker.[2] The countdown was going smoothly. Armstrong, Aldrin, and Collins had trained for over a year for this mission. Now it was about to begin. Collins thought they had about a fifty-fifty chance of completing the mission successfully. Armstrong and Aldrin thought their chances were a little better. The three had never discussed the subject with each other.[3]

The countdown swept toward the final minute, then the final seconds. Armstrong wrapped his gloved hand around the abort handle in case the launch went badly. Aldrin looked at Armstrong and then turned to grin at Collins. They were finally going!

Collins remembered walking to the pad just a while ago. He had watched the frosty steam rolling off the rocket's sides when the warm air met the rocket filled with super-cooled liquid oxygen and hydrogen. He remembered thinking the rocket almost seemed *alive*.[4] Seconds from now, it would indeed rumble to life.

[2] Apollo 11, *Technical Air-to-Ground Voice Transcription*, Manned Spacecraft Center, Houston, Texas, July 1969. All in-flight communications which follow come from this source.

[3] "Spaceflight Part 3: One Giant Leap," narrated by Martin Sheen, PBS Video (1985).

[4] Michael Collins, *Carrying the Fire: An Astronaut's Journey* (New York: Farrar, Straus & Giroux, 1974), p. 418.

Apollo 11 Commander Neil A. Armstrong leads astronauts Michael Collins and Edwin E. Aldrin to the van that will take them to the launchpad.

Spectators witness the blast off of the Saturn V rocket.

The loudspeaker at the Cape kept the thousands of onlookers counting toward the launch. "We are still go with *Apollo 11.* Thirty seconds and counting. Astronauts reported, feel good . . . T minus twenty seconds and counting. T minus fifteen seconds, guidance is internal."

All power was now on in the *Apollo 11* spacecraft. Armstrong, Aldrin, and Collins were excited, but their minds were focused on the many tasks that had to be done.[5] "Twelve, eleven, ten, nine, ignition sequence starts." Flame and smoke gushed from the five main engines of the Saturn V rocket. "Six, five, four, three, two, one, zero, all engines running." The controllers at the Cape pushed the engines to the proper thrust of 7.5 million pounds, equal to the power of more than 92,000 locomotives. Then they released the pad's hold-down clamps.

The mighty Saturn V, all 3,000 tons of it, rose from the launchpad.

"LIFT-OFF! We have a lift-off! Thirty-two minutes past the hour. Lift-off on *Apollo 11.*" It was 9:32 A.M. The rocket's deafening rise through the sky could be seen and heard for miles around the Cape. The huge flaming thrust of the engines created a shock wave that could be *felt* for just as far. The powerful Saturn V climbed through the sky, pushing the three astronauts toward space while the whole world watched.

[5] Michael Collins, *Carrying the Fire: An Astronaut's Journey* (New York: Farrar, Straus & Giroux, 1974), p. 419.

The exciting launch was a great success. Still, it was hard to believe what was about to happen. In four days, the men of *Apollo 11* would try to land on the Moon.

By Day Four of the mission the Moon's appearance had changed dramatically in the astronauts' eyes. Armstrong, Aldrin, and Collins saw the Moon as a three-dimensional thing for the first time. It was the most awesome sphere they had ever seen. It completely filled their window. Armstrong tried to describe what they were seeing.

"The view of the Moon . . . is really spectacular," he said. "We can see the entire circumference even though part of it is in complete shadow and part of it is in Earthshine (sunlight reflected off the Earth). It's a view worth the price of the trip."

"We're able to see stars again and recognize constellations for the first time on the trip," Collins added. "The Earthshine coming through the window is so bright you can read a book by it."

The Moon as viewed from *Apollo 11*.

They could not linger by the windows for long. They were about to pass behind the dark side of the Moon. They would lose contact with Earth for more than thirty minutes. During that time they would fire Columbia's engines to slow themselves down and get into lunar orbit. If it worked, their next step would be to prepare *Eagle* for its descent to the Moon.

Apollo 11 swung around the dark side of the Moon, losing radio contact with Mission Control. During this first radio blackout the three astronauts and their spacecraft were now in orbit around the Moon.

"The *Eagle* has wings," announced Armstrong as the lunar module separated from the command module.

Coming around on their first orbit, *Apollo 11* regained radio contact. The astronauts got their first view of some important sights on the Moon's surface. "We're getting our first view of the landing site approach," Armstrong said. "The pictures brought back by *Apollos 8* and *10* have given us a pretty good preview of what to look at here. It looks very much like the pictures, but . . . there's no substitute for actually being here."[6]

So far the mission was going incredibly well. Armstrong, Aldrin, and Collins settled down to rest before the big day tomorrow. They slept only five or six hours, the shortest rest period of the flight. When they awoke on Sunday, it was time to do what they had been practicing to do for over a year. But this time it would be for real.

Aldrin crawled down the tunnel and through the hatch into *Eagle.* He powered up the spacecraft and ran through a series of systems checks. Armstrong joined him a short time later. The checks continued and everything was go.

"*Apollo,* Houston. We're go for undocking," reported Mission Control. The radio again blacked out, and they swung around the Moon's dark side on their thirteenth orbit. Armstrong and Aldrin extended the landing legs on *Eagle.* After nearly ten years of hard work, the goal of the manned space program was about to be realized. They were ready to go for the landing.

[6] *Apollo 11, Technical Air-to-Ground Voice Transcription,* Manned Spacecraft Center, Houston, Texas, July 1969. All in-flight communications which follow come from this source.

Collins pressed a button in the command module. Latches clicked open, and *Eagle* floated gently away from *Columbia*. Mission Control waited for the signal to come through again. As *Eagle* again came into radio contact, Armstrong announced through the static, "The *Eagle* has wings."

The two ships flew in formation while Collins inspected the lunar module for any problems or damage. "Looks like you've got a mighty good-looking flying machine there, *Eagle*," he said, "despite the fact that you're upside down." Collins later gave *Columbia* a burst from its engine. This boosted him ahead to give *Eagle* some flying room. "OK *Eagle* . . . you guys take care."

"See you later," Armstrong said.

Eagle was again on the dark side, in radio blackout. It began its long arcing descent toward the landing site. The site was in an area on the Moon called the Sea of Tranquility. This place was chosen as a landing site because the area was wide-open and very flat. If all went well, Armstrong and Aldrin would land there in about seventeen minutes. They came out of the radio blackout with everything going fine. *Eagle* had now descended to about ten miles above the lunar surface.

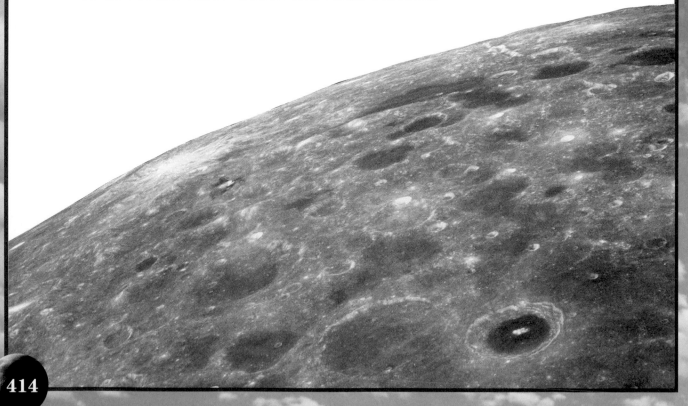

"You are go to continue powered descent," Mission Control said. "You're looking good."

"Got the Earth right out our front window," Aldrin said. Armstrong had turned *Eagle* into position; its landing legs were pointed toward the lunar surface. This enabled the landing radar to lock on and feed altitude and velocity data to the onboard computer. The landing proceeded perfectly as Armstrong and Aldrin descended to 3,000 and then 2,000 feet from the surface. Then things got very tense. An alarm light flashed on their instrument panels.

"Twelve alarm," Aldrin said, "1201." This meant that one of the landing computers was overloaded with data. It was feeding Armstrong and Aldrin faulty information about their descent.

"Roger," said Mission Control, "1201 alarm." The controllers at Houston assured them the computer would reset. They were to continue the descent despite the alarm.

"We're go," Aldrin replied. "Hang tight. We're go. Two thousand feet." Aldrin continued to read out the data. Armstrong watched out his left window as they approached the landing site. "Seven hundred feet, 21 down," Aldrin said. This meant *Eagle* was seven hundred feet above the Moon and was descending at twenty-one feet per second. "Four hundred feet, down at 9. We're pegged on horizontal velocity. Three hundred feet, down 3 and a half."

The controllers in Houston were on the edge of their seats. Nearly every astronaut in the astronaut program was gathered behind the viewing window in the control room. They were all nervously watching the television screen and listening to Aldrin call out the landing data.[7]

"Altitude-velocity lights. Three and a half down, 220 feet. Thirteen forward, 11 forward, coming down nicely. Two hundred feet, 4 and a half down, 5 and a half down."

The landing site came into view outside *Eagle*'s two windows. As Armstrong looked, he saw something that made his heartbeat begin to race.[8] The computer was leading *Eagle* to the intended landing site. But that site was littered with boulders the size of automobiles! There was no way they could make a safe landing among those boulders.

Armstrong grasped the rocket control handle with his right hand and overrode the automatic landing system. *Eagle* skimmed over the large field of boulders as Armstrong searched the lunar surface for a smoother landing area. He knew he had to find it in a hurry. *Eagle* was now only one hundred feet above the Moon, and its landing engine was running very close to the end of its fuel.

[7] John Barbour, *Footprints on the Moon* (New York: The Associated Press, 1969), p. 205.

[8] Peter Bond, *Heroes in Space: From Gagarin to Challenger* (New York: Basil Blackwell, Inc., 1987), p. 191.

The controllers at Mission Control in Houston were anxiously awaiting the lunar landing.

"Seventy-five feet," Aldrin continued. "Down a half, 6 forward."

"Sixty seconds," Mission Control said, meaning there was only one minute of fuel left in *Eagle*'s landing engine. The controllers in Houston were unaware of the boulders Armstrong had seen. They were anxious for Armstrong to set *Eagle* down.[9]

"Forty feet, down 2 and a half," Aldrin read out to Armstrong, who was flying *Eagle* toward a spot he saw several hundred yards to the right of his window. Getting there would be cutting it very close. "Picking up some dust. Thirty feet . . . faint shadow. Four forward, drifting to the right a little."

"Thirty seconds," said Mission Control.

"Six forward. Drifting right." *Eagle* was now kicking up a lot of dust on the surface. "Contact light." This meant that one of the feelers on the legs of the lunar module had touched the Moon. The cloud of dust moved away from them. Armstrong and Aldrin sensed that they and *Eagle* had come to a complete stop. They were motionless.

Almost out of habit, Aldrin continued to read out the information from his panel. "Okay, engine stop. . . . descent engine command override, off. Engine arm, off."

[9] Barbour, p. 206.

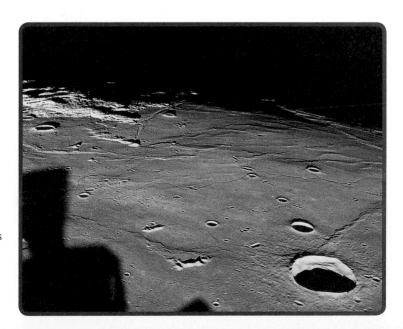

View of the approaching landing site on the Moon, as seen by the astronauts aboard *Apollo 11*.

All of Mission Control's instruments told the controllers that the lunar module was down. "We copy you down, *Eagle*," came the communicator's voice.

"Houston," Armstrong replied, hesitating for a moment, "Tranquility Base here. The *Eagle* has landed."

Mission Control erupted in cheers. "Roger Tranquility," the communicator said through the noise, "we copy you on the ground. You've got a bunch of guys about to turn blue. We're breathing again. Thanks a lot."

Aldrin reached across his instrument panel and he and Armstrong shook hands firmly. They had done it! Looking out their windows, they stared with awe at the stark and lonely alien landscape.[10] It was hard to believe they were really on the Moon.

A quarter of a million miles away, people all over the Earth were slowly realizing what had just happened. Human beings had for the first time landed upon another world.

Mission Control was still loud with the excitement of the landing. "Be advised there are lots of smiling faces in this room and all over the world. Over," the communicator told the astronauts.[11]

"There are two of them up here," Armstrong replied.

"And don't forget one in the command module," Collins broke in on the circuit.

[10] Harry Hurt, III, *For All Mankind* (New York: Atlantic Monthly Press, 1988), p. 169.

[11] *Apollo 11, Technical Air-to-Ground Voice Transcription*, Manned Spacecraft Center, Houston, Texas, July 1969. All in-flight communications which follow come from this source.

A manager at Mission Control studies his console during the *Apollo 11* landing mission.

"Tranquility Base, it sure sounded good from here. You guys did a fantastic job."

"Thank you," Armstrong replied. "Just keep that orbiting base ready for us up there now."

Armstrong and Aldrin were scheduled for a four-hour rest period after the landing systems check. They were simply too excited. They requested to go ahead with preparations for the Moon walks now.[12] Houston agreed. The two astronauts ate their first meal on the Moon. Then they spent the next two hours getting suited up for the Moon walks.

The suits Armstrong and Aldrin wore included a backpack that would keep a person alive on the Moon for four hours. It carried oxygen for them to breathe, water to cool the special garment they wore beneath the suit, and communications equipment. As soon as Armstrong and Aldrin sealed their helmets and gloves, they depressurized the cabin. Armstrong dropped to his hands and knees and began to back out of the open hatch. He stepped onto the ladder on one of *Eagle*'s landing legs.

[12] Edwin E. "Buzz" Aldrin, Jr., with Wayne Warga, Return to Earth (New York: Random House, 1973), pp. 232–233.

Back on Earth, millions breathlessly watched their televisions. A camera placed near the base of the lunar module brought them live pictures of Armstrong's ghostly image coming down the ladder. People all over the world were amazed that astronauts were on the Moon. And most of them found it just as amazing that they were able to watch live television pictures of it.

"Okay Neil, we can see you coming down the ladder now," Mission Control said.

Armstrong carefully stepped down each rung of the ladder. It was tricky. He was still getting used to the bulky suit and the Moon's gravity, which is one-sixth the gravity of Earth. "I'm at the foot of the ladder," Armstrong reported. "The LM footpads are only depressed in the surface about one or two inches. Although the surface appears to be very, very fine grained, as you get close to it. It's almost like a powder."

Stepping down from the lunar module to the Moon was tricky. Featured on these two pages is Buzz Aldrin descending the ladder.

The Mission Control room was completely silent. They were fascinated by every word of Armstrong's description of the Moon's landscape around him. They knew they were witnessing history.

"I'm going to step off the LM now." Armstrong moved his left leg away from *Eagle*'s footpad and planted his boot in the lunar soil—the first human step on another world. "That's one small step for a man . . . one giant leap for mankind."

Millions of people on Earth witnessed this moment of history. It was a moment unlike any other. It gave many people a sense of awe and a feeling of pride that humanity had accomplished such a feat. It left many people, including the famous CBS television news anchor Walter Cronkite, completely speechless.

Armstrong walked around the landing area. His walk looked more like a bouncy skip or a hop. The Moon's gravity allowed him to bound lightly from one foot to the other. He took out a scoop with a long handle to collect the first sample of Moon soil. He collected some soil and rocks in a bag and placed it in a pocket just above his left knee. Then he looked out across the lunar landscape.

"It has a stark beauty all its own," he said. "It's different, but it's very pretty out here."

A few minutes later, Aldrin joined Armstrong on the surface. "Beautiful view!" Aldrin said when he stepped away from the ladder.

"Isn't that something?" Armstrong said. "Magnificent sight out here."

"Magnificent desolation," Aldrin added.

They practiced different methods of walking in Moon's gravity and reported their sensations to Mission Control. Then they unveiled a plaque attached to *Eagle*'s landing leg. Armstrong read it for the viewers back on Earth.

"'Here Men from the planet Earth first set foot upon the Moon, July 1969 A.D. We came in peace for all mankind.' It has the crewmembers' signatures and the signature of the President of the United States."

Next they planted the United States flag near *Eagle* and received a special telephone call from President Richard Nixon.

"For one priceless moment, in the whole history of man," Nixon said, "all the people of Earth are truly one. One in their pride in what you have done. And one in our prayers that you will return safely to Earth."

Two and a half days later, on Thursday, July 24, 1969, *Apollo 11* reentered the Earth's atmosphere. After the fiery reentry, huge red and white parachutes sprang from the nose of the capsule. Neil Armstrong, Edwin E. "Buzz" Aldrin, and Mike Collins came to a soft splashdown in the Pacific Ocean. *Apollo 11* had returned.

They were recovered by the aircraft carrier U.S.S. *Hornet.* President Nixon was waiting to welcome them. Scientists were afraid that the astronauts might have brought dangerous organisms back from the Moon. So the men had to wear strange airtight overalls with headgear that looked like gas masks.

The *Apollo 11* crew awaits pickup by a helicopter from the U.S.S. *Hornet.*

As soon as a helicopter landed them on the carrier, they entered a large van that looked like a camper trailer. It was a comfortable quarantine facility. They took off the suits and looked out a window to participate in a welcoming ceremony with President Nixon. They stayed in the trailerlike facility for three days. Then it was flown by cargo plane to Houston. There it was pulled into the Lunar Receiving Laboratory (LRL). There the astronauts were let out of the trailer and scientists checked them out thoroughly.

For the next three weeks, Armstrong, Aldrin, and Collins lived in the LRL. They debriefed NASA people about the flight and were continually examined for the effects of any possible alien organisms. After three weeks, on August 10, 1969, the quarantine was over. The astronauts were released to the outside world.

For the next two months, Neil Armstrong, Buzz Aldrin, and Mike Collins rode in parades and gave speeches to hundreds of thousands of people on a tour that took them to six continents. They were heroes, and now an important part of history. Eventually the celebrations died down and plans for the next trip to the Moon, *Apollo 12,* continued. But there would never be another Moon mission like *Apollo 11.*

President Richard M. Nixon proudly greets the three astronauts who were being quarantined aboard the U.S.S. *Hornet.*

It is difficult to know the true meaning or importance of humanity's first voyage to another world. Perhaps Buzz Aldrin stated it best in his words to a joint session of Congress, fifty-four days after *Apollo 11* had returned from the Moon:

I say to you today what no men have been privileged to say before: We walked on the Moon. But the footprints at Tranquility Base belong to more than the crew of Apollo 11. . . . *Those footprints belong to the American people . . . who accepted and supported the inevitable challenge of the Moon. And, since we came in peace for all mankind, those footprints belong also to all the people of the world.*

The first step on the Moon was a step toward our sister planets and ultimately the stars. 'A small step for a man' was a statement of fact, 'a giant leap for mankind' is a hope for the future.[13]

[13] Douglas MacKinnon and Joseph Baldanza, *Footprints* (Washington, D.C.: Acropolis Books Ltd., 1989), p. 21.

The city of Chicago welcomes Armstrong, Collins, and Aldrin home with a ticker tape parade.

Meet the Author

Michael D. Cole

Michael D. Cole dreamed of being an astronaut as a child. His fascination with outer space has continued into his adult life. He has written many books about the exploration of space, including *Vostok 1: First Human in Space, Columbia: First Flight of the Space Shuttle,* and other books about Apollo and space shuttle missions. His books give readers a window into the technology and people involved in these amazing space adventures.

Our Corner of the Universe

Theme Connections

Within the Selection

1. Why did *Apollo 11* lose contact with Earth each time it traveled to the dark side of the moon?

2. What kind of preparations were needed for *Apollo 11* to be a success?

Across Selections

3. How is the surface of the moon like the surface of Mars?

4. Which spacecraft from "Apollo 11: First Moon Landing" is most like *Pathfinder*?

Beyond the Selection

5. Why did people from other countries share in the excitement of the moon landing?

6. Why do you think it was important to send humans to the moon?

Write about It!

Describe what it might be like to walk on the moon.

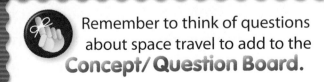

Remember to think of questions about space travel to add to the **Concept/Question Board.**

Space Messengers

The universe is filled with seventy sextillion stars (seven followed by twenty-two zeros). Like our solar system, many of them probably have planets. Soon the *Voyager 1* and *2* spacecraft will leave our solar system. In the near future they may contact another life form.

Voyager 2's journey began when it entered space propelled by a rocket launched on August 20, 1977. *Voyager 1* followed two weeks later. They were headed for Jupiter and Saturn.

Timing was everything on this mission. Jupiter, Saturn, Uranus, and Neptune were positioned in a way that happens only once every 176 years. This alignment was important. As each craft approached a planet, it would get caught in the planet's gravity. The planet, caught by the sun's gravity and orbiting through space, carried the spacecraft along. Soon the craft was flying at the same rate as the planet.

This new speed propelled *Voyager 1* and *2* on to the next planet, which was waiting in just the right place. This process cut the time it would take to reach Neptune from thirty years to twelve.

Voyager 1 and *2* sent back amazing photos of Jupiter. Scientists were in awe of the images. One image showed Jupiter's largest moon, Io. It had nine volcanoes erupting across its surface.

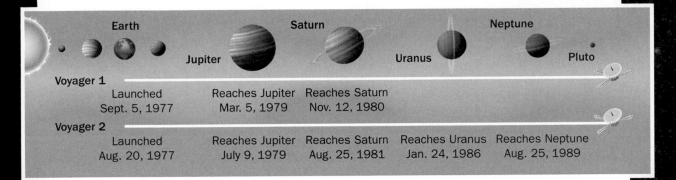

	Earth		Saturn			Neptune	
		Jupiter			Uranus		Pluto

Voyager 1

| Launched
Sept. 5, 1977 | Reaches Jupiter
Mar. 5, 1979 | Reaches Saturn
Nov. 12, 1980 | | |

Voyager 2

| Launched
Aug. 20, 1977 | Reaches Jupiter
July 9, 1979 | Reaches Saturn
Aug. 25, 1981 | Reaches Uranus
Jan. 24, 1986 | Reaches Neptune
Aug. 25, 1989 |

Saturn was the next stop. *Voyager 1* passed by Saturn's largest moon, Titan, then headed off into space. *Voyager 2*, though, continued on to Uranus and Neptune. Among its many discoveries, ten new moons were found orbiting Uranus. *Voyager* also showed that Neptune, like Saturn, was ringed.

The spacecraft are still traveling today. *Voyager 1* will leave our solar system around 2015. *Voyager 2* will follow around 2020.

They both carry record albums made of copper and gold. These records hold greetings spoken in fifty-five languages.

Think Link

1. When did *Voyager 2* reach Saturn?
2. Which planet has a moon named Io?
3. Which planets did *Voyager 1* reach?

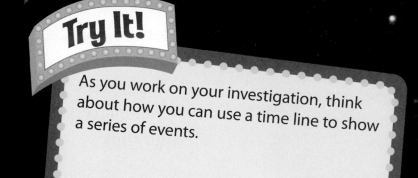

Try It!

As you work on your investigation, think about how you can use a time line to show a series of events.

Vocabulary Strategy

Sometimes you can use **word structure** to help you find the meanings of words. Look at the word *discouraged*. Use word structure to find the word's meaning.

Vocabulary

Warm-Up

Becca was tired of waiting. In fact, she was starting to lose confidence, which was an odd thing for her. Becca usually had great faith in her abilities. It had now been three weeks, though, since she had sent in her application. The judges at the citywide science fair were using it to decide whether Becca would be asked to join the competition. The most important part of the form was where she had to describe her project.

Becca was planning a presentation about eclipses. One kind of eclipse happens when the moon blocks all or part of the sun. The amount of sun varies depending on where the moon is in the sky during its orbit around Earth. Becca had already calculated the precise times eclipses would be occurring around the planet. She knew exactly where and when they would be taking place for the next five years.

One of Becca's responsibilities for the science fair would be designing a visual demonstration of her topic.

She wanted to build a miniature eclipse. A flashlight would act as the sun. It would shine onto a moon and Earth made of paper. Becca worried about transferring the model to the fair. It needed to be sturdy so that it would not break during the move.

Becca knew that the judges liked seeing the processes that students went through to create their projects. If they thought students did not spend enough time researching and developing their presentations, the judges would not advance them to the next round.

Becca looked up and saw her mother enter the room smiling. She held a thin envelope in her hand that she quickly gave to her daughter. The size of the envelope discouraged Becca. She had been hoping for a thick envelope filled with information. She expected the worst.

Taking a deep breath, Becca tore into the envelope. *Congratulations!* the letter read. *You have been accepted. More information will arrive later this week.* Becca grinned with relief.

GAME

Substituting Synonyms

Using a thesaurus, find a synonym for each selection vocabulary word. On a separate sheet of paper, rewrite the sentences from the selection that contain vocabulary words, but substitute a synonym for each vocabulary word.

Concept Vocabulary

The concept word for this lesson is **perseverance**. *Perseverance* means having the strength to keep going even when you might feel like quitting. For instance, inventors usually fail many times before finally finding a solution, but they never give up. Difficult tasks always require perseverance.

Genre

Biography is written about a real person's life by someone else.

Comprehension Strategy

☆ **Predicting**
As you read the selection, make predictions about what will happen next. Revise these predictions when necessary.

Ellen Ochoa: Reaching for the Stars

by Claire Daniel

Focus Questions

What kind of education is required to become an astronaut? How do astronauts help us understand the universe?

Ellen became a real expert with the RMS. In a NASA interview, Ellen explained that the robot arm is "a lot like your own arm." She said, "It has wrists and joints. It has an elbow joint, and it has a shoulder joint. And we can operate it in a variety of ways. The most common way is that we have two hand controllers—kind of like a video game where we're trained to operate the arm to move all the joints at once so we can move from one position to any other position by moving these two hand controls."

Ellen performed many other duties during her second space mission. For example, she used extremely precise instruments to measure the energy of the sun. These experiments were conducted to investigate how the sun's energy, which varies from year to year, affects Earth's climate and environment. This important research continued the work Ellen began during her first mission.

Mission 3: STS-96

The ISS is the largest space station ever built, with room for several people to live and work inside for months at a time. This makes longer and more complicated experiments possible. The ISS is made up of individual units, called modules, and has places for the space shuttle and other vehicles to dock. The United States and many other countries began constructing the ISS in 1998. In 1999, Ellen Ochoa was ready to do her part.

Ellen with the members of the STS-66 crew

In May and June of 1999, STS-96 undertook the first mission in which the space shuttle docked with the ISS. Ellen was in charge of transferring important supplies from the shuttle Discovery to the space station. These supplies would be needed by the astronaut members of the first ISS crew in 2000. The supplies included crew clothing, computers, cables, medical equipment, camera equipment, and electronic parts. The shuttle crew also unloaded two cranes that would be needed on the station in the future.

Tammy Jernigan anchored on a mobile foot restraint connected to Discovery's RMS

During a space walk for the STS-96 mission, astronauts Tammy Jernigan and Dan Barry ventured outside the spacecraft to move some bulky and unwieldy equipment. This operation needed more than four arms, so Ellen operated the RMS to assist. Her job was difficult because she could not see the robot arm. Instead, she had to rely on camera views of the RMS to do the job. Her previous experience operating the RMS to catch and retrieve satellites helped her, and the mission was successful.

Ellen was enthusiastic about helping to build the first permanent space station. She explained, "We're going to be performing research in many areas that should benefit people here on Earth. Secondly, we're using it to test technologies that can be used when we advance human space exploration, including possible trips to the moon or Mars. And third, it's really leading the way in terms of international cooperation, where countries are all working together focused on a common goal that benefits people around the world."

Mission 4: STS-110

In April 2002, Ellen Ochoa went into space for the fourth time, aboard the shuttle Atlantis. The goal of mission STS-110 was to install the truss, a structure that includes a sort of railroad running on the outside of the space station. The truss is designed to transport a robotic arm and carts with astronauts from one end of the ISS to the other. The truss also carries electrical power from one part of the station to another. The truss was needed to make the ISS a more useful place to do scientific research and other work.

Ellen worked in a module aboard the ISS to install the first section of the truss. She used the station's RMS to gently lift the truss out of the shuttle's payload bay. Then she and another crew member moved the truss onto a clamp at the top of the ISS Destiny laboratory. This was difficult work that required a great amount of concentration. It took the astronauts four hours to complete the job.

International Space Station

During the remainder of the mission, Ellen and her crewmates used the station's RMS to move astronauts from one place to another on the ISS. The astronauts connected a power supply to the truss, installed floodlights, and built a platform to work on.

Interview with Ellen Ochoa

Question: How do you spend your free time in space?

Ellen: Often there is not very much free time. If there is, we get together as a crew to eat dinner. Of course, looking outside the window towards views of the Earth is a favorite pastime. We do have access to e-mail. So in the evenings I read the daily news or a note from my husband.

Question: What is the funniest thing that happened to you in space?

Ellen: On my last flight, my kids were watching me on video. They love those goldfish [crackers]. We had some onboard with us, and I was putting them out in front of me. They were floating, and I was eating them out of the air. My two-year-old thought that that was the funniest thing he'd ever seen. He didn't understand how I could do that.

Question: What's the best thing about being in space?

Ellen: I can think of three things. First, having the opportunity to view the Earth from space is one. It's a spectacular view, and it's always changing. You launch during different seasons and during different times of the day, so you see different areas of the earth and different lighting. Also, the opportunity to experience weightlessness is very interesting and unlike anything that you can do on Earth. And then there's the opportunity to work with a crew and accomplish a task that you really find rewarding and challenging. That's a really special part of being on the space shuttle.

Question: What's the hardest thing about being on a mission?

Ellen: I guess the hardest thing is making sure that you're adequately prepared. You have to learn about a lot of different areas before you fly.

Question: What was your most exciting mission?

Ellen: That's like asking which of your children you love the best. They were all exciting, and they all had special things about them.

Conclusion

If someone had told Ellen Ochoa when she was a little girl that one day she would be working aboard a space station, she probably would have laughed. Space travel was so new and strange that it seemed impossible for a small girl in La Mesa, California. But Ellen grew up to become a famous astronaut as well as a great engineer. Her work has helped us see space more clearly and understand our world better. Ellen proves that when someone works hard, anything is possible.

Meet the Author

Claire Daniel

Claire Daniel is the pen name of the author of "Ellen Ochoa: Reaching for the Stars." A pen name, or pseudonym, is a fictitious name used by an author to conceal his or her identity. An author may want to conceal his or her identity to draw attention to the work rather than to him or herself. Book and magazine publishers sometime use a pseudonym for one author of a series of stories that would be shared by multiple authors.

For example, Dr. Seuss, author of *The Cat in the Hat* and other children's books, was a pen name for Theodore Seuss Geisel. Mark Twain, the author of *Huckleberry Finn* and *Tom Sawyer*, was a pen name for Samuel Langhorne Clemens. Rev. Charles Lutwidge Dodgson wrote *Alice in Wonderland* under the pen name Lewis Carroll, but used his real name when writing academic papers.

Our Corner of the Universe
Theme Connections

Within the Selections

1. What is one task that Ellen Ochoa performed while in space?

2. What do we use on Earth that was originally designed for space exploration?

Across Selections

3. Besides being an astronaut, what else does Ellen Ochoa have in common with the men of *Apollo 11*?

4. What has Ellen Ochoa done that was also done by the Native Americans in "Circles, Squares, and Daggers"?

Beyond the Selection

5. Why is the selecting and training of astronauts done so carefully?

6. Why are most astronauts also scientists?

Write about It!

Describe how you think the International Space Station might be used.

Remember to look for newspaper or magazine articles about NASA to add to the **Concept/ Question Board.**

Cosmonaut Yuri Gagarin

After World War II, the United States and the Soviet Union became locked into the Cold War. No shots were fired, but tensions were high. Each country wanted to prove that it was superior to the other. Most Americans were sure that the U.S. was the more advanced nation. Then, on October 4, 1957, the Soviets launched *Sputnik 1*—Earth's first human-made satellite. Fear and insecurity swept America. Would the Soviets now be able to spy— or worse—from space?

Four months later, the U.S. answered with its own satellite. The Space Race had begun. The next big goal was putting a person into space. Once again, the Soviets were first. On April 12, 1961, *Vostok 1* carried cosmonaut Yuri Gagarin into orbit. It was a historic milestone for humankind.

Communist leaders promoted Gagarin's flight as an example of Soviet superiority. They stressed that Gagarin was a "peasant" who had become a national hero because of the fairness of the Communist system. Gagarin had been born on a farm, but he had also studied physics, attended college, and flew in the Soviet Air Force.

Gagarin's flight had lasted barely two hours—enough time to circle the planet once—but he became an instant celebrity around the world. Gagarin wanted to keep working as a cosmonaut, but this path was discouraged. He was now an important Communist symbol. Flying was too dangerous.

Instead, Gagarin designed spacecraft. He also became a leader in the Soviet space program. Gagarin never lost his desire to fly, though. By 1967 he was training once again to fly jets.

Then tragedy struck. While on a flight with his trainer, Gagarin's plane crashed. The heroic cosmonaut died in 1968 at the age of thirty-four.

Since 2001, people around the world have been celebrating Yuri Night on April 12. Parties are held to honor Gagarin's historic deed and to inspire a new generation to take part in space exploration.

Think Link

1. Why was Yuri Gagarin considered an important symbol for Communism?

2. Why did the author use scare quotes around the word *peasant* in the third paragraph?

3. Who do you think won the Space Race?

Try It!

As you work on your investigation, think about how you could use quotation marks as *scare quotes*.

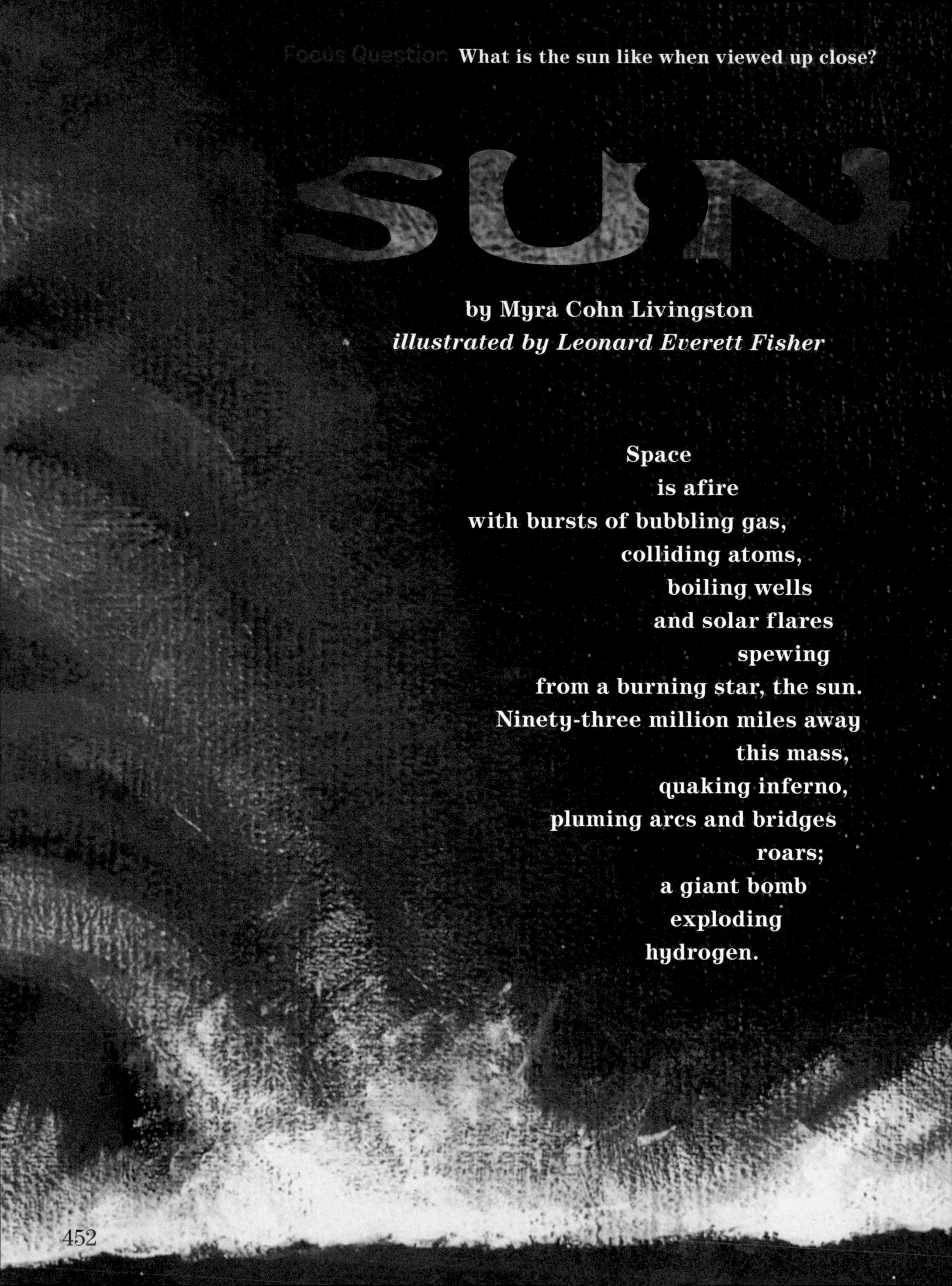

Focus Question **What is the sun like when viewed up close?**

SUN

by Myra Cohn Livingston
illustrated by Leonard Everett Fisher

Space
is afire
with bursts of bubbling gas,
colliding atoms,
boiling wells
and solar flares
spewing
from a burning star, the sun.
Ninety-three million miles away
this mass,
quaking inferno,
pluming arcs and bridges
roars;
a giant bomb
exploding
hydrogen.

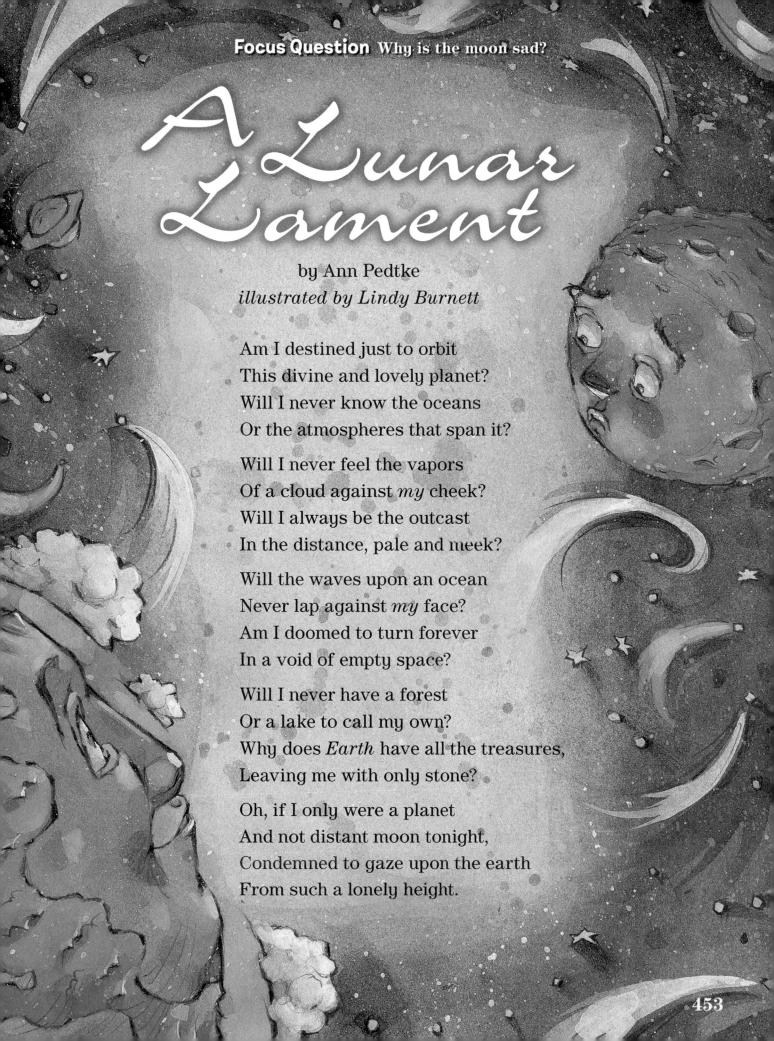

A Lunar Lament

by Ann Pedtke

illustrated by Lindy Burnett

Am I destined just to orbit
This divine and lovely planet?
Will I never know the oceans
Or the atmospheres that span it?

Will I never feel the vapors
Of a cloud against *my* cheek?
Will I always be the outcast
In the distance, pale and meek?

Will the waves upon an ocean
Never lap against *my* face?
Am I doomed to turn forever
In a void of empty space?

Will I never have a forest
Or a lake to call my own?
Why does *Earth* have all the treasures,
Leaving me with only stone?

Oh, if I only were a planet
And not distant moon tonight,
Condemned to gaze upon the earth
From such a lonely height.

Test-Taking Strategy: Skimming and prioritizing items

Some items on a test are easier than others. You might find it helpful to skim all the questions and answer the easiest ones first.

Skimming and prioritizing items

Good test takers look at each group of questions. They answer the easiest questions first. Then they go back and answer the harder items.

Read the questions below. Decide which one seems hard and which seems easy.

1. **In this story, Lisa was late because she**

   walked the dog   was sick

   helped her mother   missed the bus

2. **What is the author's main purpose for writing this story?**

   - to explain the difference among different kinds of clouds

   - to inform the reader about how clouds are formed

   - to show how some clouds are more likely to cause rain

   - to persuade the reader to spend more time watching clouds

The first question seems easy. It has fewer words and asks a question about a character. The second question is harder. It will take longer to read. You might want to skip this item and answer all the easier ones. You can come back to the harder items after you do the easier ones.

Collision in Space

Imagine that you are an astronaut on board a space station. You are near Jupiter, the largest planet in the Solar System. You look out the window. The giant brown and red planet fills your vision. Its surface is blanketed with thick clouds. You wonder what it would be like to be on Jupiter, looking at these clouds from the other side.

Suddenly, a huge spinning piece of ice and rock flashes past! You stare in amazement. You see more of these bodies streaking through space. They are on course to collide with Jupiter. "Look out the window!" you call to the others on board. Then you prepare to view an awesome series of impacts.

In 1994, a comet really *did* crash on Jupiter. There is not actually a space station near the planet, but telescopes on Earth and in space recorded the event. This was very exciting, not just for scientists, but for everyone. It was the first time humans got to witness and record the collision of two bodies in the Solar System.

GO ON

In some ways, comets are like very small planets. Like planets, they almost always orbit the sun. Comets that get close to the sun begin to warm up. Since a comet is made of ice, rock, and dust, it can leave behind a "tail" of gas and particles. In fact, the word *comet* is Greek for "long-haired star."

The comet that hit Jupiter was called *Shoemaker-Levy*. It was named for the people who discovered it. The comet was unusual in some ways. Though most comets orbit the sun, this one orbited Jupiter. Some people think this was because Jupiter's powerful gravity "captured" the comet when it passed by.

Jupiter's strong gravity probably tore the comet into more than twenty pieces. Many of these fragments were over a mile across! All of them ended up crashing on Jupiter.

Back in the imaginary space station, you see the first spinning comet fragment approach Jupiter. It hits the planet's atmosphere. The friction of the air heats the comet into a fireball. A moment later, there is a flash of light as the comet strikes the planet. You will later learn that the plume from the impact rose more than one thousand miles. As the first impact fades, the next comet fragment hits. Over time, the series of falling pieces leaves behind a chain of fading fireballs.

Today, scientists continue to watch Jupiter closely. They wonder if another comet will get caught in its gravity. If one does, it will be another spectacular event.

1. Read these sentences from the passage.

   Suddenly, a huge spinning piece of ice and rock flashes past! You stare in amazement.

   Which word means the same as *amazement*?

   Ⓐ fright
   Ⓑ pleasure
   Ⓒ interest
   Ⓓ surprise

Test Tips
- Choose the best answer to the question.
- Mark your answer carefully.
- Skip difficult items and come back to them later.

2. How was the *Shoemaker-Levy* comet DIFFERENT from most comets?

   Ⓕ It left behind a "tail."
   Ⓖ It orbited the planet Jupiter.
   Ⓗ It was made of ice, rock, and dust.
   Ⓘ It became cold as it neared the sun.

3. What is believed to have caused the *Shoemaker-Levy* comet to break into pieces?

   Ⓐ heat from the sun
   Ⓑ its long tail
   Ⓒ Jupiter's strong gravity
   Ⓓ the plume from the impact

4. Describe what it looked like when the comet hit Jupiter. Use details and information from the passage to support your answer.

STOP

457

Unit 5

Going West

What do you think about when you hear the phrase "going West"? Why did pioneers explore the American West? Does the American West make you think of adventure and exploration? Does it make you think about America's wild history, cowboys, or the Gold Rush?

Fine Art Theme Connection

Look at the painting *Surveyor's Wagon in the Rockies* by Albert Bierstadt.

- How do your ideas about the unit theme compare to the images in the painting?

- What images would you add to the painting to illustrate the theme Going West?

Albert Bierstadt. *Surveyor's Wagon in the Rockies.* 1859.

Oil on canvas. $7\frac{1}{4}$" × $12\frac{7}{8}$". St. Louis Art Museum, gift of J. Lionberger Davis.

458

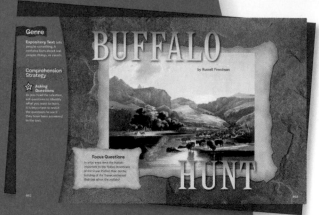

Read the article to find the meanings of these words, which are also in "Buffalo Hunt":

+ banners
+ pitched
+ stampede
+ lurking
+ ladles
+ procession
+ cow
+ elders
+ legends
+ sacred

Vocabulary Strategy

An **appositive** is a noun that follows another noun to modify or name it. Authors sometimes use apposition to clarify the meanings of words. Look at the word *ladles*. Find how the author uses apposition to define the word.

Vocabulary
Warm-Up

Hi, Mario!

Our vacation to South Dakota has been awesome so far. Yesterday we arrived at the Double B Ranch (the *Bs* stand for *Buffalo Bonanza*). Banners that hang at the entrance and along the main drive directed us to the campsite. It sits inside a fenced area because more than one thousand buffalo roam around the ranch! One family tried to set up their tent outside the fenced area, but Mr. Saunders, the owner, said, "Tents have to be pitched inside here. If something spooks that herd and they begin to stampede, trust me, you'll be glad you are inside the fence!" Then he explained the dangers of hiding in bushes or behind a tree like a lurking predator. "Don't sneak up on these guys. You don't want to startle them."

Last night we ate barbecued buffalo meat and baked beans under the stars. The ranch hands used ladles, or giant spoons, to scoop out the grub. There are a lot of people here, and I ended up clear at the end of the procession.

By the time I made it through the long line, I was feeling a little guilty. Buffalo meat is supposed to be a delicacy, but a cow kept staring at me the whole time I was waiting to get food!

I will write again and let you know what else happens this week.

Your friend,
Hector

Hi, Mario!

Yesterday was the coolest day yet! We visited one of the nearby Indian reservations. The campers met inside a museum filled with Native American crafts. Then we listened to a couple of the tribe's elders explain their culture and legends. One of the older men, Harvey Brown Bull, told us the story of the white buffalo. It is a Lakota Sioux legend about respecting Earth and other people. Today when a white buffalo is born, it is seen as a sacred event that should be treated with respect.

I will see you in just a few days.
Hector

Substituting Synonyms
Using a thesaurus, find a synonym for each selection vocabulary word. On a separate sheet of paper, rewrite the sentences from the selection that contain vocabulary words, but substitute a synonym for each vocabulary word.

Concept Vocabulary

The concept word for this lesson is **devastation.** *Devastation* occurs when something is ruined or destroyed by violence. Natural disasters, like earthquakes, can result in devastation to a city. In what other ways can devastation occur?

461

Genre

Expository Text tells people something. It contains facts about real people, things, or events.

Comprehension Strategy

Asking Questions

As you read the selection, ask questions to identify what you want to learn. It is important to revisit the questions to see if they have been answered in the text.

Focus Questions

In what ways were the buffalo important to the Native Americans of the Great Plains? How did the building of the Transcontinental Railroad affect the buffalo?

FALO

by Russell Freedman

HUNT

Buffalo Hunter. c.1844. **Artist Unknown.**
Oil on canvas. Santa Barbara Museum of Art.

A Gift from the Great Spirit

Over blazing campfires on winter nights, Indian storytellers spoke of the buffalo. They told tales of buffalo giants and buffalo ghosts, of buffalo that changed magically into men, of children who were raised by buffalo and understood their language.

In olden times, it was said, buffalo used to eat Indians. They ate so many Indians that a legendary figure called Old Man had to put a stop to it. He organized a race between the buffalo and the Indians to decide who should eat whom. The Indians won.

On the Great Plains of North America, every Indian tribe had a rich and ready store of buffalo tales and legends. According to the Comanche, buffalo came from gigantic caves somewhere on the windswept ranges of the Texas Panhandle. Each spring, the Great Spirit sent throngs of buffalo from those hidden caves onto the open plains, as a gift to the Indian people.

Up North, the Blackfoot said that a lake in Canada was the place where the buffalo began. They were born beneath the water, in the darkest depths of the lake. If you could visit that sacred spot on the right night, at exactly the right time, you would hear an eerie rumbling coming from the middle of the lake. Then you would see the buffalo rise out of the water and crowd onto the shore, their shaggy fur wet and dripping, their curved horns gleaming in the moonlight.

To the Plains Indians, the buffalo, or American bison, was the most important animal on Earth. This snorting, lumbering beast provided almost everything the Indians needed to stay alive. The buffalo kept their bellies full and their bodies warm. It supplied raw materials for their weapons, tools, ornaments, and toys. The rhythm of their daily lives was ruled by the comings and goings of the great buffalo herds.

It is little wonder that the Indians worshipped the buffalo as a sacred animal. Before and after every hunt, they praised the spirit of the buffalo and thanked him for giving his meat. Men, women, and children carried buffalo-shaped rocks and fossils for good luck. They believed in the powerful magic of buffalo dreams. When they died, they hoped to go to a happy hunting ground in the sky where buffalo flourished. Looking into the night sky, the Pawnee believed that the Milky Way was formed by dust left behind by the spirit-buffalo.

Catching the Wild Horse. **George Catlin.** The Thomas Gilcrease Institute of American History and Art, Tulsa, Oklahoma.

As recently as 150 years ago, countless millions of buffalo still roamed the prairies and plains. They ranged from the Mississippi River westward to the Rockies, and from Canada down to the Rio Grande. Native American hunters had been stalking the animals for many thousands of years. During most of that time, the Indians had neither horses nor guns. They hunted on foot, and they killed their prey with stone-tipped arrows and spears. They knew how to creep up on a grazing herd, how to surround the buffalo, and how to drive them into corrals or stampede them over cliffs.

Without horses, the Indians had to travel on foot whenever they moved their encampments. Back then, they used big shaggy dogs as pack animals to help carry their tipis and other belongings. Sometimes on a long journey the dogs would grow tired and begin to droop and lag and hang their tongues. Then someone would cry, "Buffalo ahead! Fresh meat in plenty!" And the dogs would bound forward as though they had just set out. Later, the Indians would remember that era as their Dog Days.

The first horses were brought to North America by Spanish explorers in the 1500s. Within a century or so, runaway horses had drifted northward from Spanish settlements in Mexico and were roaming the plains in wild herds. The Indians learned to capture and tame those wild horses, and the horses changed their lives.

Now they could travel long distances to find the buffalo. They could chase the herds and kill the choicest animals. And with pack horses, they could carry bigger tipis and more possessions with them as they traveled across the plains. In time, the Indians became some of the world's finest horsemen, experts at hunting and fighting on horseback.

When white trappers and traders began to visit the Great Plains in the early 1800s, about 250,000 Indians were living in the region. They belonged to some two dozen distinct tribes, each with its own language and customs. Many of these tribes had migrated from the woodlands of the East, but only a few, like the Pawnee of Kansas and Nebraska, still practiced the old arts of farming and fishing.

Most of the Plains Indians had given up the settled life of farmers and fishermen to follow the buffalo herds. They spent the winter in sheltered camps. But in spring they folded their tipis and roamed the plains. They hunted other animals besides the buffalo, of course—deer, antelope, elk, and an occasional bear. But buffalo meat was their staple food, buffalo hunting their main occupation.

A Plains tribe was made up of many small, independent bands. Once or twice a year, all the bands belonging to a tribe would assemble for a great religious ceremony, a tribal council, or a communal hunt.

But mostly, the bands moved about on their own. Each band had its own encampments, or villages. And each band hunted in a different part of the tribal territory.

Hunting was a man's responsibility. Every able-bodied boy was taught that he should become a fearless hunter and warrior. Small boys ran about yip-yapping in play hunts, dreaming of the day when they would be big enough to ride after a herd of stampeding buffalo. A successful hunter could provide for many people. He became a man of influence, entitled to honors and privileges.

Women were responsible for putting the buffalo and other game to good use. It was a woman's job to skin and butcher the buffalo, to preserve the meat and tan the hides. As Indian girls grew up, they learned from their mothers and grandmothers the art of transforming a dead buffalo into a thousand practical and useful objects.

Painted elkskin robe. Late 19th Century. Crow. The National Museum of the American Indian, Smithsonian Institution.

The buffalo was the biggest animal on the plains. A full-grown bull stood six feet tall at the humped shoulders and weighed a ton or more. An angry bull could stab a bear to death. He could toss a wolf so high into the air that the wolf would be killed by the fall.

While buffalo were somewhat dim-sighted, they could hear the faintest sounds and smell enemies from three miles away. And when they sensed danger, they moved fast. A bull or cow could wheel about on its slim hind legs and run as fast as a horse. When a whole herd stampeded, the earth trembled.

White explorers were astonished at the size of the herds they saw as they crossed the Great Plains. There were times when buffalo stretched endlessly across the countryside as far as the eye could see. Artist George Catlin described these herds when he traveled west during the 1830s to study and paint the Indians. "Buffalo graze in immense herds and almost incredible numbers," he wrote. "And they roam over vast tracts of country."

No one really knows how many buffalo roamed the prairies and plains before the white man came. The Indians thought there were enough buffalo to last forever. It seemed impossible that they could ever disappear.

The Hunt

On the day set for starting a hunt, everyone was up at sunrise. The women went right to work, packing their household belongings and getting everything ready for the move. Youngsters rounded up the horses and dogs. The men gathered in small groups to discuss the day's plans.

After a quick morning meal, the leaders of the hunt, the marshals, assembled. They took their feathered banners in their hands, mounted their horses, and gave the signal to break camp.

With that, the Indian village disappeared almost like a puff of smoke. Tipis dropped to the ground as the women removed the buffalo-skin walls and took down the long poles that held the tipis erect.

The poles were now put to a different use. Lashed to the sides of a horse so they trailed behind on the ground, the poles supported a sturdy rawhide platform called a travois (tra-VOY). This platform held the folded tipi walls and the family's household goods. Sometimes small children or sick people sat on top of the pile to be hauled along by a strong packhorse. Dogs also worked as pack animals, pulling travois designed to fit their size and strength.

When the horses and dogs were harnessed and loaded and ready to go, the people and their animals moved out across the plains. The warriors, mounted on the best hunting horses, rode along in front. They were followed by boys and girls driving the herd of extra horses. Behind them came the women leading the packhorses, along with the small children and the old folks, some riding, some walking, and some being carried on the travois. Every woman had a heavy pack on her back. The men never carried packs. They kept their arms free to use their weapons in case of a surprise attack.

Scouts rode far ahead of the marching people, and far to either side, watching for signs of buffalo or lurking enemies. Other warriors acted as a rear guard. They followed the group at a distance, seeing that no one lagged behind.

Strung out across the prairie, the Indians formed a grand procession. People sang as they marched along, dogs barked, horses whinnied, bells jingled. They moved forward each day by easy stages, so their horses would be in good condition when they found the buffalo.

At the end of a day's march, the marshals picked the spot where they would pitch camp. The women quickly put up the tipis and prepared the evening meal as the men gathered to chat and smoke.

On the open plains, the Indians usually camped in a circle, with the doorway of each tipi facing east to catch the morning sun.

When they reached the territory where they expected to hunt, the scouts fanned out across the countryside, looking for buffalo. Everyone else waited in the hushed camp. Marshals moved quietly from one tipi to the next. They reminded people in low tones not to sing or shout or make any loud noise that might scare off the buffalo, which could hear weak and distant sounds.

The scouts, meanwhile, searched for buffalo signs. Sometimes they relied on animal helpers. The Comanche watched for ravens. They thought that if a raven circled four times overhead and cawed, it would then fly off toward the buffalo. A Cheyenne hunter would find a cricket, hold it in his hand, and wait to see which way its antennae pointed. The buffalo, he believed, would be found in that direction.

Buffalo Chase with Bows and Lances. 1832–33. **George Catlin.** Oil on canvas. National Museum of American Art, Smithsonian Institution.

When a herd was sighted, the successful scout rushed back to camp. As he arrived, people crowded around, greeting him with congratulations and thanks. First he smoked a ceremonial pipe with one of the band's elders. Then he reported what he had seen.

The chase usually started the next morning. As soon as it was light enough to see, the hunters mounted their horses. Riding close together, they stayed downwind from the herd, so the buffalo would not catch their scent.

When they were as close as they could get without disturbing the buffalo, they paused and waited. The marshals looked over the area and selected the best spot to launch the attack. Silently, they led the hunters forward and spaced them evenly, so that each would have a fair start. Then one of the marshals rode out in view of both hunters and buffalo. He waved his hand above his head, and the chase began.

Bending low over their horses, the Indians galloped toward the grazing herd. At first the buffalo paid little attention. Often the hunters would almost reach the herd before the buffalo became alarmed and started to run.

The Buffalo Hunt No. 39. 1919. **Charles M. Russell.**
Oil on canvas. Amon Carter Museum, Fort Worth, Texas.

Each man acted on his own now. Holding his bow in his left hand, urging his horse on with the whip strapped to his right wrist, a hunter picked his target and went after it at full speed. His horse was trained to approach the buffalo from the right, so the rider could shoot his arrow to the left, toward the animal. As he closed in, he aimed for a spot just behind the buffalo's last rib, where the arrow would pierce the animal's lungs. A single well-aimed arrow could kill the biggest buffalo.

Sometimes an arrow would strike with such force that it would be completely buried. It might pass all the way through the animal, come out the other side, and drop to the ground. If an arrow failed to go deep enough, the hunter might reach over, pull it out of the buffalo, and use it again.

Once an arrow hit its mark, the hunter instantly took off after another buffalo. His horse understood exactly what to do. Running free, guided only by words or knee pressure, a trained hunting pony would leap away from a buffalo's horns as soon as it heard the twang of the bowstring.

Some men found the bow and arrow too tame. They preferred to use spears, for it took more strength and courage to spear a buffalo. To carry only a spear on the hunt was a mark of daring and pride.

With any weapon, the chase was risky. Horses stumbled in prairie-dog holes. Wounded buffalo lashed out with their horns. Sometimes an enraged bull crashed headlong into a horse and rider. The buffalo claimed many victims as hunters were trampled in the dust or died of broken bones.

While the chase was thrilling, it wasn't always the best way to hunt. During a typical chase on horseback, each hunter might bring down two or three buffalo. Under the right conditions, the Indians could get better results with less danger by hunting in the old way—on foot.

In that case, they would stake their horses and creep up
on the buffalo, crawling on hands and knees through tall
grass. As long as the Indians were hidden, the buffalo would
go right on grazing, even as arrows flew silently around
them. Each man might shoot several buffalo in quick
succession before the others became frightened and ran off.

In winter, when the grass offered little cover, a hunter
might sneak up on a herd disguised in a buffalo robe. Or he
could drape himself in the skin of a white wolf. Healthy
buffalo in herds did not fear wolves and didn't run when they
saw one.

If a herd was small enough, the Indians sometimes
surrounded the buffalo on foot. Approaching downwind, they
fanned out, moved in from all sides, and formed a tight ring.
Then they ran in circles around the herd, whooping and
yelling and waving their arms as the terrified animals milled
about in confusion. Slowly the Indians closed the circle until
they were close enough to let go with their arrows and
spears.

The first buffalo to be hit would fall near the outside of the
circle, blocking the path of those inside the ring. As more
buffalo fell, their bodies trapped the others. Sometimes not
a single animal escaped alive.

On horseback, the Indians could surround bigger herds, galloping around them in a circle. One afternoon in 1832, the artist George Catlin, armed with his pencil and sketchbook, watched from a distance as 500 Sioux horseman surrounded a herd near the present site of Pierre, South Dakota. By sundown, the hunters had killed 1,400 buffalo.

From the Brains to the Tail

A successful hunt called for a feast. Beside the campfire that evening, a medicine man offered prayers of thanksgiving. He thanked the spirits for their aid during the chase, and he thanked the buffalo for giving his meat to the people. Choice bits of meat were sliced off, held up for the spirits to see, then buried as an offering.

There was plenty for everyone to eat. A single fat buffalo cow supplied enough meat to feed a hundred hungry people. They gorged themselves on fresh tongue roasted over the open fire, on tasty morsels cut from the buffalo's hump. They ate hot, dripping ribs and steaks. And they feasted on yards of roasted gut, turned inside out, stuffed with chunks of meat, and seared over glowing coals. The sweet, nutritious bone marrow was saved for the old folks. It was the only meat their toothless gums could chew.

Most of the meat taken during a big hunt was preserved for the future. The women cut the meat into strips and hung it over high poles to dry.

Comanche Village in Texas, Women Dressing Robes and Drying Meat. 1834–35. **George Catlin.** Oil on canvas. National Museum of Art, Smithsonian Institution.

After several days, this sun-dried meat, called jerky, was so well preserved that it would last for months. It could be carried anywhere and would not spoil, even during the hottest months.

Some of the dried meat was pounded to a pulp, mixed with buffalo fat, and flavored with crushed nuts, berries, and fruit. This was called pemmican. Packed in buffalo-skin bags, pemmican would last for years without spoiling. Sliced and dipped in wild honey, it was nourishing and delicious, a favorite food among the Indians, and later the white fur traders as well.

Every part of the buffalo that could be chewed, swallowed, and digested was used for food. And every other part was put to some use.

Indian women spent a great deal of time and effort tanning buffalo hides. After a hunt, the fresh hides were spread out on the ground, hairy side down, and pegged in place. Using scrapers made of buffalo bone, the women scraped all the flesh, fat, and blood from the hides. They cured and bleached the hides in the sun, and soaked them in a tanning fluid of buffalo brains, liver, and fat mixed with water. Then they worked the hides for several days—rubbing, kneading, squeezing, stretching—to make them soft and supple. A good hunter might have several wives working on hides taken from the animals he had killed.

Buffalo Chase, A Single Death. 1832–33. **George Catlin.** National Museum of American Art, Smithsonian Institution, Washington, DC.

If the hides were to be used as winter robes, the hair was left in place. Thick-furred buffalo robes made warm and comfortable cloaks and bedding. They could be cut and stitched into caps, earmuffs, leggings, and mittens. The finest robes came from buffalo killed during the winter, when nature gave the animal a full coat to protect it from snow and cold.

With the hair scraped off, the hides were smoked over fires to make them waterproof. They could then be fashioned into dozens of useful articles. They were used for the walls of tipis, for clothing and moccasins, for pouches, purses, and saddlebags. Babies were carried in cradleboards lined with the softest buffalo calfskin. The dead were laid to rest wrapped in buffalo-hide winding sheets.

Thick rawhide from the necks of old bulls was stretched to make tough war shields and the soles of winter moccasins. Strong sinews from the neck and back of the buffalo provided bowstrings and thread. The buffalo's hair was twisted into ropes and bridles, woven into ornaments, stuffed into leather balls. Its stomach became a water jug, its tail a flyswatter.

Buffalo horns were used for cups, ladles, and spoons, and to carry hot coals to the next campground. The hooves produced glue; the fat, soap. The bones were shaped into knives, spears, and tools of many kinds. On the northern plains, the backbone with ribs attached made a toboggan for children in winter.

Even the buffalo's droppings were valuable. On the treeless plains, firewood was scarce. But there was an endless supply of sundried buffalo dung left behind by the grazing herds. These prized "buffalo chips" burned slowly, produced a hot fire, and were ideal for cooking. They were used for that purpose by the Indians, and later by white settlers too.

A fall buffalo hunt would continue until the band had all the hides and meat it needed for the winter. Then the Indians would settle down in their winter camps. Every band had its favorite winter camping sites near woods, in a sheltered canyon, or along a river bottom. Instead of camping in a circle, as they did on the open plains, the Indians pitched their winter tipis in a line that sometimes stretched for miles along the canyon floor or the river's banks.

The Herd on the Move. 1862. **William J. Hays.** Toned lithograph. Amon Carter Museum, Fort Worth, Texas.

A tipi provided a warm and cozy winter home. Because it was shaped like a cone, it could withstand the most violent winds and blizzards. Its walls were waterproof. An open fire in the center of the tipi furnished heat, light, and a stove for indoor cooking. The smoke spiraled up through an adjustable smoke hole at the top of the tipi. At night, firelight would shine through the translucent buffalo-skin walls, and from the outside, the tipi glowed like a lantern.

Tipis were usually owned by the women who made them. A typical tipi measured perhaps fifteen feet across at the base, allowing sufficient living space for the family and its possessions. It could be put up in fifteen minutes by the women of the household. It could be taken down in five minutes. And it could be packed on a horse travois and carried anywhere.

When the hunting was good, the Indians went into winter camp with tons of sun-dried buffalo meat. They didn't have to hunt day after day, all winter long, for fear of starving. Between hunts, they were free to do as they wished. "It was a great life," said Tom Le Forge, a white man who lived several years with the Crows. "At all times I had ample leisure for lazy loafing and dreaming and visiting."

With the Buffalo Gone

Year after year without fail, the buffalo drifted back and forth across the plains in tune with the seasons. Usually they traveled in small bands. But during the late summer rutting season, they gathered in enormous herds that numbered hundreds of thousands of animals. A truly great herd might be fifty miles long and take days to pass by.

Indians had hunted the buffalo for thousands of years without making much of a dent in the herds. Sometimes they killed more animals than they could use. When they drove a herd over a cliff, they could not always carry away all the meat. But for the most part, the Indians were not wasteful. They hunted when they needed meat and hides.

As white people came to the plains, the buffalo herds began to dwindle. By the early 1800s, trading posts were springing up all over the West. White traders wanted buffalo robes and tongues for profitable markets in the East. In exchange, they offered guns, tools, tobacco, whiskey, and trinkets. The Indians had always hunted for their own needs. Now, by killing a few more buffalo, they could obtain the white man's goods.

Soon the Indians were killing buffalo for their hides and tongues alone. Tongues packed in salt were shipped in barges down the Missouri River, to be sent to the cities of the East, where they were sold as an expensive delicacy. Buffalo robes became fashionable as lap robes and blankets. White people had them made into fur coats. During the 1830s and 1840s, hundreds of thousands of robes were shipped east.

By then, white hunters were beginning to kill more buffalo than the Indians. Pioneers traveling westward in covered wagons shot the animals for food along the way, scaring off entire herds. Before long, few buffalo could be found along the great trails leading west. Then the United States Army hired professional hunters to supply buffalo meat to western military posts. And as railroads were built across the prairies and plains, white hunters furnished buffalo meat for the railroad construction crews.

Buffalo hunting became a popular sport. Many travelers felt that a trip west wasn't complete unless they had shot themselves a buffalo. American millionaires and European noblemen toured the West in style, with servants to hand them their guns and champagne to drink after the hunt. Railroads began to feature special excursion trains through buffalo country. As the trains chugged along, passengers could poke their guns through the open windows and fire away at the grazing herds.

By the 1860s, Indian tribes found that the buffalo were disappearing from their traditional hunting grounds. When they went elsewhere to hunt, they were followed almost immediately by white hunters, soldiers, and settlers. "Wherever the whites are established, the buffalo is gone," complained the Sioux Chief White Cloud, "and the red hunters must die of hunger."

Indians who once had been friendly to white people vowed to go on the warpath. Alarmed by the large-scale slaughter of their herds, angry warriors from many tribes banded together. They began to attack wagon trains, ranch houses, and railroad construction crews.

There were still about eight million buffalo left on the plains in 1870, when a newly invented tanning process sealed the fate of the remaining herds. For the first time, commercial tanneries in the East could turn buffalo hides into expensive leather. A single hide now brought as much as $3—more than a factory worker earned in a week in those days. A professional hide hunter could bag as many as two hundred buffalo in one day.

Organized bands of hide hunters shot their way south from Kansas to Texas. Armed with powerful long-range rifles with telescopic sights, they began to slaughter buffalo at the rate of a million a year. As the animals fell, gangs of skinners stripped them of their valuable hides and left the carcasses to rot on the prairie.

Indian war parties attacked the hide hunters wherever they found them, but the hunters could not be stopped. Within a few years, the Indians saw their main source of food, clothing, and shelter vanish.

At one time, perhaps sixty or seventy million buffalo had roamed the plains. By the early 1880s, the endless herds had been wiped out. Only a few hundred wild buffalo were still hiding out in remote mountain valleys.

With the buffalo gone, the proud and independent Plains Indians became a conquered people. Their way of life was destroyed, their hunting grounds taken over by white ranchers and settlers. Swept by starvation and disease, the great hunting tribes were confined to reservations, where they depended on government food rations. Their children were sent to boarding schools to learn the language and customs of the white man.

The days of the buffalo hunters had faded like a dream. But Indian storytellers still gather on winter nights to keep the old tales alive. They speak of a time when buffalo ruled the plains, and Indian warriors rode out to meet them.

I go to kill the buffalo.
The Great Spirit sent the buffalo.
On hills, in plains and woods.
So give me my bow; give me my bow;
I go to kill the buffalo.

—SIOUX SONG

Meet the Author

Russell Freedman

Russell Freedman seemed destined to be a writer. He grew up in a home frequently visited by authors. He later became a reporter and stumbled across a story about a sixteen-year-old boy who invented the braille typewriter. The story inspired his first book, *Teenagers Who Made History*. Freedman travels widely to do the research for his books. When he is not writing, he enjoys attending films, concerts, and plays.

Theme Connections

Within the Selection

1. Other than for food, what is one way the Plains Indians used the buffalo they hunted?

2. What is something from the Plains Indians' culture that shows that buffalo were sacred to them?

Beyond the Selection

3. Do you think any Native Americans hunt buffalo today? Why or why not?

4. Do we use animals today as completely as the Plains Indians used the buffalo? Why or why not?

Write about It!

Imagine you are part of a Plains Indian tribe preparing for a buffalo hunt. Describe what your day would be like.

Remember to look for pictures of buffalo to add to the **Concept/Question Board.**

491

Red Cloud

Driven by a belief in Manifest Destiny,* European Americans spread westward throughout the 1800s. Many Native American tribes moved westward as well, trying to stay ahead of the settlers. The tribes that did not relocate were forcibly removed. By mid-century, many Native Americans decided it was time to fight back.

Red Cloud, an Oglala Sioux, was born around 1821 in Nebraska. As a young man, he earned his reputation as a fierce warrior during battles with other tribes. European Americans saw him as a Sioux leader because of his status.

In the early 1860s a gold rush started in Montana. European Americans began pouring into the area. Most of them used the Bozeman Trail, which led settlers north from Colorado. The trail ran straight through Sioux territory. Red Cloud knew that the miners were only the first step toward losing Sioux lands and their way of life. Leading a group of warriors, he attacked forts built along the trail.

*An influential idea during the 1800s that the United States not only had the right, but was morally required, to take over all of the West.

492

By 1868, Red Cloud's successful campaign forced the United States to sign treaties. Red Cloud signed a treaty for his people, but the complicated language was unclear to him. It required the Sioux to move onto reservations scattered across South Dakota. Red Cloud felt tricked, but at least the Sioux were promised control over large areas of land. Or so they thought.

South Dakota Native American Reservations

Gold was soon discovered in the Black Hills. According to the treaty, this land belonged to the Sioux. However, the United States broke the treaty and its promises. U.S. General George Custer led his men into the area to secure it for mining. Many Indian warriors fought for this land, although Red Cloud did not.

As he got older, Red Cloud saw that the United States was too powerful to fight. He and his tribe's elders strove for peaceful solutions that would avoid bloodshed. In 1909, Red Cloud died on the Pine Ridge Reservation in South Dakota.

Think Link

1. Why did General Custer lead his army into the Black Hills?

2. Why do you think the author said that Red Cloud was born *around* 1821?

3. Reread the footnote at the bottom of the first page. Discuss the idea of Manifest Destiny.

Try It!

As you work on your investigation, think about how you can use footnotes.

The Journal of Wong Ming-Chung

by Laurence Yep
Illustrated by Karen Jerome

Focus Questions
Why does Wong Ming-Chung emigrate from China to the Western United States? How does he accomplish what he came to do?

Read the article to find the meanings of these words, which are also in "The Journal of Wong Ming-Chung":

+ immigrants
+ endure
+ rationed
+ squat
+ theory
+ registered
+ burden
+ raggedy
+ investment
+ boast

Vocabulary Strategy

An **appositive** is a noun that follows another noun to modify or name it. Authors use apposition to sometimes clarify the meanings of words. Look at the word *rationed*. Find how the author uses apposition to define the word.

494

Vocabulary
Warm-Up

I would like to tell you about my friend, Asmina Deng, and her family. They are immigrants, or new residents, from Sudan. They had to endure a lot of hardships before coming to America.

A civil war has raged in Sudan for many years. The Dengs are part of a large clan— a group of people descended from the same ancestors. Armies traveled through the countryside trying to kill or injure the Dengs' clan, so they fled to a camp for protection.

Life in the camp was not much easier. Food was rationed to ensure that everyone would get some. Each family received only a small amount per day. The Dengs' tent had no furniture, so they slept on the floor, and they either ate standing up, or they had to squat near the ground.

The Dengs' dream was to reach America. Their theory was that life would be better here. They registered with aid workers at the camp, and were selected for relocation. They started a new life in our town.

Of course, life here was still challenging. They had the burden of learning a new language and culture, and Asmina's parents would have to find jobs.

One day I was invited over to the Dengs' home. I saw that some of their furniture was broken, and Asmina's little sister wore raggedy clothes. They were thrilled with everything they had, but I wanted to help.

The principal of my school, Mrs. Austin, helped me organize a fund drive. All of the schools in our district participated. We raised almost $5000! A local bank even made an investment in the Dengs' name. It will grow in value over the years and help pay for Asmina's and her sister's college educations.

I am very proud of what I did, but it does not seem right to boast. I only wanted to help my friend.

GAME

Blank Out
Use the following clues to fill in the blanks with selection vocabulary words. Write your answers on a separate sheet of paper.

1. A statement in which one brags _ _ _ _ _ _
2. Limited to fixed portions _ _ _ _ _ _ _ _
3. People who live in countries in which they were not born _ _ _ _ _ _ _ _ _ _
4. To crouch down with the knees bent

   _ _ _ _ _
5. To put up with _ _ _ _ _ _
6. Worn-out _ _ _ _ _ _ _
7. Something hard to bear _ _ _ _ _ _
8. Officially recorded _ _ _ _ _ _ _ _ _ _

Concept Vocabulary

The concept word for this lesson is *aspiration. Aspiration* is the strong desire to achieve a goal. Most people's lives are guided by their aspirations. What do you aspire to be when you are an adult? What are you doing today that will help you reach that goal?

Genre

Historical Fiction is a story set in the past and includes events, problems, and possibly even characters from that time period.

Comprehension Skill

⭐ **Sequence**
As you read the selection, think about the order in which things occur and how this helps you understand the story.

The Wong

Journal of Ming-Chung

by Laurence Yep

illustrated by Karen Jerome

Focus Questions

Why does Wong Ming-Chung emigrate from China to the Western United States? How does he accomplish what he came to do?

Wong Ming-Chung's family has sent him to America to help his uncle strike it rich on the "Golden Mountain." In 1852 he joins his uncle on a gold claim outside of San Francisco. He works there with a company of Chinese immigrants led by the Fox. He also befriends an American boy named Hiram and comes to love the beauty of northern California. However, his company must constantly endure the raids of American "bullies." The company is able to keep its claim because the Fox comes up with clever ways to disguise their gold from the raiders. He hides it in a chamber pot and molds it into chopsticks. However, a mob finally runs the company off their claim. The Fox does not lose hope. He decides to take his company to the Sacramento delta to build levees. Wong Ming-Chung and his uncle agree to join them. However, his uncle, who is known back home for his big ideas and bad luck, is beginning to lose heart.

April 23

We followed the river all day without seeing anyone else.

It's like the end of the world. The only signs that humans had been here were the rotting rockers and ruined shacks.

We've camped for the night on an abandoned claim. The shack's roof is gone. A broken rocker sits beside the bank. Holes dot the banks. It looks like a battlefield.

The bank juts out like a finger, forming a breakwater. The river forms a lazy eddy behind it, which the Fox said would be a good spot for gold to drop out.

It's a good thing we've stopped, too. My feet are so sore that I soaked them in the river. For once, I'm grateful the water is icy cold.

Uncle sat like a lump beside me. He said he didn't see how we'd ever get really rich piling up dirt for levees. It's like we're in prison and every day we have to do hard work.

I reminded him of what the Fox said—that we'll still be sending home something. It might be less but it will still be a lot by Chinese standards. But Uncle just kept staring at the river.

The cook fixed a quick meal. Since we can eat only what we could carry away, everything's rationed. The meals are small—about what they'd be back in China.

But we're alive. That's the important thing.

April 24

I can hardly write these words. Uncle's left me.

This morning he told the Fox that he was going to stay and prospect. He bought his own ticket here, so he was free to leave like any employee. The Fox didn't need a carpenter anymore.

The Fox thought he'd lost his senses. After all, we'd just gotten chased off our claim by a mob. Uncle might not survive the next mob.

Uncle said he would search around here for a new claim. The Fox had said it was safe enough.

The Fox tapped his nose and said, "That's because there's no gold, or this would have told me."

Uncle has plans for home. He can't carry them out piling up dirt.

The Fox shook his head but suggested that I go with him.

I was scared at the idea of staying in the gold country. However, I thought of Uncle left alone in the mountains with his bad luck. He wouldn't last a week.

So I said I was going to help Uncle.

Uncle tried to use his authority as the head of the family and tell me to go with the Fox.

I refused.

Uncle said I was useless to him. He didn't want me hanging around his neck anymore like a stone.

I started to cry. Even if Father and Mother didn't need me, I had been sure Uncle did.

Uncle kept saying a lot of hurtful things. I tried to remind him that he had been glad when I came.

He insisted that had been a lie and said I was nothing but a burden on him.

The Fox came over and put his hands on my shoulders. As we walked away, he told the cook to leave some supplies and a few tools with Uncle.

The others made their farewells to Uncle, but I stood by the path ready to go. When we left Uncle, I didn't even look back.

We've made camp for our noon meal. However, I've had no appetite. I have to talk to someone, even if it's only my diary.

How could Uncle say those things? How?

Evening

I am writing this quickly by moonlight. I tossed and turned for hours. I can't let Uncle die in the mountains. Even if he doesn't love me, he is still family.

Everyone is asleep. I'm going to leave a note for the Fox and then sneak away and find Uncle.

April 25

About an hour after midnight last night, I reached the shack where we had left Uncle.

Uncle was sitting by the river. His shoulders were silvery in the moonlight.

I hesitated, expecting him to say more hurtful things. However, I'd had time to rehearse a speech. So I told him I'd try my best not to be a burden.

Uncle came rushing toward me before I could finish. He gave me a big hug. He told me he hadn't meant what he said.

I asked him why he had said it then.

Uncle thought I would be safer with the Fox. Those hurtful words were maybe the hardest things he'd ever had to say.

I'm not ashamed to say that we both wept. When we finished, we decided to look for gold in the morning.

To change our luck, I spun on my heel and recited, "Spin around, turn around, luck changes."

With a chuckle, Uncle copied me.

When we entered the shack to go to sleep, I had to laugh. There isn't any roof. We might just as well sleep outside.

However, the shack does have a fireplace. After we had gathered branches, I got a good fire roaring in the fireplace. Then we lay down in our blankets.

As I stared at the flickering flames, I thought of Mother. I used to squat by the front of the stove feeding the fire while she cooked. She used to like to hum, and the flames seemed to dance to her tune.

When will I see her again?

Later

Just had the worst nightmare. The mob was chasing me. I tried to run, but there was mud all around. I kept slipping and sliding and the mob kept gaining.

I must not have slept for very long, though, because the fire is just now dying. There are little dots of light all over the dirt floor of the cabin. They look like the torches the mob carried.

We're safe. We're safe. For now.

Still later

I'm trembling so badly I can barely write these words.

As I stared at the glittering floor, my curiosity got the better of my fear. What was reflecting the light?

So I crawled out of my blanket and crept across the floor with my nose almost touching the dirt.

I smelled gold. After spending all that time drying it and weighing it with the Fox, I know its smell by now.

That's it. Drying it!

The owner of the claim probably got the gold from the river. That means he had to dry it at night just as the Fox did with his gold.

There is gold dust scattered all around us.

I've got to wake Uncle and tell him.

Night

When I first told Uncle my theory, he didn't get excited.

Instead, he said it was an interesting idea, but why didn't the owner pick up the gold?

I said that maybe the light had to be just right from the fireplace.

Uncle looked thoughtful. He admitted that he hadn't noticed it when he first came in here. And it had still been day then.

I tried another explanation. The Fox had said this area had been worked in the early months of the gold rush.

There was still plenty of easy gold then.

Uncle eagerly agreed. He said that maybe the owner thought the floor wasn't worth the time.

I said that the owner had probably thought there would be nuggets just waiting to be picked upriver.

"Maybe even big as melons," Uncle had to laugh.

His boast in the village seems so long ago now.

We'll wait until sunrise. One of the walls should give us the lumber to build a rocker. Then we'll know.

I don't know how much sleep I'll get, though.

April 26

It took half the day to build the rocker. Then Uncle dug up a shovelful of soil by the fireplace. Carefully he carried it over to the rocker. I used my hat to pour water in.

Gently we began to make the rocker sway. Water ran through the holes at the bottom.

Then we held our breaths as the water poured out.

Uncle got discouraged right away when he didn't see anything.

I leaned my head this way and that, studying the wooden cleats from all angles. "Wait," I said. There was a faint gleam of light.

I ran my fingertips along the edge and held it up. Bits of gold clung to it.

April 27
Evening

We're rich!

It took only one and a half days to get a small pouch of gold! Uncle says we'll make our melon-sized nuggets the hard way, one flake at a time.

April 29

We went into town to buy supplies and tools like pails and things, but we were careful not to bring too much gold with us. Uncle let me do the talking since I've learned more American than he has.

The Americans laughed at us when we registered our claim. Then they told us there is no gold up there.

Uncle was curious when I insisted on buying a big chamber pot but he gave in.

Later, when I told him what the Fox used his chamber pot for, Uncle had a good chuckle.

May 4

We've cleaned out the cabin floor.

Uncle says our method of mining is worth more than the gold itself. We have to protect it.

I agree, so we've filled in the holes and smoothed over the dirt floor with branches. When we were finished, it looked just as we had first seen it.

Now it's on to the next abandoned claim.

May 24

We stop only at abandoned claims where there was likely to have been gold at one time. Uncle and I have picked up a lot from the Fox and his nose for gold. We look for spots where the river widens and the water slows, or behind breakwaters like our first claim. Sometimes we look inside the bends of the river or in the pool of slow water that forms just before the rapids.

So far we've tried ten more abandoned claims on this side of the river. Not every miner was careless, but two more have paid off. One of them was the richest of all.

Every time we file a new claim in town, they laugh at us some more. We're just the crazy Chinese to them.

We just smile.

While we work, I tell Uncle about some of the investment schemes I heard from my friends and some of the miners' letters. Uncle agrees with me that a store might be a good idea sometime in the future.

Uncle says that maybe once we have the store, we'll bring some of our cousins over from China.

May 26

We're going to take our gold into Sacramento. It's time to bank it.

May 27

En route to Sacramento

It's so strange to be riding a wagon back to Sacramento. The wagon's going directly there, so the trip is much shorter than when I first went into the gold fields.

Our gold is in a basket that I'm sitting on. No one looks twice at two dirty, raggedy guests. And we muddied up our basket to look just as run-down as us.

The hills are green from the winter rains. In the dells where the water gathers, flowers are blooming. I think you could grow anything here.

Hiram's right. It's the soil here that's the real gold in America. Once the metal's gone, it's gone. The earth will keep bringing up new crops each year.

I wonder what happened to Hiram and his dream of a farm?

May 31
Sacramento

I am writing this while the clerk in the American bank finishes weighing and recording our deposits.

When we arrived on the wagon in Sacramento, I saw that it was all new. About a month after I came through here, a terrible fire burned down everything.

When we opened our basket in the American bank, the bank clerk was very curious. He kept wanting to know if we had made a big strike. On the way down here, though, Uncle and I had already decided to just smile and say as little as possible.

Once we get our bank draft, we'll go over to Chinatown to the headquarters of our district back in China.

Then we can send some of the money in the American bank back to China. I wish I could hear the clan when our money gets there. They'll say Uncle must have luck as big as a mountain.

Meet the Author

Laurence Yep

Laurence Yep was born in San Francisco, California. His Chinese American family lived in an African American section of the city, so he had to commute to a bilingual school in Chinatown. Yep says he never encountered white culture in America until high school, and he always felt like an outsider. Growing up, he found few books that dealt with being a Chinese American. Because of this, he uses his own writing to fight racial stereotypes. He likes to write about this feeling of being an outsider and believes this is the reason he is so popular with young adult readers.

Meet the Illustrator

Karen Jerome

Karen Jerome teaches drawing and painting to children when she is not illustrating books. "We draw from photographs, famous painters' artwork, stuffed animals, horse statues, mirrors, and much more. That's how I learned to improve my skills as an artist, and that's how my students are improving theirs." Karen also likes to fish, ski, play tennis, take photographs, paint landscapes, and write children's stories.

Theme Connections

Within the Selection

1. How does Wong Ming-Chung help his uncle?
2. Why would prospectors leave gold behind on the floor of the shack?

Across Selections

3. How do you think Native Americans felt about Chinese immigrants in the West?
4. What is something that buffalo and gold had in common in the Old West?

Beyond the Selection

5. For what reason might an immigrant leave one country for another?
6. Before an entire immigrant family moves to a new country, often just one or two family members will move there first. Why do you think this happens?

 **Write about It!**

Describe how you would feel if you moved to a new country.

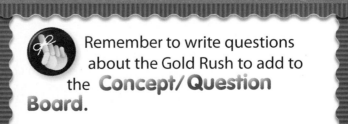 Remember to write questions about the Gold Rush to add to the **Concept/Question Board.**

511

Many Kinds of Californians

Through the years, the people who have called California home are as diverse as its landscape.

The first inhabitants were, as you might guess, Native Americans. Tribes such as the Mohave, the Chumash, and the Modec lived there for centuries before Europeans arrived. Each tribe thrived within its part of the state and traded with other tribes to get the things their land could not provide.

The first Europeans came to California by sea during the 1500s. Juan Cabillo, a Portuguese sailor, claimed what is known today as Baja California for Spain. A few years later, in 1579, Sir Francis Drake landed his ship in Northern California. He claimed the land around San Francisco for England. European immigrants, though, did not begin settling there for almost two more centuries.

Genre

Expository Text tells people something. It contains facts about real people, things, or events.

Feature

Sidebars contain information that enhances the main text. The sidebar's text is often set inside a box.

Trading was very common among California's Native Americans. Inland tribes traded items such as animal hides and stone tools for things like dried fish or salt that could be found only on the coasts. When tribes did not have items to trade, they used *wampum*, a form of money made from shells, to get the things they needed. The Chumash, whose name means roughly "the ones who make shell bead money," supplied wampum used throughout the region.

During that time, the Spanish Empire kept growing. By the mid-1700s, it stretched north from Peru into the American Southwest. The first Spanish settlements in California were missions run by the Catholic Church.

When Mexico won its freedom from Spain in 1821, the northern regions of the empire also became part of Mexico. The Mexican government gave most of it to wealthy Mexican families who already lived there, and the era of the *rancho* began. These giant cattle ranches employed many poor Mexicans and Native Americans as cowboys and laborers.

Mexico, 1821

Soon a steady stream of U.S. citizens from the East began coming to California. They did not like living under Mexican laws, so when the Mexican-American War broke out in 1846, they sided with the United States. The war ended two years later with an American victory, and California became a U.S. territory.

Think Link

1. How did the Chumash get their name?

2. In what year did Mexico win independence from Spain?

3. Using an encyclopedia or the Internet, find the difference between a territory and a state. What year did California become a territory?

Try It!

As you work on your investigation, think about how you can use sidebars.

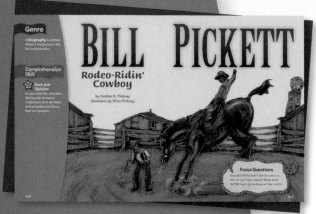

Read the article to find the meanings of these words, which are also in "Bill Pickett: Rodeo-Ridin' Cowboy":

- ✦ challenge
- ✦ trek
- ✦ association
- ✦ prospering
- ✦ enslaved
- ✦ bundled
- ✦ straddled
- ✦ stunt
- ✦ rickety
- ✦ lasso

Vocabulary Strategy

Sometimes you can use **word structure** to help you find the meanings of words. Look at the word *enslaved*. Use word structure to find the word's meaning.

Vocabulary

Warm-Up

Jacob knew that sailing from Philadelphia to the West would be a challenge. Being cooped up in his cabin or staring at the sea would quickly become boring, and, like any ocean trek, the trip would take a long time—probably a whole year. What Jacob had not expected were pirates.

Just one month into the voyage, an association of thieving sailors attacked. They were prospering from unlucky ships that crossed their path.

It was now three weeks later, and Jacob knew that most of the passengers were, in fact, lucky. The pirates had only robbed them. He and two other men had been kidnapped and held as enslaved captives by these vultures of the sea.

For fourteen hours each day, the men performed hard labor. At sunset, they were marched below deck, where each man's hands were tied to the others. Jacob and Tom were bundled together. Then, sitting in the dark, they planned their escape.

Finally the day arrived. A blazing afternoon sun bore down on the ship, and the lazy pirates began dozing off. Jacob straddled a cannon and pretended to clean it. He caught Tom's eyes first, then Burton's. The three of them barely nodded toward one another. Jacob knew this stunt was their only chance.

Quietly, Jacob swiveled the cannon toward the ship's interior. With his back to the pirates, Tom began cutting ropes that held a rickety raft alongside the ship.

BOOM!

Jacob's cannon blasted across the deck as the raft dropped into the water. The startled pirates bounced off one another, trying to figure out what had happened. Burton grabbed a rope with a large loop tied at one end. Like a skilled cowhand down at the ranch, Burton managed to lasso four pirates with one toss.

As the thieves tried to tackle them, the three men raced to the rail and jumped overboard. Now they just had to find that raft. . . .

GAME

Vocabulary Shuffle
Using a dictionary, find definitions for the selection vocabulary words and write each one on a separate index card. Shuffle the cards, and give half of them to another student. Take turns reading the definitions and trying to determine which word is being defined.

Concept Vocabulary

The concept word for this lesson is **spirited.** *Spirited* people are energetic, active, and courageous. In fiction, the hero is often a spirited character who does whatever it takes to solve a problem. You may know a spirited person in real life. He or she can usually get everyone excited and involved, whether it is for work or fun.

BILL

Rodeo-Ridin' Cowboy

by Andrea D. Pinkney

illustrated by Brian Pinkney

PICKETT

Focus Questions

How did Bill Pickett's family come to live on the Texas plains? What skills did Bill learn by working on the ranch?

Folks been tellin' the tale
since way back when.

They been talkin' 'bout
that Pickett boy.

Growed up to be a rodeo-ridin' man.

His story keeps spreadin' on
like swollen waters in the wide Red River.

Yeah, folks been tellin' the tale
since way back when.

And they'll keep on tellin' it
till time's time ends.

—A.D.P.

Long before Bill Pickett was born, a wagon train traveled west, all the way from South Carolina. It was 1854. Eager Americans were packing up their belongings and wheeling on to the Great Plains. Some of these pioneers were white folks, looking for a new life in a new land. The rest were black—enslaved people forced to follow their masters.

The men, women, and children loaded everything they owned into those covered wagons: croaker-sacks, homespun duds, and bedclothes bundled tight. To pass the time on the slow, steady trek, the southerners sang traveling songs:

> *Westward ho, where the gettin's good.*
> *On to the land of opportunity.*
> *Westward ho, gonna stake my claim.*
> *On to Texas, the Lone Star State.*

519

During this long journey a baby boy was born. His name was Thomas Jefferson Pickett. He was a free-spirited young'un. But he wasn't free. Born into slavery, he had to wake when his master said *wake,* work when his master said *work,* sleep when his master said *sleep.*

On the Texas plains Thomas grew up learning to brand cattle and swing a lariat. He and his family worked for the white folks, helping them tame the parched soil into prospering feed crops.

Then the Civil War ravaged the United States. And when the war ended, all enslaved people were declared free—as free as the bluebonnet blossoms that covered the Texas prairie.

Thomas married a woman named Mary Virginia Elizabeth Gilbert. They settled with other freed slaves at Jenks-Branch, a small community just north of Austin, Texas. Heaven blessed Thomas and Mary with thirteen children.

Their second-born child was Willie M. Pickett, but folks called him Bill. A young'un who took after his father, Bill was the feistiest boy south of Abilene. He was quick as a jackrabbit, more wide-eyed than a hooty owl—and curious.

Bill's parents now owned a small plot of land, where they raised chickens and pigs and grew sweet corn, tomatoes, and collards. They sold the vegetables and fruits in town to earn their living.

Bill's brothers and sisters helped tend the crops. But Bill was always wandering off. Most days he straddled the rickety corral gate to watch cattle drives tramp along the Chisholm Trail, a gritty stretch of road that snaked from the Rio Grande to the heart of Kansas.

Bill watched as the cowboys drove thousands of ornery longhorn steers past his parents' farm to stockyards in Kansas. Each trail crew had a trail boss, a cook, and a slew of cowboys. Bill always offered them a friendly "How do?" Some cowboys tipped their hats to signal hello. But they hardly ever stopped. And behind them they left hoof-beaten dirt and the smell of adventure.

In the evenings, after the last batch of corn pone had been eaten, Bill and his family would gather round the stove fire for a night of story swapping.

Bill had two cousins, Anderson Pickett and Jerry Barton, who were trail-driving horsemen. When they came to visit, they bragged about roping steer, breaking ponies, and protecting their trail crews against buffalo stampedes. Bill and his family loved to learn their campfire songs about nights on the trail, when Anderson and Jerry slept under the black western sky with nobody watching them but the stars.

All these songs and stories sparked Bill's imagination. They made him more up-jumpy than ever. He would lie in his bed and dream of the day when he'd be old enough to rope mossback cattle and help stray dogies keep up with the herd.

One afternoon Bill was straddling the gate as usual when he spotted an eye-popping sight. A bulldog was holding a restless cow's lower lip with its fangs. Bill moved closer to get a good look at how the dog's bite kept the squirming cow down. Soon Bill got to wondering: *If a small bulldog can bite-hold a big-lipped cow, why can't I do the same?*

Days later, on his way to school, Bill passed a band of cowboys from the Littlefield Cattle Company. The men were having a hard time branding their calves.

"Want some help?" Bill called to them. The cowboys looked at this brazen boy and went back to their work.

"I can hold one of them calves by the lip with my teeth, just like a bulldog," Bill went on. "I can do it sure as my name's Bill Pickett."

The cowboys turned out a rip-roarin' laugh.

But one of them put forth a challenge: "Let the boy go 'head and try it, if he dares."

The men roped the calf and threw it to the ground. Bill put his face down and sunk his teeth into the animal's lip. Then Bill held the calf firm while the cowboys pressed a hot branding iron into its side.

"Bulldoggin'—done by a young'un!" The cowboys cheered. Invented there and then by feisty Bill Pickett, that was bulldogging, bite-'em style.

When he was no more than fifteen and still itching for adventure, Bill set out to find his own way. Like many young'uns who came from large families, Bill had to go out and earn a living to help make ends meet.

Bill found work as a cowhand on ranches all over Texas. He spent long days saddling horses and mucking out their stalls. During the winter it was Bill's job to watch for wolves that crept up to the henhouses.

Bill learned to lasso and ride like the cowboys he'd seen pass by on the Chisholm Trail. He practiced bulldogging by catching steers that charged off into the mesquite brush. Soon Bill could tame broncs better than almost any other ranch hand. And every now and then, when work was slow, Bill went home to his mama and daddy's farm. Each time he had a new story of his own to tell his family.

Word of Bill's fearless riding spread from ranch to ranch. On Sundays folks gathered at local barnyards to watch Bill snatch a fire-eyed steer by the horns. Men, women, and young'uns rode on horseback and in their buggies to admire Bill's skill. They dropped coins in his hat to show how much they liked his horsemanship.

One morning, while he was working at a ranch in Taylor, Texas, Bill heard that the Williamson County Livestock Association had brought a fair to town. The fair included a full-scale rodeo. Men from the association had parked their wagons on a hill a few miles south of Taylor. Their rodeo was going to be a big event. Bill was determined to compete.

For the first time Bill performed his bulldogging stunt before a large rodeo crowd. As the steer thundered into the arena, Bill jumped from the back of his horse and grabbed it by the horns. Then, before the beast knew what was coming, Bill dug his teeth into the animal's tender upper lip. He raised his hands in victory as the grizzly critter went down without a fight.

Somebody let out a holler. "*Hooeee! Hooeee-hi-ooooh!*" All the folks watching the rodeo clapped and stomped.
"He throwed that beast but good!"
"That cowboy's brave clear down to his gizzards!"
"*Hot-diggity-dewlap!*"

After that Bill bulldogged at rodeos throughout the West. When he wasn't bulldogging for show, he still worked on ranches to make ends meet. But stories about Bill's rodeo ridin' kept on keeping on—from Texas to Arkansas to Oklahoma to Kansas to Colorado and on up through the hills of Wyoming. Now everybody wanted to see Bill perform his special bulldogging feat.

In 1905, when Bill was performing in the Texas Fort Worth Fat Stock Show, he was taken by surprise. After the rodeo a fine-talkin' man named Zack Miller approached Bill and shook his hand.

Zack Miller and his brothers, Joe and George, owned one of the biggest ranches in the West. Their 101 Ranch spread over three towns—White Eagle, Red Rock, and Bliss—in Oklahoma. The Miller brothers also owned a traveling Wild West show, a spectacle greater than the small-time rodeos where Bill usually performed. The 101 Ranch Wild West Show had ninety cowboys and cowgirls, three hundred animals, and sixteen acts.

The Millers' show was famous. But to make it the best, they had to have a cowboy who could draw crowds and keep folks yip-yapping for more. The Millers had heard about Bill Pickett. After seeing Bill perform that day, Zack knew Bill was just the cowboy they needed. He asked Bill to join the 101 Ranch Wild West Show. He even told Bill that Maggie and their children would be welcome to live at the 101 Ranch while Bill traveled.

Bill didn't have to think twice. Zack's offer was the best he'd ever got. It wasn't long before Bill and his show horse, Spradley, became the 101's star attraction.

Soon Bill began to take his bulldogging to the far corners of the world. Crowds stood up and cheered when Bill bulldogged at Madison Square Garden in New York City.

In Mexico City townspeople filled the stands at El Toro, the national building, to watch the Dusky Demon face a fighting bull that was meaner than ten bulls in one.

Bill bulldogged in Canada and in South America, too. And in 1914 he performed in England for King George V and Queen Mary!

Bill's bulldog act helped turn the 101 Ranch Wild West Show into a high-falutin' wonder. Even more important, Bill helped make rodeo one of the best-loved sports of his time.

After years of bulldogging with the 101 show, Bill decided to give traveling a rest. He wanted to spend more time with Maggie and their children. So he returned to the 101 Ranch, where he lived and worked as a cowhand. To keep his skills strong, he bulldogged in rodeos closer to home.

Bulldogging lived on long after Bill died in 1932. But nobody could snatch a steer the way Bill did. When Bill's children were grown, they gathered up their own young'uns and told them about their grandfather, Bill Pickett—the feisty cowboy-child from south of Abilene who grew up to be the Dusky Demon.

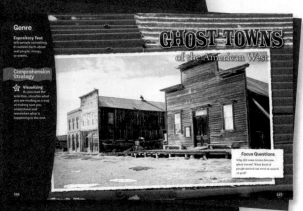

Read the article to find the meanings of these words, which are also in "Ghost Towns of the American West":

+ evidence
+ centuries
+ minerals
+ tattered
+ traces
+ territory
+ inhabitants
+ prosperity
+ trough
+ longed

Vocabulary Strategy

An **appositive** is a noun that follows another noun to modify or name it. Authors sometimes use apposition to clarify the meanings of words. Look at the word *evidence*. Find how the author uses apposition to define the word.

544

Vocabulary
Warm-Up

The car rolled slowly through the mall's empty parking lot. As it passed each storefront window, the bright afternoon sunshine reflected into the passenger's eyes. Inside the car, Ryan thought, "It might as well be midnight." He saw no evidence of life, proof that one of the stores might still be in business.

The car stopped in front of Johnson's Booksellers. A few months earlier, Ryan had gone there for his birthday. The mall was already mostly empty, but he remembered that the Fossil Shop had still been operating. His brother, Brandon, liked the insects and fish frozen into rock centuries ago. The store also carried crystals, pyrite or fools' gold, and other minerals. Now it was gone too.

Ryan and his grandmother approached the bookstore's entrance. A sign taped to the glass thanked the customers for many years of loyalty.

Grandma shook her head. "I remember when this mall opened. It is hard to believe the stores are all gone."

Blocking the reflections with his hands, Ryan peered inside the vacant space. Two tattered posters hung on the wall. The shredded ads were the only traces remaining of what had once been a thriving bookstore.

Ryan surveyed the territory in which the mall was located. The area had other businesses, but cars just zipped past them. The drivers were probably racing to the new mall a few miles farther west.

Ryan's grandmother sighed. "Like the city's inhabitants, I guess prosperity moves from one part of town to the next," she observed. She described how successful the mall had been when it opened. Then, as new malls were built, the customers went elsewhere.

At the far end of the building, a trash container sat in front of an old grocery store. Ryan imagined it as a huge feeding trough for dinosaurs that would soon arrive to eat the contents.

As Ryan and his grandmother zoomed off to the new mall, he longed for his favorite old bookstore.

GAME

Define It! Form two teams with your classmates. Have a volunteer define a vocabulary word. The first team to guess the word being defined gets a point. Spell the word correctly to receive a bonus point. If the team is unsuccessful, the other team can spell the word for a point. The game is over when all of the words have been defined and spelled.

Concept Vocabulary

The concept word for this lesson is *abandon.* To *abandon* something means "to give it up or leave it behind." Abandoned things usually fall into disrepair, but sometimes new uses can be found for things that have been discarded. Buildings, cars, and furniture can be abandoned, but so can goals, ideas, and beliefs.

Genre

Expository Text tells people something. It contains facts about real people, things, or events.

Comprehension Strategy

★ Visualizing

As you read the selection, visualize what you are reading as a way of making sure you understand and remember what is happening in the text.

GHOST TOWNS
of the American West

by Raymond Bial

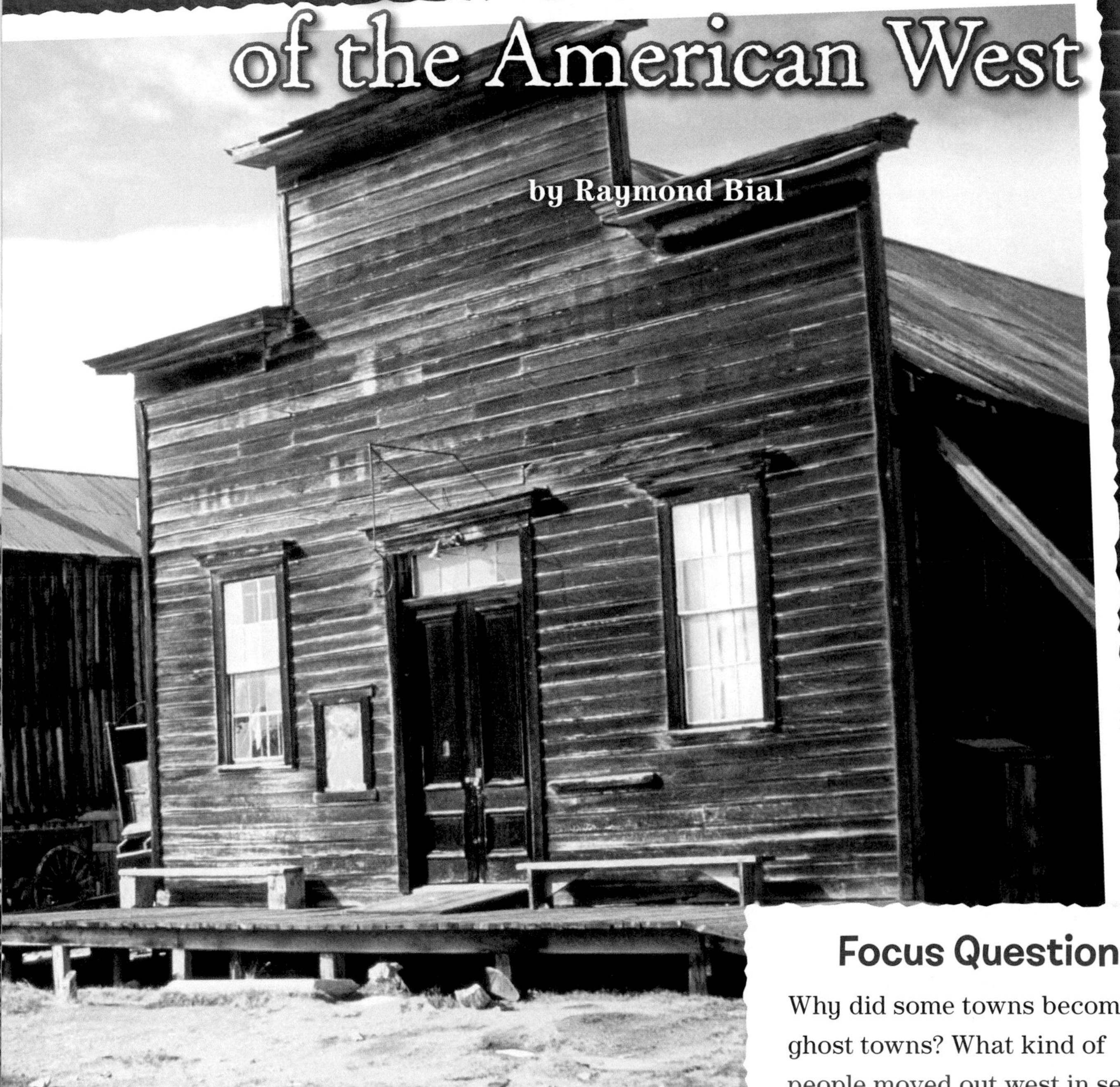

Focus Questions

Why did some towns become ghost towns? What kind of people moved out west in search of gold?

Towns sprang up overnight. Charles B. Gillespie, a miner who worked near Coloma, California, described the typical main streets of these towns as "alive with crowds." To him, the miners were ragged, dirty men who were otherwise good-natured. They were a mix of Americans and immigrants—Germans, French, and other Europeans, and gold seekers from China and Chile, along with British convicts from Australia. Mark Twain declared, "It was a driving, vigorous, restless population in those days . . . two hundred thousand *young* men—not simpering, dainty, kid-gloved weaklings, but stalwart, muscular, dauntless young braves, brimful of push and energy."

In 1851, when a Scottish artist named J. D. Borthwick arrived to try his luck as a prospector, he wrote that the main street of Hangtown, later renamed Pacerville, "was in many places knee-deep in mud, and was plentifully strewn with old boots, hats, and shirts, old sardine-boxes, empty tins of preserved oysters, empty bottles, worn-out pots and kettles, old ham-bones, broken picks and shovels, and other rubbish." Borthwick described the town as "one long straggling street of clapboard houses and log cabins, built in a hollow at the side of a creek, and surrounded by high and steep hills." Along the creek, he said, "there was continual noise and clatter, as mud, dirt, stones, and water were thrown about in all directions, and the men, dressed in ragged clothes and big boots, wielding picks and shovels . . . werc all working as if for their lives."

In the typical western town, the buildings were often skirted with a sidewalk of wooden planks, along with hitching posts and water troughs for horses. There might be a bank made of solid brick to assure depositors that their hard cash or gold dust was safe from robbers. There might also be a mercantile store, an early version of the department store, as well as a general store. The town certainly had to have a blacksmith shop and livery stable, as well as corrals for horses and cattle. Some towns had a telegraph office and their very own newspaper. The town might be lucky enough to be on a stagecoach route, a Pony Express station, or, better yet, a railroad stop.

"The Americans have a perfect passion for railroads," wrote Michel Chevalier, a French economist, in the 1830s. If the railroad bypassed the village, it quickly became a ghost town. Helen Hunt Jackson described Garland City, Colorado, where she lived: "Twelve days ago there was not a house here. Today, there are one hundred and five, and in a week there will be two hundred." However, the town lasted only a few months, at least at that site. When the railroad passed thirty miles to the west, folks moved the entire town—walls and windows, as well as sidewalks, furnishings, and goods—to the railroad tracks. Railroads laid down thousands of miles of gleaming tracks across the grasslands, with a transcontinental link completed in 1869.

The waves of western migration reached a peak between 1860 and 1880. Over time, some towns grew into large cities, such as Denver and Phoenix, while many others were abandoned and forgotten in the desert sands or mountain snows. Most went bust because of economic failure—all the gold or silver was mined or the cattle were driven to another market town. A few people got rich, but others suffered heartbreak, hunger, and plain bad luck, then abandoned the town. Perched on mountain cliffs, tucked into a wooded valley, or baking in the desert sun, these ghost towns are so remote that they are almost impossible to find.

People often have to travel to them by four-wheel-drive vehicles and then hike several miles up rocky slopes or over cactus-studded deserts. Finding the ghost towns may be as difficult as the search for gold that led to the founding of the towns.

John Steele described Washington, California, in the 1840s, just six months after it had been founded: "With a large number of vacant cabins it contained several empty buildings and quite a large hotel, closed and silent." Once ringing with the voices of cheerful people, the towns have now fallen silent. They have become little more than empty shells of their former selves. There may be a handful of old false-front buildings, weathered to a haunting gray, with open doorways and broken windows. But little else remains; few people even remember the place. Even the memories, along with the hopes and dreams of the inhabitants, have blown away, like so much dust in the wind.

Meet the Author

Raymond Bial

As a child, Raymond Bial was never quite sure what he wanted to be when he grew up. His mother encouraged him to be a lawyer or a teacher. In the fifth grade, after sending in bubble gum wrappers to get his first camera and having his first story published in the newspaper, Bial decided writing and photography would be interesting career paths. He has combined these two skills to create more than eighty books. Bial shares his stories with his wife, two daughters, and son.

Theme Connections

Within the Selection

1. Why did people abandon some towns in the American West?

2. Why did the towns in the selection grow so quickly at first?

Across Selections

3. What other story in this unit deals with miners searching for gold?

4. Contrast ghost towns with the small villages of the Yup'ik Eskimos.

Beyond the Selection

5. What do you think you would find if you visited a ghost town in the West?

6. What might cause a town to be abandoned today?

Write about It!

Imagine you are one of the last people still living in a nearly deserted town. What would it be like, and how would you feel?

Remember to write questions about abandoned buildings to add to the **Concept/Question Board.**

JOHN CHARLES FRÉMONT

John Charles Frémont (1813–1890) was an explorer, soldier, and politician. Frémont played a big part in America's westward growth during the 1800s.

The Louisiana Purchase of 1803 nearly doubled the size of the United States. This vast new territory had to be explored. Lewis and Clark's journey of 1804–06 was just the start. During the next fifty years, Frémont and many others helped map the area as well.

In 1838–39, Frémont teamed up with Frenchman Joseph Nicollet. They explored the land that sat between the Missouri and Mississippi Rivers. Frémont spent 1841 mapping the Des Moines River. By 1846, this area would become Iowa—the twenty-ninth state. In 1842, Frémont followed the Oregon Trail, mapping it along the way. In 1845–46, Frémont and his guide, Kit Carson, hiked through the Sierra Nevada Mountains of eastern California. Frémont and his wife wrote a famous book about this trip. It made Kit Carson an American folk hero.

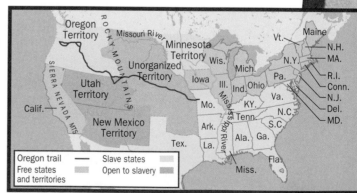

United States in 1850

While Frémont was in the West, he joined the army and fought in the Mexican-American War. In 1846, Frémont led his men into California and helped the United States win the war. After California became a state in 1850, Frémont was one of its first two senators. In 1856, Frémont was chosen as the new Republican Party's first candidate for president. In his speeches, he spoke out against slavery. Frémont lost the race to James Buchanan.

Frémont joined the army again during the Civil War. He also governed the Arizona Territory from 1878 to 1883. Frémont died in New York City in 1890.

BIBLIOGRAPHY

Maynard, Charles. *John Charles Frémont: The Pathfinder.* New York: PowerKids Press, 2003.

Souza, D. M. *John C. Frémont.* New York: Scholastic, 2004.

Witteman, Barbara. *John Charles Frémont: Western Pathfinder.* Minneapolis: Capstone Press, 2002.

Think Link

1. Who was Frémont's guide in his travels through California?
2. Who wrote *John Charles Frémont: The Pathfinder?*
3. Which states had joined the union by 1850?

Try It!

As you work on your investigation, remember to include a bibliography if necessary.

Read the article to find the meanings of these words, which are also in "McBroom the Rainmaker":

+ predict
+ accurate
+ drought
+ desperately
+ sowing
+ dispositions
+ regard
+ heaved
+ merciful
+ prairie

Vocabulary Strategy

Context Clues are hints in the text that help you find the meanings of words. Look at the words *predict* and *drought*. Use context clues to find each word's meaning.

Vocabulary

Warm-Up

Pa's leg could always predict rain. Whenever wet weather was about to arrive, it ached where he had busted it once. Even when the sky was as blue as Ma's Sunday dress, if his leg got to hurting, you knew clouds hovered behind the horizon. That leg was more accurate than the watch Pa carried in his overalls.

During the summer of '38, though, Pa's leg felt fantastic. That was bad news for us. Our family farmed back then, and we sure needed rain. A monthlong drought had left our crops thirstier than a man traveling through the desert. Every morning Pa would squint into that vast emptiness hanging above our farm. After a while, he would just shake his head. It was obvious how desperately he wished for rainfall. Pa was beginning to lose hope.

Back in the springtime, I had worked right alongside the farmhands sowing seeds in the fields. It was plenty wet, so everyone had good dispositions. Everyone except Mitch, the oldest farmhand.

When I asked him why he was not in a good mood, he reminded me that planting seeds was the easiest part. A long season still stretched ahead before any celebrating was in order. Unfortunately, Mitch was right in that regard.

Finally, a morning arrived when Pa heaved himself out of bed and limped downstairs. His leg throbbed with pain and made movement difficult. Despite his aching, Pa grinned from ear to ear. He took the soreness as a merciful sign.

Later that day, we watched enormous black clouds sweep over the prairie. At first the grasses just swayed, but suddenly they collapsed as the forceful storm rolled over them. As the first few drops of rain reached our dry, brown fields, they sent up puffs of dust. Soon, however, the dust disappeared, and the fields began splashing and bubbling with mud. The dry spell was finished—just like Pa's leg had predicted.

GAME

Fill in the Blanks

On a separate sheet of paper, complete the following sentences with selection vocabulary words.

1. I admire people who have good ____ even when they are busy and stressed.

2. The only way Shawna could ____ how well she would do on a test was if she had studied hard beforehand.

3. The farmer ____ one straw bale after another into the back of his pickup.

Concept Vocabulary

The concept word for this lesson is **hyperbole**. *Hyperbole* is an obvious exaggeration that is used for emphasis or entertainment. For example, if you say you have heard a song "a million times," no one thinks you mean it literally. Tall tales often use hyperbole as a form of entertainment.

A **tall tale** uses humor and exaggeration to tell the adventures of a fictional character.

Comprehension Skill

 Cause and Effect

As you read the selection, remember that a cause is why something happened and an effect is what happened.

564

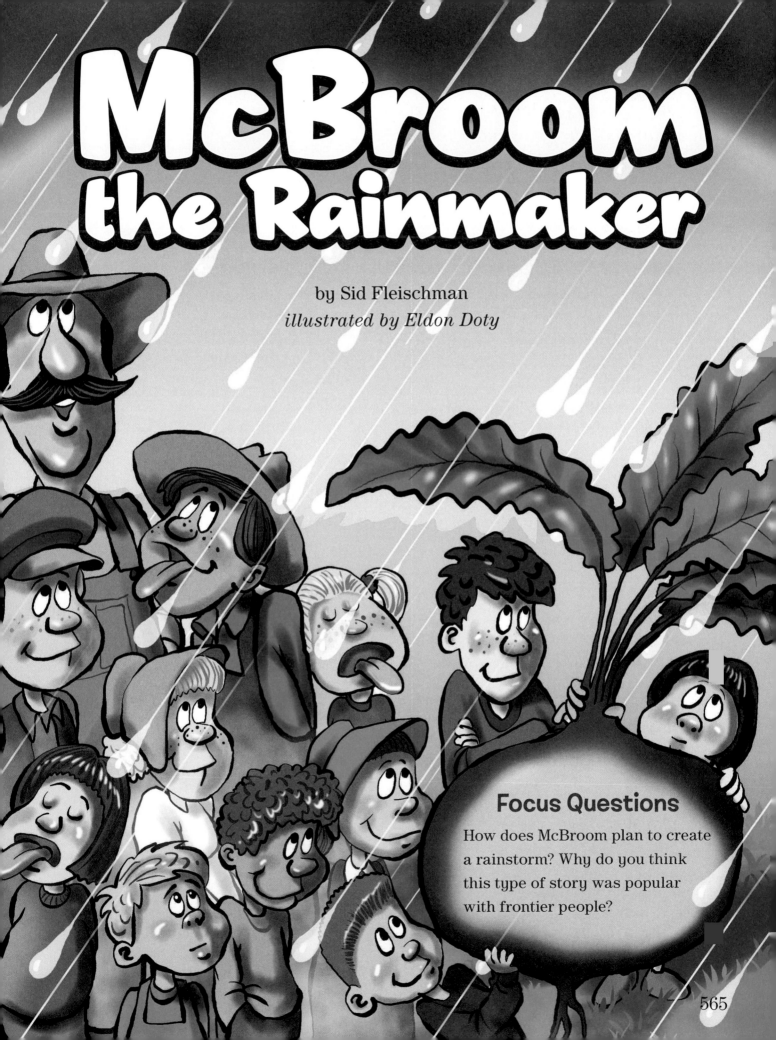

McBroom the Rainmaker

by Sid Fleischman

illustrated by Eldon Doty

Focus Questions

How does McBroom plan to create a rainstorm? Why do you think this type of story was popular with frontier people?

565

I dislike to tell you this, but some folks have no regard for the truth. A stranger claims he was riding a mule past our wonderful one-acre farm and was attacked by woodpeckers.

Well, there's no truth to that. No, indeed! Those weren't woodpeckers. They were common prairie mosquitoes.

Small ones.

Why, skeeters grow so large out here that everybody uses chicken wire for mosquito netting. But I'm not going to say an unkind word about those zing-zanging, hot-tempered, needle-nosed creatures. They rescued our farm from ruin. That was during the Big Drought we had last year.

Dry? Merciful powers! Our young'uns found some tadpoles and had to teach them to swim. It hadn't rained in so long those tadpoles had never seen water.

That's the sworn truth—certain as my name's Josh McBroom. Why, I'd as soon grab a skunk by the tail as tell a falsehood.

Now, I'd best creep up on the Big Drought the way it crept up on us. I remember we did our spring plowing, as usual, and the skeeters hatched out, as usual. The bloodsucking rapscallions could be mighty pesky, but we'd learned to distract them.

"Will*jill*hester*chester*peter*polly*tim*tom*mary*larry*andlittle-*clarinda!*" I called out. "I hear the whine of gallinippers. We'd better put in a patch of beets."

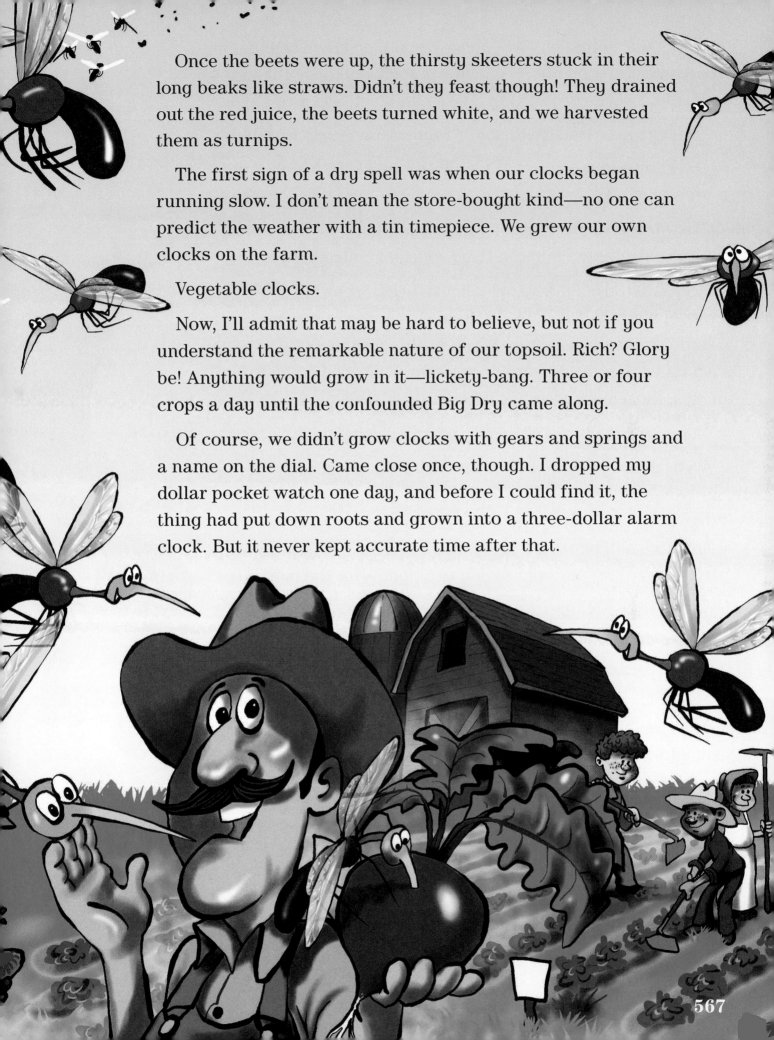

Once the beets were up, the thirsty skeeters stuck in their long beaks like straws. Didn't they feast though! They drained out the red juice, the beets turned white, and we harvested them as turnips.

The first sign of a dry spell was when our clocks began running slow. I don't mean the store-bought kind—no one can predict the weather with a tin timepiece. We grew our own clocks on the farm.

Vegetable clocks.

Now, I'll admit that may be hard to believe, but not if you understand the remarkable nature of our topsoil. Rich? Glory be! Anything would grow in it—lickety-bang. Three or four crops a day until the confounded Big Dry came along.

Of course, we didn't grow clocks with gears and springs and a name on the dial. Came close once, though. I dropped my dollar pocket watch one day, and before I could find it, the thing had put down roots and grown into a three-dollar alarm clock. But it never kept accurate time after that.

567

It was our young'uns who discovered they could tell time by vegetable. They planted a cucumber seed, and once the vine leaped out of the ground, it traveled along steady as a clock.

"An inch a second," Will said. "Kind of like a second hand."

"Blossoms come out on the minute," Jill said. "Kind of like a minute hand."

They tried other vegetable timepieces, but pole beans had a way of running a mite fast and squash a mite slow.

As I say, those homegrown clocks began running down. I remember my dear wife, Melissa, was boiling three-and-a-half-minute eggs for breakfast. Little Clarinda planted a cucumber seed, and before it grew three blossoms and thirty inches, those eggs were hard-boiled.

"Mercy!" I declared. "Topsoil must be drying out."

Well, the days turned drier and drier. No doubt about it—our wonderful topsoil was losing some of its get-up-and-go. Why, it took almost a whole day to raise a crop of corn. The young'uns had planted a plum tree, but all it would grow was prunes. Dogs would fight over a dry bone—for the moisture in it.

"Will*jill*hester*chester*peter*polly*tim*tom*mary*larry*andlittle-clarinda!*" I called. "Keep your eyes peeled for rain."

They took turns in the tree house scanning the skies, and one night Chester said, "Pa, what if it doesn't rain by Fourth of July? How'll we shoot off firecrackers?"

"Be patient, my lambs," I said. We used to grow our own firecrackers, too. Don't let me forget to tell you about it. "Why, it's a long spell to Fourth of July."

My, wasn't the next morning a scorcher! The sun came out so hot that our hens laid fried eggs. But no, that wasn't the Big Dry. The young'uns planted watermelons to cool off and beets to keep the mosquitoes away.

"Look!" Polly exclaimed, pointing to the watermelons. "Pa, they're rising off the ground!"

569

Rising? They began to float in the air like balloons! We could hardly believe our eyes. And gracious me! When we cut those melons open, it turned out they were full of hot air.

Well, I was getting a mite worried myself. Our beets were growing smaller and smaller, and the skeeters were growing larger and larger. Many a time, before dawn, a rapping at the windows would wake us out of a sound sleep. It was those confounded, needle-nosed gallinippers pecking away, demanding breakfast.

Then it came—the Big Dry.

Mercy! Our cow began giving powdered milk. We pumped away on our water pump, but all it brought up was dry steam. The oldest boys went fishing and caught six dried catfish.

"Not a rain cloud in sight, Pa," Mary called from the tree house.

"Watch out for gallinippers!" Larry shouted, as a mosquito made a dive at him. The earth was so parched, we couldn't raise a crop of beets and the varmints were getting downright ornery. Then, as I stood there, I felt my shoes getting tighter and tighter.

"Thunderation!" I exclaimed. "Our topsoil's so dry it's gone in reverse. It's *shrinking* things."

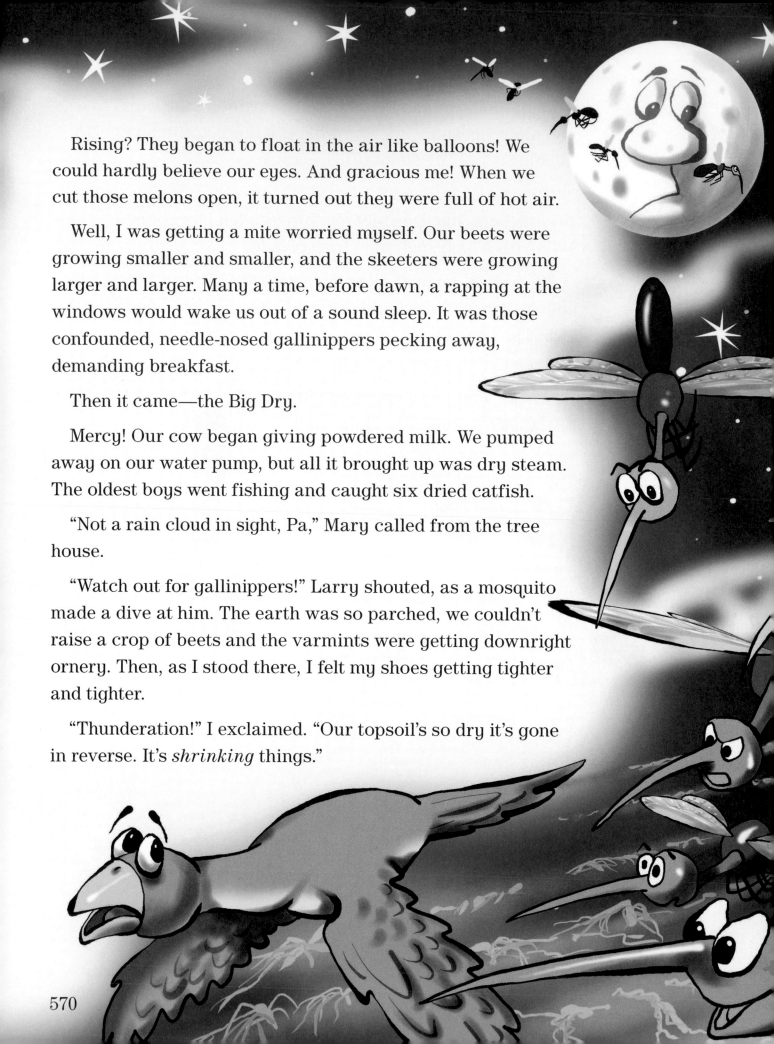

Didn't I lay awake most of the night! Our wonderful one-acre farm might shrink to a square foot. And all night long the skeeters rattled the windows and hammered at the door. Big? The *smallest* ones must have weighed three pounds. In the moonlight I saw them chase a yellow-billed cuckoo.

Didn't that make me sit up in a hurry! An idea struck me. Glory be! I'd break that drought.

First thing in the morning I took Will and Chester to town with me and rented three wagons and a birdcage. We drove straight home, and I called everyone together.

"Shovels, my lambs! Heap these wagons full of topsoil!"

But Larry and little Clarinda were still worried about Fourth of July. "We won't be able to grow fireworks, Pa!"

"You have my word," I declared firmly.

571

Before long, we were on our way. I drove the first wagon, with the young'uns following along behind in the other two. It might be a longish trip, and we had loaded up with picnic hampers of food. We also brought along rolls of chicken wire and our raincoats.

"Where are we going, Pa?" Jill called from the wagon behind.

"Hunting."

"Hunting?" Tom said.

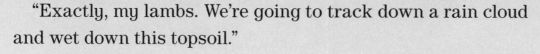

"Exactly, my lambs. We're going to track down a rain cloud and wet down this topsoil."

"But how, Pa?" asked Tim.

I lifted the birdcage from under the wagon seat. "Presto," I said, and whipped off the cover. "Look at that lost-looking, scared-looking, long-tailed creature. Found it hiding from the skeeters under a milk pail this morning. It's a genuine rain crow, my lambs."

"A rain crow?" Mary said. "It doesn't look like a crow at all."

"Correct and exactly," I said, smiling. "It looks like a yellow-billed cuckoo, and that's what it is. But don't folks call 'em rain crows? Why, that bird can smell a downpour coming sixty miles away. Rattles its throat and begins to squawk. All we got to do is follow that squawk."

But you never heard such a quiet bird! We traveled miles and miles across the prairie, this way and the other, and not a rattle out of that rain crow.

The Big Dry had done its mischief everywhere. We didn't see a dog without his tongue dragging, and it took two of them to bark at us once. A farmer told us he hadn't been able to grow anything all year but baked potatoes!

Of course, we slept under chicken wire—covered the horses, too. My, what a racket the gallinippers made!

Day after day we hauled our three loads of topsoil across the prairie, but that rain crow didn't so much as clear its throat.

The young'uns were getting impatient. "Speak up, rain crow," Chester muttered desperately.

"Rattle," Hester pleaded.

"Squawk," said Peter.

"Please," said Mary. "Just a little peep would help."

Not a cloud appeared in the sky. I'll confess I was getting a mite discouraged. And the Fourth of July not another two weeks off!

We curled up under chicken wire that night, as usual, and the big skeeters kept banging into it, so you could hardly sleep. Rattled like a hailstorm. And suddenly, at daybreak, I rose up laughing.

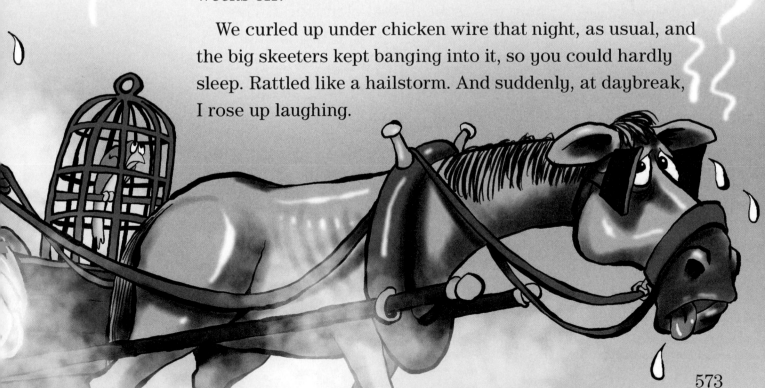

"Hear that?"

The young'uns crowded around the rain crow. We hadn't been able to hear its voice rattle for the mosquitoes. Now it turned in its cage, gazed off to the northwest, opened its yellow beak, and let out a real, ear-busting rain cry.

"K-*kawk*! K-*kawk*! K-*kawk*!"

"Put on your raincoats, my lambs!" I said, and we rushed to the wagons.

"K-*kawk*! K-*kawk*! K-*kawk*!"

Didn't we raise dust! That bird faced northwest like a dog on point. There was a rain cloud out there and before long Jill gave a shout.

"I see it!"

And the others chimed in one after the other. "Me, too!"

"K-*kawk*! K-*kawk*! K-*kawk*!"

We headed directly for that lone cloud, the young'uns yelling, the horses snorting, and the bird squawking.

Glory be! The first raindrops spattered as large as quarters. And my, didn't the young'uns frolic in that cloudburst! They lifted their faces and opened their mouths and drank right out of the sky. They splashed about and felt mud between their toes for the first time in ages. We all forgot to put on our raincoats and got wet as fish.

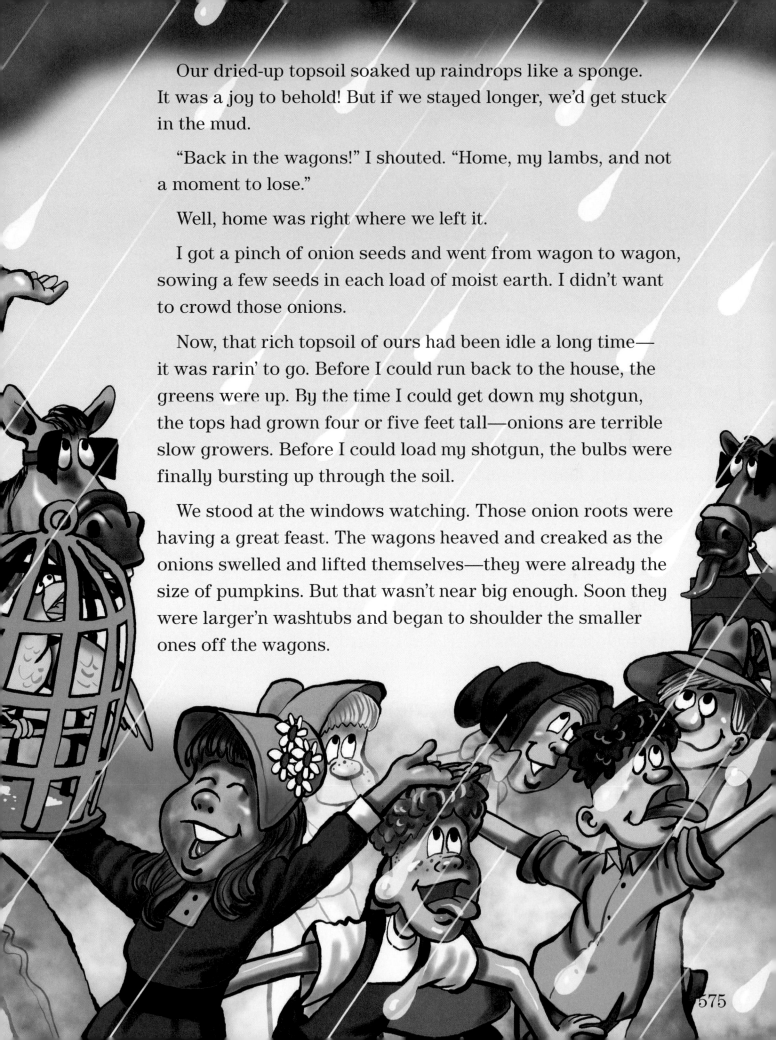

Our dried-up topsoil soaked up raindrops like a sponge. It was a joy to behold! But if we stayed longer, we'd get stuck in the mud.

"Back in the wagons!" I shouted. "Home, my lambs, and not a moment to lose."

Well, home was right where we left it.

I got a pinch of onion seeds and went from wagon to wagon, sowing a few seeds in each load of moist earth. I didn't want to crowd those onions.

Now, that rich topsoil of ours had been idle a long time— it was rarin' to go. Before I could run back to the house, the greens were up. By the time I could get down my shotgun, the tops had grown four or five feet tall—onions are terrible slow growers. Before I could load my shotgun, the bulbs were finally bursting up through the soil.

We stood at the windows watching. Those onion roots were having a great feast. The wagons heaved and creaked as the onions swelled and lifted themselves—they were already the size of pumpkins. But that wasn't near big enough. Soon they were larger'n washtubs and began to shoulder the smaller ones off the wagons.

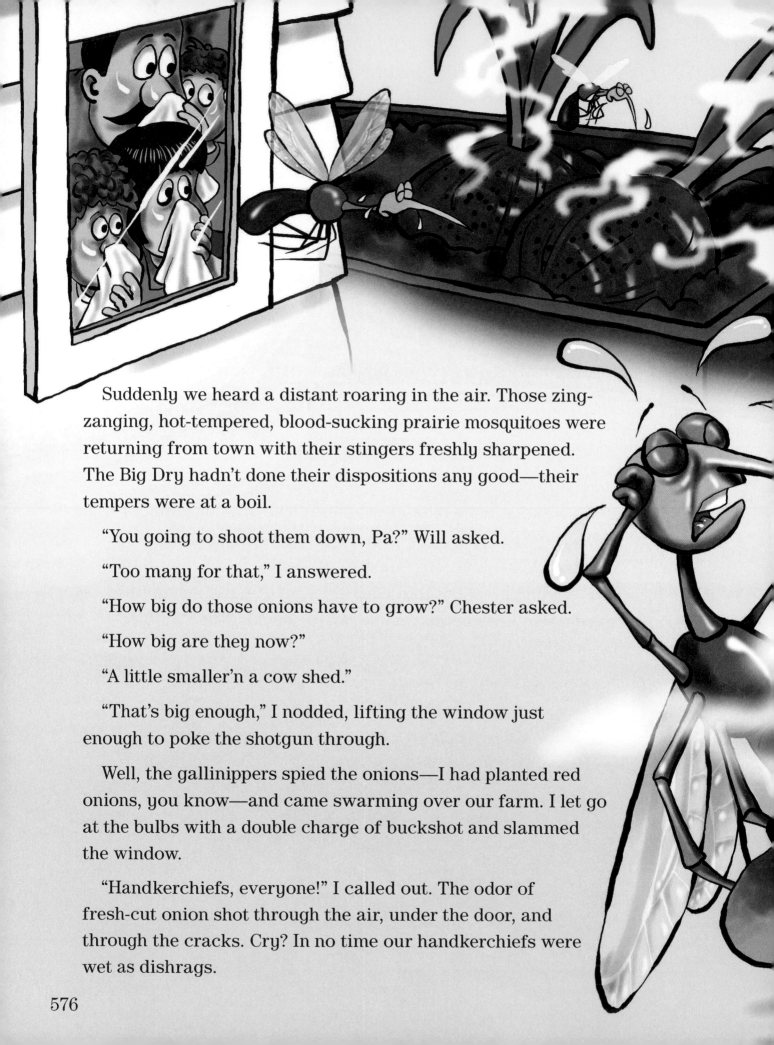

Suddenly we heard a distant roaring in the air. Those zing-zanging, hot-tempered, blood-sucking prairie mosquitoes were returning from town with their stingers freshly sharpened. The Big Dry hadn't done their dispositions any good—their tempers were at a boil.

"You going to shoot them down, Pa?" Will asked.

"Too many for that," I answered.

"How big do those onions have to grow?" Chester asked.

"How big are they now?"

"A little smaller'n a cow shed."

"That's big enough," I nodded, lifting the window just enough to poke the shotgun through.

Well, the gallinippers spied the onions—I had planted red onions, you know—and came swarming over our farm. I let go at the bulbs with a double charge of buckshot and slammed the window.

"Handkerchiefs, everyone!" I called out. The odor of fresh-cut onion shot through the air, under the door, and through the cracks. Cry? In no time our handkerchiefs were wet as dishrags.

Well! You never saw such surprised gallinippers. They zing-zanged every which way, most of them backwards. And weep? Their eyes began to flow like sprinkling cans. Onion tears! The roof began to leak. Mud puddles formed everywhere. Before long, the downpour was equal to any cloudburst I ever saw. Near flooded our farm!

The skeeters kept their distance after that. But they'd been mighty helpful.

With our farm freshly watered we grew tons of great onions—three or four crops a day. Gave them away to farmers all over the country.

The newspaper ran a picture of the whole family—the rain crow, too.

The young'uns had a splendid Fourth of July. Grew all the fireworks they wanted. They'd dash about with bean shooters—shooting radish seeds. You know how fast radishes come up. In our rich topsoil they grew quicker'n the eye. The seeds hardly touched the ground before they took root and swelled up and exploded. They'd go off like strings of firecrackers.

And, mercy, what a racket! Didn't I say I'd rather catch a skunk by the tail than tell a fib? Well, at nightfall a scared cat ran up a tree, and I went up a ladder to get it down. Reached in the branches and caught it by the tail.

I'd be lying if I didn't admit the truth. It was a skunk.

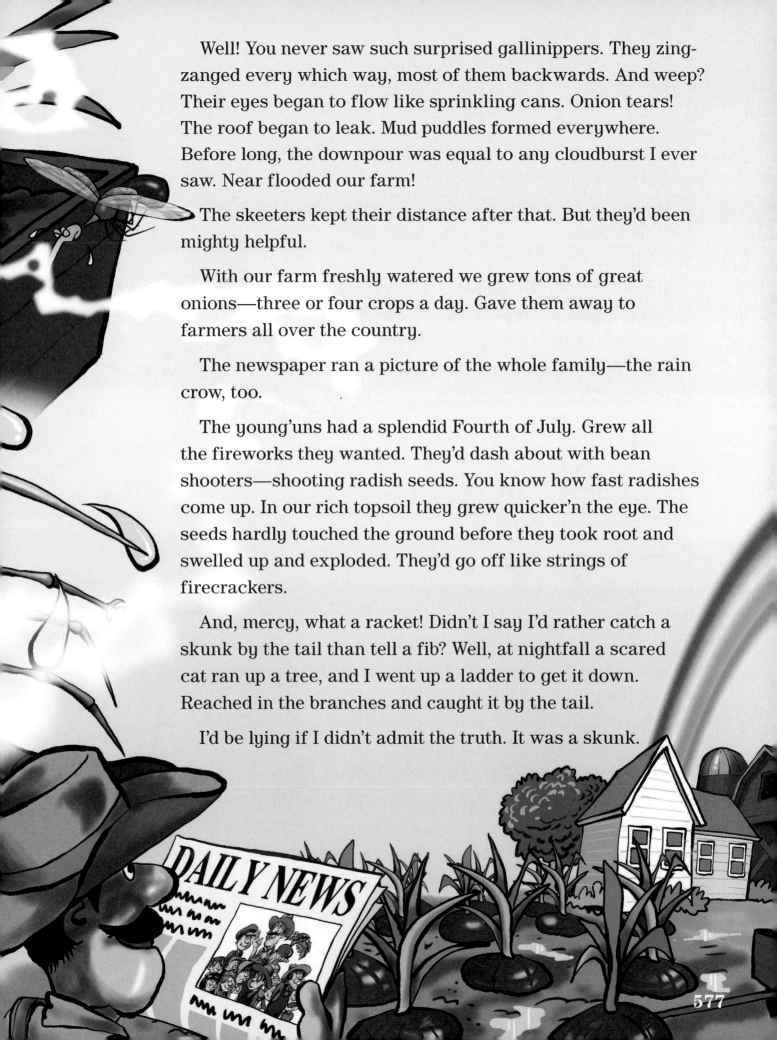

577

Meet the Author

Sid Fleischman

Sid Fleischman was fascinated with sleight-of-hand performers during his school years. After graduating at the age of seventeen, he had a traveling act of his own, performing tricks countrywide. He later went to college, after which he became a reporter and writer for the San Diego paper. He started writing for young readers by making up stories for his own children. He writes at a huge table stacked with story ideas, library books, research, letters, notes, pens, pencils, and a typewriter.

Meet the Illustrator

Eldon Doty

Eldon Doty did not start out as an artist. After college, he worked as a police officer. This was interesting, but he had other dreams. Doty decided to turn his love of art into a career and studied at an art school in San Francisco. Doty first drew cartoons by hand, but now illustrates using a computer. After illustrating for twenty-five years Doty says, "It's probably a job I will never retire from . . . it's too much fun!"

Theme Connections

Within the Selection

1. Which part of this story might actually be true?
2. What does it mean when McBroom catches a skunk at the end of his story?

Across Selections

3. What previous selection also deals with natural disasters?
4. Why do you think people like Wong Ming-Chung and the McBrooms moved out West?

Beyond the Selection

5. The McBrooms and other people in the Old West often grew their own food. How does this compare with how we get our food today?
6. Why did farmers usually have big families?

Write about It!

Tell your own tall tale about something that happened in your life.

Remember to write questions about farming to add to the **Concept/Question Board.**

The Long Trail West

The following comments about the Oregon Trail were taken from an interview with Dr. William Bautch, professor of American History at Wellstone University. Dr. Bautch's knowledge about the dispositions of pioneers helps us understand how tough it was to travel across the prairie.

Sean Logan: Why did the pioneers make such a long, difficult journey?

Dr. Bautch: For many of them it was about farming. During the 1830s, Americans in the East began to hear rumors about perfect farmland in Oregon and California. They could easily acquire land on the dry, treeless Great Plains, but most Easterners found life there difficult. By heading farther west, they hoped to find an environment closer to what they were leaving behind.

SL: What was the trip like?

DB: Just like you had said: Long and difficult! (laughter) Actually, the land route took less time than traveling by ship.

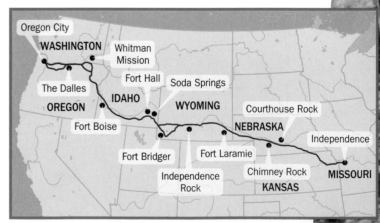

Landmarks along the trail helped the pioneers keep track of their progress as they moved westward.

Most pioneers lived too far from the coasts, anyway. It made no sense to travel by ship. The land route took only four or five months, but it was tough. Pioneer families did not ride in their wagons, which were pulled along by mules or oxen. Most people walked the entire 2,000-mile journey—many of them barefoot! The wagons were stuffed with their supplies and possessions. Heading west in those days was a brutal undertaking—one in ten people did not survive the trip.

SL: What killed them?

DB: Illness, especially cholera. It was responsible for more deaths than anything else. Most pioneers traveled in big groups called *wagon trains*. A bad cholera outbreak could kill half the people in a wagon train. Accidents and weather were also deadly. One misstep and a person could be crushed beneath a wagon's wheel. Lightning strikes and blizzards took many lives as well.

Think Link

1. How does the caption below the map make the map more useful?

2. What obstacles did the pioneers face as they headed west?

3. What animals did the pioneers use to pull their wagons?

Try It!

As you work on your investigation, think about how you might use captions.

The Whole World Is Coming

a Sioux Indian poem
illustrated by Stella Ormai

The whole world is coming,

A nation is coming, a nation is coming,

the eagle has brought the message to the tribe.

Over the whole earth they are coming;

the buffalo are coming, the buffalo are coming,

the crow has brought the message to the tribe.

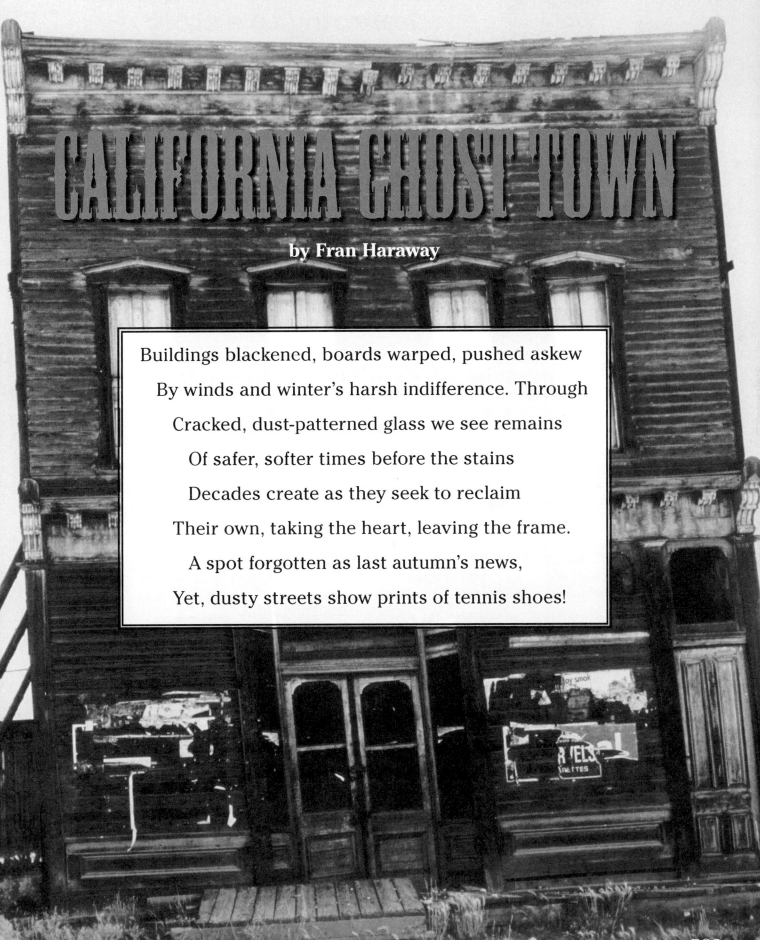

Focus Question Why are there shoe prints in the streets of the ghost town?

CALIFORNIA GHOST TOWN

by Fran Haraway

Buildings blackencd, boards warped, pushed askew

By winds and winter's harsh indifference. Through

Cracked, dust-patterned glass we see remains

Of safer, softer times before the stains

Decades create as they seek to reclaim

Their own, taking the heart, leaving the frame.

A spot forgotten as last autumn's news,

Yet, dusty streets show prints of tennis shoes!

**Test-Taking Strategy:
Referring to a story
to answer questions**

To answer some questions
on a test, you may have to
read a story. You must use
the information in the story
to answer the question.

Referring to a story to answer questions

Sometimes you will read a story on a test. You will answer questions about the story. It is very important that you use the information in the story to answer the questions.

Read this story. Use the story to decide which answer is correct.

> It was a cool morning. The swimmers were wearing warm clothes. Practice would start in a few minutes, and they all wanted to be ready. The big meet was only a few days away.
>
> **The swimmers in this story want to be ready for practice because**
>
> - the pool would get crowded.
> - it was a cool morning.
> - a big meet is coming up.
> - the coach is strict.

To answer the question, you should look back at the story. The story mentions that a big meet is just a few days away. That's why the swimmers wanted to be ready. The story says nothing about crowds or a strict coach. The morning was cool, but this didn't make the swimmers any more ready. The third answer is correct.

You should always use the information in the story to answer the question.

The First National Park

Three men dressed in buckskin are riding on horseback. They sit easily in their saddles. They take in their surroundings as they go. Emerging from a grouping of trees, the men come upon an area that is flat and barren.

The ground here is chalky white. The air smells of minerals. The men dismount. They lead their horses forward on foot. The surface of the ground is hard and crusty here. The horses' hooves make quiet crunching sounds on it. Ahead, plumes of steam come from a wide, shallow pool of water.

The men feel a rumble beneath their feet. They stop. They watch in amazement as the steaming hot water boils then surges upward. The men retreat to a safe distance. Then they continue to watch the show. A fountain builds from the geyser. It gets bigger and bigger and turns into a loud, gushing  eruption. Astounded, the men watch it spout upward. The fountain goes higher than they would have believed possible. It shoots a hundred feet in the air! With hoots and shouts, the men laugh and throw their hats in the air.

These three men were among the first scouts to explore what is now Yellowstone National Park. The geyser they saw was the Great Fountain Geyser. Though it can spout water two hundred feet in the air, few people knew of it until a short time before the men arrived.

Of course, Native Americans lived in the Yellowstone area for thousands of years. But most other people in the United States knew little or nothing of this wilderness area in Montana and Wyoming. Those who had heard of it knew it through the tall tales of its petrified forests, amazing animals, and giant geysers.

It was 1869 when the three men journeyed into the wilderness. The explorers could hardly believe their eyes. They came upon many more geysers. They saw Old Faithful and Steamboat, the tallest geyser in the world. They found hundreds of waterfalls and a canyon more than a thousand feet deep. They found dozens of animal species. There were wolves, bison, bears, eagles, and cranes.

When the explorers returned, they told of grand mountains, mighty canyons, and geysers unlike anything anyone had seen before. They agreed that it was not possible to fully describe the area's wonders with words. Yellowstone had to be *seen* to be appreciated.

By 1872, a law was passed. It protected two million acres of the Yellowstone area, making it the United States' first national park. People began to explore the area more and more. People today still experience the thrill of discovering Yellowstone's natural treasures. It is a true wonder of the natural world.

1. Read this sentence from the article.

   Astounded, the men watch it spout upwards. The fountain goes higher than they would have believed possible.

   What does the word *astounded* mean in the first sentence?

   (A) disturbed

   (B) proud

   (C) surprised

   (D) weary

2. Why did so many tall tales come out of the Yellowstone area?

   (F) Yellowstone had many amazing sights.

   (G) Many storytellers lived in Yellowstone.

   (H) Native Americans knew of Yellowstone.

   (I) Yellowstone was the first national park.

3. What was the author's main purpose for writing this article?

   (A) to encourage more people to visit Yellowstone

   (B) to describe what early visitors to Yellowstone saw

   (C) to explain how the geysers of Yellowstone work

   (D) to compare two of the biggest Yellowstone geysers

4. What did the explorers mean when they said that Yellowstone had to be *seen* to be appreciated? Use details and information from the passage to support your answer.

Call of Duty

What does it mean to follow the call of duty? What makes people do extraordinary things to help their neighbors or to fight for something they believe in? What things are worth fighting for? Read these stories to find out more about the call of duty.

Theme Connection

Look at the illustration of the Iwo Jima memorial. What qualities do you think are portrayed in the illustration? What emotions come to mind when you look at the illustration? How does the illustration relate to the theme Call of Duty?

589

Read the article to find the meanings of these words, which are also in "Founders of the Children's Rain Forest":

+ equator
+ macaw
+ biologist
+ horrified
+ tropics
+ designed
+ species
+ monument
+ grateful
+ donations

Vocabulary Strategy

Sometimes you can use **word structure** to help you find the meanings of words. Look at the word *biologist*. Use word structure to find the word's meaning.

Vocabulary
Warm-Up

After a bumpy descent out of the clouds, Bryan's plane rolled to a stop near the end of a grassy runway. He was south of the equator for the first time in his life. Everywhere he looked there were colorful birds like the macaw, and green slopes that disappeared into a misty sky. Bryan thought, *I cannot believe it. I am in the jungle!*

Bryan had just graduated from college. He had studied to be a biologist. In high school, Brian had been horrified to learn that a lot of rain forest plants and animals were already extinct. Since then his goal had been to study biology, travel to the tropics, and help preserve the rain forest.

Just before graduating, Bryan heard about a group of scientists in Brazil. They had designed a study showing how plant and animal species from the rain forests helped humans.

Their goal was to convince the local government that the jungle was important to save. Each acre they preserved would be a monument to their hard work.

Bryan wrote to the scientists, and they invited him to join them. The plane tickets to Brazil, though, were very expensive. Bryan thought he would not be able to go. Then a surprising thing happened.

A few weeks earlier, Bryan's mother invited him to dinner. They arrived at the restaurant and found it filled with people. Bryan quickly realized he knew almost everyone there and that they were there for him! He was so grateful that he began to cry. It was a very dramatic moment. The donations given to him that night paid for the airplane tickets.

As Bryan waited for the pilot to bring him his bags, he remembered the generosity of his friends and family. The thought made Bryan even more optimistic about his chances of saving the jungle.

Matching Game
Unscramble the letters to discover the selection vocabulary word that matches the definition. Write your answer on a separate sheet of paper.

1. a region of Earth near the equator — sotiprc
2. something that honors a memory — munntome
3. caused a feeling of great fear — driefohir
4. gifts — satinnood
5. created — gnidsede

Concept Vocabulary

The concept word for this lesson is *driven.* Being *driven* means wanting to accomplish something badly enough that you stick to your goal no matter what. The greatest athletes suffer through the pain and frustration of hours of training because they are driven to be the best. Scientists will conduct unsuccessful experiments for years because they are driven to find the one combination that cures a disease. What drives some people to succeed?

Genre

Narrative Nonfiction is a story that includes real people, places, and events.

Comprehension Skill

 Author's Purpose

As you read the selection, identify whether the author's purpose for writing is to inform, entertain, or persuade.

FOUNDERS OF THE CHILDREN'S RAIN FOREST

by Phillip Hoose

illustrated by Jim Effler and Fred Willingham

Focus Questions

How can ordinary people make a difference worldwide? Do they need to possess any special abilities?

It all began in the first week of school when Eha Kern, from the Fagervik School, in the Swedish countryside, showed her forty first- and second-grade students pictures of hot, steamy jungles near the Equator. It was there, she said, that half the types of plants and animals in the whole world could be found. She read to them about monkeys and leopards and sloths, about snakes that can paralyze your nerves with one bite, about strange plants that might hold a cure for cancer, about the great trees that give us oxygen to breathe and help keep the earth from becoming too hot.

And then she told them that the world's rain forests were being destroyed at the rate of one hundred acres a *minute*. In the past thirty years, she said, nearly half the world's rain forests have been cut down, often by poor people who burn the wood for fire. Sometimes forests are cleared to make pastures for cattle that are slaughtered and sold to hamburger chains in the U.S. and Europe. Sometimes the trees are sold and shipped away to make furniture and paper. More often they are just stacked up and burned. At this rate, there might not be any rain forests left in thirty years!

The children were horrified. The creatures of the rain forest could be gone before the students were even old enough to have a chance to see them. It didn't matter that they lived thousands of miles away in cold, snowy Sweden. It seemed to them that their future was being chopped and cleared away.

During the autumn, as the sunlight weakened and the days became short, the Fagervik children continued to think about the rain forest. Whenever they went on walks past the great fir trees on the school grounds, they imagined jaguars crouched in the limbs just above them, their long tails twitching impatiently.

They begged Mrs. Kern to help them think of something—anything—they could do to rescue the creatures of the tropics. And then one afternoon during a music lesson, a student named Roland Tiensuu asked suddenly, "Can't we just *buy* some rain forest?"

The lesson stopped. It was a simple, clear idea that all the others understood at once. The class began to cheer, and then they turned to their teacher. "Please, Mrs. Kern," they said. "Please, won't you find us a forest to buy?"

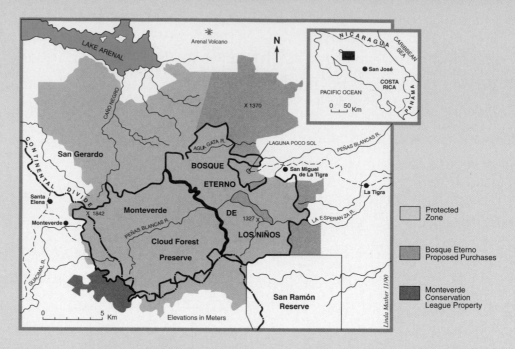

Protected Zone

Bosque Eterno Proposed Purchases

Monteverde Conservation League Property

"Please Buy Mine."

Mrs. Kern had no idea how to find a rain forest for sale. But then, the very weekend after Roland's idea, she was introduced to an American biologist named Sharon Kinsman. As they chatted, Ms. Kinsman explained that she had been working in a rain forest called Monteverde, or Green Mountain.

When Mrs. Kern told Ms. Kinsman of the nearly impossible mission her students had given her, she expected the biologist to laugh. Instead her expression turned serious. "Oh," she said quickly, "please buy mine."

Ms. Kinsman said that some people in Monteverde were trying desperately to buy land so that more trees wouldn't be cut. Much land had already been protected, but much more was needed. Land was cheap there, she said—only about twenty-five dollars per acre.

Ms. Kinsman agreed to visit the Fagervik School. She would bring a map and slides of the Monteverde forest and tell the children where they could send money to buy rain forest land. When Mrs. Kern told the children what had happened, they didn't even seem surprised. As they put it, "We knew you would find one."

"There Are No Bad Ideas."

In the days before Sharon Kinsman's visit, the Fagervik students began to think about how to raise money. They asked Mrs. Kern to write down all their ideas. As she picked up a piece of chalk, several children spoke at once.

"Pony rides!"

"Let's collect old things and sell them!"

"What about a rain forest evening here at school?"

"Dog washing!"

Dog washing? They began to laugh. "That would never work," someone said. "Who would give money for that?" Mrs. Kern put her chalk down. "Look," she said. "Let's make this our rule: there are no bad ideas. The only bad thing is if you have an idea and don't say it. Then we can't use it." She returned to the blackboard. Were there more ideas?

"A rabbit jumping contest!"

"Rabbit jumping?" said Mrs. Kern. "Be serious. You can't *make* a rabbit jump."

"Oh, yes, we all have rabbits. We can train them. We can. We *can!*"

Mrs. Kern tried to imagine someone actually paying money to watch children try to make rabbits jump. She couldn't. This idea was crazy.

"Mrs. Kern . . . there's no such thing as a bad idea . . . remember?" She did. "Rabbit jumping," she wrote, dutifully putting her doubts aside.

Giant Spiders and Deadly Snakes

On November 6, 1987, Sharon Kinsman arrived at the Fagervik School. She was just as enthusiastic as the students. They put on skits for her about rain forests and showed her the many books they had written about tropical creatures. Then at last, it was her turn to show them slides of the Monteverde forest.

First she unfolded a map of the forest and pointed to the area their money could preserve from cutting. She told them that 400 bird species live in the forest, more than in all of Sweden, as well as 490 kinds of butterflies and 500 types of trees. Monteverde is also the only home in the world, she said, for the golden toad, a creature that seems to glow in the dark.

Then she showed her slides. As the room became dark, the students were swept into a hot, steamy jungle half the world away. The slides took them sloshing along a narrow, muddy trail, crisscrossed with roots and vines. A dark canopy of giant trees, thick with bright flowering plants, closed in above them.

They saw giant spiders and deadly snakes. Ms. Kinsman's tape recorder made the forest ring with the shriek of howler monkeys calling to each other and with the chattering of parrots above the trees. They saw the golden toad, the scarlet macaw, and the red-backed poison-arrow frog.

And they saw the forest disappearing, too. They saw hard-muscled men, their backs glistening with sweat, pushing chain saws deep into the giant trees. They could almost smell the smoke of burning tree limbs and feel the thunder of thick, brown trunks crashing down. Behind great piles of ragged wood, the tropical sky was hazy with smoke. Time seemed very short.

When the lights came on, the students were back in Sweden, but they were not the same. Now they had seen their forest—and the danger it faced. There was no time to lose. Mrs. Kern had inspired them with a problem, and Roland had given them an idea they could work with. Sharon Kinsman had shown them their target. Now it was up to them.

"We Knew What We Wanted."

Two weeks later, more than a hundred people crowded into an old schoolhouse near the Fagervik School for a rain forest evening. Students stood by the door and collected ten crowns (about $1.50) from each person. Special programs cost another crown. Even though it was winter, rain splattered steadily onto the roof, just as it must have been raining in the Monteverde forest. To the students, rain was a good sign.

First they performed a play containing a dramatic scene in which trees of the rain forest were cut and creatures killed. That way guests would understand the problem they were trying to help solve. As the applause died down, the children passed an old hat around, urging audience members to drop money in it.

Then they sold rain forest books and rain forest poems. "We were not afraid to ask for money," remembers Maria Karlsson, who was nine. "We knew what we wanted was important." One boy stood at a table keeping track of how much they were making. Whenever a classmate would hand over a fresh delivery of cash, he would count it quickly and shout above the noise, "Now we've got two hundred crowns!!" "Now it's three hundred!!"

Here are the children from the Fagervik School in Sweden who started a multimillion-dollar effort to preserve rain forest habitats for endangered plants and animals.

The evening's total came to 1,600 crowns, or about $240. The next day, they figured out that they had raised enough money to save about twelve football fields worth of rain forest. It was wonderful . . . but was it enough space for a sloth? A leopard? They all knew the answer. They needed more.

They filled up another blackboard with ideas and tried them out. Everything seemed to work. Mrs. Kern brought in a list of prominent people who might make donations. Two girls wrote a letter to the richest woman on the list. A few days later, a check arrived. Someone else wrote to the king of Sweden and asked if he would watch them perform plays about the rain forest. He said yes.

One day they went to a recording studio and made a tape of their rain forest songs. From the very beginning, Mrs. Kern and a music teacher had been helping them write songs. They started with old melodies they liked, changing them a little as they went along. As soon as anybody came up with a good line, they sang it into a tape recorder so they wouldn't forget it by the end of the song. They rehearsed the songs many times on their school bus before recording them, then designed a cover and used some of their money to buy plastic boxes for the tapes. Within months, they had sold five hundred tapes at ten dollars each.

The more they used their imaginations, the more money they raised. They decided to have a fair. "We had a magician and charged admission," remembers Lia Degeby, who was eight. "We charged to see who could make the ugliest face. We had a pony riding contest. We had a market. We had a lady with a beard. We had the strongest lady in the world. We tried everything." The biggest money maker of all was the rabbit jumping contest, even though each rabbit sat still when its time came to jump! Even carrots couldn't budge them. One simply flopped over and went to sleep, crushing its necklace of flowers.

Soon they needed a place to put all the money they had earned. Mrs. Kern's husband, Bernd, helped them form an organization called Barnens Regnskog, which means Children's Rain Forest. They opened a bank account with a post office box where people could continue to mail donations.

By midwinter, they had raised $1,400. The children addressed an envelope to the Monteverde Conservation League, folded a check inside, and sent it on its way to Costa Rica. Weeks later, they received a crumpled package covered with brightly colored stamps. It contained a map of the area that had been bought with their money. A grateful writer thanked them for saving nearly ninety acres of Costa Rican rain forest.

In the early spring, the Fagervik students performed at the Swedish Children's Fair, which led to several national television appearances. Soon schools from all over Sweden were joining Barnens Regnskog and sending money to Monteverde. At one high school near Stockholm, two thousand students did chores all day in the city and raised nearly $15,000. And inspired by the students, the Swedish government gave a grant of $80,000 to Monteverde.

"I Think of My Future."

After another year's work, the children of Fagervik had raised $25,000 more. The families who could afford it sent their children to Costa Rica to see Monteverde. Just before Christmas, ten Fagervik children stepped off the plane, blinking in the bright Costa Rican sunlight. It was hot! They stripped off their coats and sweaters, piled into a bus, and headed for the mountains.

A few hours later, the bus turned onto a narrow, rocky road that threaded its way through steep mountains. The children looked out upon spectacular waterfalls that fell hundreds of feet. Occasionally they glimpsed monkeys swinging through the trees.

Ahead, the mountaintops disappeared inside a dark purple cloud. For a few moments they could see five rainbows at once. Soon it began to rain.

The next morning, they joined ten Costa Rican children and went on a hike through the Monteverde rain forest. Sometimes the thick mud made them step right out of their boots. But it didn't matter. "There were plants everywhere," says Lia. "I saw monkeys and flowers."

On Christmas day, the children of the Fagervik School proudly presented the staff of the Monteverde Conservation League with their check for $25,000. They said it was a holiday present for all the children of the world.

The Monteverde Conservation League used their gift, and funds that had been donated by other children previously, to establish what is now known as El Bosque Eterno de los Niños, or the Children's Eternal Forest. It is a living monument to the caring and power of young people everywhere. So far, kids from thirty nations have raised more than two million dollars to preserve nearly 33,000 acres of rain forest, plenty of room for jaguars and ocelots. The first group of Fagervik students have now graduated to another school, but the first- and second-graders who have replaced them are still raising great sums of money. The school total is now well over $50,000.

The Fagervik students continue to amaze their teacher. "I never thought they could do so much," Mrs. Kern says. "Sometimes I say to them, 'Why do you work so hard?' They say, 'I think of my future.' They make me feel optimistic. When I am with them, I think maybe anything can be done."

Meet the Author

Phillip Hoose

Phillip Hoose likes to spend time with his family. When his daughter Hannah was younger, the Hooses had a family band in which they sang and wrote songs. One of their songs, "Hey Little Ant," later became a book by the same title. They got the idea for the song when they saw Hannah's younger sister squashing ants in their driveway. The book asks readers to question whether or not it is right to kill bugs. Mr. Hoose is a staff member of the Nature Conservancy and a founding member of the Children's Music Network.

Meet the Illustrators

Jim Effler

Jim Effler has been drawing since he was two years old. He has illustrated several children's books about animals and his work has won awards from the Society of Illustrators. He lives in Cincinnati with his wife Debbie and daughters, Jenna and Ariana.

Fred Willingham

Fred Willingham has loved drawing for as long as he can remember, but did not consider making art his career until he received encouragement from his high school art teacher. He loves expressing himself artistically, and feels lucky to get paid to do something he would have a lot of fun doing for free.

Call of Duty

Theme Connections

Within the Selection

1. Why do you think the Swedish children were able to succeed in their goal?

2. What is one reason the rain forests are being destroyed?

Beyond the Selection

3. Can you think of another area of the world that needs to be protected?

4. Do think it is okay for humans to do whatever they want to Earth? Why or why not?

Write about It!

Tell about a fund-raising activity you were a part of or a fund-raising idea you have.

Remember to look for pictures of rain forests to add to the **Concept/Question Board**.

Science Inquiry

Water in the Sky

Clouds supply much of the water you use each day. But how do clouds form in the first place?

Water molecules are always moving through the surrounding air. When the temperature drops, this moisture gathers onto anything nearby. Dew on a cool morning demonstrates this process.

Most clouds form high above Earth's surface, where the atmosphere is much colder. The difference in temperature creates unequal atmospheric, or air, pressures. Warm air has high pressure, so it always flows toward cooler air, like compressed air escaping from a balloon.

Warm air near Earth's surface rises into the cooler air above, carrying moisture with it. As the temperature drops, water molecules cling to small dust particles floating in the atmosphere, and a cloud is born.

Please complete the following experiment, which was designed to demonstrate how clouds form.

Materials needed: one clear plastic 2-liter bottle with cap, one cup of warm water, one 2′ × 2′ piece of black paper, matches (and an adult to help you light the match!)

altocumulus   cirrus   cumulus   stratus

Instructions

1. Fill the bottle with one inch of warm water.

2. Cap the bottle tightly, and give it a good shake.

3. Squeeze the bottle hard ten times. Then squeeze it again, and hold it for a few seconds before letting go.

4. Place the bottle in front of the black construction paper. Do you see a cloud?

5. Now remove the cap, and have an adult light the match.

6. Let the match burn for a few seconds, and then blow it out.

7. Tip the bottle slightly (but don't spill the water!), and hold the match so that smoke gets inside.

8. Quickly recap the bottle to preserve the smoke. Then wait until the smoke disappears.

9. Repeat Steps 3 and 4. Do you see a cloud now?

Think Link

1. Why does a hot-air balloon float?

2. Why does dew form on a cool morning?

3. High, mountainous areas of rain forests are often called *cloud forests* because they are always covered with clouds. Why do you think this happens?

Try It!

As you work on your investigation, think about the instructions you have been given to help you to complete your task.

Genre

Myths explain imaginatively why something in nature happens or why people act the way they do.

Comprehension Strategy

Clarifying As you read the selection, remember that it is important to monitor your reading for words and ideas that you do not understand and to clarify them right away.

JASON
AND THE
GOLDEN FLEECE

retold by Geraldine McCaughrean
illustrated by Emma Chichester Clark

Focus Questions
Why did Jason go out to find the Golden Fleece? How does he accomplish his goal?

612   613

Read the article to find the meanings of these words, which are also in "Jason and the Golden Fleece":

- ✦ glistening
- ✦ strait
- ✦ throb
- ✦ hideous
- ✦ assassins
- ✦ pity
- ✦ gaping
- ✦ worthy
- ✦ challenged
- ✦ destiny

Vocabulary Strategy

An **appositive** is a noun that follows another noun to modify or name it. Authors sometimes use apposition to clarify the meanings of words. Look at the word *pity*. Find how the author uses apposition to define the word.

610

Vocabulary
Warm-Up

An intense sun beat down on Marcus and the other guards as fifty oarsmen below deck rowed the ship forward. Beads of sweat dotted Marcus's face, each one like a glistening diamond reflecting the sunlight.

The soldiers circled the ship's perimeter and watched for signs of trouble. Each of them—including Marcus—had sworn to protect King Leo as he traveled to neighboring Bildonia.

Up ahead, Marcus saw that the ship was approaching a strait. The narrow channel ran between two high cliffs and led to the safer, open sea. Marcus knew that the biggest threat of attack waited between those rocky walls.

Suddenly a steady throb of drumbeats filled the air, coming from the top of one of the cliffs. The hideous villain, Lothar, and his equally horrible men were about to attack.

Marcus knew that Lothar's assassins would try to kill the king. He also knew they took no pity—no sorrow or sympathy—on anyone who stood in the way.

As the king's ship entered the strait, the soldiers searched the cliffs above for the source of the sound. Instead, Lothar's men scrambled up from the water! The drums were a distraction. The king's men were quickly surrounded.

Lothar climbed aboard last. He scanned the captured soldiers one by one before settling his gaze on Marcus. An ugly laugh erupted from his gaping mouth, and Lothar declared Marcus to be a worthy opponent. He challenged Marcus to a duel.

Marcus accepted it as his destiny to fight the feared villain. He had been chosen by fate. The soldiers began chanting "Marcus! Marcus! . . . "

Then cold water hit his face. Marcus opened his eyes and found himself lying next to the pool. His sister had just splashed him.

"Marcus!" she called once more from the water. "Wake up! You'll get a sunburn."

Marcus quickly looked for Lothar before deciding it was safe to get into the pool.

GAME

Substituting Synonyms
Using a thesaurus, find a synonym for each selection vocabulary word. On a separate sheet of paper, rewrite the sentences from the selection that contain vocabulary words, but substitute a synonym for each vocabulary word.

Concept Vocabulary

The concept word for this lesson is **courageous.** Being *courageous* means having the inner strength, or courage, to ignore your fears so that you can accomplish difficult tasks. It takes courage to save someone whose life is in danger, but it also takes courage to perform onstage, especially if you are shy. Can you think of a time when you were courageous, even though you were scared?

Genre

Myths explain imaginatively why something in nature happens or why people act the way they do.

Comprehension Strategy

☆ Clarifying
As you read the selection, remember that it is important to monitor your reading for words and ideas that you do not understand and to clarify them right away.

JASON
AND THE
GOLDEN FLEECE

retold by Geraldine McCaughrean

illustrated by Emma Chichester Clark

Focus Questions

Why did Jason go out to find the Golden Fleece? How does he accomplish his goal?

It's sad, but sometimes brothers hate each other. Pelias hated his older brother, Aeson, because Aeson was the king of Thebes. *"I* want to be king," said Pelias, and took the throne from his brother and put him in prison. But Aeson had a son, and after many years that son came back to fight for his father's rights. His name was Jason.

When Pelias heard that Jason had arrived, he did not send assassins to kill him. He challenged him to a dare. "I'll give up the crown without a fight, if you can prove you are worthy to take it from me. I dare you to go and find the famous Golden Fleece. If you can bring it to me, the crown goes back to your father."

"I accept! I'll do it!" said Jason.

Then Pelias smiled a wicked smile. For he knew that many had tried to take the fiercely guarded Golden Fleece belonging to King Medea—but none had lived to tell the tale.

Jason's first task was to search out the finest shipbuilder in the land.

"Build me a ship finer than any that ever sailed the seas. I'm going in search of the Golden Fleece!"

"But they say the Fleece is guarded by a dragon that never sleeps!" whispered the shipbuilder.

"Then I must put that dragon to sleep forever!" cried Jason.

He called his ship *Argo,* which means swift, and he mustered a crew from all the heroes of the world and called them his Argonauts. But when he climbed aboard, he did not even know where to start looking for the Golden Fleece. Resting his hand on the wooden figurehead—carved from a magical oak tree—he could feel a throb, like a heartbeat. Suddenly the figurehead turned, and the carved eyes opened, and the carved mouth spoke: "King Phineas will tell you where. Ask poor, poor Phineas!"

Phineas was old and blind. He had chests full of robes and larders full of food. But when Jason and the Argonauts visited him he was as thin as a twig and his clothes hung in rags.

Servants brought delicious food. But no sooner was the table set than in through the windows swooped a flock of hideous birds, their claws snatching, their wings clacking. They had women's heads, with flying hair and munching mouths, and they stole the supper out of the very hands of the Argonauts and slashed at their faces.

"The Harpies! Shelter under the table, sirs!" cried King Phineas. "You'll be safer there."

But Jason drew his sword and cried, "Up, men, and fight!"

He and his crew fought the Harpies until feathers and hair fell like snow. The creatures beat at Jason with their leathery wings, but he cut them out of the air with his sword and jumped on them with his two feet. At last the Harpies fled shrieking across the rooftops and out to sea, never to return.

Jason filled a plate with food and set it in front of the king. "Eat, friend, then tell us how to find the Golden Fleece."

"Don't try it!" begged Phineas. "The Fleece hangs in the Land of Colchis, beyond the Clashing Cliffs. Think of that and tremble!"

"Tremble? I, tremble? Ha!" said Jason grandly. And he gathered his men together and the *Argo* set sail for the Clashing Cliffs.

But the cliffs were a terrifying sight. Two walls of rock, on either side of a narrow strait, crashed together like cymbals. Fire streamed down and sparks flew up, while boulders plunged into the churning sea below.

"We shall be ground to dust!" cried the Argonauts.

"No! Watch the sea gulls, men!" cried Jason. "They know when the way ahead is safe. Lean on your oars, and follow the gulls!"

And between one clash of cliffs and the next, the *Argo* sped through, swift as the darting sea gulls. Soon they had reached Colchis, Land of the Golden Fleece.

The next day Jason presented himself to the king of the island and told him his story. "I must have the Golden Fleece—it's my destiny," he said.

The king's lip curled. "Well, of course *I* shall let you take my Golden Fleece . . . but the soldiers who guard it might try to stop you. Ha ha!"

Out of his deep purple pockets he pulled handfuls of sharp white teeth. Dragon's teeth! He tossed them in among the Argonauts. As each tooth touched the ground, a warrior sprang up, bristling with weapons. Soon these soldiers outnumbered Jason's men a hundred to one.

"We fought the Harpies, didn't we?" cried Jason to his men. "Surely we can knock out a mouthful of teeth!"

"Kill them!" the king raged at his dragon-tooth army. But soon there was no army left to hear him. The Argonauts had wiped it out. Now nothing stood between Jason and the Golden Fleece.

Except the dragon.

The Fleece hung in a lovely garden. By the gate of the garden stood a woman—the king's daughter. "I watched you fight the dragon-tooth warriors," said Princess Medea to Jason. "You are a true hero, I can see that. But you'll need my magic if you are going to win the Golden Fleece. Marry me and I'll help you."

"You're so beautiful that I'll willingly marry you," said Jason. "But I must lift down the prize by my own strength or I would be cheating."

He set out through flowery groves, across streams, past bushes hung with blossom. But here and there he passed piles of bones. Other heroes had entered the garden before him . . . and met the dragon.

At last Jason found the prize he had come for. The Golden Fleece rested over the branch of a tree—as thick and heavy as a carpet, glistening with golden curls, soft, soft, soft. And around the tree coiled the dragon set to guard it. The monster had no eyelids, it had no name, and it had no pity. It looked at Jason with eyes scorched red by sunshine and moonlight. Then it pounced on him with gaping jaws.

Jason drew his sword, but its blade shattered like glass against the dragon's scales. Teeth tore his clothes and fiery breath scorched his hair. Up into the tree he clambered to escape. And when the dragon opened its mouth to lick him down, Jason plunged in his broken sword. The beast gave a terrible roar. Smoke billowed around Jason. Again and again he stabbed, until black smoke dirtied all the king's garden.

The Argonauts, watching from the shore, saw the smoke gather in the sky.

"Where's Jason? Why doesn't he come?" they cried.

Then the sun glinted on a splash of gold—a sheep's fleece. It was draped over Jason's shoulder as he came running down the beach. Alongside him ran a woman as beautiful as the Fleece.

"Aboard, men!" cried Jason. "I've stolen the king's Golden Fleece and his daughter!"

So Jason and Princess Medea returned to Thebes—much to the amazement and fury of Pelias. Jason's father, Aeson, was freed from prison, but he refused to put on the crown of Thebes again.

"I'm too tired to rule, Son," he said. "You must be king in my place."

But Medea said gently, "Trust me, father-in-law. I have magic to make you strong and young again."

She poured him a peculiar potion, which sent Aeson to sleep for three days. When he awoke, he had the body of a young man and the wisdom of an old one—and all the energy he needed to rule Thebes.

When wicked old Pelias saw this amazing transformation, he went to Medea and offered her all his money if she would do the same for him. "Make me young again, Medea," he said. "I'd give anything for that!"

So Medea gave him a potion, too, and he fell asleep for three days. Three months. Three years. In fact he never woke up again, because Medea had put him to sleep forever.

So Jason and Medea lived together as man and wife, and although Jason dressed in simple clothes, his cloak was lined with a golden fleece.

Meet the Author

Geraldine McCaughrean

Geraldine McCaughrean was very shy as a child in London, but she loved to make up stories. When her 14-year-old brother wrote a book, she wanted to be an author too. She continued to write while working many other jobs. In 1988, she finally became a full-time author. McCaughrean loves drama. She sometimes gets story ideas from plays. She lives in Berkshire, England, with her husband and daughter. Her dog, Daisy, likes to eat her stories instead of read them.

Meet the Illustrator

Emma Chichester Clark

Emma Chichester Clark was born in London, England. She draws the eyes of most of her characters in a very distinctive way—as circles with pupil dots. This gives the character a childlike, curiously expressive appearance. Many of Clark's books, such as *Tea with Aunt Augusta,* show characters wearing wide-brimmed hats. Expressive eyes and wide-brimmed hats are Emma Chichester Clark's trademarks.

Theme Connections

Within the Selection

1. Why does Jason refuse help from Princess Medea?
2. Do you think Jason would be a good king? Why or why not?

Across Selections

3. How is Jason similar to the schoolchildren in "Founders of the Children's Rain Forest"?
4. How is Jason different from the schoolchildren in "Founders of the Children's Rain Forest"?

Beyond the Selection

5. What kinds of heroic acts do people perform today?
6. Can you think of a reason why someone would go on a journey in real life?

Write about It!

Tell about someone who you think is a hero, and explain why.

Remember to look for newspaper or magazine articles about heroes to add to the **Concept/Question Board.**

Newton's Law

For hundreds of years, philosophers and scientists believed that everything in the universe wanted to be at rest. Whenever they observed something that was moving, it would, sooner or later, come to a stop. They concluded that this must be the natural way of things. Then, in 1687, Isaac Newton published his Laws of Motion. They challenged this belief.

Newton's First Law of Motion states that inertia, not rest, is an object's natural state. Inertia means that things are lazy. Objects at rest want to stay at rest, and objects in motion want to keep moving. Newton knew that when things do slow down and stop, it is not just a natural event. It happens because forces like gravity, friction, or other objects made them stop.

Imagine a boat on a perfectly still, windless lake. As long as you do not touch that boat, it will sit there forever. Give it a shove, though, and it will move in the direction you pushed it. With no other forces affecting it, the boat would float along steadily forever.

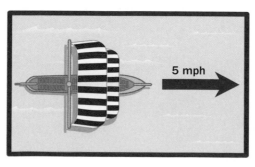

5 mph

As long as no other force acts upon the boat, it will move forward forever at a constant speed.

Of course, a real lake has wind, water, and other boats. Wind will cause the boat to drift in a different direction. Friction caused by the water will slow the boat down until it stops. If the boat bumps into another boat, the boats will affect each other. The bigger boat will have more force on the smaller boat. If one of the boats is big enough, the smaller boat will not affect its movement at all.

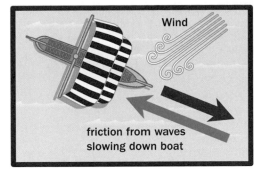

Forces like gravity, friction, and wind will alter the boat's speed and direction.

Objects that seem to be at rest are usually at rest only because two equal forces are canceling each other out. A pencil lying on a desk actually wants to move. Gravity is pulling it downward. However, the table is pushing upward with equal force. The pencil stays put. Remove the table, though, and that pencil will immediately accelerate toward the next object in its way—the floor.

Think Link

1. When did Isaac Newton publish his Laws of Motion?

2. If a boat is pushed across the water and there are no forces acting against it, how long will it float?

3. What force pulls objects toward Earth?

Try It!

As you work on your investigation, think about how you might use captions.

Read the article to find the meanings of these words, which are also in "The Quest for Healing":

+ task
+ quest
+ sport
+ lumbered
+ loyalty
+ descended
+ exhausted
+ spring
+ fitter
+ beaded

Vocabulary Strategy

Context Clues are hints in the text that help you find the meanings of words. Look at the words *descended, exhausted,* and *beaded.* Use context clues to find each word's meaning.

Vocabulary

Warm-Up

Blue trotted down the trail, pausing to sniff logs and clumps of grass scattered along the side. When he got too far ahead, Myn called his name. Blue waited impatiently for his human to catch up.

Myn and Blue were searching for a hot spring. It was not exactly on the trail. Myn's friends had told her to watch for certain landmarks so that the task of finding the spring would not be too hard. So far, though, Myn had not seen them. She wondered if her quest for a warm soak in a natural watering hole would be unsuccessful. *At least it is a nice hike,* she thought.

In the woods to Myn's left, something skittered through the leaves. Startled for a moment, Myn and Blue froze, but then the dog leapt off the trail and raced after the sound.

"Blue!" Myn yelled, as he disappeared into the thick greenery. Blue liked chasing squirrels for sport—he never actually caught them—but this could be something dangerous.

Heading into the woods, Myn kept calling Blue's name. She lumbered across the uneven ground, slowly and awkwardly following her dog's barking. Going off the trail was not a great idea, but Myn's loyalty toward Blue was equal to the love she had toward her family.

Myn carefully descended a small, rocky slope. She found Blue waiting at the bottom in a small clearing. The chase had exhausted Myn—she felt the tiredness throughout her body—but Blue looked unaffected.

"You silly dog," Myn said as she approached him.

Looking around the clearing, Myn could not believe what she saw: the hot spring! Tiny wisps of steam rose off the spring water's surface.

After soaking for nearly an hour, Myn felt much fitter. Before leaving, she took a long drink from her plastic bottle. It was beaded with tiny water droplets. Myn was ready to head home, but first she put a leash on Blue.

GAME

Searching for Synonyms Look at the list of words below. Using a dictionary or a thesaurus, find the selection vocabulary word that has the same or nearly the same meaning, and write your answers on a separate sheet of paper.

trudged	dotted
expedition	fountain
depleted	stronger
plummeted	entertainment
chore	faithfulness

Concept Vocabulary

The concept word for this lesson is **devotion.** *Devotion* is dedicating your time and effort to a person or an idea. People show devotion to their country by taking part in civic duties, such as voting or volunteering. Have you ever shown devotion to a cause or to a person?

Genre

A **folktale** is an old story handed down by word of mouth from generation to generation. It often contains a moral, or lesson about life.

Comprehension Strategy

 Making Connections

As you read the selection, make connections between what you are reading and what you already know from past experience or previous selections to help you understand story events and characters.

Focus Questions

What did Nekumonta set out to find? Why did the Manitou help Nekumonta in his quest?

The Quest for Healing

by Philip Ardagh

illustrated by Diana Magnuson

Nekumonta patted her gently and said, "Everyone in my village is dying, and my beautiful wife, Shanewis, is among them. If you know where the Manitou has planted the healing herbs, please lead me to them. They are our only hope."

But the doe didn't know where the Manitou had planted the herbs, so she twitched her ears and disappeared into the forest. The story was the same with every animal he met after that. None of them could help him.

On the third night Nekumonta was near to giving up. Weak and exhausted, he wrapped himself in his blanket and fell asleep.

While he slept, the animals of the forest held a meeting.

"Nekumonta is a good human," said the grizzly bear. "He only kills when he has to, as is the way with us animals."

"And he treats our homes with respect, too," said the rabbit. "He cares about the trees and plants around him."

"Do you think we should help him?" asked the doe.

"Yes," said the rabbit. "But how can we?"

"Perhaps we could call to the great Manitou for his help?" suggested the grizzly bear. "Then he will realize that all living things want Nekumonta to succeed in his quest."

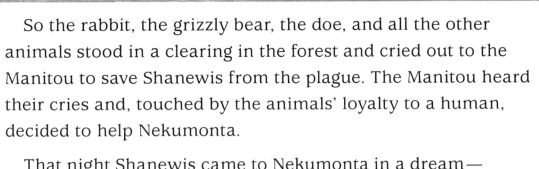

So the rabbit, the grizzly bear, the doe, and all the other animals stood in a clearing in the forest and cried out to the Manitou to save Shanewis from the plague. The Manitou heard their cries and, touched by the animals' loyalty to a human, decided to help Nekumonta.

That night Shanewis came to Nekumonta in a dream—pale-faced and very thin. She began to sing him a strange and beautiful song, but he could not understand the words, and they soon turned into the music of a waterfall.

Meet the Author

Philip Ardagh

While he has toured the United States only once, Philip Ardagh stays busy writing and promoting his books in Great Britain and Ireland. He is as unique as his books—he stands 6'7" tall and sports a long beard. He has written over sixty books, but he has not always been a writer. He has also cleaned hospitals, worked in a library, and made tapes of books for people who are blind. When not writing, he enjoys watching the wildlife in his garden, which includes woodpeckers, owls, squirrels, and badgers.

Meet the Illustrator

Diana Magnuson

Diana Magnuson has lived in many places, including Germany and parts of Africa. When she was little, she loved playing football. Magnuson also drew pictures of pretend worlds. Now she spends her time drawing pictures for stories and textbooks. She does not play football as often now, but Magnuson loves to hike and ski. She and her family live in Michigan near Lake Superior.

Theme Connections

Within the Selection

1. Why were the animals willing to help Nekumonta?

2. Why do you think Native Americans believe that the same spirit is found inside all things?

Across Selections

3. How is this story similar to "Founders of the Children's Rain Forest"?

4. How is this story different from "Founders of the Children's Rain Forest"?

Beyond the Selection

5. Can you think of a way that this myth relates to our world today?

6. Should people be allowed to have as much as they want of everything? Why or why not?

Write about It!

Tell about a time when you helped a friend or family member.

Remember to look for pictures of animals that live in your neighborhood to add to the **Concept/Question Board.**

People of the Long House

Did you know that a representative government existed in North America years before the American Revolution? It was the League of Five Nations, better known as the Iroquois.

The name *Iroquois* was actually an insult. Their enemies, the Algonquin, called them *iroqu*, which means "rattlesnakes." The Iroquois call themselves *Haudenosaunee* (Ho-dee-no-show-nee), meaning "people of the long house."

The Mohawk, Onondaga, Oneida, Cayuga, and Seneca lived in what is today New York. For hundreds of years, they fought one another. Then a

The five nations of the Haudenosaunee in 1650

peacemaker named Deganawida and the Mohawk war chief, Hiawatha, convinced the tribes to pledge loyalty to one another. An agreement called the Great Law of Peace was made, but no one is certain exactly when. Most likely it happened during the 1500s.

The Great Law of Peace created something like Congress. Each nation chose representatives to be part of a group that governed all the Haudenosaunee. At the same time, each nation still made many decisions for itself, much as the states do in our country.

The Haudenosaunee became very powerful. Their enemies were no match for the Five Nations working together.

The Haudenosaunee were mainly farmers. When the colonists arrived, though, hunting became a priority. Beaver pelts could be traded for European goods, especially guns.

Guns made hunting much easier. They also quickly reduced the number of beavers on Iroquois land. In the mid-1600s, the Five Nations began attacking their neighbors—and enemies—the Huron, to get more land.

The Five Nations also raided French settlements. France was the Huron's main trading partner. Soon the French army joined the conflict. Then England, the Five Nations' trading partner, began helping the Haudenosaunee. Known as the Beaver Wars, this bloody conflict lasted nearly fifty years.

In 1701, France, England, and dozens of Native American chiefs signed the Great Peace, ending the Beaver Wars.

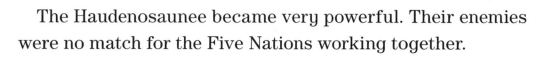

Think Link

1. What does the word *Haudenosaunee* mean?

2. Why do you think England supported Native Americans who were attacking France, another European nation?

3. The Huron lived to the northeast of the Haudenosaunee. Which of the Five Nations was most likely to attack them?

Try It!

As you work on your investigation, think about how you might be able to use maps.

Read the article to find the meanings of these words, which are also in "The White Spider's Gift":

+ irritably
+ murmur
+ scowls
+ Paraguay
+ murals
+ pleading
+ intricate
+ burdened
+ rare
+ noble

Vocabulary Strategy

Context Clues are hints in the text that help you find the meanings of words. Look at the words *irritably, murmur,* and *Paraguay.* Use context clues to find each word's meaning.

Vocabulary

Warm-Up

As Gabrielle ate breakfast, Mrs. Rivera clomped into the kitchen and headed to the sink without saying a word.

Oh no, Gabrielle thought, *she's acting irritably again.* Lately, Gabrielle's mother often seemed impatient and angry.

Mrs. Rivera shook her head and frowned at the sink full of dirty dishes. She began to murmur in Spanish, quietly complaining about her messy family.

She scowls so much these days, Gabrielle thought. Gabrielle knew that dirty dishes were not the only cause of her mother's frustrations.

The Riveras had recently moved to the U.S. from Paraguay—a South American country. Gabrielle and her father learned English in school there, but Mrs. Rivera had picked up only a few words.

In Paraguay, Gabrielle's mother had been a successful painter of murals in people's homes. Customers were always pleading with her, begging her to create colorful and intricate scenes on their walls.

Since the family had moved, though, Mrs. Rivera had painted just one mural. It was a forest scene in Gabrielle's bedroom. It showed a spring of bubbling water coming out of the ground and birds swooping in for a drink.

Gabrielle knew that her mother wanted to start working again but was worried about her English. Then Gabrielle had an idea.

In Spanish, she asked, "Mom, could I help you with your English?"

At first, Mrs. Rivera refused. "Honey, you do not need to be burdened by me. You already have plenty to do."

Gabrielle insisted. "Please let me help. You have a rare talent. Few people paint as well as you do."

"Gabrielle," Mrs. Rivera began, "you are a noble child—generous and quite special. I will let you help me. . . ," she smiled, " . . . wash the dishes."

Gabrielle laughed and joined her mother.

Word Charades
Divide into two teams, and choose one student from each team to sit facing the class. Reveal a vocabulary word to everyone but the two seated students. Then have the class describe the word without saying the word itself. The first of the two students to predict the word scores a point for his or her team. Continue with different vocabulary words and different students until all words have been used.

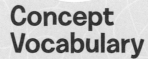

Concept Vocabulary

The concept word for this lesson is **virtue.** *Virtue* is doing what is morally right, even when it may be difficult. Telling the truth, protecting the weak, and helping people who are in trouble are behaviors that show virtue. Have you ever shown virtue during a difficult time?

Genre

A **Play** is a story that uses actors to speak dialogue and is performed for an audience.

Comprehension Strategy

⭐ **Predicting**
As you read the selection, make predictions about what will happen next. Revise these predictions when necessary.

The White Spider's Gift

by Jamie Turner

illustrated by Judith Nelson

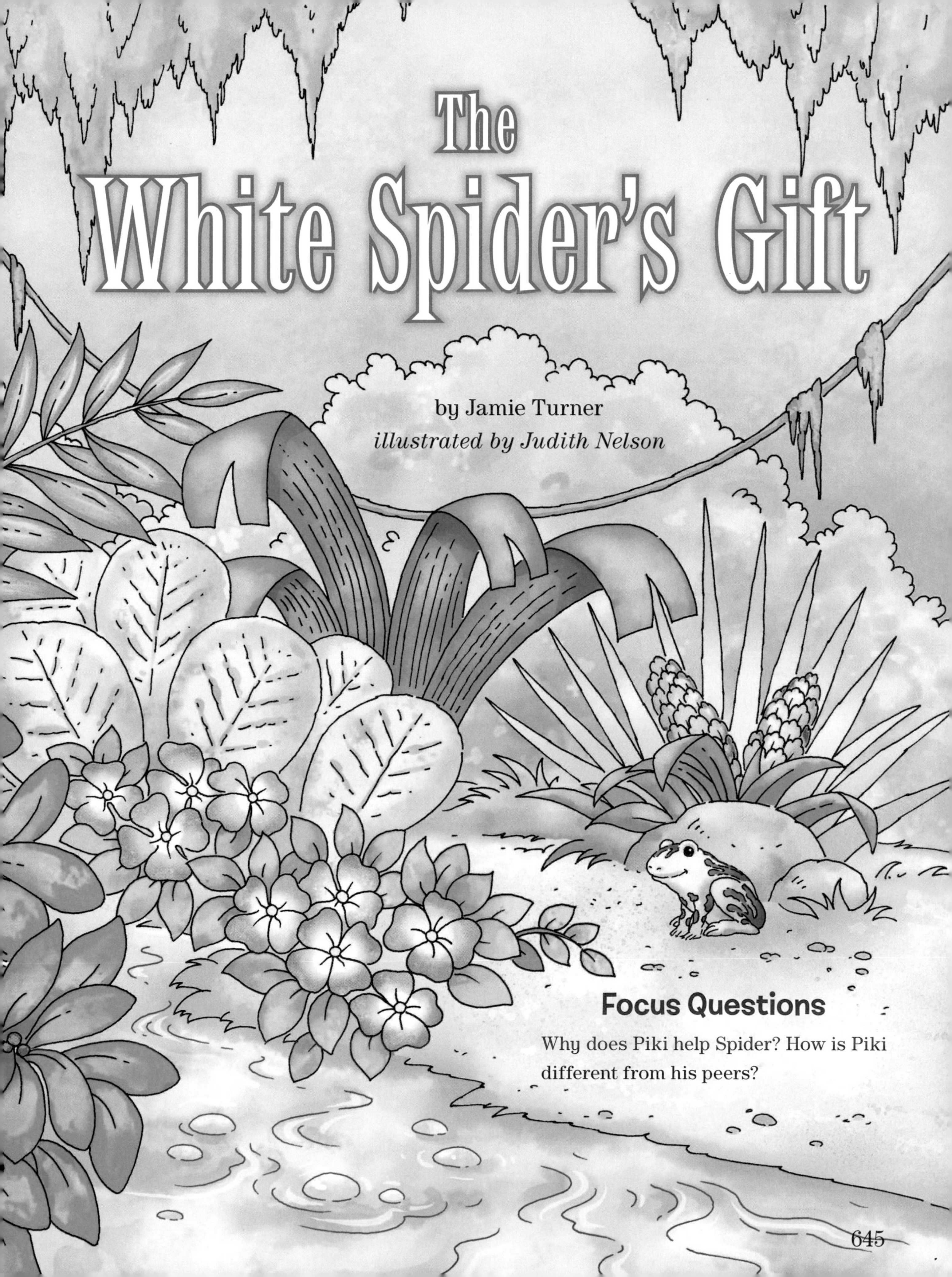

Focus Questions

Why does Piki help Spider? How is Piki different from his peers?

645

Characters

WHITE SPIDER, offstage voice	**CHIEFTAIN**
KUMA, Guarani boy	**MESSENGER**
TWO GIRLS	**DIKA** ⎤
OLD WOMAN	**DABU** ⎟
PIKI, Guarani boy	**KINTA** ⎬ Guarani boys
MOTHER, Piki's mother	**MUNGA** ⎦
TUKIRA, Chieftain's daughter	
THREE WOMEN	

SCENE 1

TIME: *Long ago.*

SETTING: *Forest of Paraguay. Played before curtain. Murals on walls flanking stage depict trees and undergrowth. One large bush, displayed on right wall outside curtain, represents spider's home. Bush must be visible throughout the play. A large spider's web of white yarn covers most of the bush.*

BEFORE RISE: *KUMA enters left, and runs toward spider's web.*

SPIDER *(From offstage):* Help me! Please, I am over here in the spring!

KUMA *(Stopping; irritably):* What? Who are you? *(Peers over stage apron)*

SPIDER: Please, will you bend down here and lift me out? I have fallen into the spring.

KUMA: What? Help a spider? I cannot stop for such a small matter. I must go find tea leaves for my father. I have already wasted much time, and he will be angry.

SPIDER *(Pleading):* Oh, please. I would not trouble you if I were not so tired. The water bubbles up so, and I cannot reach the edge.

KUMA *(Looking up at sky):* I must hurry. Father is waiting. *(Runs out. 1ST GIRL enters at side, looks along floor as if hunting.)*

SPIDER: Please, little girl, help me! See, I am here in the spring.

1ST GIRL *(Stooping):* Where? Oh, I see—why, you are a spider! I am afraid of spiders! And you are a white one, besides; I have never seen a white spider. You must be ill. I cannot help you; I might get hurt.

SPIDER: I am harmless, little girl. Please help me. My strength is almost gone.

1ST GIRL: Oh, but I could not bear to touch a spider. Swim to the edge and climb out yourself. Spiders are good climbers.

SPIDER: I cannot! The water swirls around me with great force; it is stronger than I am.

1ST GIRL: If I remember, I will send a friend to help you when I get back to the village. I am looking for the beautiful nandari flower now. I cannot stop. *(Exits, humming and stooping to examine flowers. OLD WOMAN with walking stick enters, shuffles toward spider web, dragging burlap sack behind her.)*

SPIDER *(Calling):* Kind woman! Please help me! *(OLD WOMAN cocks head, puts hand to ear)*

OLD WOMAN: What is it that I hear?

SPIDER: It is I, the little white spider who lives in the yerba bush beside the spring.

OLD WOMAN *(Looking up at web):* Eh? Who? Where?

SPIDER: No, not up there. I am down here in the water! I fell from my web and cannot get out. Please help me!

OLD WOMAN *(Looking over edge of stage; shaking head, sadly):* Ah, yes, life is full of trouble, little spider. And the older one gets, the more burdened with care he becomes.

SPIDER: But will you not help me, Guarani woman? Will you not hold your stick down and let me crawl upon it so that you may lift me out?

OLD WOMAN: I am old, little spider. I must help myself. I must look for twigs so that I may have a fire tonight. *(Exits, mumbling)* Trouble, trouble. Life is full of trouble. *(PIKI and MOTHER enter, carrying large earthen jars, and walk across stage.)*

SPIDER: Help! Oh, please! I am growing weak! Please help me!

PIKI: Do you hear a cry for help?

MOTHER: Yes, Piki, I do. *(Calls)* Where are you?

SPIDER: Here in the spring! *(Voice grows fainter.)* I cannot swim any longer. My legs are . . .

PIKI *(Dropping to knees and looking over edge of stage):* Oh, Mother, it is a spider. She is sinking! *(Reaches down. "Spider" [see Production Notes] may be concealed in PIKI's hand when he first enters or hidden on ledge near spring.)*

MOTHER: Can you reach her, Piki?

PIKI *(Rising, cupping hand gently):* Yes. Oh, I hope she's still alive!

MOTHER: Oh, Piki, see—she opens her eyes!

PIKI *(Patting inside hand with finger):* Little spider, are you really alive? I am so happy I could catch you before the water pulled you down.

MOTHER: Is this the little white spider who lives in the yerba bush there beside the spring? *(Looks up at web)*

PIKI: Yes. I see her each day when I come to fill the water jars. She lives so quietly and peacefully, spinning her beautiful web of silk. I am pleased that I could help her.

SPIDER *(Weakly):* Thank you, kind Piki. You are a good, strong young Guarani.

PIKI: Strong? But it does not take strength to lift a small spider.

SPIDER: No, it does not take a strong body, Piki, but it takes a strong heart. A selfless heart is the strongest of all. I am feeling better now. Will you please place me back in my web so that I may rest?

PIKI: Certainly. *(Places SPIDER in center of web)* Rest quietly, little friend. I will visit you tomorrow to see if you are well. Goodbye.

SPIDER: Goodbye, Piki. Someday I shall help you as you have helped me this day. *(PIKI stoops as if filling jar with water. MOTHER takes it from him and gives him another to fill. TUKIRA enters at side, pretending to gather berries, placing them into basket. PIKI looks up and sees her; he stands slowly, gazing in wonder. TUKIRA sees him, looks down quickly, turns and runs off.)*

PIKI: Mother! Who is she?

MOTHER: She is Tukira, the chieftain's daughter.

PIKI: But why have I never seen her before?

MOTHER: When Tukira was a small child, her mother died, and the chieftain sent her to live with an aunt in a distant village. She is sixteen now and has come back to our village to live. The chieftain will soon choose a husband for her.

PIKI: How will he do that?

MOTHER: Tomorrow he will assemble the young men from our village and announce his plan. You will be among them.

PIKI *(Lifting jar to his shoulder):* Tukira . . . what a beautiful name.

MOTHER *(Lifting other jar):* Yes. A beautiful name for a beautiful princess. Let us start home now, Piki. It is growing late. *(They exit. Curtain)*

SCENE 2

TIME: *The next day.*

SETTING: *Chieftain's home. Cloth-covered wooden frame center has leafy branches laid across the top. Large earthen jars, weaving frame, and wood for fire are on either side. Background mural shows forest.*

AT RISE: *CHIEFTAIN sits on floor beneath frame. 1ST WOMAN pretends to cook over open fire. 2ND WOMAN, carrying earthen jar, crosses stage and exits. CHILDREN run across, laughing as they play tag. 3RD WOMAN pretends to weave on loom. MESSENGER enters and bows before CHIEFTAIN.*

CHIEFTAIN: Have the six youths received my message to come today?

MESSENGER *(Bowing):* Yes, Chieftain. They come now. *(PIKI, DIKA, DABU, KINTA, MUNGA, and KUMA enter, carrying bows and arrows. All but CHIEFTAIN, MESSENGER, and boys exit. Boys stand on either side of CHIEFTAIN, with backs to audience.)*

CHIEFTAIN: I have chosen you six youths to have a contest. The winner of the contest may have the hand of my daughter Tukira in marriage and perhaps may rule our village when I grow old. *(Speaks to each of six in turn)* You, Kuma, are tall and strong. Dika, you swim and fish with the skill of your father. With your swift arrows, Dabu, you have fed your family well. You, Kinta, have the wisdom of your ancestors. Munga, you are brave in times of war. And you, Piki, are good and noble. The contest will begin now and will end in three days. Today you will compete in running, shooting, and wrestling. First will be the foot race. The course is clearly marked through the forest and back to our village. You may take a moment to prepare. My messenger will signal the start. *(MESSENGER sits, beats on small drum. Boys lay down bows and arrows and prepare to run.)*

KUMA *(Boastfully):* I shall surely win the race, for I am the oldest.

DABU: You may be the oldest, but I have seen young Piki run—and he is very fast. He saves his energy by running steadily, and then his feet seem to grow wings as he nears the end of a race.

KUMA: He will not pass me. You will see. *(Boys line up in front of MESSENGER, facing left. Drum grows louder. MESSENGER shouts, and race begins. Boys run offstage and follow prescribed course through audience, with KUMA in the lead. With PIKI right behind, KUMA returns to stage slightly ahead of others. KUMA glances back and deliberately trips PIKI. CHIEFTAIN stares straight ahead, apparently not seeing the incident. PIKI rises, brushes off knees and hands. KUMA looks exultant. Other boys return to stage, panting, and CHIEFTAIN motions for all to sit.)*

CHIEFTAIN: You all ran well, but you, Kuma, finished first. *(PIKI drops his head briefly but raises it again.)* Next is the shooting contest. *(Points off left)* Do you see the red feather on the trunk of the old tree beside the river? *(Boys nod.)* The one whose arrow pierces the tip of the feather will win this contest. *(MESSENGER stands far left, announcing results of each boy's shot.)* Munga, you may try first. *(One at a time boys stand, facing left, and raise their bows slowly as if to aim an arrow.)*

MUNGA *(Shooting):* How close is it?

MESSENGER: It is very close, only a hand's length from the feather's tip. *(MUNGA runs out left. KINTA shoots next and runs out left.)* That was a good shot, but the first arrow is still closer.

DABU: Surely I can shoot closer. I will pretend the feather is the forehead of a wild boar. *(Shoots, exits)*

MESSENGER: Dabu's arrow is only a finger's width from the tip of the feather! *(DABU shouts joyfully.)*

DIKA: Save your joy, Dabu. There are three more of us to try. *(Shoots)*

MESSENGER: Your arrow did not fly true, Dika. It fell far beneath the feather. *(DIKA exits, disappointed.)*

KUMA *(Boastfully):* With my new bow I can easily win. Watch how straight my arrow will fly! *(Shoots)* I won, did I not?

MESSENGER: No, Kuma, your arrow has fallen near the bottom of the feather's stem, not its tip. Now, Piki, it is your turn. *(KUMA stalks angrily right and sits, sulking.)*

KUMA: You will never win, Piki. You are the youngest of us. Have you ever even held a bow before?

PIKI: I have held a bow for many years, Kuma. This was my father's bow, and it has never failed me. *(Shoots. Boys and MESSENGER shout excitedly and run back onstage, with MESSENGER holding feather aloft. Feather is large and may be made out of red construction paper, cut partway down the middle as if split by the arrow.)*

MESSENGER: See, Piki, your arrow pierced the feather's tip, dividing it exactly in half. You have won! *(KUMA scowls angrily.)*

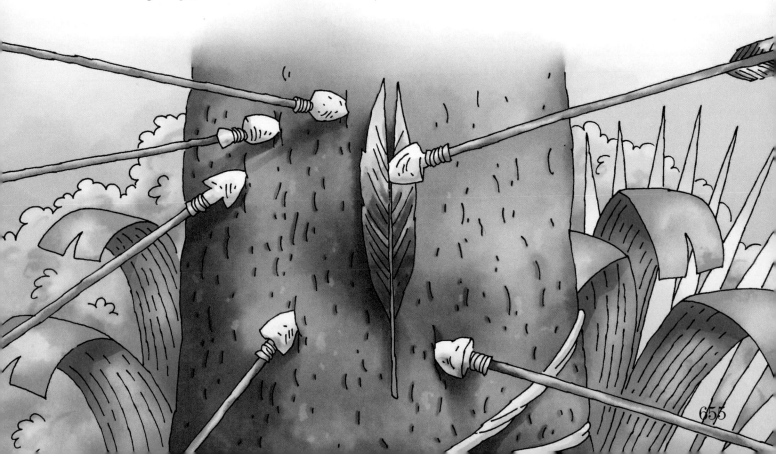

CHIEFTAIN: Kuma has won the foot race, and Piki has won the shooting contest. Now you will all wrestle. *(MESSENGER hands CHIEFTAIN a stick.)* You will hold this stick between you, and you must keep both hands on the stick at all times. You may not move your feet once the contest begins. The one who can force the other to lose his balance will win. Kuma and Dika will fight first. *(KUMA and DIKA face each other with stick between them, each grasping it with both hands. They plant their feet firmly.)*

MESSENGER: Begin. *(KUMA and DIKA begin their "fight." After brief struggle, DIKA loses balance, and KUMA wins. Next, DABU and KINTA fight, and DABU wins. Then MUNGA and PIKI fight, and PIKI wins.)*

CHIEFTAIN: Now the three winners will fight. First, Piki and Dabu. *(PIKI and DABU face each other and begin. Others form semicircle behind them, upstage, facing audience, but KUMA stands in back of others, drops to ground, takes tube out of his waistband, and aims at PIKI's ankle, as if blowing stone or dart.)*

PIKI winces and grabs his ankle, losing his balance. No one else appears to see what KUMA did.) Dabu has won. Now, Dabu, you and Kuma will fight. *(DABU and KUMA fight, and DABU wins after a struggle.)*

KUMA *(Throwing stick down angrily):* It was not fair! I was not ready to start!

CHIEFTAIN: Dabu is the winner. *(Looks around at boys)* You have all done well today, but only three have won. Kuma, Piki, and Dabu will now compete in another contest, which will end in three days. The winner will marry my daughter Tukira on that day. *(DIKA, KINTA, and MUNGA exit; CHIEFTAIN addresses remaining three.)* Each of you must find a beautiful gift to present to my daughter. Return in three days with your gifts, and she will choose the best. Go now and may your search be rewarded. *(Drum beats as KUMA, DABU, and PIKI exit. Curtain)*

SCENE 3

TIME: *Two days later.*

SETTING: *The forest; before curtain.*

BEFORE RISE: *PIKI enters, carrying jar. He approaches spring, kneels down as if to fill jar, then sets jar beside him and sits, looking sad.*

SPIDER *(From offstage):* Piki, Piki, why do you look so sad?

PIKI *(Looking up at bush in surprise):* Oh, it is you, little spider. *(Sighs)* My heart is heavy because I shall not win the beautiful Tukira for my wife. I ran well, I shot well, and I fought well. But now I have no hope. Tukira will surely become the wife of Kuma or Dabu.

SPIDER: You can win the final contest with my help.

PIKI: Do you know of the contest?

SPIDER: Yes. I listen as I sit quietly in my yerba bush spinning my web. The women talk as they come to fill their water jars. I heard them speak of the gifts for the lovely princess.

PIKI: Yes, the lovely princess . . . but she will never be mine. Tomorrow we must present our gifts. It is said that Dabu will bring a headdress woven of colorful feathers from rare birds. And Kuma boasts openly of his gift, a necklace of gold, encrusted with the lovely topaz stones of the highlands. But I . . . I have nothing. My mother and I are poor, unlike the families of Dabu and Kuma.

SPIDER: Piki, did you not hear me? I shall help you win Tukira's hand.

PIKI: But how can you help, little spider?

SPIDER: Go home to your mother, Piki, but return to the spring at sunrise. Your special gift for Tukira will be ready. Be joyful, Piki, for the morning will dawn bright.

PIKI (*Puzzled yet hopeful*): I shall do as you say, little friend. Bless you for giving me hope.

SPIDER: Bless you, Piki, for taking time to save me from the bubbling spring. I promised on that day to repay your kindness, and I will. (*PIKI exits, looking back in wonder at spider's bush. Lights dim and music plays softly, indicating nighttime.*) I will spin my most delicate thread and sprinkle it with moon dust. In the center I will form the beautiful guava flower . . . the loveliest I have ever spun.

And then, rare orchids of many designs. Then I shall spin stars to twinkle around the edges, and then I shall weave all the designs together with a fine, intricate lace. Now I will begin my work, for I must finish before the sun reaches the horizon. *(Music continues for 30 seconds, with lights gradually coming up. Music stops.)*

PIKI *(Entering left, approaching bush):* The new day has dawned, and I have returned as you said, friend.

SPIDER: Look beneath the bush, Piki. I have finished your gift.

PIKI *(Removing lace mantle from bush; holding it up):* Oh, it is beautiful! Never have I seen such delicate lace! It is fit for a princess.

SPIDER: It will be Tukira's bridal veil. Now, hurry home to show it to your mother, and then take it to the chieftain at the appointed time.

PIKI: How I thank you, White Spider! *(Gently folds lace and turns to exit, but KUMA enters, blocks his way. PIKI hides lace behind his back.)*

KUMA: Piki, what makes you rise so early? Surely you are not still searching the forests for a gift worthy of the princess? *(Laughs)*

PIKI: No, Kuma, I am no longer searching. But I cannot talk; I must go now. *(PIKI starts to move on, but KUMA stops him roughly.)*

KUMA: The women of the village say you have no gift to bring. *(Laughs rudely)* I have fashioned gold into a necklace for Tukira.

PIKI: Yes, Kuma, I have heard of it. The whole village has heard.

KUMA: And soon Tukira will wear my necklace and become my bride. What will you bring, Piki? Perhaps a bowl of tea leaves? *(Laughs)* Or a dish of berries? *(Laughs harder)* Or perhaps the lovely princess would like a new mat woven from dried grass. *(Laughs more)* Go, Piki, and I shall meet you soon as we stand before the chieftain—unless you decide not to come. I would not blame you.

PIKI *(Passing KUMA)*: I shall be there, Kuma. *(Exits, followed by KUMA, laughing. Curtain rises.)*

TIME: *Later that morning.*

SETTING: *Chieftain's home.*

AT RISE: *CHIEFTAIN and TUKIRA sit side by side. 2ND GIRL combs and arranges flowers in TUKIRA's hair. MESSENGER sits behind them, tapping a drum as they talk.*

CHIEFTAIN: The morning has come, daughter. Soon the three young braves will hear the drum and arrive to present their gifts.

TUKIRA: Father, what if I cannot decide which is the most beautiful gift?

CHIEFTAIN: You will know. Your heart will tell you. And after you choose, I shall give one final test to prove the worthiness of your husband. Stand, now. Here come the youths. *(CHIEFTAIN and TUKIRA stand as DUBA, KUMA, and PIKI enter, carrying gifts behind their backs. MESSENGER stops beating drum, and VILLAGE PEOPLE enter, gather around. CHIEFTAIN addresses boys.)* The three days have ended, and now Tukira will choose among you. Present your gift first, Duba. *(DUBA steps forward, kneels, holds out feathered headdress. PEOPLE murmur approval.)*

TUKIRA *(Taking headdress; with admiration)*: It is lovely. Such rare feathers and such brilliant colors! Thank you, Dabu. *(TUKIRA hands headdress to 2ND GIRL. DABU rises and moves back.)*

CHIEFTAIN: Now your gift, Kuma. *(KUMA steps forward, kneels, presents necklace to TUKIRA. PEOPLE murmur even louder and lean forward for closer look. KUMA glances back at PIKI scornfully.)*

TUKIRA *(In admiring tone):* What fine gold! And such glowing topaz stones! Thank you, Kuma. *(TUKIRA hands necklace to 2ND GIRL.)*

KUMA *(Pompously):* The topaz stones do not compare to the beauty of your eyes, lovely princess. *(TUKIRA lowers her eyes, and CHIEFTAIN motions KUMA back. KUMA speaks to DUBA and PIKI.)* I can see in her eyes that she admires the necklace above all else.

CHIEFTAIN: Piki, you may present your gift now. *(PIKI steps forward, kneels, presents lace mantle. PEOPLE gasp, reach forward to touch it, murmuring loudly at its beauty. TUKIRA takes mantle, unfolds it, studies it silently.)*

TUKIRA *(After a moment):* Never have I held such beautiful lace. It is clearly a miracle, for no hands could spin such glistening threads and intricate patterns—so delicate yet so strong. I choose Piki's lace mantle as the best gift, Father. *(PIKI bows head gratefully, rises, steps back. KUMA scowls angrily.)*

CHIEFTAIN: You have chosen well, daughter. *(Addresses boys)* Before I give up my daughter, however, there is one final test.

KUMA *(Aside):* Aha! Perhaps I shall win yet!

CHIEFTAIN: It is said that the spirit of a great tiger roams throughout our forest. Only the wisest and noblest among the Guaranis can see the spirit. *(Motions toward audience)* Look into the forest and tell me what the tiger wears around his neck. *(PEOPLE murmur. DABU, KUMA, and PIKI gaze out silently.)*

DABU *(Questioningly):* I believe he wears around his neck a . . . a cord of twisted vines?

KUMA *(Boastfully):* Yes, yes, I see the spirit clearly, but you are wrong, Dabu. He wears about his neck a beaded leather strap. He turns his head now and gazes at me, recognizing me as one of the wise and noble. *(Kneels and bows toward "spirit")*

CHIEFTAIN: Piki, what can you see?

PIKI *(Puzzled):* I have looked and looked, Chieftain, but I see no tiger spirit at all. *(PEOPLE murmur.)*

CHIEFTAIN: You have shown yourself worthy, young Piki, for it is also said that the tiger spirit never reveals himself where many people are gathered. I do not know what you saw, Dabu, nor you, Kuma, but it was not the great spirit tiger. You alone, Piki, have been truthful. Surely you are the wisest and noblest of all the young Guaranis. You have competed with honor and have won the hand of my daughter in marriage. Let us make ready for the ceremony. It will be tonight.

TUKIRA: And I shall wear the lovely lace mantle for my veil.

PIKI: Yes, you shall. Just as my friend said you would. *(PIKI gently places mantle over TUKIRA's head as curtain falls.)*

THE END

Meet the Author

Jamie Turner

Jamie Turner adapted the selection "The White Spider's Gift," a South American folktale, into a play. She says she enjoys writing stories that convey a moral truth "using the wonderful vehicle of fiction." She is the author of several novels and teaches Creative Writing and Poetry Writing at Bob Jones University in South Carolina.

Meet the Illustrator

Judith Nelson

Judith Nelson divides her time between homes in Massachusetts and Tucson, Arizona where she works as a freelance illustrator. Nelson loves the challenge that a new project presents and the opportunity to be creative. Although she often works with the same characters, she never tires of them because she enjoys making each illustration come to life in a different way.

Theme Connections

Within the Selection

1. What is the most important thing Piki did that helped him win the contest?

2. Why did the Chieftain ask the youths about an invisible tiger?

Across Selections

3. How does this story fit into the theme Call of Duty?

4. How is Piki similar to Nekumonta in "The Quest for Healing"?

Beyond the Selection

5. What are some characteristics of a good leader?

6. Why do you think cultures have folktales and myths?

Write about It!

Tell a folktale, myth, or story from your own culture.

Remember to look for pictures of spiders to add to the **Concept/Question Board.**

The Maya:
Ancient Timekeepers

For nearly two thousand years, the Maya flourished in Central America. At the height of their power, around A.D. 500, Mayan lands spread from southern Mexico down into present-day Honduras.

The Maya were among the most advanced people in the Americas at that time. They built massive stone pyramids, lived in complex cities, and created a written language. Above all, though, these noble people excelled at math and astronomy. Their calendars prove it.

Mayan calendars are some of the world's most accurate timekeeping systems. Their two main calendars worked together to give every day a unique name and number. Another calendar tracked the passage of Venus through the skies.

The two main Mayan calendars were the *tzolkin* and the *haab*. The tzolkin had 260 days. Each day had a name and a number. There were twenty different names for days, and each one was numbered one through thirteen.

With twenty names, but only thirteen numbers, the names had to go through thirteen cycles, or 260 days, before the same names and numbers combined again.

Genre

Expository Text tells people something. It contains facts about real people, things, or events.

Feature

Charts help readers see ideas at a glance and organize the information in their minds.

The *haab* was a solar calendar with 365 days. It had eighteen "months" with twenty days each, plus a five-day month called *Wayeb*. Wayeb marked the end of the year. It was seen as a very unlucky time, so many Maya stayed indoors to avoid trouble.

The names and numbers from both calendars were used to name each day. Using this method, fifty-two years passed before the same combinations began again. For most Maya, this event only happened once in their lifetimes and brought a lot of fear. Would the Mayan gods allow the next cycle to begin?

Cycle 1		Cycle 2	
Day Name	**Number**	**Day Name**	**Number**
Imix	1	Imix	8
Ik	2	Ik	9
Akbal	3	Akbal	10
Kan	4	Kan	11
Chikchan	5	Chikchan	12
Kimi	6	Kimi	13
Manik	7	Manik	1
Lamat	8	Lamat	2
Muluk	9	Muluk	3
Ok	10	Ok	4
Chuwen	11	Chuwen	5
Eb	12	Eb	6
Ben	13	Ben	7
Ix	1	Ix	8
Men	2	Men	9
Kib	3	Kib	10
Kaban	4	Kaban	11
Etznab	5	Etznab	12
Kawak	6	Kawak	13
Ajaw	7	Ajaw	1

This chart shows how the names and numbers worked together in the tzolkin. After thirteen cycles, the combinations begin to repeat.

Think Link

1. Which Mayan calendar—the tzolkin or the haab—is closest to the calendar we use today?

2. How does the chart help the reader understand the text?

3. Do you think the Mayan calendar could still be used today? Why or why not?

Try It!

As you work on your investigation, think about how you might use charts to display information.

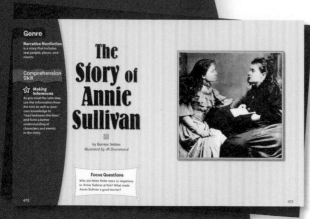

The Story of Annie Sullivan

by Bernice Selden
illustrated by JK Drummond

Focus Questions
Why did Helen Keller react so negatively to Annie Sullivan at first? What made Annie Sullivan a good teacher?

672   673

Read the article to find the meanings of these words, which are also in "The Story of Annie Sullivan":

+ imitating
+ lunged
+ amusing
+ soiled
+ remark
+ disturbed
+ sulking
+ distract
+ aromas
+ insistently

Vocabulary Strategy

Context Clues are hints in the text that help you find the meanings of words. Look at the words *amusing*, *soiled*, and *disturbed*. Use context clues to find each word's meaning.

Vocabulary

Warm-Up

Although my brother, Sam, is two years younger than I am, we hang out together constantly. Before I do anything else after school, I rush home to see how his day went and to play a game or two with him. The weekends are even better. Sam and I spend a few hours each day messing around in the yard. If he were not my brother, I would call him my best friend.

At home Sam follows me everywhere, and he loves imitating the things I do. Just last Saturday we were tossing a baseball back and forth when one of his throws fell a little short. I lunged forward to catch it, and the next thing I knew, I was lying face-first in a muddy patch of grass. Sam laughed and laughed, finding the whole thing very amusing. Suddenly, he ran over and dove right next to me! We both ended up with soiled clothes and a scolding remark from our mother, but it was worth it.

Sam is normally really happy, but it is a struggle for him to learn new things, which makes him upset. I can always tell when he is disturbed because of his sulking. He gets really quiet, and the angry expression on his face makes it obvious that he is unhappy. All I want to do then is find some way to distract him. I look for an activity that will take his mind off his frustration.

One of the best solutions is heading to the bakery at the end of our block. The minute we enter the store, the aromas of baking bread, cookies, and cakes hit us and Sam begins to smile. Over and over, he insistently asks the owner for the same thing—a pecan roll. By the time we get home, Sam has a huge grin shining out from his sticky face.

You know, brother or not, Sam is my best friend.

GAME

Creative Correction Each sentence below contains a selection vocabulary word that has been used incorrectly. Work with a partner to rewrite the sentences using the vocabulary words correctly.

1. The ballet instructor was imitating her students how to perform the steps.
2. Sulking in the bathtub soothed Shareen's sore muscles.
3. Fresh aromas were sold in a booth at the market.
4. As soon as Hank surfaced from the water, he lunged in mouthfuls of air.

Concept Vocabulary

The concept word for this lesson is *fellowship.* Fellowship occurs between people who share the same concerns, beliefs, or feelings. People in a fellowship are good companions who treat each other as equals and try hard to help one another. Fellowships can be formal, like the members of a club, or they can be informal, like a group of good friends. Where would you find a fellowship?

671

The Story of Annie Sullivan

by Bernice Selden

illustrated by JK Drummond

Focus Questions

Why did Helen Keller react so negatively to Annie Sullivan at first? What made Annie Sullivan a good teacher?

As they came closer to the house, Annie saw a child half-hidden in the doorway. She was well formed and had a beautiful face. But her apron was soiled, her hair uncombed, and the white laces on her black shoes were mostly untied.

"There she is," Captain Keller said. "She has known all day that someone was expected, and she has been wild ever since her mother went to the train station to get you."

"How could she have known someone was expected?" Annie asked.

"Oh, she knows a great deal," Mrs. Keller offered. "She can feel the vibrations of people, and also of animals, about the house."

Meanwhile, Helen lunged at Annie, nearly knocking her backward against Captain Keller. She put her hands to Annie's face, then touched her dress and the small traveling bag she was carrying. She pulled at the catch to see if the bag would open.

"She wants to know if you have any candy there," Mrs. Keller said. "Sometimes our guests bring little gifts. Here, let me take it."

"Just wait . . ." Annie pulled out a watch to distract Helen, who was beginning to get flushed and make angry sounds because she could not have the bag.

Annie showed her how to release the cover of the watch by putting her fingers on the spring. She did this several times. She also managed to "tell" Helen, by placing her hand on the trunk, that there *was* a treat in store for her later, if she would be patient.

In Annie's room Helen helped her put her things away. She groped for and found Annie's hat as soon as she had removed it, and put it on her own head. It was amusing to see her primp in front of the mirror, just as if she could actually see herself in it. No doubt she was imitating someone she had felt going through those motions.

Then Helen reached into the trunk and pulled out the gift doll from the blind girls at Perkins.

Annie decided to start her lessons right then. Curling her fingers against the palm of Helen's hand, she spelled out D-O-L-L in the manual alphabet she had learned with Laura Bridgman.

She pulled the doll gently away from Helen, intending to return it when she got Helen to spell D-O-L-L herself. Helen's face again got red, and she grabbed the doll from Annie's hand. She was used to getting her way. For a few seconds there was a tug-of-war as Annie tried to get hold of the doll.

"You don't understand . . ." Annie began, before she realized this child could not hear. She tried to get Helen into a chair so that she could start the lesson over again, but gave up, exhausted. She had to try something else.

Down in the Keller's big kitchen she saw a large cake, only half eaten. She cut a piece, wrapped it in a cloth napkin, and brought it upstairs where she found Helen sulking.

Into Helen's hand she spelled C-A-K-E, allowing her to unwrap the sweet bundle only after Helen had made the same motions in Annie's hand. Helen ate the cake very quickly, afraid it would be taken away from her.

The next morning Annie came down to a peaceful family scene in the Keller's dining room. While Captain Keller ate his breakfast slowly and thoughtfully, Mrs. Keller was chatting with her stepsons, James and Simpson. James was just a little younger than Annie, and Simpson looked about age twelve or thirteen. In a corner of the room, in a cradle, baby Mildred lay sleeping.

Suddenly Helen came thundering into the room behind Annie. Annie took her seat, but Helen remained standing and sniffing the aromas of the food. To Annie's horror, Helen began going from place to place, taking a bit of food from each person's plate and stuffing it into her mouth. To her even greater shock, not one person in the family did anything about it, much less make some remark.

When Helen tried to take a piece of bread from Annie's plate, Annie moved her plate out of reach.

Helen then pinched Annie.

Helen lay down on the floor, kicking and grunting and trying to pull Annie's chair out from under her. She was determined to have her way.

Confused and disturbed about these goings-on, the family one by one tiptoed out.

Helen returned to her chair and started to eat—but with her hands instead of a spoon. Annie insistently placed a spoon in her hand. When the meal was over, Helen threw her napkin on the floor. They struggled until, at Annie's insistence, Helen folded it. Finally Annie let her run out and play while she went up to her room and had herself a good cry.

"I suppose I shall have many such battles with the little woman," Annie wrote Mrs. Hopkins, "before she learns two essential things—obedience and love." But she wished in her heart it could be otherwise.

This was a difficult time for Annie. Often she wondered if she could find the jewel of a child buried under the resistant wild creature.

Helen's movements were so angry that once her hand flew up and knocked out one of Annie's front teeth.

"To get her to do the simplest thing, such as combing her hair or washing her hands," Annie reported to Mrs. Hopkins, "it is necessary to use force." But then the family would get upset, particularly Captain Keller, who could not bear to see his daughter cry.

Something had to be done—Annie thought—and quickly.

Was there a place she and Helen could be by themselves? she asked the Kellers. Surprised by this request, they promised to think it over.

Finally Captain Keller made available to them a garden house some distance away from Ivy Green. "But only for two weeks," he said firmly. "Then we want her back home."

Day by day Helen became easier to work with. But it was an up and down struggle. One morning, during the first week in the garden house, Captain Keller passed by and looked in the window. He saw Helen still in her nightgown long after the breakfast hours. He was outraged. "I've got a good mind to send that Yankee girl back to Boston," he told a relative.

He had no idea what progress this "Yankee girl" was making. Helen was learning to sew, knit, and string beads. On her daily visits to the barnyard, she was beginning to identify living creatures.

"I spell into her hand everything we do all day long, although she has no idea yet what the spelling means," Annie wrote.

The two weeks in the garden house passed quickly, and soon teacher and student were back in the Keller home.

Helen was beginning to associate some of the words with some objects out there in the world. It was a kind of game that she played, partly to please Annie. But she was mixed up about a lot of things.

For instance, she knew that the words *mug* and *milk* had something to do with drinking. But she kept using one in place of the other. Now, when she was washing her hands, she asked to know the word for *water.* She did this by pointing to the water and patting her teacher's hand.

Annie took her out to the pumphouse in the garden. Helen felt the cold water pouring into her mug and all over her fingers. Annie spelled W-A-T-E-R into her free hand. Helen froze. She looked as if she was remembering something from very long ago. As Annie reported it: "The word coming so close upon the sensation of cold water rushing over her hand seemed to startle her. She dropped the mug . . . A new light came into her face."

Helen had suddenly realized that she was not just playing games, but that *words* stood for *things*. And if she could identify those things with words, she had the power to know anything she wanted to—out there in the world of light and sound.

She touched the ground and immediately wanted to know the word for it. Then the pump. When her baby sister was brought out for her to hold, she wanted to know what she was called. And finally she wanted to know Annie's name.

"T-E-A-C-H-E-R," Annie spelled out. From that day on, Annie was called "Teacher" and nothing else.

A key had been turned in Helen's mind. Within an hour she had memorized thirty words.

"When I got into bed," Annie wrote, "she stole into my arms of her own accord and kissed me for the first time, and I thought my heart would burst, so full was it of joy!"

Meet the Author

Bernice Selden

Bernice Selden focuses on three important things in her books—facts, people, and history. Research is very important to her work so she can share correct information. She has written biographies on well-known people such as Annie Sullivan and Walt Disney.

Meet the Illustrator

JK Drummond

JK Drummond has been drawing and painting since she was a child. Since her father is a painter, she grew up around the profession and her career as an artist seemed like a natural choice. Drummond has fun researching the characters and the setting of a story she is about to illustrate. She says, "It's like a treasure hunt." She thinks the best part of her job is creating new things that have the potential to be around for many generations.

Theme Connections

Within the Selection

1. Why do you think Annie needed the two weeks alone with Helen?

2. Why was Helen so angry and frustrated most of the time?

Across Selections

3. Which story from this unit has the most in common with "The Story of Annie Sullivan"? Why?

4. How is Annie Sullivan like Piki, the boy from "The White Spider's Gift"?

Beyond the Selection

5. What can you learn from Annie Sullivan's experience?

6. What is one way you could help someone in your community?

Write about It!

Describe something you have done that was difficult, and explain why the hard work was worth it.

 Remember to think of questions about Helen Keller to add to the **Concept/Question Board.**

Louis Braille Presents

A hush fell over the room as Louis entered. Louis's distinctive footsteps were enough to distract them from their work. They knew what he was about to do.

Louis made his way toward Monsieur Pignier's desk, where the school's director conversed quietly with Captain Barbier. Louis guessed that they were discussing methods for teaching the blind. Only fifteen years old, Louis was about to announce that he had changed—and greatly improved—the captain's invention.

Months earlier, Captain Barbier had introduced his special writing system to the Royal Institution for Blind Youth. The series of raised dots and dashes had originally been intended for soldiers to help them communicate silently in the dark. However, the captain saw that his system might also help the blind read. Excited by the captain's idea, Monsieur Pignier had demonstrated it to his students.

Louis immediately saw its benefits. He also saw right away that each symbol contained too many dots to be read easily with one touch. Louis had spent every free moment tweaking the captain's idea. Then one day he had a breakthrough. He needed only six dots— few enough for a fingertip to feel—to create a symbol for each letter of the alphabet.

Next, Louis and his best friend, Gabriel, traded notes written with the raised dots. They could not believe how quickly they learned the system. Now it was time for Louis to present his changes.

"Excuse me, sirs," Louis began, and showed them his writing system. Once he finished, the room remained eerily quiet. Then Monsieur Pignier spoke.

"Louis, I am quite disturbed by your brashness," he said sternly. "The honorable captain does not need some youngster telling him what is wrong with his ideas."

This reaction was exactly what Louis had feared.

A	B	C	D	E	F	G	H	I	J	K	L	M
N	O	P	Q	R	S	T	U	V	W	X	Y	Z

Capital letter follows	Number follows	Full stop/ period	Comma	Semicolon

Exclamation point	Opening quotation mark	Closing quotation mark	Parenthesis (opening and closing)	Hyphen

Think Link

1. Why did Captain Barbier invent a new writing system?

2. Use the chart from the article to translate the following sentence:

3. Who was Monsieur Pignier?

Try It!

As you work on your investigation, think about how you might use charts to display information.

685

DUTY

by Edwin Markham
illustrated by Tom Herzberg

When Duty comes a-knocking at your gate,
Welcome him in; for if you bid him wait,
He will depart only to come once more
And bring seven other duties to your door.

Jim

by Gwendolyn Brooks
illustrated by Marni Backer

There never was a nicer boy
Than Mrs. Jackson's Jim.
The sun should drop its greatest gold
On him.

Because, when Mother-dear was sick,
He brought her cocoa in.
And brought her broth, and brought her bread.
And brought her medicine.

And, tipping, tidied up her room.
And would not let her see
He missed his game of baseball
Terribly.

Test-Taking Strategy: Taking the best guess when unsure of the answer

Sometimes you won't know which answer is correct. When this happens, take your best guess.

Taking the best guess when unsure of the answer

Sometimes you might not be able to decide which answer is correct when taking a test. When this happens, take your best guess. When you guess, you will be right some of the time.

Try not to guess too often. It is always better to think about the question, look at the answer choices, and choose the one you think is correct.

Read the sentence below. Think about the answer that means the same as *concerned*.

> **The captain of the ship was *concerned* about the weather. Both the wind and the rain were getting worse.**
>
> worried   happy
>
> writing   pleased

How do you know which answer fits best? Think about the second sentence. It says *Both the wind and the rain were getting worse*. The sentence helps you know that *worried* is the correct answer.

There's one other thing you should keep in mind. Stay with your first answer. Don't change an answer unless you are sure the one you chose is wrong and another answer is better.

A Surprising Choice

With less than a minute to go, Luke knew the game was lost. Despite his older brother's effort, Seacoast State was not going to be the national champion.

After the buzzer sounded, Luke and his mother waited for a few minutes for the floor to clear. The players and fans from North Utah College were enjoying the moment. The team had won the NCAA Division III National Basketball Championship. For Seacoast State, it was an unhappy end to a great season.

The floor began to clear. Luke and his mother walked slowly down the steps. Will was sitting on the bench, obviously dejected after losing.

"Not a bad season," he muttered. "A few more minutes and we might have won."

The loudspeaker came on, and for the next few minutes, the championship and runner-up trophies were awarded. The All-Tournament Team was named, and Will made first team. Luke thought this was fabulous, but he knew that Will would have given it up if it meant his team would have won. He was that kind of guy.

The next day, the three of them flew home to Orlando. A reporter met them at the airport and interviewed Will. Luke and his mother stood nearby and listened carefully.

"Do you think you have any chance to make it in the NBA?" asked the reporter.

"I doubt it. Besides, that is not what I want to do." Will answered slowly and thoughtfully.

GO ON

The reporter looked up. A few other people had gathered around.

"What do you want to do instead?" The reporter raised her eyebrows as she spoke.

"I want to be a police officer or maybe go into the Secret Service," said Will. "I have thought about it for a long time. I have never wanted to do anything else"

The reporter wrote quickly and then smiled as she spoke. "That is an answer that I really did not expect." She turned to Luke and asked, "You must be Will's little brother. What do you think he should do?"

Luke moved a step closer to his mother. He felt a little embarrassed and spoke quietly. "Being a police officer is really important. Will should do what he thinks is best. I think he will be a great police officer. I hope he gets a job near us so he can help coach my basketball team."

Luke's mother gave him a hug, and Will messed up his hair. Luke was pretty sure he had given a good answer.

1. Read these sentences from the story.

   Will was sitting on the bench, obviously dejected after losing.

   What does the word *dejected* mean in this sentence?

   Ⓐ hot

   Ⓑ busy

   Ⓒ late

   Ⓓ sad

Test Tips

• If you do not know an answer, guess.

• Skim the questions and do the easiest ones first.

• Look for important words in the questions and answers.

2. Luke probably felt embarrassed when he spoke to the reporter because

   Ⓕ Will's team did not win the championship.

   Ⓖ he had never spoken to a reporter before.

   Ⓗ the people at the airport were not very nice to them.

   Ⓘ it would have been nice for Will to be in the NBA.

3. What happens RIGHT AFTER the trophies were awarded?

   Ⓐ The All-Tournament Team was named.

   Ⓑ Will, Luke, and their mother fly to Orlando.

   Ⓒ Luke and his mother walked down the steps.

   Ⓓ The reporter met them in the airport.

4. Based on the story, do you think that Will is a nice person or not? Use details and information from the story to help explain your answer.

STOP

Pronunciation Key

a as in **a**t
ā as in l**a**te
â as in c**a**re
ä as in f**a**ther
e as in s**e**t
ē as in m**e**
i as in **i**t
ī as in k**i**te
o as in **o**x
ō as in r**o**se

ô as in b**o**ught and r**aw**
oi as in c**oi**n
o͞o as in b**oo**k
o͞o as in t**oo**
or as in f**or**m
ou as in **ou**t
u as in **u**p
ū as in **u**se
ûr as in t**ur**n; g**er**m, l**ear**n, f**ir**m, w**or**k

ə as in **a**bout, chick**e**n, penc**i**l, cann**o**n, circ**us**
ch as in **ch**air
hw as in **wh**ich
ng as in ri**ng**
sh as in **sh**op
th as in **th**in
t͟h as in **t͟h**ere
zh as in trea**s**ure

The mark (ˊ) is placed after a syllable with a heavy accent, as in **chicken** (**chik**ˊ ən).

The mark (ˋ) after a syllable shows a lighter accent, as in **disappear** (**dis**ˊ ə **pēr**ˋ).

692

Glossary

A

abandoned (ə ban´ dənd) *v.* Past tense of **abandon:** to leave and not return.

abolish (ə bol´ ish) *v.* To end, stop.

absorbs (əb sorbs) *v.* Takes in.

accomplishment (ə kom´ plish ment) *n.* Achievement.

accumulate (ə kyo͞om´ yə lāt´) *v.* To gather or pile up.

accurate (ak´ yər it) *adj.* Correct; exact.

accurately (ak´ yər it lē) *adv.* With few mistakes; correctly.

adjourned (ə jûrnd´) *v.* Past tense of **adjourn:** To stop work.

advance (ad vans´) *v.* To help the progress or growth of; further.

agent (ā´ jənt) *n.* A person who acts for some other person or company.

alarming (ə lär´ ming) *adj.* Causing alarm or fear.

alert (ə lûrt´) *adj.* Awake and prepared to act.

alerting (ə lûr´ ting) *v.* Warning of possible danger.

algae (al´ jē) *n.* Simple living things that are composed of one or more cells. Most algae are plants that do not have roots or flowers.

allegiance (ə lē´ jəns) *n.* Faithful support of a country, person, group, or cause.

aloft (ə lôft´) *adv.* Far above the ground.

ammunition (am´ yə nish´ ən) *n.* Material used with weapons; for example, bullets.

amusing (ə mū´ zing) *adj.* Entertaining.

analyze (an´ ə līz´) *v.* To find out what something is made of by taking it apart.

ancestors (an´ ses´ tərs) *n.* A person from whom one is descended.

ancient (ān´ shənt) *adj.* Of or having to do with times very long ago.

anvil clouds (an´ vil klouds) *n.* Plural of **anvil cloud:** a type of cloud with a flat top that is mostly ice. These clouds often form in the upper parts of thunderstorms.

anxiously (ang´ shəs lē) *adv.* Nervously or with fear.

apparently (ə par´ ənt lē) *adv.* As far as one can judge by the way things appear.

appetite (ap´ ə tīt´) *n.* A desire for food.

693

Pronunciation Key: at; lāte; câre; fäther; set; mē; it; kīte; ox; rōse; ô in bought; coin; bŏŏk; tōō; form; out; up; ūse; tûrn; ə sound in about, chicken, pencil, cannon, circus; chair; hw in which; ring; shop; thin; there; zh in treasure.

application (ap´ li kā´ shən) *n.* A request, especially for a job.

Word Derivations

Below are some words related to *application*.

applicant	apply	applied
applying	applicable	applicatory

archaeology (är´ kē ol´ ə jē) *n.* The study of the way humans lived a long time ago. Archaeologists dig up the remains of ancient cities and towns and then study the tools, weapons, pottery, and other things they find.

Word History

Archaeology, or archeology, came into English in the year 1837. It is from the Latin word *archaeologia*, meaning knowledge gained through the study of ancient objects. This Latin word's origins are with the Greek words *arch*, meaning "beginning," and *logos* meaning "word."

arms (ärms) *n.* Plural of **arm:** weapon.

Word Derivations

Below are some words related to *arms:*

arm	armor	armed
armory	armament	arming

aromas (ə rō´ məs) *n.* Plural of **aroma:** a pleasant or agreeable smell.

ascend (ə send´) *v.* To climb.

assassins (ə sas´ ins) *n.* Plural of **assassin:** a person who murders a public figure, such as a government leader.

assigned (ə sīnd´) *v.* Past tense of **assign:** to give out as a task.

associate (ə sō´ sē āt´) *v.* To connect in one's mind.

association (ə sō´ sē ā´ shən) *n.* A group of people joined together for a common purpose.

assumed (ə sōōmd´) *v.* Past tense of **assume:** to take for granted.

assure (ə sûr´) *v.* To give confidence to.

astronomy (ə stron´ ə mē) *n.* The science that deals with the sun, moon, stars, planets, and other heavenly bodies.

atmosphere (at´ mə sfir´) *n.* The layer of gases that surrounds a planet.

Word History

Atmosphere came into English in the year 1677. It is from the Latin word *atmosphera*, which was made from the Greek word *atmos* and the Latin word *sphaera*. *Atmos* means "vapor," and *sphaera* means "sphere."

attitude (at´ ə tōod´) *n.* A way of acting, thinking, or feeling.

attracted (ə trak´ təd) *v.* Past tense of **attract:** to cause to come near.

awe (ô) *n.* Great wonder, fear, and respect.

banners (ban´ ûrs) *n.* Plural of **banner:** a piece of cloth that has a design and sometimes writing on it.

barrack (bar´ək) *adj.* Providing temporary housing; very plain and uniform.

beaded (bēd´ əd) *adj.* Covered with drops.

bear (bâr) *v.* To put up with patiently; stand.

beckoned (bek´ ənd) *v.* Past tense of **beckon:** to make a sign or signal by moving the hand or head.

benefit (ben´ ə fit) *n.* Something that helps a person or thing; advantage.

besides (bi sīdz´) *prep.* In addition to.

biologist (bī o´ lə jəst) *n.* A person who studies the way in which plants and animals and other living things live and grow and where they are found.

black holes (blak hōls) *n.* Plural of **black hole:** an invisible object in space that has a pull of gravity so strong that nothing can escape from it, not even light.

black hole

blistering (blis´ tər ing) *adj.* Extremely intense or severe.

boast (bōst) *n.* A statement in which one brags.

bombarded (bom bärd´ əd) *v.* Past tense of **bombard:** to attack with bombs or heavy fire from big guns.

booming (bōōm´ ing) *adj.* Deep and loud.

brand (brand) *v.* To mark the skin of cattle with a hot iron to show who owns the animal.

brand

Pronunciation Key: at; l**ā**te; c**â**re; f**ä**ther; s**e**t; m**ē**; **i**t; k**ī**te; **o**x; r**ō**se; **ô** in b**ou**ght; c**oi**n; b**oo**k; t**oo**; f**or**m; **ou**t; **u**p; **ū**se; t**û**rn; **ə** sound in **a**bout, chick**e**n, penc**i**l, cann**o**n, circ**u**s; **ch**air; **hw** in **wh**ich; ri**ng**; **sh**op; **th**in; **th**ere; **zh** in trea**s**ure.

break down (brāk doun) *v.* To separate into smaller parts; digest.

brilliant (bril´ yənt) *adj.* Extremely intelligent.

Word History

Brilliant came into English in the year 1696. It is from the French word *brillant*, a derivative of the verb *briller*, meaning "to shine."

bulges (bəl´ jez) *n.* Plural of **bulge:** a rounded part that swells out.

bulky (bəl´ kē) *adj.* Large and puffy.

bull's-eye (boolz´ ī´) *n.* The center of a circle or target.

bull's-eye

bundled (bun´ dəld) *v.* Past tense of **bundle:** to tie or wrap together.

burden (bûr´ dən) *n.* Something hard to bear.

burdened (bûr´ dend) *adj.* Weighed down with a heavy load.

calculations (kal´ kyə lā´ shəns) *n.* Plural of **calculation:** the result of counting, computing, or figuring.

carnivore (kär´ nə vor´) *n.* An animal that eats only the flesh of other animals.

central (sen´ trəl) *adj.* Main; chief.

centuries (sen´ chə rēs) *n.* Plural of **century:** a period of one hundred years.

certificate (sər tif´ i kət) *n.* A written statement accepted as proof of certain facts.

challenge (chal´ ənj) *n.* A call to take part in a difficult task or contest.

challenged (chal´ ənjd) *v.* Past tense of **challenge:** call to take part in a contest.

character (kâr´ ək tər) *n.* All the qualities that make a person or thing different from others.

charged (chärjd) *v.* Past tense of **charge:** to fill with electricity.

chaser fatigue (chā´ sər fə tēg´) *n.* The condition of being very tired after chasing a storm.

chests (chests) *n.* Plural of **chest:** a large, strong box used for holding things.

churning (chûrn´ing) *adj.* Stirring or moving with a forceful motion.

civilians (sə vil´yənz) *n.* Plural of **civilian:** a person not in the military.

civilizations (si´və lə zā´shənz) *n.* Plural of **civilization:** an advanced human society in which agriculture, trade, government, art, and science are highly developed.

claim (klām) *v.* To declare as one's own.

clan (klan) *n.* A group of families descended from the same ancestor.

clarity (klâr´i tē) *n.* Clearness.

climax (klī´maks) *n.* The most exciting moment.

clusters (klus´tərz) *n.* Plural of **cluster:** a number of things of the same kind that are grouped together.

coiled (koild) *v.* Past tense of **coil:** to wind round and round.

collapse (kə laps´) *v.* To fall in; break down.

collide (kə līd´) *v.* To crash against each other.

colonies (ko´lə nēz) *n.* Plural of **colony:** a territory ruled by another country.

commander (kə man´dər) *n.* A leader.

communal (kə myoo´nəl) *adj.* Belonging to a group or community.

compact (kəm pakt´) *adj.* Tightly packed together.

company (kəm´pə nē) *n.* A group of people gathered together.

composition (kom´pə zish´ən) *n.* Something put together or created, especially something written.

Word Derivations

Below are some words related to *composition:*

composite   compose   composing
composer   compositional

comrade (kom´rad´) *n.* A friend who shares the same work as another.

concern (kən sûrn´) *n.* Something important to a person.

concert (kon´sûrt´) *n.* A musical performance.

conclusions (kən kloo´zhəns) *n.* Plural of **conclusion:** something decided after thinking and experimenting.

conductors (kən duk´tərs) *n.* Plural of **conductor:** a material that carries an electric charge.

confederation (kən fe´də rā´shən) *n.* A group of countries or states joined together for a common purpose.

confidence (kon´fə dəns) *n.* Faith in oneself.

697

Pronunciation Key: at; lāte; câre; fä**ther**; s**e**t; m**ē**; **it**; k**ī**te; **o**x; r**ō**se; **ô** in b**ou**ght; c**oi**n; b**oo**k; t**oo**; f**or**m; **ou**t; **u**p; **ū**se; t**û**rn; **ə** sound in **a**bout, chick**e**n, penc**i**l, cann**o**n, circ**u**s; **ch**air; **hw** in **wh**ich; ri**ng**; **sh**op; **th**in; **th**ere; **zh** in trea**s**ure.

consent (kən sent´) *n.* Permission.

constitution (kon´ stə too´ shən) *n.* The document containing the law and plan of government.

Continental Congress (kon´ tə nen´ təl kong´ gris) *n.* The group of delegates from the American colonies who met during and after the American Revolution to issue the Declaration of Independence and to set up a national government after the United States won its freedom.

contribute (kən trib´ yoot) *v.* To give.

controlled (kən trōld´) *v.* Past tense of **control:** to command or regulate by using power or authority.

convention (kən ven´ shən) *n.* A formal meeting for some special purpose.

converts (kən vûrts´) *v.* Changes something into something different.

converted (kən vûrt´ əd) *v.* Past tense of **convert:** to change something into something different.

cooperating (kō op´ ə rāt´) *v.* Working together.

Word History

Cooperating came into English in the year 1582. It is the gerund form of the word *cooperate*, from the Latin *cooperari*. *Cooperari* can also be divided into the word parts *co-*, meaning "with," and *operari*, meaning "to work."

cosmic (koz´ mik) *adj.* Of or relating to the universe.

cow (kou) *n.* The fully grown female of some large mammals, such as buffaloes, elephants, or whales.

cowhand (kou´ hand´) *n.* A person who works on a cattle ranch.

crane (krān) *n.* A large machine with a long arm that can be moved up and down and in a circle. Cables at the end of the crane's arm are used to lift and move heavy objects.

cubic (kyoo´ bik) *adj.* Describing or measuring length, width, and thickness.

cuckoo (koo´ koo´) *n.* A bird with a long tail and a call that sounds like its name.

cuckoo

cultivate (kəl´ tə vāt´) *v.* To plant and help grow.

currents (kûr´ ənts) *n.* Plural of **current:** a flow of electricity.

D

daggers (dag´ ərz) *n.* Plural of **dagger:** a small weapon that looks like a knife.

dare (dâr) *n.* A test of courage or ability; a challenge.

dawn (dôn) *n.* Daybreak.

dawn

debate (di bāt´) *n.* A discussion between two groups that do not agree.

debriefed (dē brēfd´) *v.* Past tense of **debrief:** to question in order to obtain knowledge or information.

declarations (dek´ lə rā´ shəns) *n.* Plural of **declaration:** written statements that make something known.

dedication (ded´ i kā´ shən) *n.* A ceremony that involves setting aside something for a specific purpose.

defenses (di fens´ es) *n.* Plural of **defense:** a person or thing that guards against attack.

defiance (di fī´ əns) *n.* Refusal to obey.

deflated (di flāt´ əd) *v.* Past tense of **deflate:** to let the air out of something.

delegates (de´ li gəts) *n.* Plural of **delegate:** a person who is chosen to act for others.

Word History

Delegates came into English more than 600 years ago. It is the plural form of the word *delegate*, from the Latin *delegare*. *Delegare* can also be divided into the word parts *de-*, meaning "from," and *legate*, meaning "to send."

delicacy (de´ li kə sē) *n.* Something fine and delicious, especially a food.

delicate (de´ li kət) *adj.* Small, or dainty.

demonstration (de´ mən strā´ shən) *n.* Something that explains, proves, or shows something clearly.

Word Derivations

Below are some words related to *demonstration:*

demonstrate   demonstrable
demonstrative   demonstrated
demonstrator

Pronunciation Key: at; lāte; câre; fäther; set; mē; it; kīte; ox; rōse; ô in bought; coin; book; too; form; out; up; ūse; tûrn; ə sound in about, chicken, pencil, cannon, circus; chair; hw in which; ring; shop; thin; there; zh in treasure.

depict (di pikt´) v. To show in pictures.

depressed (di prest´) v. Past tense of **depress:** to cause to sink below the surrounding region.

descended (di send´ əd) v. Past tense of **descend:** to come down.

designed (di zīnd´) v. Past tense of **design:** to create.

despair (dis pâr´) n. A complete loss of hope.

desperately (des´ pə rət lē) adv. Hopelessly.

destiny (des´ tə nē) n. What happens to a person, especially when it seems to be determined in advance; fortune.

detect (di tekt´) v. To find out or notice; discover.

determined (di tûr´ mənd) adj. Firm in sticking to a purpose; showing determination.

devised (di vīzd´) v. Past tense of **devise:** to think out, invent, or plan.

diet (dī´ it) n. The food and drink eaten by an animal.

digest (dī jest´) v. To change food into a form that can be used by the body.

dike (dīk) n. A dam or high wall of earth built to hold back the waters of a sea or river.

disastrous (di zas´ trəs) adj. Extremely bad.

discharge (dis´ chärj) n. Dismissal from service or a job.

discouraged (dis kûr´ ijd) v. Past tense of **discourage:** to try to keep a person from doing something.

disks (disks) n. Plural of **disk:** a flat, thin, round object.

dispositions (dis´ pə zi´ shəns) n. Plural of **disposition:** a natural way of acting; mood.

dissolve (di zolv´) v. To mix into liquid.

distract (dis trakt´) v. To draw one´s attention away from what one is doing or thinking.

district (dis´ trikt´) n. A region that is part of a larger area such as a city or county.

disturbed (dis tûrbd´) adj. Upset or confused.

document (dok´ yə mənt) n. A written statement that gives information about something.

doe (dō) n. A female deer.

donations (dō nā´ shəns) n. Plural of **donation:** a gift or contribution.

donned (dond) *v.* Past tense of **don:** to put on.

donors (dō´ nərs) *n.* Plural of **donor:** a person who gives something.

draft (draft) *n.* A rough copy of something written.

dramatic (drə ma´ tik) *adj.* Exciting or interesting.

drought (drout) *n.* A period of time when there is very little rain or no rain at all.

duct tape (dukt´ tāp) *n.* A type of silver adhesive tape.

duds (dədz) *n.* Plural of **dud:** clothing.

durable (dûr´ ə bəl) *adj.* Able to last a long time.

dutifully (doo´ ti fəl ē´) *adv.* Out of a sense of obedience.

eavesdroppers (ēvz´ drop´ rz) *n.* Plural of **eavesdropper:** a person who listens to other people talk without letting them know they are listening.

eclipse (i klips´) *n.* A darkening or hiding of the sun, a planet, or a moon, by another heavenly body.

eclipse

economical (ek´ ə nôm´ i kəl) *adj.* A good use of resources; not wasteful.

ecosystem (ē´ kō sis´ təm) *n.* All the living and nonliving things in a certain area.

edible (ed´ ə bəl) *adj.* Fit or safe to eat.

Word History

Edible came into English in 1594. It is a derivative of the Latin verb *edere*, meaning "to eat." (Also note that edible contains the –ible suffix, which in this word means "able to be.")

elders (el´ dərs) *n.* Plural of **elder:** a person who is older.

electrocuted (i lek´ trə kyoot´ ed) *v.* Past tense of **electrocute:** to kill by means of a very strong electric shock.

Word Derivations

Below are some words related to *electrocuted:*

electric   electricity   electrify
electrician   electrocute   electronic

electromagnets (i lek´ trō mag´ nits) *n.* Plural of **electromagnet:** a piece of iron with wire wound around it. It becomes a magnet when an electric current is passed through the wire.

Pronunciation Key: at; lāte; câre; fäther; set; mē; it; kīte; ox; rōse; ô in bought; coin; book; too; form; out; up; ūse; tûrn; ə sound in about, chicken, pencil, cannon, circus; chair; hw in which; ring; shop; thin; there; zh in treasure.

emancipator (i man´ sə pā´ tûr) *n.* Someone who sets others free from slavery or control.

employee (em ploi´ ē´) *n.* A person who works for a business for pay.

Word Derivations

Below are some words related to *employee:*

employ	employed	employing
employable	employment	employer

encrusted (en krus´ təd) *adj.* Covered or coated with something.

endure (in dûr´) *v.* To put up with.

energy (en´ ər gē) *n.* Power; the capacity to do work.

engineer (en´ jə nir´) *n.* A person who is trained in engineering, the work that uses scientific knowledge for practical things, such as designing machines.

enrich (en rich´) *v.* To make better by adding something.

enslaved (in slāvd´) *adj.* Held in slavery.

enthusiastic (in thoo´ zē as´ tik) *adj.* Full of excitement; eager.

equator (i kwā´ tər) *n.* The imaginary line that circles Earth's center halfway between the North and South Poles.

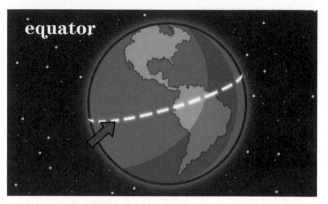
equator

essential (i sen´ shəl) *adj.* Very important or necessary.

eventually (i ven´ chə wəl lē) *adv.* Finally.

evidence (e´ və dəns) *n.* Proof of something.

exhausted (ig zost´ əd) *adj.* Weak or tired.

expands (ik spandz´) *v.* Becomes larger.

exposing (ik spōz´ ing) *v.* Leaving open or without protection.

extraordinary (ik stror´ dən âr´ ē) *adj.* Very unusual; remarkable.

exultant (ig zul´ tənt) *adj.* Triumphant; very joyful.

faint (fānt) *adj.* Not clear or strong; weak.

fangs (fangz) *n.* Plural of **fang:** a long, pointed tooth.

fangs

farewell (fâr wel´) *n.* Good-bye and good luck.

federal (fed´ ər əl) *adj.* Having to do with a central government of the United States, thought of as separate of the government of each state.

ferocious (fər ō´ shəs) *adj.* Fierce; strong and violent.

fiercely (firs´ lē) *adv.* In a strong and violent way.

finest (fī´ nəst) *adv.* Best; most excellent.

fitter (fit´ ər) *adj.* Healthier; in better physical shape.

flanking (flangk´ ing) *adj.* At the sides of.

flatterer (fla´ tər ər) *n.* A person who praises too much, or insincerely.

fleet (flēt) *n.* A group of warships under one command.

flickering (flic´ kər ing) *adj.* Burning or shining in an irregular way.

flint (flint) *n.* A very hard, gray stone.

flourished (flû´ risht) *v.* Past tense of **flourish:** to grow or develop strongly and with vigor.

fluent (floo´ ənt) *adj.* Able to speak effortlessly.

Word History

Fluent came into English in 1585. It is a derivative of the Latin verb *fluere*, meaning "to flow."

focused (fō´ kəst) *v.* Past tense of **focus:** to direct attention to someone or something.

food chain (food chān) *n.* A group of living things that form a chain in which the first living thing is eaten by the second, the second is eaten by the third, and so on.

food web (food web) *n.* A group of food chains in an ecosystem that are connected.

fooling (fool´ ing) *v.* Being silly, joking, or teasing.

forbidden (fər bi´ dən) *adj.* Off-limits.

force (fors) *n.* Power or strength used against a person.

Word History

Force came into English more than 700 years ago. It is a derivative of the Latin word *fortis*, meaning "strong."

fossil fuels (fôs´ əl fyoo´ əls) *n.* Plural of **fossil fuel:** A fuel formed from the remains of plants and animals. Coal and petroleum are fossil fuels.

Pronunciation Key: at; l**ā**te; c**â**re; f**ä**ther; s**e**t; m**ē**; **i**t; k**ī**te; **o**x; r**ō**se; **ô** in b**ou**ght; c**oi**n; b**oo**k; t**oo**; f**o**rm; **ou**t; **u**p; **ū**se; t**û**rn; **ə** sound in **a**bout, chick**e**n, penc**i**l, cann**o**n, circ**u**s; **ch**air; **hw** in **wh**ich; ri**ng**; **sh**op; **th**in; **th**ere; **zh** in trea**s**ure.

freighter (frā´ tər) *n.* A ship used for carrying cargo.

freighter

fright (frīt) *n.* A sudden fear or alarm.

frontier (frən tir´) *n.* The far edge of a country, where people are just beginning to settle.

funnel cloud (fun´ əl kloud) *n.* A type of rotating cloud that extends down from a thunderstorm. When funnel clouds extend to the ground, they become tornadoes.

galaxy (gal´ ək sē) *n.* A very large group of stars.

galloping (gal´ əp ing) *v.* Moving or riding at a gallop, the fastest gait of a horse.

gaping (gā´ ping) *adj.* Wide open.

genuine (jen´ yə wən) *adj.* Being what it seems to be.

geologist (jē o´ lə jist) *n.* One who specializes in the study of geology, the science that deals with the structure of Earth.

gleam (glēm) *n.* A flash or beam of light.

glimmer (glim´ ər) *n.* Faint light.

glistening (glis´ ən ing) *adj.* Shining with reflected light.

gossipy (gos´ ə pē) *adj.* Full of talk or rumors, often untrue.

grabs (grabz) *v.* Takes hold of.

grand (grand) *adj.* Very good or excellent.

grandly (grand´ lē) *adv.* In an arrogant or overly confident way.

grant (grant) *n.* A gift of money for a specific purpose.

grateful (grāt´ fəl) *adj.* Full of thanks for a favor.

grizzly (griz´ lē) *adj.* Mean.

groundnuts (ground´ nuts´) *n.* Plural of **groundnut:** peanut.

gusts (gusts) *n.* Plural of **gust:** a sudden, strong rush of wind or air.

gusty (gus´ tē) *adj.* Blowing in strong, sudden bursts.

habitable (hab´ ət ə bəl) *adj.* Suitable to live in or on.

Word Derivations

Below are some words related to *habitable*:

habitat	inhabitant	habitation
habit	inhabit	habitability

harmony (här´ mə nē) *n.* Friendly agreement or cooperation.

Word History

Harmony came into English in the fourteenth century. *Harmony* came from the Middle English word *armony*, a derivative of the Greek word *harmos*, meaning "harmony."

harnessed (här´ nisd) *v.* Past tense of **harness:** to control or make use of.

harsh (härsh) *adj.* Severe.

hatch (hach) *n.* An opening in the deck of a ship or spacecraft that leads to other decks.

haze (hāz) *n.* Mist, smoke, or dust in the air.

heaved (hēvd) *v.* Past tense of **heave:** to make a sound with a lot of effort or strain.

herbivore (hûr´ bə vor´) *n.* An animal that eats only plants.

hesitated (hez´ ə tāt´ əd) *v.* Past tense of **hesitate:** to wait or stop a moment, especially because of feeling unsure.

hideous (hid´ ē əs) *adj.* Extremely ugly; horrible.

holler (hol´ ər) *n.* A yell, shout, or call.

honorable (ä´ nər ə bəl) *adj.* Honest; worthy of respect.

horizon (hə rī´ zən) *n.* The line where the sky and the ground or the sea seem to meet.

horrified (hor´ ə fīd) *v.* Past tense of **horrify:** to cause a feeling of great fear and dread.

hospitable (hos´ pi´ tə bəl) *adj.* Welcome and comfortable; friendly.

humidity (hū mid´ i tē) *n.* The amount of moisture in the air.

hypothesis (hī poth´ i sis) *n.* Something that is suggested as being true for the purposes of further investigation.

identify (ī den´ tə fī´) *v.* To recognize.

idle (īd´ l) *adj.* Not busy.

ignores (ig norz´) *v.* Pays no attention to.

imagine (i maj´ in) *v.* To picture a person or thing in the mind.

imitating (i´ mi tāt´ ing) *v.* Acting just as another person does; copying.

Pronunciation Key: at; l**ā**te; c**â**re; f**ä**ther; s**e**t; m**ē**; **i**t; k**ī**te; **o**x; r**ō**se; **ô** in b**ou**ght; c**oi**n; b**oo**k; t**oo**; f**o**rm; **ou**t; **u**p; **ū**se; t**û**rn; **ə** sound in **a**bout, chick**e**n, penc**i**l, cann**o**n, circ**u**s; **ch**air; **hw** in **wh**ich; ri**ng**; **sh**op; **th**in; **th**ere; **zh** in trea**s**ure.

immigrants (i´ mi grənts) *n.* Plural of **immigrant:** a person who comes to live in a country in which he or she was not born.

impact (im´ pakt´) *n.* The force of one object striking against another.

income (in´ kəm´) *n.* Money received for work or from things that are owned.

inefficient (in´ ə fish´ ənt) *adj.* Not offering a good use of money or effort.

infinity (in fin´ i tē) *n.* The condition of having no limits.

inflated (in flā´ tid) *v.* Past tense of **inflate:** to cause to swell by filling with air or gas.

influence (in´ floo´ əns) *n.* Power to produce an effect on others.

inhabit (in ha´ bət) *v.* To live in or on.

inhabitants (in ha´ bə tənts) *n.* Plural of **inhabitant:** A person or animal that lives in a place.

insistently (in sis´ tənt lē) *adv.* In a strong or firm manner.

inspiration (in´ spə rā´ shən) *n.* The stirring of the mind, feelings, or imagination, especially so that some good idea comes.

inspired (in spīrd´) *v.* Influenced.

insulators (in´ sə lā´ tərs) *n.* Plural of **insulator:** a material that does not carry an electric charge.

internal (in tûr´ nəl) *adj.* Having to do with or on the inside.

internment (in tûrn´ mənt) *adj.* Confined or impounded, especially during a time of war.

intricate (in´ tri kit) *adj.* Involved or complicated, complex.

intrigued (in trēgd´) *v.* Past tense of **intrigue:** to make curious.

invaders (in vād´ ərz) *n.* Plural of **invader:** a person who breaks into something or some place without being asked or wanted.

invading (in vād´ ing) *v.* Entering by force.

investment (in vest´ mənt) *adj.* Using money to buy something that will make more money.

irritably (ir´ i tə blē) *adv.* In an angry or impatient way.

jolt (jōlt) *n.* Shock.

junkyard (jungkʹ yärd) *n.* A place where junk is collected and stored, especially a place for cars that are old and wrecked.

KIA/DIA (kīa dīā) *n.* Know-It-All, Do-It-All.

kimono (ki mōʹ nə) *n.* A loose robe that is tied with a sash.

ladles (lāʹ dəlz) *n.* Plural of **ladle:** a spoon with a long handle and a bowl shaped like a cup. It is used to scoop up liquids.

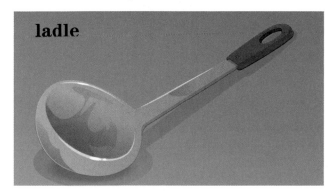

ladle

lagoon (lə go͞onʹ) *n.* A shallow body of water usually connected to a larger body of water.

landscape (landʹ skāpʹ) *n.* Scenery.

larvae (lärʹ vē) *n.* Plural of **larva:** The newly hatched form, of some insects and other animals without backbones.

lasso (laʹ sōʹ) *v.* To catch an animal using a long rope with a loop.

latrines (lə trēnzʹ) *n.* Plural of **latrine:** a toilet.

lavender (laʹ vən dər) *n.* A plant with fragrant purple flowers.

layer (lāʹ ər) *n.* One thickness of something.

lead (led) *n.* A heavy, soft, gray metal.

league (lēg) *n.* A number of people, groups, or countries joined together for a common purpose.

ledge (lej) *n.* A narrow surface on a cliff or rock wall.

legislature (lejʹ i slāʹ chər) *n.* A body of persons that has the ability to make or pass laws.

legends (lejʹ əndz) *n.* Plural of **legend:** a story passed down through the years that many people believe, but that is not entirely true.

lessen (lesʹ ən) *v.* To make or become less.

liberty (libʹ ər tē) *n.* Freedom from control of another country.

Word History

Liberty came into English in the 1300s. *Liberty* comes from the Latin word *liber,* meaning "free." The French word *liberté,* which means "liberty," is also derived from the Latin.

Pronunciation Key: at; l**ā**te; c**â**re; f**ä**ther; s**e**t; m**ē**; **i**t; k**ī**te; **o**x; r**ō**se; **ô** in b**ou**ght; c**oi**n; b**ŏŏ**k; t**ōō**; f**or**m; **ou**t; **u**p; **ū**se; t**û**rn; **ə** sound in **a**bout, chick**e**n, penc**i**l, cann**o**n, circ**u**s; **ch**air; **hw** in **wh**ich; ri**ng**; **sh**op; **th**in; **th**ere; **zh** in trea**s**ure.

light-years (līt yirs) *n.* Plural of **light-year:** the distance that light travels through space in one year. Since light moves at a speed of about 186,000 miles per second, it travels about 5,880,000 miles in one year. If a star is 30 light-years away, it takes 30 years for its light to reach Earth.

lilting (lilt´ ing) *adj.* Having cheerful rhythm or beat.

linen (lin´ ən) *adj.* Made of linen. Linen is a cloth woven from fibers of flax.

lingered (lin´ gərd) *v.* Past tense of **linger:** to be slow in leaving.

logic (lo´ jik) *n.* A way of thinking about something.

longed (longd) *v.* Past tense of **long:** to want very much; yearn.

loom (lōōm) *n.* A machine or frame for weaving thread into cloth.

looting (lōōt´ ing) *v.* Stealing valuable things from others.

loyal (loi´ əl) *adj.* Having or showing strong and lasting support for someone or something.

loyalty (loi´ əl tē) *n.* Strong and lasting affection and support; allegiance.

lumber (lum´ bər) *n.* Boards cut from logs.

lumbered (lum´ bərd) *v.* Past tense of **lumber:** to move about in a clumsy, noisy way.

lunar (lōō´ nər) *adj.* Of or having to do with the moon.

lunged (lunjd) *v.* Past tense of **lunge:** to move forward suddenly.

lurking (lûr´ king) *adj.* Lying hidden and quiet, preparing to attack.

luxury (lug´ shōō rē) *adj.* Expensive.

macaw (mə kô´) *n.* A long-tailed parrot.

macaw

magnificent (mag ni´ fə sənt) *adj.* Outstanding; excellent.

magnified (mag´ ni fīd) *v.* Past tense of **magnify:** to make something look bigger than it really is.

mankind (man´ kīnd´) *n*. Human beings as a group; the human race.

mantle (man´ təl) *n*. A loose, sleeveless cape.

market (mär´ kit) *n*. A place where food or goods are for sale.

master list (mas´ tər list) *n*. A list containing all of the information for a certain project.

merciful (mûr´ si fəl) *adj*. Kind or forgiving.

messin' up (mes´ in up) *v*. Making mistakes; misbehaving.

meteorologist (mē´ tē ə rol´ ə jist) *n*. A person who studies Earth's atmosphere and the changes that take place within it. One important branch of meteorology is the weather.

microscopic (mī´ krə skop´ ik) *adj*. So small it can only be seen through a microscope.

migrated (mī´ grātəd´) *v*. Past tense of **migrate:** to move from one place to another.

migration (mī grā´ shən) *n*. The movement of people from one area of a country or region to another.

militia (mə lish´ ə) *n*. A group of citizens trained to fight and help in emergencies.

millstones (mil´ stōns´) *n*. Plural of **millstone:** a pair of cylinder-shaped stones used in a mill for grinding grain.

minerals (min´ ər əls) *n*. Plural of **mineral:** A substance found in nature that is not an animal or plant. Salt, coal, and gold are minerals.

mission (mish´ ən) *n*. A special job or task.

mist (mist) *n*. A cloud of tiny drops of water or other liquid in the air; fog.

mob (mob) *n*. A large number of people who are so angry or upset about something that they break the law and cause damage.

models (mäd´ ls) *n*. Plural of **model:** a thing that is a good example of something and is copied.

module (mä´ jəl) *n*. A part of a spacecraft that has a special use and can be separated from the rest of the craft.

moisture (mois´ chər) *n*. Water or other liquid.

monument (mon´ yə mənt) *n*. A building or statue that is made to honor a person or event.

monument

mount (mount) *v*. To get up on a horse.

Pronunciation Key: at; lāte; câre; fäther; set; mē; it; kīte; ox; rōse; ô in bought; coin; book; tōo; form; out; up; ūse; tûrn; ə sound in about, chicken, pencil, cannon, circus; chair; hw in which; ring; shop; thin; there; zh in treasure.

muffled (muf´ əld) *adj.* Made softer or less loud.

muggy (mug´ ē) *adj.* Warm and damp.

munchkin (munch´ kin) *n.* A very small person.

murals (myŏŏr´ əls) *n.* Plural of **mural:** a picture that is painted on a wall. A mural usually covers most of a wall.

murmur (mûr´ mûr) *v.* To make or say with a low, soft sound.

mythology (mi thol´ ə jē) *n.* A group or collection of myths and legends.

nature (nā´ chər) *n.* The basic characteristics of a thing.

navigation (nav´ i gā´ shən) *n.* The act of navigating a ship or aircraft.

necessities (nə ses´ i tēz) *n.* Plural of **necessity:** something that is needed.

negative (neg´ ə tiv) *adj.* **1** Saying or indicating "no." **2** Having one of two opposite kinds of electric charge.

nerves (nûrvz) *n.* Plural of **nerve:** a bundle of fibers that carries messages between the brain and spinal cord and other parts of the body.

noble (nō´ bəl) *adj.* Having greatness of inner nature.

nutrients (noo´ trē ənts) *n.* Plural of **nutrient:** something that is needed by people, animals, and plants for life and growth.

nutritious (noo trish´ əs) *adj.* Giving nourishment; useful as food.

O

obedience (ō bē´ dē əns) *n.* To obey or carry out the orders, wishes, or instructions of.

observatories (əb zûr´ və tor ēz) *n.* Plural of **observatory:** a place or building that has telescopes for observing and studying the sun, moon, planets, and stars.

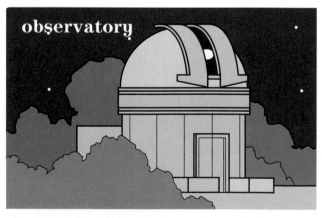

observatory

observe (əb zûrv´) *v.* To make a careful study of.

ocelots (o´ sə lotz´) *n.* Plural of **ocelot:** a wildcat of medium size that has yellow fur with black stripes on its face and spots on its body.

ocelot

odor (ō´ dər) *n.* Smell; scent.

omnivores (om´ nə vors´) *n.* Plural of **omnivore:** an animal that eats both animal flesh and plants.

opposing (ə pōz´ ing) *adj.* Opposite; completely different.

Word Derivations

Below are some words related to *opposing:*

oppose	opposition	opposite
opposed	opposable	opponent

optimistic (op´ tə mis´ tik) *adj.* Tending to look on the favorable side of things and believe that everything will turn out for the best.

Word Derivations

Below are some words related to *optimistic:*

optimism	optimist	optimize
optimization	optimum	optimal

orbit (or´ bit) *v.* To move in a path around a heavenly body.

Word History

Orbit came into English more than 600 years ago. The English word is derived from the Latin word *orbita*, meaning "path," "rut," or "orbit."

orderly (or´ dər lē) *adj.* Not causing or making trouble.

organisms (or´ gə niz´ əmz) *n.* Plural of **organism:** a living thing.

pace (pās) *n.* The rate of speed in walking, running, or moving.

pale (pāl) *adj.* Skin color that is lighter than usual.

pamphlets (pam´ flitz) *n.* Plural of **pamphlet:** a small book that has a paper cover.

panels (pa´ nəls) *n.* Plural of **panel:** A board containing the dials, instruments, and controls for running something.

Paraguay (par´ ə gwā´) *n.* A country in central South America.

paralyze (pa´ rə līz´) *v.* To take away the power to move or feel in a part of the body.

particles (pär´ ti kəlz) *n.* Plural of **particle:** A very small bit or piece of something.

pass (pas) *n.* A written permission.

passion (pash´ ən) *n.* A strong liking.

Word Derivations

Below are some words related to *passion*:

impassioned   passionate
dispassionate   passionately
passionless   disimpassioned

patch (pach) *n.* A small piece of ground where something grows.

patent (pa´ tənt) *n.* A piece of paper issued to a person or company by the government. It gives someone the right to be the only one to make, use, or sell a new invention for a certain number of years.

permanently (pûr´ mə nənt lē) *adv.* Lasting or meant to last.

persecuted (pûr´ si kūt´ əd) *v.* Past tense of **persecute:** to treat in a cruel and unjust way.

phonograph (fō´ nə graf´) *n.* An instrument that reproduces sound from records.

pitched (pitchd) *v.* Past tense of **pitch:** to set up.

pity (pit´ ē) *n.* A feeling of sorrow and sympathy for the troubles of another.

pitiful (pi´ ti fəl) *adj.* Causing feelings of sorrow and sympathy.

plague (plāg) *n.* A very serious disease that spreads quickly among the people in a certain area.

plateau (pla tō´) *n.* An area of flat land higher than the surrounding country.

plateau

pleading (plē´ ding) *v.* Making a sincere request; begging.

poised (poizd) *adv.* Balanced or steady.

portrait (por´ trit) *n.* A likeness of a person that is created by a painter or photographer.

positive (po´ zi tiv) *adj.* Having one of two opposite kinds of electric charge.

potential (pə ten´ shəl) *adj.* Capable of becoming something; possible but not yet actual.

practically (prak´ tik lē) *adv.* Nearly; almost.

prairie (prâ´ rē) *n.* A large area of level or rolling land with grass and few or no trees.

precautions (pri kô´ shənz) *n.* Plural of **precaution**: something done beforehand to prevent harm or danger.

precise (pri sīs´) *adj.* Exact; definite.

predators (pre´ də tərz) *n.* Plural of **predator**: an animal that hunts and kills other animals for food.

predict (pri´ dikt) *v.* To tell beforehand.

Word History

Predict came into English in 1609. *Predict* is derived from the Latin verb *praedicere*, which can also be divided into the word parts *prae-*, meaning "before," and *dicere*, meaning "to say." (Also note that predict contains the prefix *pre-*, which in this word means "before.")

prediction (pri dik´ shən) *n.* The act of telling something before it happens.

preserve (pri zərv´) *v.* To keep from being lost; protect.

pressure (pre´ shər) *n.* Force caused by one thing pushing against another thing.

prey (prā) *n.* An animal that is hunted by another animal for food.

pride (prīd) *n.* A feeling that one has worth and importance.

primary producers (prī´ mer´ ē prə dōō´ sərs) *n.* Plural of **primary producer**: the first food-makers in a food chain or web.

primitive (pri´ mə tiv) *adj.* Having to do with an early or first stage of development.

primp (primp) *v.* To dress oneself in a careful and precise way.

processes (prä´ se səz´) *n.* Plural of **process**: a series of actions performed in making or doing something.

procession (prə sesh´ ən) *n.* A group of persons moving forward in a line or in a certain order.

professional (prə fesh´ ə nəl) *adj.* Having to do with a career that requires special schooling.

prompt (prompt) *adj.* Quick or on time.

propel (prə pel´) *v.* To cause to move forward.

Word Derivations

Below are some words related to *propel*:

propeller   propelled   propelling
propellant   propels

propped (propd) *adj.* Supported by something under or against.

Pronunciation Key: at; lāte; câre; fäther; set; mē; **it**; kīte; **ox**; rōse; **ô** in b**ou**ght; c**oi**n; b**oo**k; t**oo**; f**or**m; **ou**t; **up**; ūse; tûrn; ə sound in **a**bout, chick**e**n, penc**i**l, cann**o**n, circ**u**s; **ch**air; **hw** in **wh**ich; ri**ng**; **sh**op; **th**in; **th**ere; **zh** in trea**s**ure.

prospering (pros´ pər ing) *v*. Doing extremely well.

prosperity (pros per´ i tē) *n*. Success, wealth, or good fortune.

protest (prō´ test) *n*. An objection to.

protested (prō´ test´ əd) *v*. Past tense of **protest**: to object to.

published (pub´ lisht) *v*. Past tense of **publish**: to print a newspaper, magazine, book, or other material and offer it for sale.

pursuing (pər soo´ ing) *v*. Finding ways to accomplish goals, as in a career.

Q

quarantine (kwor´ ən tēn´) *n*. The keeping of a person, animal, or thing away from others to stop the spreading of a disease.

quest (kwest) *n*. A search or pursuit.

quivers (kwi´ vərz) *v*. Shakes slightly.

radiosondes (rā´ dē ō sondz´) *n*. Plural of **radiosonde**: an instrument carried upward by a balloon that gathers and sends data about the weather.

raggedy (rag´ i dē) *adj*. Torn or worn-out.

raged (rājd) *v*. Past tense of **rage**: to talk or act in a violent way.

raging (rā´ jing) *adj*. Very active and unpredictable.

ranged (rānjd) *v*. Past tense of **range**: to wander or roam.

rare (râr) *adj*. Not often found.

rationed (rash´ ənd) *v*. Past tense of **ration**: to limit to fixed portions.

reach (rēch) *n*. Touch or grasp.

reality (rē al´ i tē) *n*. Something actual or real.

reconstruction (rē´ kən struk´ shən) *n*. A structure, such as a building or model, that has been made again by putting parts together.

recycle (rē sī´ kəl) *v*. To make fit to be used again.

regard (re gärd´) *n*. Thought or care.

region (rē´ jən) *n.* Any large area or territory.

Word History

Region came into English in the 1300s and is derived from the Latin word *regio*, which means "direction" or "arca." *Regio* is a variation of the Latin verb *regere*, which means "to direct."

registered (re´ jə stərd) *v.* Past tense of **register:** to officially record.

rehearse (ri hûrs´) *v.* To practice what to say before speaking to someone.

related (ri lā´ tid) *adj.* Belonging to the same family.

reliable (ri lī´ ə bəl) *adj.* Able to be depended on.

Word Derivations

Below are some words related to *reliable:*

reliant	rely	reliance
reliability	self-reliant	

relying (ri lī´ ing) *v.* Trusting or depending.

remark (ri märk´) *n.* A short statement or comment.

remote (ri mōt´) *adj.* Far from cities or towns.

Word History

Remote came into English in the fifteenth century and is derived from the Latin adjective *remotus* of the same meaning. *Remotus* comes from the Latin verb *remov, re-* meaning "to remove."

renewable (ri nōō´ ə bəl) *adj.* Able to be made new or as if new again.

representation (rəp´ ri zen tā´ shən) *n.* The right or privilege of having someone that speaks and acts for a group of people in a legislative body.

representing (rəp´ ri zen´ ting) *v.* Speaking or acting for.

reproduce (rē´ prə dōōs´) *v.* To produce offspring.

requirements (ri kwīr´ mənts) *n.* Plural of **requirement:** something that is necessary.

reservations (rez´ ər vā´ shənz) *n.* Plural of **reservation:** land set aside by the government for a special purpose.

resistant (ri zis´ tənt) *adj.* Going against the wishes of someone in charge.

resources (rē´ sors ez) *n.* Plural of **resource:** something used for help or support.

Pronunciation Key: at; l**ā**te; c**â**re; f**ä**ther; s**e**t; m**ē**; **i**t; k**ī**te; **o**x; r**ō**se; **ô** in b**o**ught; c**oi**n; b**oo**k; t**oo**; f**o**rm; **ou**t; **u**p; **ū**se; t**û**rn; **ə** sound in **a**bout, chick**e**n, penc**i**l, cann**o**n, circ**u**s; **ch**air; **hw** in **wh**ich; ri**ng**; **sh**op; **th**in; **th**ere; **zh** in trea**s**ure.

responsibilities (ri spon´ sə bil´ i tēz) *n.* Plural of **responsibility:** something that is a person's job, duty, or concern.

Word Derivations

Below are some words related to *responsibilities*:

response   responsible
responsibly   responsive
responsiveness   responsibility

retirement (ri tīr´ mənt) *n.* The act of taking oneself away from a job or occupation.

retreat (ri trēt´) *v.* To move back.

revealed (ri vēld´) *v.* Past tense of **reveal:** to make visible.

revealing (ri vēl´ ing) *v.* Making known.

revolution (re´ və loo´ shən) *n.* The overthrow of a system of government and the setting up of a new or different system of the government.

revolving doors (ri vôl´ ving dors) *n.* Plural of **revolving door:** a door at the front of a building that moves in a circle around a central point.

rickety (ri´ ki tē) *adj.* Likely to fall or break; shaky.

ridges (ri´ jes) *n.* Plural of **ridge:** a raised, narrow strip.

rights (rīts) *n.* Plural of **right:** a just, moral, or lawful claim.

rodeo (rō´ dē ō´) *n.* A show with contests in horseback riding, roping, and other similar skills.

role (rōl) *n.* A position or function.

role model (rōl´ mod´ l) *n.* A person whose behavior is imitated, or copied, by others.

roll call (rōl kôl) *n.* The act of calling off a list of names to check attendance.

roused (rouzd) *v.* Past tense of **rouse:** to wake up.

rumors (roo´ mərz) *n.* Plural of **rumor:** a story or statement passed from one person to another as truth with no proof.

sacred (sā´ krid) *adj.* Regarded as deserving respect.

Word History

Sacred has been in English for over 700 hundred years. It came from the Middle English word *sacren* which means "to consecrate." The word *sacren* came from the Anglo French word *sacrer*, which was derived from the Latin word *sacrare* meaning "sacred."

satellite (sat´ e līt´) *adj.* From a spacecraft that moves in an orbit around Earth that is used to help predict the weather.

scanning (skan´ ing) *v.* Looking closely and carefully.

scattered (skat´ erd) *adj.* Spread throughout various places.

scavenger (ska´ vən jər) *n.* An animal that feeds on dead animals.

scientific method (sī´ ən tif´ ik meth´ əd) *n.* The accepted process for scientific investigation that involves creating a hypothesis, experimenting to test the hypothesis, and then drawing conclusions based on the results of the experiments and research.

scold (skōld) *v.* To speak sharply to.

scorched (skorcht) *v.* Past tense of **scorch:** to burn slightly on the surface.

scowls (skoulz) *v.* Frowns in an angry way.

seasonal (sē´ zə nəl) *adj.* Happening in a certain season of the year.

secluded (si klōōd´ əd) *adj.* Removed from others.

section (sek´ shən) *n.* A part of an area.

Senegal (Sen´ i gôl) *n.* A country in Africa.

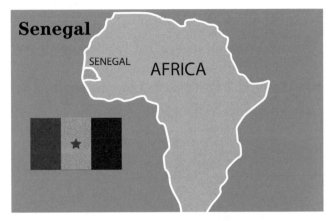

Senegal

sensations (sen sā´ shənz) *n.* Plural of **sensation:** a feeling.

Word Derivations

Below are some words that are related to *sensations*:

sensation	sense	senses
sensational	sensationalize	sensate

sense (sens) *v.* To feel or understand.

setting (set´ ing) *n.* A description of the location, time, and place where a play takes place.

settlers (set´ lərz) *n.* Plural of **settler:** a person who makes his or her home in a new land or country.

severe (sə vir´) *adj.* Very serious; dangerous.

sewage (sōō´ ij) *n.* Waste that is carried off in sewers and drains.

ship (ship) *v.* To send by ship, train, truck, or airplane.

Word History

Ship, as a verb, has been in English since the fourteenth century. The verb tense of the word is derived from the Old English noun *scip*, meaning "a large seagoing vessel."

shoot-outs (shŏŏt´ outs´) *n.* A shooting competition that is used to decide the winner of a game.

shoots (shŏŏts) *n.* Plural of **shoot:** a new or young plant stem.

skin bottle (skin bôt´ əl) *n.* A bottle, made from animal skin, for drinking liquid.

skits (skitz) *n.* Plural of **skit:** a short play.

slopes (slōpz) *n.* Plural of **slope:** a section of ground that is not flat.

snatch (snach) *v.* To seize or grab suddenly or quickly.

soiled (soild) *v.* Past tense of **soil:** to make or become dirty.

solar (sō´ lər) *adj.* Having to do with or coming from the sun.

solar system (sō´ lər sis´ təm) *n.* The sun and all the planets, satellites, asteroids, and comets that revolve around it.

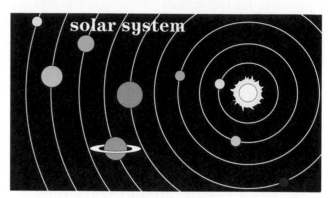

solar system

soloed (sōl´ ōd) *v.* Past tense of **solo:** to dance or perform alone.

sowing (sō´ ing) *v.* Planting.

species (spē´ sēz) *n.* A group of animals or plants that have many characteristics in common.

spectacular (spek tak´ yə lər) *adj.* Out of the ordinary; impressive.

spellbound (spel´ bound) *adj.* Fascinated; filled with delight or wonder.

spindly (spind´ lē) *adj.* Long and lean.

spiral (spī´ rəl) *n.* A curve that keeps winding. A spiral may wind inward and outward or downward and upward.

Word History

Spiral came into in English in 1551. It is derived from the Latin word *spira*, meaning "coil."

spiraling (spī´ rəl ing) *v.* Moving in the shape of a spiral.

spokes (spōks) *n.* Plural of **spoke:** One of the rods or bars that connect the rim of a wheel to the hub.

sport (sport) *n.* Amusement; fun.

spread (spred) *v.* To make or become known by more people.

spring (spring) *adj.* From a place where underground water comes out of the earth.

spurted (spûrt´ əd) *v.* Past tense of **spurt:** to pour out suddenly in a stream.

squat (skwot) *v.* To crouch or sit with the knees bent and drawn close to the body.

squinted (skwint´ əd) *v.* Past tense of **squint:** to partially close the eyes.

stalking (stôk´ ing) *v.* Following someone or something quietly and carefully in order to catch it.

stampede (stam pēd´) *v.* To cause a sudden, wild running of a frightened herd of animals.

standard (stan´ dərd) *adj.* Widely used or usual.

stargazers (stär´ gā zerz) *n.* Plural of **stargazer:** a person who studies the stars.

startle (stär´ tl) *v.* To cause to move suddenly.

startled (stär´ tld) *adj.* Excited by sudden surprise or alarm.

stationed (stā´ shənd) *v.* Past tense of **station:** to place in a post or position.

stirred up (stûrd up) *v.* Past tense of **stir up:** to arouse or excite.

stooping (stoop´ ing) *v.* Bending forward and downward.

straddled (stra´ dəld) *v.* Past tense of **straddle:** to sit with one's legs on each side of an object.

stovepipe (stōv´ pīp´) *n.* A thin pipe connected to a stove that directs smoke or fumes out of an area.

strait (strāt) *n.* A narrow channel between two larger bodies of water.

striving (strīv´ ing) *v.* Making a great effort.

stunt (stunt) *n.* An act of skill or strength.

sulking (sulk´ ing) *v.* Acting angry and silent.

supercells (soo´ pir sels) *n.* Plural of **supercell:** the strongest type of thunderstorm.

supreme (su prēm´) *adj.* Greatest in power or authority.

surrounded (sə round´ əd) *v.* Past tense of **surround:** to be on all sides.

survey (sûr´ vā) *n.* An inspection or investigation.

> **Pronunciation Key: a**t; lāte; câre; fä́ther; set; mē; it; kīte; **o**x; rōse; **ô** in b**ou**ght; **c**oin; b**oo**k; t**oo**; form; **out**; up; ūse; tûrn; ə sound in **a**bout, chick**e**n, penc**i**l, cann**o**n, circ**u**s; **ch**air; **hw** in **wh**ich; ri**ng**; **sh**op; **th**in; **th**ere; **zh** in trea**s**ure.

swarming (swôrm´ ing) *v.* Moving in a large group.

sweltered (swel´ tərd) *v.* Past tense of **swelter:** to suffer, sweat, or become faint from heat.

tackle (tak´ əl) *v.* To stop and bring to the ground.

tadpoles (tad´ pōlz) *n.* Plural of **tadpole:** a very young frog or toad when it still lives underwater and has gills, a tail, and no legs.

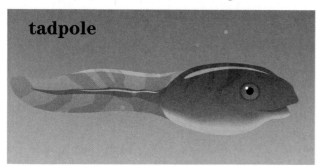

tadpole

task (task) *n.* A piece of work to be done.

tattered (tat´ ərd) *adj.* torn into shreds.

tenants (ten´ ənts) *n.* Plural of **tenant:** a person who pays money

to use a house, apartment, office, or land that belongs to someone else.

terminal (tur´ mə nəl) *n.* Either end of a battery, through which electricity is conducted.

territory (ter´ i tôr´ ē) *n.* A large area or region of land.

texture (teks´ chər) *n.* The look and feel of something.

theory (thēr´ ē) *n.* An opinion based on some evidence but not proved.

throb (throb) *n.* A heavy, fast beat or sensation.

thrust (thrust) *n.* A sudden, strong push or force.

thundered (thun´ dərd) *v.* Past tense of **thunder:** to make a noise like thunder.

tilted (tilt´ ed) *v.* Past tense of **tilt:** to raise one side of.

topsoil (top´ soil) *n.* The upper layer of the soil.

traces (trās´ ez) *n.* Plural of **trace:** A small bit or sign left behind showing that something was there.

traders (trā´ dərz) *n.* Plural of **trader:** a person who buys and sells things as a business.

traitor (trā´ tər) *n.* A person who does something to harm his or her own country.

tranquility (tran kwil´ ə tē) *n.* The absence of motion or disturbance.

Word Derivations

Below are some words related to *tranquility*:

tranquil tranquilize tranquilly
tranquilizer tranquilized

transferring (trans fər´ ing) *v.* Moving from one place to another.

transformation (trans´ fər mā´ shən) *n.* A major change in how someone looks, usually for the better.

transforming (trans form´ ing) *v.* Changing.

treason (trē´ zən) *n.* The betraying of one's country by helping the enemy.

treaty (trē´ tē) *n.* A formal agreement between two countries.

trek (trek) *n.* A long, slow journey.

trench (trench) *n.* A long narrow ditch.

tribute (trib´ ūt) *n.* Something done or given to show respect or thanks.

trolley (trol´ ē) *n.* A streetcar that runs on tracks and gets its power from an electric wire overhead.

trolley

troop (trōop) *adj.* Soldier.

tropics (trop´ iks) *n.* A region of Earth that is near the equator.

trough (trôf) *n.* A long narrow container that holds water or food for animals.

trudging (truj´ ing) *v.* Walking slowly and with effort.

tyranny (tir´ ə nē) *n.* Unjust use of power; harsh or cruel government.

Word Derivations

Below are some words related to *tyranny*:

tyrant tyrannize tyrannical
tyrannicide tyrannic tyrannized

unjustly (un just´ lē) *adv.* Unfairly.

Word History

Unjustly is the adverb form of the word *unjust*, which came into English in the 14th century. The word *just* is derived from the Anglo French word *juste* and the Latin word *justus*, both meaning "right" or "just." (Also note that unjust contains the prefix *un-*, which in this word means "not.")

unanimous (yōō nan´ ə məs) *adj.* In or showing total agreement.

Pronunciation Key: at; lāte; câre; fäther; set; mē; it; kīte; ox; rōse; ô in bought; coin; bŏŏk; tōō; form; out; up; ūse; tûrn; ə sound in about, chicken, pencil, cannon, circus; **ch**air; **hw** in **wh**ich; ring; **sh**op; **th**in; **th**ere; **zh** in treasure.

uproariously (up ror´ ē əs lē) *adv.* Noisily; loudly.

utter (ut´ ər) *v.* To express out loud.

vacant (vā´ kənt) *adj.* Not having anyone or anything in it; empty.

Word Derivations

Below are some words that are related to *vacant*:

vacancy	vacate	vacation
vacantly	vacantness	vacationer

Word History

Vacant came into English in the 14th century. *Vacant* is derived from the Latin verb *vacare*, meaning "to be empty" or "to be free." Anglo French and Middle English also have similar words derived from this Latin root.

varies (vâr´ ēz) *v.* Changes; makes or becomes different.

vast (vast) *adj.* Great in size.

velvet (vel´ vit) *n.* A fabric made of soft, thick fibers.

vents (vents) *n.* Plural of **vent:** an opening through which a gas passes.

versions (vûr´ zhəns) *n.* Plural of **version:** a form of something that is changed from an earlier form.

vertical (vûr´ ti kəl) *adj.* Straight up and down.

veteran (vet´ ər rən) *n.* A person who has had a lot of experience.

vibrations (vī brā´ shənz) *n.* Plural of **vibration:** a slight or quick shaking, which is felt rather than seen or heard.

wall cloud (wôl kloud) *n.* A type of cloud that hangs below the base of the thunderstorm. These clouds sometimes become funnel clouds.

weathercock (weth´ ər kôk´) *n.* A weathervane.

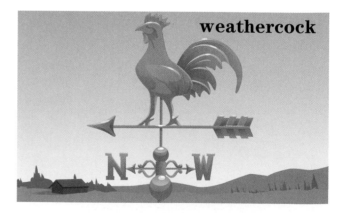

weathercock

whistles (wis´ əls) *v.* Moves with a sound like a whistle.

winding (wīnd´ ing) *adj.* To move in one direction and then another.

windmill (wind´ mil) *n.* A machine that uses the power of the wind to turn sails at the top of a tower.

wind turbines (wind tûr´ bīns´) *n.* Plural of **wind turbine:** a modern-day windmill.

withered (with´ ərd) *v.* Past tense of **wither:** to dry up from a loss of moisture.

witness (wit´ nis) *v.* To be present to see or hear something.

worthy (wûr´ thē) *adj.* Having enough value; deserving.

Acknowledgments *(continued)*

MCBROOM THE RAINMAKER TEXT COPYRIGHT © 1973 BY SID FLEISCHMAN. Used by permission HarperCollins Publishers.
"The Whole World is Coming" from SONGS OF THE DREAM PEOPLE: Chants and Images from the Indians and Eskimos of North America. Edited and illustrated by James Houston. Atheneum, New York, copyright © 1972 by James Houston. Stella Ormai.
"California Ghost Town" by Fran Haraway from MY AMERICA edited by Lee Bennett Hopkins. Used by permission of the author. Fran Haraway, a retired junior high reading skills teacher, is currently an aide in a public library.

Unit 6—Call of Duty

"Founders of the Children's Rain Forest" from IT'S OUR WORLD, TOO! by Phillip Hoose. Copyright © 1993 by Phillip Hoose. By permission of Little, Brown and Company (Inc.).
"Jason and the Golden Fleece" reprinted with the permission of Margaret K. McElderry Books, an imprint of Simon & Schuster Children's Publishing division, from GREEK MYTHS by Geraldine McCaughrean, illustrated by Emma Chichester Clark. Text copyright © 1992 Geraldine McCaughrean. Illustrations copyright © 1992 Emma Chichester Clark.
"The Quest for Healing" from NORTH AMERICAN MYTHS AND LEGENDS by Philip Ardagh. Used by permission.
"The White Spider's Gift" by Jamie Turner from PLAYS, THE DRAMA MAGAZINE FOR YOUNG PEOPLE © March 2005, reprinted with the permission of the publisher PLAYS/ Sterling Partners, Inc., PO Box 600160, Newton, MA 02460.
From THE STORY OF ANNIE SULLIVAN: HELEN KELLER'S TEACHER by Bernice Selden, copyright © 1987 by Parachute Press. Used by permission of Dell Publishing, a division of Random House, Inc.
"Jim" from BRONZEVILLE BOYS AND GIRLS by Gwendolyn Brooks. COPYRIGHT © 1956 by GWENDOLYN BROOKS BLAKELEY. Used by permission of HarperCollins Publishers.

Photo Credits

38 © Kristi J. Black/CORBIS; **38–39** © J Marshall - Tribaleye Images/Alamy; **94–95** © Time Life Pictures/ Getty Images; **99, 107** © Jesuit Oregon Province Archives, Gonzaga University; **100–120** © Aylette Jenness; **132–133** © Bettmann/CORBIS; **136–137** Getty Images, Inc.; **138** Library of Congress; **139** North Wind Picture Archives; **145** Taxi/Getty Images, Inc.; **148** © numb/Alamy; **148–149** © Robert Harding World Imagery/CORBIS; **184–185** © Jeffrey Coolidge/Getty; **188–189** Dennis MacDonald/Photoedit, Inc.; **190** Gacin Hellier/Robert Harding World Imagery/Getty Images, Inc.; **192** AKG-Images; **194** Getty Images, Inc.; **195** Spencer Grant/PhotoEdit, Inc.; **196–197** James P. Blair/National Geographic/Getty Images, Inc.; **198** © Royalty-Free/CORBIS; **198–199** © PCL/Alamy; **202–203** © Royalty-free/CORBIS; **204** © Royalty-Free/CORBIS; **205** Digital Vision/Getty Images, Inc.; **208** Thomas Schmitt/The Image Bank/Getty Images, Inc.; **208** (bl)Dr. Pail Zahl/Photo Researchers, Inc, (br) © Les David Manevitz/Superstock; **209** Anna Zuckerman-Vdovenko/Photoedit, Inc.; **210** Digitial Vision/Getty Images, Inc.; **211** Digital Vision/Getty Images, Inc.; **212** Steven Kazlowski/Peter Arnold; **213** (t)Animals Animals, (bl) David Dennis/Animals Animals, (br) Animals Animals; **214** Macduff Everton/CORBIS; **216–217** © Image Source/Alamy; **217** © Jim West/Alamy; **224–225** © Library of Congress; **245** © Bettmann/CORBIS; **246** (t, c, bl, br) © North Wind Picture Archives, (bc) © Stock Montage; **247** (t, bl) © North Wind Picture Archives, (br) © Culver Pictures, Inc.; **248** © North Wind Picture Archives; **280** © Corcoran Gallery of Art, Washington, DC/CORBIS; **281** © North Wind Picture Archives; **282** © John B.Martin/The Valentine Museum, Richmond, VA; **291** Courtesy of the Virginia Historical Society, Richmond, Virginia; **297** © Darlene Bordwell; **320** © Matthew Cavanaugh/epa/CORBIS; **320–321** © The Granger Collection; **326** © Hulton Archive/Getty Images, Inc.; **328** © The Granger Collection; **331** © Library of Congress; **332** © The Granger Image Collection, New York; **333** © Library of Congress; **334** © The Granger Collection, New York; **335** © Library of Congress; **336** © The Granger Collection; **338–339** © John Lawrence/Getty; **339** © Micheal Newman/PhotoEdit; **348–349** © Gabe Palmer/CORBIS; **352–353** © NASA/|The Hubble Heritage Team (AURA/STScI); **354** © C. Butler/Photo Researchers, Inc.; **354–361** NASA; **355** © Royal Observatory, Edinburgh/AAO/Photo Researchers, Inc.; **356** © Mark McCaughrean (MPIA)/C. Robert O'Dell (Rice University)/NASA; **357** © StockTrek/Getty Images, Inc.; **358** © StockTrek/Getty Images, Inc.; **359** © NASA/Roger Ressmeyer/CORBIS; **360** © NASA/JPL-Caltech/The Hubble Heritage Team (STScI/AURA); **361** © C. Butler/Photo Researchers, Inc.; **362–363** NASA; **380–381** @ Courtney Milne; **386–387** © StockTrek/Getty Images, Inc.; **388** Time Life Pictures/NASA/Getty Images, Inc.; **388–389** NASA/JPL/Caltech; **389–397** NASA/JPL/Caltech; **398** file photo; **398–399** STScI/NASA/Photo Researchers, Inc.; **400–401** © Trip/Alamy; **406–409** NASA; **410** © Bettmann/CORBIS; **411** NASA; **412** © Dennis di Cicco/CORBIS; **413–415** NASA; **416** © Bettmann/CORBIS; **417–424** NASA; **425** © NASA/Science Photo Library/Photo Researchers, Inc.; **426** NASA; **432–433** © NASA/Getty Images, Inc.; **434** © NASA/Getty Images, Inc.; **435** © San Diego Historical Society; **436–438** © NASA/CORBIS; **440** © NASA/Roger Ressmeyer/CORBIS; **441–442** © NASA/CORBIS; **443** © NASA/Getty Images; **444–445** © NASA/Getty Images, Inc.; **447** © NASA Marshall Space Flight Center; **449** (bkgd) © NASA/H. Hicher(University of British Columbia); **458–459** © The Granger Collection; **462–463** © Historical Picture Archive/CORBIS; **464** Santa Barbara Museum of Art. Gift of Harriet Cowles Hammett Graham, in memory of Buell Hammett; **469** The National Museum of The American Indian, Smithsonian Institution. 3249; **470** National Museum of American Art, Smithsonian Institution/Art Resource, NY; **473** National Museum of American Art, Smithsonian Institution/Art Resource, NY; **475** Amon Carter Museum, Fort Worth, Texas. 1931.146; **477** Amon Carter Museum, Fort Worth, Texas. 1961.135; **479** National Museum of American Art, Smithsonian Institution/Art Resource, NY; **480** National Museum of American Art, Smithsonian Institution/Art Resource, NY; **482** Amon Carter Museum, Fort Worth, Texas. 1967.40; **490** file photo; **492** © Library of Congress; **512–513** © Trevor Wood/Getty; **542** © Kansas State Historical Society; **546–457** © Stone/Getty Images, Inc.; **546–547, 550–551, 554–555,** (bkgd) © Roger Cope/Alamy Images; **548** © Getty Images, Inc.; **549** © Bettmann/CORBIS; **550–551** © Bettmann/CORBIS; **552** © Bettmann/CORBIS; **553** © Bettmann/CORBIS; **554–555** © CORBIS; **558–559** © The Granger Collection, New York; **560–561** © David R. Frazier Photolibrary, Inc./Alamy; **583** © Library of Congress; **592–593** © Sue Cunningham Photographic/Alamy; **601** Bernd Kern; **605** © NOAO/Gatley/Merrill/Ressmeyer/CORBIS; **608–609** © Ron Chapple/Getty Images, Inc.